How to Use This Book

Lotus Notes is a complex environment that includes a built-in application development environment and a powerful server, the Domino server, that opens the Notes environment to the Internet and the World Wide Web. Some of the techniques taught in this book require a full Notes client, the same software that is used for application development. However, most functions are available with a Notes Desktop license, or even a Notes Mail client. And some of the functionality, such as the Weblicator functionality, does not even require Notes software.

The book was written based on a Lotus Notes 4.5 running in a Windows 95 environment on an IBM PC. However, the Notes environment allows documents to be shared across platforms, and has virtually the same functionality on a UNIX workstation or a Macintosh as it has on the IBM PC. And you can use Notes, and do most of the exercises, in a stand-alone environment as well in a networked environment.

Teach Yourself LOTUS NOTES® 4.5 in 14 days

Teach Yourself
LOTUS NOTES® 4.5
in 14 days

Don Child

201 West 103rd Street
Indianapolis, Indiana 46290

This book is dedicated to my wonderful parents, Bob and Tee Child.

Copyright © 1997 by Sams Publishing

FIRST EDITION

All rights reserved. No part of this book shall be reproduced, stored in a retrieval system, or transmitted by any means, electronic, mechanical, photocopying, recording, or otherwise, without written permission from the publisher. No patent liability is assumed with respect to the use of the information contained herein. Although every precaution has been taken in the preparation of this book, the publisher and author assume no responsibility for errors or omissions. Neither is any liability assumed for damages resulting from the use of the information contained herein. For information, address Sams Publishing, 201 W. 103rd St., Indianapolis, IN 46290.

International Standard Book Number: 0-672-31080-5

Library of Congress Catalog Card Number: 97-65459

2000   99   98   97   4   3   2   1

Interpretation of the printing code: The rightmost double-digit number is the year of the book's printing; the rightmost single-digit, the number of the book's printing. For example, a printing code of 97-1 shows that the first printing of the book occurred in 1997.

Composed in AGaramond and MCPdigital by Macmillan Computer Publishing

Printed in the United States of America

Trademarks

All terms mentioned in this book that are known to be trademarks or service marks have been appropriately capitalized. Sams Publishing cannot attest to the accuracy of this information. Use of a term in this book should not be regarded as affecting the validity of any trademark or service mark. Lotus Notes is a registered trademark of Lotus Development Corporation.

Publisher and President   Richard K. Swadley
Publishing Manager   Dean Miller
Director of Editorial Services   Cindy Morrow
Director of Marketing   Kelli Spencer
Product Marketing Manager   Wendy Gilbride
Assistant Marketing Manager   Jen Pock

Acquisitions Editor
Grace M. Buechlein

Development Editor
Brian-Kent Proffitt

Production Editor
Heather Kaufman Urschel

Indexer
Johnna VanHoose

Technical Reviewer
David Hatter

Editorial Coordinator
Katie Wise

Technical Edit Coordinator
Lynette Quinn

Resource Coordinator
Deborah Frisby

Editorial Assistants
Carol Ackerman
Andi Richter
Rhonda Tinch-Mize

Cover Designer
Tim Amhrein

Book Designer
Gary Adair

Copy Writer
Peter Fuller

Production Team Supervisors
Brad Chinn
Charlotte Clapp

Production
Mona Brown
Cynthia Davis
Ian A. Smith
Mary Ellen Stephenson

Overview

Introduction		xxi
Week 1 At a Glance		**1**
Day 1	Understanding Notes	3
2	Exploring the Notes Workspace	25
3	Using Notes Help	57
4	Creating Notes Documents	81
5	Working with Rich Text in Documents	105
6	Working with Objects	137
7	Exploring a Notes Database	165
Week 1 In Review		**195**
Week 2 At a Glance		**199**
Day 8	Searching for Information in Notes Databases	201
9	Notes Mail Basics	227
10	Notes Mail Advanced Features	255
11	Calendaring and Scheduling	277
12	Mobile Notes: Using Notes When You're Out of the Office	307
13	Automating Notes with Agents and Actions	339
14	Notes and the Internet	363
Week 2 In Review		**401**
Appendix		
A	Workshop Answers	405
	Index	419

Contents

Week 1 At a Glance   1

What's Ahead? 2

Day 1 Understanding Notes   3

What Is Lotus Notes? 3
    Communication 4
    Collaboration 5
    Coordination 6
The Notes Environment 7
    Domino Server 8
    Notes Client 8
    Web Browser 9
How Notes Data Is Stored 11
    Using Local Notes Databases 13
    Using Notes Databases on the Domino Server 15
Understanding Notes Security 16
    The Notes UserID 18
    The Password 19
    The Access Control List 21
The Role of the Public Address Book 22
Summary 22
Workshop 23
    Q&A 23
    Quiz 23
    Exercises 24

2 Exploring the Notes Workspace   25

How to Launch Notes 26
Layout of Notes Workspace 26
    Title Bar 28
    Menu Bar 28
    Working with SmartIcons 29
    Placing Database Icons on the Workspace 33
    Working with Tabbed Workspace Pages 39
    Using the Status Bar 42
Setting Up User Preferences 44
    Setting Preferences on the Basics Page 44
    Setting the Environment for International Users 50

	Setting Mail Preferences	51
	Setting Port Preferences	52
	How to Close Notes	53
	Summary	53
	Workshop	54
	Q&A	54
	Quiz	55
	Exercises	55
3	**Using Notes Help**	**57**
	Putting the Help Database on Your Workspace	58
	Opening Help	60
	Exploring the Help Index View	60
	Displaying the Preview Pane	61
	Expanding Categories	62
	Looking for Help on a Topic Using the Index View	63
	Reading a Help Document	64
	Saving Commonly Used Help Documents in a Folder	66
	Looking at the Contents Views of the Help Database	67
	Using the Visual Index View	69
	Using the Search View	70
	Using the Printed Books View	72
	Other Ways to Access Help	73
	Using Context-Sensitive Help	73
	Accessing Help from Buttons	74
	Database Level Help	75
	Document Level Help	75
	Field-Level Help	77
	What to Do If You Still Need Help	77
	Summary	78
	Workshop	78
	Q&A	78
	Quiz	79
	Exercises	79
4	**Creating Notes Documents**	**81**
	Putting Databases on the Desktop	82
	Creating a Simple Document	83
	Getting Started	84
	What to Look for in the View	84
	Creating a Main Topic	87
	Responding to a Document	89

	What Types of Data Do Notes Documents Accept?	90
	Text	90
	Rich Text	91
	Keywords	91
	Numbers	93
	Time	94
	Authors	94
	Readers	95
	Names	95
	Which Fields Can You Edit?	96
	How Notes Checks for Required Data	98
	Looking at a Complex Document	99
	Closing a Notes Document	100
	Editing Existing Documents	101
	Summary	102
	Workshop	103
	Q&A	103
	Quiz	104
	Exercises	104
5	**Working with Rich Text in Documents**	**105**
	Working with Text in a Rich Text Field	106
	Displaying the Text Properties InfoBox	107
	Working with Tables in a Rich Text Field	118
	Creating a Table	119
	Using the Table Properties InfoBox to Format the Table	119
	Creating Page Breaks	127
	Using Collapsible Sections in Your Document:	
	The 20 Percent Solution	128
	Creating a Collapsible Section	129
	Defining Section Properties	130
	Deleting a Section	133
	Moving a Section	134
	Summary	134
	Workshop	134
	Q&A	135
	Quiz	136
	Exercises	136
6	**Working with Objects**	**137**
	Using Graphics in Rich Text Fields	138
	Importing Data into Notes	140
	Importing Data into a Notes View	140
	Importing Data into a Document	140
	Exporting Notes Data to a File	141

| Creating and Using Embedded Objects 142
| Creating an Embedded Object from Scratch 143
| Creating an Embedded Object from a File 145
| Working with Linked Objects 147
| Creating a Linked Object 148
| Managing Links 148
| Editing a Linked Object 151
| Working with Attached Files 151
| Attaching Files 151
| Linking to Other Notes Documents, Views, and Databases 153
| Other Ways to Link within Notes Documents 155
| Buttons 155
| Other Hotspots 158
| Editing Hotspots 161
| Removing a Hotspot 162
| Summary 162
| Workshop 163
| Q&A 163
| Quiz 164
| Exercises 164

7 Exploring a Notes Database 165

Using Your Notes Password 166
    Changing Your Password 167
Touring the Database 169
    Looking at Default Opening Pages in the Database 169
    How to Use Views 170
    Working with Folders 177
    Creating a Private View 180
Printing Notes Documents 181
    Printing an Individual Document 181
    Setting Up a Default Printer 182
    Setting Page Specifications for a Notes Database 183
    Headers and Footers for Printed Documents 184
Looking at the Database Characteristics 187
    Examining the Database Properties InfoBox 187
Summary 191
Workshop 192
    Q&A 192
    Quiz 193
    Exercises 193

Week 1 In Review 195

Week 2 At a Glance	**199**
What's Ahead?	199

Day 8 Searching for Information in Notes Databases — 201

- Getting Started with a Simple Search 202
- Find and Replace Text in a Document 203
- What Is a Full Text Search? 204
  - Displaying the Search Bar 204
  - Examining the Search Bar 205
  - Creating a Full Text Index 206
- Using a Full Text Search 210
  - Controlling How Documents Are Displayed 211
  - Looking at the Search Results 213
  - Performing Boolean Searches Using the Search Builder 214
  - Launching a Search after Using the Search Builder 218
  - Saving a Search 219
  - Deleting a Saved Search 219
- Searching for Documents in More than One Database 219
  - Setting Up Databases for Inclusion in a Site Search 220
  - Setting Up the Search Site Database 221
  - Doing a Search on Your Site 222
- Summary 224
- Workshop 224
  - Q&A 224
  - Quiz 225
  - Exercises 225

9 Notes Mail Basics — 227

- Notes Mail Overview 227
- A Tour of the Notes Mail Database 228
- Sending an E-Mail Message 230
  - Addressing an E-Mail Memo 231
  - Completing Your Memo 233
  - Sending the Memo 233
  - Selecting Delivery Options 234
  - Making Delivery Options Applicable to All Outgoing Mail 236
- Opening and Reading Your Mail 238
  - Forwarding a Document 239
  - Replying to a Memo and Replying with History 240
- Creating Special Mail Documents 241
  - Creating Mail Bookmarks 241
  - Creating Phone Messages 242
  - Creating Serial Route Memos 242

  Create a Temporary Export Certificate 244
  Creating a Memo for the Database Manager 246
 Working with Mail Views 246
  Using the Views and Folders 247
  Using the Discussion Threads View 247
  Archiving Documents 248
 Summary 253
 Workshop 253
  Q&A 253
  Quiz 254
  Exercises 254

10   Notes Mail Advanced Features   255

 Addressing Users Using the Name and Address Books 255
  Using the Public Address Book 256
  Using a Personal Address Book 257
  Defining Which Address Books Notes Uses 260
 Customizing Notes Mail Documents 261
  Working with Stationery 261
 Customizing Your Memos with Letterheads 264
 Letting Other Notes Users Work with Your Mail Database 265
 Sending Messages to Others Automatically When You
  Are Out of the Office 267
 Using Other Mail Systems with Notes 269
  Using cc:Mail and VIM Programs with Notes 270
  Using Microsoft Mail-Enabled Programs and
   Microsoft Exchange with Notes 272
 The Hidden Role of Notes Mail 273
 Summary 274
 Workshop 275
  Q&A 275
  Quiz 275
  Exercises 276

11   Calendaring and Scheduling   277

 Taking a Tour of the Calendar View 278
  Moving to Another Page on the Calendar 278
  Moving to a Specific Day 279
  Displaying a Day in Hourly Increments 279
 Setting Up Your Calendar Profile 280
 Defining Scheduling Options 283
 Entering Data in Your Calendar 284
  Creating a Calendar Entry 284
  Creating an Appointment 284

	Creating Invitations 288
	Creating an Event 296
	Creating a Reminder 296
	Creating an Anniversary 296
Using the Meetings View 297
Creating a To Do List 298
	Creating a Task While Reading Mail 299
	Assigning a Task to Others 299
	Looking at the To Do View 300
Working with Documents in the Calendar View 301
Summary 303
Workshop 304
	Q&A 304
	Quiz 304
	Exercises 305

12 Mobile Notes: Using Notes When You're Out of the Office 307

Sharing Data Between Different Locations 308
Setting Up Communications 309
    Setting Up a Modem Connection 310
    Setting Up an Internet Connection 312
Setting Up a Location 312
    Defining Location Basics 313
    Defining an Internet Browser 314
    Defining Servers 314
    Setting Up Phone Dialing 315
    Setting Up Mail 316
    Setting Up a Replication Schedule 317
    Working with Advanced Settings 318
Setting Up a Server Connection 318
    Verifying Your Connection 321
Understanding Replicas 322
    Creating a Replica Database 323
    Controlling What Gets Replicated 324
Replicating a Single Database 326
    Using the Replicator Page 329
    Elements of the Replicator Page 330
    Strategies for Speeding Up Replication 332
    Adding and Deleting Databases from the Replicator Page 333
Switching Locations 334
Summary 335
Workshop 336
    Q&A 336
    Quiz 336
    Exercises 337

| 13 | **Automating Notes with Agents and Actions** | **339** |

Creating and Using Agents 339
    What Is an Agent? 340
    Personal Agents and Shared Agents 341
Taking a Cautious Approach to Creating Agents 342
    Creating an Agent 342
    Naming Your Agent 343
    Defining When the Agent Should Run 345
    Define Which Documents the Agent Should Run Against 347
    Define What the Agent Should Do 348
Working with Actions 352
    Creating an Action Hotspot 353
    Creating an Action Button on a Form 353
    Creating an Action in a View 357
Summary 359
Workshop 360
    Q&A 360
    Quiz 361
    Exercises 361

| 14 | **Notes and the Internet** | **363** |

Looking at Web-Enabled Notes Applications 364
    An Intranet Example 365
    An Internet Example 366
Using a Web Browser from within Notes 367
    Setting Up Your Default Browser 368
    Setting Up the Web Navigator 370
Using the Notes Web Navigator 371
    Setting up the Notes Web Navigator 372
    Setting Internet Options for the Web Navigator 373
    Using the Personal Web Navigator 377
Weblicator: Notes Functionality without Notes 384
    Verifying the Weblicator Settings 386
    Selecting a Local Database 387
    Creating a Link to a Notes Database 387
    Setting Up Replication Schedules 389
    Enabling and Disabling Schedules 391
    Adding New Favorites to Your Weblicator 392
    Looking at Replicated Pages Offline 393
Kona and Maui: The Future of Notes 394
Summary 397
Workshop 398

	Q&A	398
	Quiz	399
	Exercises	399

Week 2 In Review — 401

Appendix

A Workshop Answers — 405

- Day 1 406
  - Quiz 406
  - Exercises 406
- Day 2 407
  - Quiz 407
  - Exercises 407
- Day 3 407
  - Quiz 407
  - Exercises 408
- Day 4 408
  - Quiz 408
  - Exercises 408
- Day 5 409
  - Quiz 409
  - Exercises 409
- Day 6 409
  - Quiz 409
  - Exercises 410
- Day 7 410
  - Quiz 410
  - Exercises 411
- Day 8 411
  - Quiz 411
  - Exercises 412
- Day 9 412
  - Quiz 412
  - Exercises 413
- Day 10 413
  - Quiz 413
  - Exercises 414
- Day 11 414
  - Quiz 414
  - Exercises 415

Day 12	415
Quiz	415
Exercises	415
Day 13	416
Quiz	416
Exercises	416
Day 14	416
Quiz	416
Exercises	417

Index   **419**

Acknowledgments

I want to thank people in four different quarters for their direct or indirect contributions to this book. First on the list are the members of the editorial team at Sams Publishing who have helped to make this into a far better book than I could have done on my own. Those deserving special thanks are Grace Buechlein, the acquisitions editor, and Brian-Kent Proffitt, the development editor during most of this effort. I also want to thank Sunthar Visuvalingam, with whom I worked on other projects, and who got me going on this book. They have coordinated an excellent team of production and technical editors who helped focus the final product.

I also want to acknowledge my professional colleagues at DataHouse, who let me bounce ideas off them. DataHouse is a Lotus Premium Business Partner. Without the knowledge I have gained working with everyone there, I could never have written this book.

Other professional colleagues include members of the Lotus Business Partner community and the folks at Lotus who continue to innovate and lead the way in the software industry with the continuing evolution of Notes. And I especially want to thank the Weblicator development team's John Immerman, who patiently led me through setup problems when I wandered into uncharted territory during my research for this book.

And finally, I want to acknowledge my wife Wyn and my son Tristan, who had to put up with my unsociable hours and no weekends while this book was being written.

About the Author

Don Child

Don Child is a senior technical writer with DataHouse, a Lotus Premium Business Partner in Honolulu. He is a Certified Lotus Professional application developer and system administrator for Notes 4.5. He has worked as a Lotus instructor, and has written documentation for numerous Notes applications. Mr. Child is a senior member and current president of the Aloha Chapter of the Society for Technical Communication (STC). He has written for other Lotus Notes books from Sams Publishing, including *Lotus Notes 4 Unleashed* and *Lotus Notes and Domino Server 4.5 Unleashed*. When he's not busy sitting in front of a computer, he likes to spend time on his family's ranch near Snowmass, Colorado, or with his wife's family in England. Mr. Child can be reached at `don_child@datahouse.com`.

Tell Us What You Think!

As a reader, you are the most important critic and commentator of our books. We value your opinion and want to know what we're doing right, what we could do better, what areas you'd like to see us publish in, and any other words of wisdom you're willing to pass our way. You can help us make strong books that meet your needs and give you the computer guidance you require.

Do you have access to CompuServe or the World Wide Web? Then check out our CompuServe forum by typing **GO SAMS** at any prompt. If you prefer the World Wide Web, check out our site at `http://www.mcp.com`.

> **NOTE** If you have a technical question about this book, call the technical support line at (800) 571-5840, ext. 3668.

As the publishing manager of the group that created this book, I welcome your comments. You can fax, e-mail, or write me directly to let me know what you did or didn't like about this book—as well as what we can do to make our books stronger. Here's the information:

    Fax: 317/581-4669
 E-mail: `opsys_mgr@sams.mcp.com`
   Mail: Dean Miller
          Sams Publishing
          201 W. 103rd Street
          Indianapolis, IN 46290

Introduction

Who Should Read This Book?

This book is directed toward the beginning or novice Lotus Notes 4.5 user who wants to attain a more thorough understanding of the Notes user environment. There is nothing in the book that requires special technical knowledge or programming skills.

Conventions Used in the Book

The book is designed so that you can read and absorb the material in a single chapter every day. Based on that, you can finish the book in two weeks. When you reach the end of each lesson, you will find a summary of the day's lesson, followed by a workshop section that includes questions and answers, a short quiz, and some exercises. These exercises are somewhat incremental. You begin by creating a database, and then you fill it with documents and learn to work with data as you gain proficiency in Notes. You should attempt to answer all of the quiz questions and do the exercises before moving on to the next day's lesson. For review, the answers to the quizzes and suggestions for doing the exercises can be found in Appendix A.

Throughout the book, you will find icons beside paragraphs that contain special information. These icons include the following:

Notes enhance the text by calling out key information that you might otherwise miss as you work your way through the text.

Tips provide hints for ways to put in practice some of the techniques you are learning.

Warnings are there to tell you to slow down and pay attention. If you ignore a Warning, you may end up losing data or getting into a situation from which it is not easy to recover.

Navigation within Notes uses easy-to-follow commands when possible. If there is a command to copy a document from the Edit menu, for example, it will be described as "Select Edit | Copy from the menu bar." You will also be directed to click on icons and buttons to initiate actions.

In some instances, you are directed toward keyboard shortcuts, but I have not attempted to exhaustively describe every shortcut. The commonly available ones are listed on menus that can be accessed from the menu bar, and you are welcome to use these keyboard shortcuts as you become more proficient. You may also want to refer to the extensive online help to find further shortcuts on your own.

After you complete this book and feel you are proficient in Notes, you may be interested in learning more about the Notes environment. There are two excellent resources you can tap into, if you want to further your Notes skills. Read other books from Sams Publishing. They have several excellent titles besides this one regarding various aspects of the Lotus Notes environment. And Lotus maintains an education connection for clients. You can contact a Lotus Authorized Education Center (LAEC) in your community directly, contact the Lotus Education Hotline at 1-800-346-6409, or visit the Lotus Web page at `http://www.lotus.com`.

Enjoy your journey through Lotus land.

At a Glance

During your first week of learning Lotus Notes 4.5, you will be learning most of the functions used every day by a majority of Lotus Notes users. But you are starting from scratch. Because you are reading this book, presumably you have Notes installed on your local workstation, and your organization probably has a Domino server installed—the Domino server is synonymous with a Notes server. You will be learning most of the fundamentals during the first week, including how to create and read Notes documents. Lessons are arranged so that one day's lesson builds on what you learned the previous day. You begin with a blank desktop, learn how to put a database on the desktop, and then you create documents in the database and learn how to work with those documents.

Each day's lesson ends with several quiz questions and some exercises to help you reinforce what you learned. You should be able to answer all the quiz questions and do the exercises based on what you learned in the lesson. Appendix A, "Workshop Answers," includes answers to all the quiz questions, and solutions to any exercises that do not include discovery in your own Notes environment. For most exercises, there are suggestions and tips to help you complete the exercise.

You will find that you get more out of this book if you make an effort to answer all the quiz questions and complete the exercises before continuing to the next day's lesson. Many of the later lessons depend on the successful understanding and completion of earlier exercises.

What's Ahead?

The first week covers the Notes environment so that you understand what you are seeing on your desktop, and can tailor it to your requirements. You will then learn how to create and work with Notes documents and Notes databases.

On Day 1, you will gain a fundamental understanding of just what Notes is, the general concepts of Notes, and the network environment in which you will be using Notes. Day 2 will extend this information to your desktop, where you will learn to tailor your personal Notes environment.

On Day 3, you learn how to use the online Notes Help. This serves two functions. First, it introduces you to a very comprehensive resource. But this lesson serves another purpose: to teach you how to read a Notes document, and how to navigate within a Notes database.

On Day 4, you learn how to create a basic Notes document. You will go deeper into the creation process on Day 5, when you learn about the word processing functions of Notes in a Rich Text field.

On Day 6, you will again be working with rich text, but this time, you will be learning about the multimedia functionality of rich text, including activities such as attaching and launching files, embedding graphics, and linking to other documents.

On Day 7, you will be working with the documents you created in the previous lessons, learning how to use views and folders to make your documents accessible to you.

By the end of this first week, you will be able to use Notes to read and create documents—the two primary functions of any document-centric application.

Week 1

Day 1

Understanding Notes

On this first day, you will learn a bit about what Lotus Notes is and how it is commonly used in an organization. You will learn many of the terms and concepts that are essential to understanding Notes, and you will begin to understand how Notes fits into the virtual world of Internet computing.

What Is Lotus Notes?

Before we go one word farther, let's get this much clear. Lotus Notes is not Lotus 1-2-3, the spreadsheet. It is entirely different, except for the name of the originating company.

Lotus Notes is *groupware*, which is collaborative technology that helps people work in groups. To understand Notes, you must understand something about the "group," something that makes Notes fairly unique in the world of computers. Members of the workgroup can be any of the following:

- Individuals who are constantly connected to each other via a local area network (LAN)
- Individuals who are sometimes connected to the LAN and are sometimes on the road

- Individuals who always work remotely and must dial in to a Notes server to exchange data with members of the workgroup
- Individuals who are on another LAN that is either constantly connected to another LAN in a wide area network (WAN), or is connected only on occasion via a dial-up connection or some other sort of connection
- Individuals who connect to other members of the workgroup using a Web browser over the Internet
- Individuals who use an IBM PC or laptop running OS/2, Windows 3.1 or Windows 95, Windows NT, AIX, Solaris SPARC and Intel Edition, HP-UX, a Macintosh, or a UNIX workstation

In short, you can be part of a Notes workgroup if you are using practically any type of computer, and you can be part of a Notes workgroup from practically any location, as long as all of the members have a way to communicate with a shared Notes server.

So, you are probably asking, what can a workgroup do?

Communication

The first thing that comes to mind when most people think of Notes is communication. The members of a workgroup must communicate with each other.

So how does a workgroup communicate if they are not using Notes? If they are in close proximity, they can pull up a chair for a quick, informal meeting. They can exchange an idea or develop a bit of team spirit with a smile and a greeting in the hallway. They can chat over the water cooler.

Add a bit of hierarchy, and the communication can become more formal, taking place primarily during scheduled meetings. Add a bit of distance, and communications are likely to become more frustrating and inefficient. Most people are probably familiar with telephone tag and memos in the company mailbox, or documents sent around the office with a routing slip.

Add even more distance. Now you are dependent on mail or a delivery service, a fax machine, long distance phone charges, different time zones, and infrequent, expensive meetings.

In every instance cited above, Notes can improve communication, because the individuals involved can share common information, and they can—within reason—choose when and where they are when they communicate with each other. No more phone tag, because you can write a message to a team member, and he can look at the e-mail message when he is ready for it, without interruptions from the phone. Information is there when it is needed, no matter where you are.

Individuals can forward mail to an individual or to everyone in the cc: field on a memo. They can forward Web pages. They can change the letterhead on their memos and they can stamp outgoing memos with "mood stamps" as a way of personalizing their mail. They can exchange mail with others who may be using cc:Mail, Exchange, or other commonly available e-mail packages.

Outside of mail, many organizations communicate with their employees using Notes databases as electronic libraries. Documents are distributed via Notes or via a Web browser, and people can read the documents whenever they want. Notes is an excellent tool when used as an online reference library, because documents can be searched using a full text index that helps you quickly find the information you need.

Okay, you say. Any good e-mail package can do quite a few of those things, if not all. But read on, and you will discover that Notes is far more than just being able to choose when and how you communicate with your colleagues.

Collaboration

The best thing about working as a member of a team is that you increase the chances of coming up with a good idea. Everyone brings their own perspective to the table, and hopefully as the members of the team interact, new ideas emerge. And, as mentioned in the previous section, you can collaborate with virtually anyone, no matter where they are.

In Notes, a prime example of collaboration takes place in interactive discussion databases, which are like bulletin boards. One person posts a message, and everyone who happens to pass that way is free to write their own opinions in response to the initial posting. Everyone can read what others have written. The discussion is controlled by Notes security, which determines who has access to the database, who can create or edit documents, and who can respond to existing documents.

NOTE This is similar to Usenet groups, which you may be familiar with if you have used the Internet before. The Notes discussion database is more accessible, but it is the same principle. If you participate in Usenet groups, you can still interact with them using the Domino server.

Of course, you can use Notes to collaborate with others in your own organization, with those people you see every day. Notes collaborative databases become an additional tool to supplement e-mail and meetings. But you begin to unleash the real power of Notes when you discover that Notes lets you quickly and easily create a virtual community. You can form ad hoc alliances with other organizations that use Notes, or you can use Notes to create an intranet so that you can collaborate using any Web browser.

>
> **NOTE**
>
> The *Internet* is a global network of computers that share a common protocol called TCP/IP. With the Internet, you can share e-mail, you can transfer files from FTP sites, and you can use the World Wide Web (also known as the Web or WWW.) An *intranet* is a network that uses Internet technology behind a firewall. If you have an intranet, you can access data via Web pages that are only available to people within your organization. If you extend the intranet to people outside your organization, it is referred to as an *extranet*. For example, you may establish a collaborative environment where your customers and suppliers have access to certain data from your legacy systems and from your intranet.

Coordination

Coordination is the third of the three C's of Lotus Notes. You can communicate directly with other users, and you can use Notes as a tool for collaboration, but you can also use Notes as a tool to automate the flow of work within your organization.

For example, suppose you have certain sensitive documents that are being prepared for release to the public. The documents have to go through an approval process that includes several edits before they get published. The old paradigm is probably all too familiar. You create a draft document and circulate a hard copy to several reviewers. Alternatively, you may give the draft to a single individual, who in turn passes the document up a hierarchical ladder. Eventually, one or more copies of the document come back to you with suggested edits. You pull up the original, make the suggested changes, and then send the document on the approval path again.

The traditional editorial review process is fraught with pitfalls and bottlenecks. Using Notes, you can coordinate the review process automatically. You create a draft document, and then define a review cycle. The document can be distributed for serial or simultaneous review, for example. Notes forwards the document to the first reviewer, and sends automatic reminders if he or she fails to respond within a set time. After a reviewer is done with the document, it is automatically forwarded to the next reviewer, and you have the option of tracking the document as it moves through the entire cycle.

This is just one simple example of how Notes can be used to coordinate the flow of work in an organization. Another prime example is how Notes might be used in a sales organization. Sales reps out in the field can look up inventory in a Notes database. When they place an order for a customer, they can dial in to headquarters with the order. The inventory can be updated automatically, and the order can be displayed in a Notes view used by the fulfillment

department. When the order is dispatched, the customer's account is updated and bookkeeping is informed that an invoice needs to be generated. Eventually, the information moves full circle. The next time the sales rep visits that customer, he or she can ask them if they need any more widgets. All of this coordination takes place within a well-designed Notes application that makes information available just in time. The flow of information is coordinated by Notes, with each member of the work team receiving just the information he or she needs to do his or her job efficiently.

The Notes Environment

It is difficult to describe a "typical" Notes environment because there are so many possible permutations. At a very high level, the Notes environment must include a Domino server and at least one Notes client. Notes runs on top of a local area network (LAN) using any of the common network protocols to carry data between Notes clients and the Domino server.

The network environment can take on a variety of configurations, including dial-in phone lines for remote or mobile Notes clients; dedicated communication lines linking multiple LANs into a wide area network; and connections to the Internet that enable Notes clients to communicate directly with the Domino server, and enable Web browsers to access data that is published to the Web through Domino.

The Notes environment is depicted in Figure 1.1.

Figure 1.1.
The Notes environment is a complex mix of Notes clients, Domino servers, and Web browsers on LANs, WANs, and the Internet.

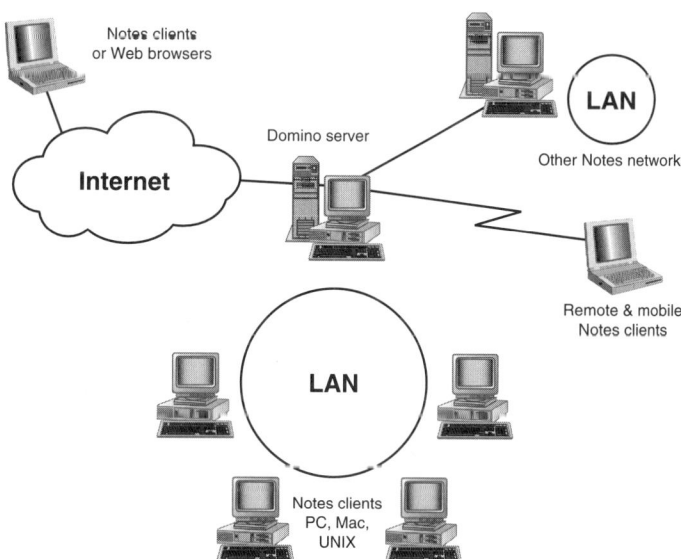

The Notes environment can include the Domino server, local and remote Notes clients, and Internet access using Notes clients or Web browsers. Local Notes clients could be on your LAN, or they could be part of wide area network (WAN) connected to the Domino server through a dedicated line. The remote clients could be part of another Notes installation that is tied to your LAN via a dial-up connection. And, of course, Internet or intranet users could be on the other side of the world.

To understand the environment, let's look at the key elements a little more closely.

Domino Server

The Domino server and the Lotus Notes server are one and the same. When Notes 4.5 was released in November 1996, Domino, originally a server task on the Notes server, was fully integrated into the Notes server and added so much Internet functionality to Notes that Lotus decided to give the new server a new identity. Therefore, the server is officially *Domino Server 4.5, Powered by Lotus Notes.*

The Domino server is what enables Notes clients to communicate, collaborate, and coordinate. The server controls access to Notes databases, controls communications within a Notes installation, handles the routing of Notes mail, replicates data with other Notes and Domino servers and with workstations. In short, the Domino server handles all the details that transform Notes from a fancy desktop environment into a groupware environment, where you can share data easily with the members of your workgroup.

Notes Client

This book focuses on teaching yourself to use the Notes client. The Notes client is the Notes environment you see when you sit at your computer and work with Notes. It is the desktop, the icons, local databases, menus, and documents, plus everything within Notes that goes on behind the scenes on your local workstation.

The Notes client looks virtually the same on any platform. There are minor differences in the way parts of the workspace are displayed for different environments, but the differences are cosmetic. You can access the same data from any Notes client, so, for example, a Notes database can be shared between users on a Windows 95 Notes client and users on a Macintosh Notes client.

What you can do with a Notes client depends on the type of Notes license you have. Notes clients can be broken down into the following basic categories:

- ☐ *Notes client on a Domino server.* When a Domino server is installed on a workstation, the server runs in a text-based environment. A Notes client is installed on the same workstation along with the server. This Notes client can be used as a full

Notes client, and is commonly used by the system administrator to perform administrative tasks within Notes.

WARNING

The Notes client on the server should be used sparingly to minimize the potential for security breaches, and to avoid impacting server performance.

- *Full Notes client.* The full Notes client can be used to develop Notes applications and perform administrative functions, as well as being used to work with Notes applications as an end user.
- *Notes Desktop client.* The Notes Desktop client provides everything the full Notes client provides, except for the application development functionality. This type of client enables you to work with Notes applications. If you are using this book, you are probably using either a desktop client or a full Notes client.
- *Notes Mail client.* The Notes Mail client was designed to provide a low cost way to use limited Notes functionality. When you have a Notes Mail client, you can only access databases created by the five templates that Lotus includes with the client. These templates include Notes mail and simple databases such as discussions and document libraries.

NOTE

At Lotusphere, an annual gathering of Notes professionals and clients, Lotus announced several new initiatives involving the Notes client. In essence, these initiatives make it possible to tailor the client more specifically to the needs of an individual user. Therefore, the items listed above are intended only as guidelines. If you are unable to perform certain exercises in this book, it may be that you have a Notes client with restricted functionality.

Web Browser

Lotus Notes is fully Web enabled. For those who are not familiar with the Internet, the *Web* is the popular World Wide Web, which provides a graphical interface for navigating the Internet. As long as the Domino server is attached to the Internet, you can browse the Web. Notes offers a choice of browsers, including two browsers that are built into Notes and two others that are bundled with Notes. The browser you select may depend on what you want to do on the Web.

Web browsing can be done by going to the Web and navigating to a specific Web site as you would with any Web navigator. But Notes goes one step further. Web addresses, known as URLs (Uniform Resource Locators), are recognized and turned into hypertext links by Notes whenever they appear in a Notes document. To visit a Web site, all you have to do is click on the underlined hypertext link. The hypertext link is a shortcut for entering a URL that points to a specific Web site. Notes will launch your Web browser and retrieve the page for you. You can also launch a Web browser from a SmartIcon, from a full text search bar, or from a Web Navigator database. These are all covered in detail later in this book.

The following paragraphs describe some of the features of the various Web browser options.

Notes Personal Web Navigator

The Personal Web Navigator runs on the Notes client. To use the Personal Web Navigator, your workstation must be connected to the Internet. You are connected to the Internet if any of these conditions are true:

- ☐ You communicate with a Web-enabled Domino server using TCP/IP protocol, the communication protocol used to communicate on the Internet.
- ☐ You communicate directly with the Internet.
- ☐ You are connected to the Internet through a dial-up connection to an Internet service provider such as America Online, or another Internet service provider (ISP).

With the Personal Web Navigator, you explore the Web from within your Notes client. When you retrieve a Web page, it is stored on your workstation as a Notes document. You can search Web pages using a full text search, you can forward Web pages via e-mail to other Notes users, you can have the pages refreshed automatically on a schedule, and you can have the Personal Web Navigator download all links from a page automatically.

Notes Public Web Navigator

The Public Web Navigator is a collaborative version of the Personal Web Navigator. Rather than retrieving Web pages directly to your desktop, Web pages are retrieved into a database on the Domino server, where they can be seen by anyone with reader access to the Web Navigator database. This has a couple of advantages for an organization.

First, you cut down on Internet traffic, because multiple Notes users can view a single Web page instead of each user having to download the page themselves.

Second, and perhaps the biggest advantage, is that users do not have to be running TCP/IP on their workstations. Notes clients can use existing protocols over the LAN—for example, NetBEUI, SPX/IPX, AppleTalk, Banyan Vines—and they can still view Web pages.

As with the Personal Web Navigator, you can still work with the Web content as a Notes document, meaning that you can take advantage of Notes functionality to perform tasks such as full text indexing the Web pages or forwarding them to other users via e-mail.

Other Web Browsers

Notes ships with Netscape Navigator and Microsoft Internet Explorer. You can use either of these Web browsers if you want. When you click on a hypertext link in a Notes document, the selected browser is launched.

You lose some of the Notes functionality, such as the capability to full text index your Web pages when you select an alternative Web browser, but much of this functionality can be regained by using the *Weblicator*, a Web application from Lotus that lets you work with Web pages no matter which Web browser you choose.

NOTE Another browser option is the JavaBean version of the Microsoft Internet Explorer. In January 1997, Lotus announced Java-based components, including a version of the Explorer interface that will run within the Notes environment. This is not included in the initial release of Notes 4.5, but should be available with later releases.

How Notes Data Is Stored

One way to visualize Lotus Notes is as a series of nested containers, as shown in Figure 1.2. The kernel of these nested containers is the data that you see as a document. As an end user of Notes, you do not need to understand every permutation of the nested containers, but there are certain concepts that you should be familiar with. So, you will get a quick tour of the nested containers, and then a more in-depth look at some of the key elements.

Figure 1.2.
Visualize Notes as nested containers. The Notes environment contains databases, which contain forms and fields through which data is displayed.

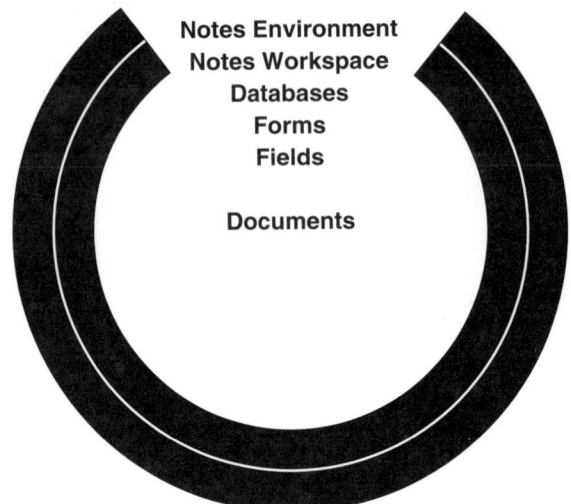

So far in today's lesson, we have looked at the Notes environment. In Day 2, "Exploring the Notes Workspace," we will be looking at the Notes workspace in detail. Before you actually open up the Notes workspace, though, let's examine the Notes database. You will be looking at the database in detail on Day 3, "Using Notes Help," but today you will get a high-level view.

Notes databases have an NSF file extension by default. The story I heard about the origin of this extension may be apochryphal, but it makes the extension easy to remember. Supposedly, the NSF stands for Notes Storage Facility. The popular microbrewries in the neighborhood of Lotus headquarters in Cambridge, Massachusetts, kept their stock in a storage facility because it was manufactured in batches too small to put in a warehouse. If this is true, then the Notes database was named in honor of the local pub. The databases can have other file extensions, but your ability to locate them will be limited if they do not have the NSF extension.

The Notes database contains various forms and views, along with a variety of other design elements. Forms, in turn, hold fields, some of them visible and some hidden. Finally, the form with its fields provides a framework for you to enter data that, when it is saved, becomes a document. When you view a document, the data is seen through the framework of a form, although not necessarily the same form you used when you created the document. And that is a Notes database in a nutshell.

Understanding Notes

The Notes database differs from most other databases you may be familiar with. The traditional database contains files and records. But Notes is document centric. That is why examples of what can be done in Notes refer to documents pinned to a bulletin board, or documents circulated with a routing slip.

Another key difference between Notes and other databases is that most databases use some sort of file locking to maintain the integrity of data. Notes does not lock its documents. A single document can be opened and edited simultaneously by multiple users, working on the same database or on multiple replicas of the database…replicas that are synchronized over time.

NOTE Replication is a key concept in Lotus Notes. Replica databases and replication will be explained in detail on Day 12, "Mobile Notes: Using Notes When You're Out of the Office."

NSF files (that is, Notes databases) can be stored in one of two places: on your local workstation or on a shared network drive that can be accessed by the Domino server. The location of a Notes database can make a big difference in how you work with data.

WARNING The shared network drive is not as secure as a Domino server, and you risk database corruption if the database is not on a Domino server.

Using Local Notes Databases

You can work with Notes databases that are stored on your local workstation. In fact, you could use the Notes client as a stand-alone product, and create Notes databases for storing documents, keeping track of names and addresses, even tracking your sports card collection. There are rules that should be kept in mind, though, if you are using a Notes database that exists only on your workstation.

First, you cannot share information directly with other users if it is stored in a local database. All shared access takes place through a Domino server. If you decide that you want to share the data, you have a few options:

- ☐ Make a copy of the local database and distribute it via the sneaker net so it can be placed on another user's workstation.
- ☐ Make a copy of the local database and place it on the Domino server.

- Make a replica copy of the local database on the Domino server. You can then create and update documents on your local copy and replicate the changes to the replica copy on the server.
- E-mail documents to other users or to another database.
- Print documents and distribute them as hard copies.

In short, if you want to share the data in a Notes database, the database should reside on the Domino server.

The second important concept to be aware of is the different way that security is handled when you use a Notes database on a local Notes client. Access to the various design elements and documents in a Notes database is defined within each database. This access security is always enforced when the database is on a Domino server. However, you can gain full and direct access to a database that resides on a Notes client.

There are a couple of exceptions to this full access on local databases:

- You cannot view encrypted data unless you have a valid key to unlock the encrypted data.
- Access control can be enforced locally, in which case you must have a valid Notes userID along with a password in order to gain access to the database. This is particularly useful for protecting Notes databases on a laptop computer that may be vulnerable to theft, or on workstations that may be shared by more than one Notes user.

What does full access to a Notes database mean? Soon, you will learn about Notes security, where you will find a more detailed discussion of access control. But, in summary, unrestricted access means that you can change the design of the database, including forms and views. You can edit any document in the database, regardless of who created the document. You can delete documents, views, and forms. You can also remove someone from the Access Control List. And you can physically delete the database file.

If you make local changes to a database, changes that you are barred from making on the server copy of the database, can you replicate the changes to the server? No way. Notes security has been tested and refined over a period of several years. You cannot do an end run around the security system. Why do you think so many banks and government agencies use Notes?

Using Notes Databases on the Domino Server

When a Notes database resides on the Domino server, it can be accessed by any authorized Notes user. The user must have a valid Notes UserID capable of accessing the server, and they must have access to the directory in which the database is stored. Beyond that, a user's ability to use a Notes database is up to the manager of the database and the type of Notes license being used.

We will look at the above paragraph one item at a time.

By default, Notes databases are kept in a DATA directory defined in a Domino server's directory tree. The database could also be stored in other directories or subdirectories as long as there is a direct path or a pointer to where the data is stored. But to you, the end user, the location of the database is entirely transparent. The key point is that you have to go through the Domino server to get to the database.

You have to be an authorized Notes user. That means that you must have a Notes UserID capable of being authenticated by the Domino server on which the database resides. The authentication process is described in greater detail in the section "Understanding Notes Security," later in this chapter, but basically, it means that the server and the ID used on your Notes client recognize each other. Once the Domino server recognizes the UserID, it gives you the ability to open any Notes database to which you have authorized access.

Once the Domino server gives you the ability to open databases, there are still a couple of things that have to happen.

First, you must have network access to the database's location, even if the location is transparent to you as a Notes user. For example, suppose your system administrator stores databases on a network drive that has more disk storage than the machine running the Domino server. The administrator will also have to set up network security so you have access to the drive and directory in which the database is stored.

Second, you must be included in the Access Control List of a database before you can open it. You can be included explicitly as an individual, you can be included as a member of a group that has access, or you can be included via the database's default level of access.

Once you get through all the security loopholes and have access to a database, you have to add a database icon to your Notes workspace so you can work with the database.

Note: There are some instances where you can open a Notes database without putting it on your Notes desktop. For example, some applications may comprise several Notes databases, which are opened from navigators within the primary database. The primary database must be on your desktop, but the developer can elect to open the other databases without putting them on your desktop. Also, many applications use other databases as repositories for mail-in data or for looking up data. You do not need to place these supplementary databases on your desktop, but they must be accessible to the Domino server.

You can work with a server-based Notes database by opening it up directly or by making a local replica copy of the database. You can work on the replica using your local Notes client, and then replicate with the server-based copy to synchronize any changes that you or others have made. You can only replicate with a replica copy of the database on a Domino server. You cannot replicate directly with a copy that is on another user's Notes client.

Note: *Replication* is the process of synchronizing the data in two databases when the two databases are *replicas* (a special type of a copy) of each other. You will learn about replication in greater detail on Day 12 when you learn about using Notes on the road.

The more you work with Notes from any location besides the office LAN, the more you will begin to appreciate the power of replication. Communication time is kept to a minimum, and you can continue working even if the network or the communication lines go down. Notes is truly information at your fingertips, no matter where you are, and no matter which type of hardware you are using.

Understanding Notes Security

Remember the Notes containers illustrated in Figure 1.2? The container was several layers thick, including the Notes environment, the Notes desktop, the database, forms and views, and fields. That same model works well when discussing Notes security, as well.

Figure 1.3 shows the same model, only this time, the various layers are rotated like tumblers on a combination lock so that access to the data is blocked.

Figure 1.3.
Gaining access to the data in Notes documents requires the right combination of security elements.

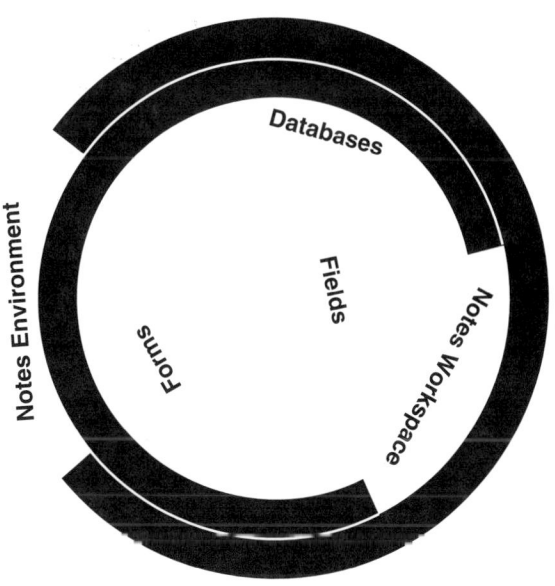

You need the right combination of security access at several levels before you can view and work with data in Notes documents. You can break down the layers in varying degrees of granularity, but basically, security is enforced at each of the following layers:

- *The network.* Before you can communicate with a Domino server, you need access to network services. This is true whether you are using a LAN, a wide area network, a dial-up connection to the network, or an Internet connection.
- *The Domino server.* The Domino server has its own Notes ID, just as if it were another Notes user. The Server ID and your Notes userID must be compatible before the server will let you open up Notes databases. In other words, they must both be certified as part of your Notes organization.
- *The Notes database.* Each Notes database has its own Access Control List that determines who can open the database and work with the data.
- *Database forms and views.* Some forms are used only for data entry, some are used only for displaying data, and some serve both purposes. Some forms are only available to certain users of the database, depending on a user's role in the database. Likewise, some views may be restricted to certain individuals. You can build private views to display most data in a database, with the exception of encrypted data and restricted access sections on forms.
- *Documents.* Individual documents can have different security settings, based on names entered into special Reader Name and Author Name fields that determine who can read or edit the document.

- *Restricted sections.* Some data may be hidden in restricted access sections to make documents more relevant to individual users. For example, suppose a database contains a library of proposals. Financial information could be put into a restricted section that is only displayed for members of the accounting department and the management team, for whom the information is most important.
- *Fields.* Fields may be hidden under certain conditions, and displayed under other conditions.
- *Encryption.* All or part of a document can be *encrypted*, which means that it is scrambled. The encrypted data is only available to users who have access to a valid encryption key that unscrambles the data.

That's a lot of gates to pass through, but the process is easy. Log on to your network. Launch Notes. Provide a Notes UserID if Notes cannot find it automatically. Enter your password once. You can then open any database to which you have authorized access. Your username is taken from your UserID, and is used throughout the Notes session to determine which databases you can access and which Reader Name fields and Author Name fields contain your name. If a document requires an encryption key, Notes gets the key from your UserID. If you need to access a database that is stored on another server in another Notes network, Notes looks in your UserID to see if there is a certificate held in common with the other server.

In other words, all you do is log in to the system. Notes does everything else. The security is built into the system at every step.

The Notes UserID

You can see from the previous paragraph that the Notes UserID holds the key to who you are in terms of the Notes environment and what you can do within Notes.

Your Notes UserID was created when the Notes administrator registered you as a user of the system. At the same time your UserID was created, Notes also created an e-mail database for you (assuming your organization uses Notes Mail) with you as the manager and only authorized user of the database, and created an entry for you in the Public Address Book.

Your Notes UserID is saved in the form of a small file that the Notes administrator can give to you on a diskette or in a directory where you can access it, or as a file attachment in the Public Address Book. The file is given the default name USER.ID.

TIP You can change the name of the ID file as long as you leave the suffix (.ID). For example, you may want to give your UserID the same name as your mail file, with the first character of your first name, plus your last name. John Smith's ID would therefore be renamed JSMITH.ID.

The UserID has embedded in it certain information, including a Notes license number, electronic certificates that indicate which Domino and Notes servers you can access, a private encryption key and any other encryption keys that have been provided to you, and a password that lets you use the UserID.

The UserID is used to authenticate you as a user, which is necessary the first time you access a Domino or Notes server during a session, or try to access a local database on which security is enforced.

When you first attempt to communicate with the Domino server, a dialog box will be displayed asking you to enter your password. Then there is an almost imperceptible delay while the server and your UserID authenticate each other.

NOTE The process of authentication, while not important for you to understand, is interesting, and worth noting. It involves a dialog between the server and your Notes client. The two parties identify themselves to each other, ensure that they both have access to certificates descended from the same recognized authority, and then they go through a process of proving to each other that they really are who they claim to be. This involves each party generating and encrypting a random number using a public encryption key from the Public Address Book, then using a private encryption key to decrypt the data, proving its authenticity to the originating party. The private encryption keys are stored in the UserID and in the ServerID.

Assuming that you pass the authentication test, you are given access to the Domino server and its services, which include the ability to open shared databases.

The Password

The UserID should always be protected with a password. The minimum length of the password can be set by the Notes administrator when they register you as a user, but the default minimum length of eight characters is recommended.

The Notes administrator should also have protected your UserID with a password before it was given to you. You should change the password as soon as you have the opportunity. How to change your password is covered on Day 2.

The password has the following characteristics:

- Passwords are case sensitive. In other words, "PassWord," "password," and "PASSWORD" are each unique.
- Passwords cannot contain any of the following characters: spaces, commas, forward or back slashes (/ \), colons, semicolons, or periods.
- Passwords can contain a combination of numbers and letters.

TIP

Consider using a phrase as password, because it is easy to remember but hard to guess. For example, your password could be "TheQuickBrownFox." Avoid using common items such as children's names, birthdates, and place names.

If security is a primary consideration, consider establishing a corporate policy requiring users to use a combination of numbers and letters in mixed case in their passwords.

NOTE

Notes UserIDs can have multiple passwords assigned to them. When extra security is required, you may want to have the Notes Administrator create a fake user, and then assign different passwords to different users. Make the ID accessible only when multiple passwords are used. In that way, the ID can only be used with the explicit consent of two or more individuals.

Passwords in Notes are not restricted to Notes UserIDs. Other Notes ID files can also have passwords assigned to them. This includes the CERT.ID file, which is used for registering new users and servers, the SERVER.ID file, which is a "user" ID for each Domino server in the organization, and IDs for other users.

WARNING

Passwords are encrypted in a way that they cannot be recovered. Be sure you do not forget your password.

The Access Control List

Looking back at the security model, you first had to access the Domino services with your UserID. Once you have access to the server, you can open Notes databases, assuming the database Access Control List (ACL) permits you to open the database.

Every Notes database has an ACL. The ACL determines what can be done by various users (including Domino servers) within that database. We will be looking at the ACL in greater detail on Day 4, "Creating Notes Documents."

The ACL is used to assign individuals, groups, and servers to one of seven levels of access. The levels and their privileges are summarized below.

- *Manager.* Manager access is required to modify the ACL or to delete a database from the Domino server. The manager also has all privileges granted to Designers, Editors, Authors, and Readers.
- *Designer.* Designer access is required to modify the design of a Notes database. The Designer also has all privileges granted to Editors, Authors, and Readers.
- *Editor.* Editor access allows a user to create or modify any document in the database, no matter who created the document. The Editor also has all privileges granted to Authors and Readers.
- *Author.* Author access allows users to create documents in a Notes database and modify documents that they themselves have created. More precisely, authors can modify any document where they are listed in an Author Name field.
- *Reader.* Reader access is required in order to be able to read any documents in a Notes database. Readers cannot create, modify, or delete documents.
- *Depositor.* Depositor access allows a user to create documents, but a depositor cannot view any documents in the database, including documents that they have previously created and saved. This level of access may be used for applications such as a ballot box, a suggestion box, or to allow individuals to create evaluations. It is also useful if you want to have temporary help input data but do not want them to view confidential data.
- *No Access.* No Access means just what it says. The database cannot be placed on the Notes desktop, and cannot be accessed by users (or servers) who have No Access.

This is only a summary, and there are a lot of permutations. But from this, you can see that your role in a particular database can be restricted. If you cannot perform a function in a particular database, check the Access Control List (File | Database | Access Control on the menu bar) to see what restrictions the database Manager has imposed.

Remember, the ACL is enforced for databases that are accessed through the Domino server. The ACL is only enforced on local databases if the database Manager has chosen to enforce the ACL on all replica copies of the database. Incidentally, that also means that only the database Manager can delete the database from within Notes.

The Role of the Public Address Book

Throughout today's introductory lesson, you have learned about communications in a Notes network, and about the role of Notes security. There is one more element that is essential for the proper functioning of Notes—the Public Address Book.

The Public Address Book must be accessible by all users and servers in the organization, because it is the nerve center of the Notes organization. Documents in the Public Address Book define all servers and users and how they are situated within the organization. The complexities of the organization are defined, such as where user mail files are located, which groups the Notes administrator can place users and servers into, and how different servers should communicate with each other. When you enter your password and authenticate with the Domino server, it is the Public Address Book that provides public encryption keys. When you send e-mail to another user, the Router on the Domino server uses the Public Address Book to determine where to deliver the mail. Without the Public Address Book, you have no Notes organization, and you cannot share data with other Notes users.

Summary

Today you learned what Lotus Notes is, and about the environment in which it operates. The Notes environment is complex, but as an end user, these complexities are more or less transparent once you understand how they can potentially affect you.

The parts of the Notes environment with which you need to be concerned are: the location of data, that is, is it on a Domino server where it can be shared with other Notes users; the importance of your Notes UserID, which you need in order to communicate with a Domino server; and the role of the Access Control List, which determines what you can do within any particular database.

Tomorrow, you will have an opportunity to begin building on this fundamental knowledge as you explore the Notes workspace.

Workshop

The Workshop section presents quiz questions to help you cement your new knowledge and exercises to give you experience using what you have learned. Try to understand the questions and exercises before moving on to the next lesson. Answers are in Appendix A.

Q&A

Q Is Notes backward compatible? In other words, can I use a Notes 4.5 client with a Notes 3.x server?

A You can open databases that are running on earlier versions of Notes servers, but you will lose some functionality. For example, you cannot use graphical navigators on databases that were created in versions earlier than Notes 4.x, and functions that depend on LotusScript (an advanced Notes programming language introduced in Notes 4.x) will not work. Also, you cannot connect directly to the Internet with earlier versions of Notes, and you cannot connect at all with versions earlier than Notes 4.x.

Q I have a Notes UserID that was created on a Notes 3.x server. Is that still good?

A Yes. The Notes security paradigm has not changed. As long as the UserID has a certificate recognized by the server, it can be used.

Q I forgot my password. Can the Notes administrator recover the password for me?

A No. The password is encrypted and cannot be recovered from the UserID, even by the Notes administrator. You have two alternatives. Some Notes administrators keep an archive of Notes UserIDs, all stored with the original default password. If your administrator has a backup copy of your UserID, you are back in business. Otherwise, the Notes administrator must delete your Person record in the Public Address Book, and then register you as a new user and give you a new UserID.

Quiz

1. What are the different types of Notes clients?
2. Can another user access Notes databases that reside on your Notes client workstation?
3. Can you enforce security on a Notes database that is on your Notes client workstation?

4. If you have a Notes document open for editing, can that document be accessed by other users?
5. Which documents can you modify if you have Author access?
6. Which documents can you read if you have Depositor access?
7. You discover that you can modify or delete any document in a database. What levels of access could you have for this database?

Exercises

1. Diagram the way Notes is deployed in your organization. Keep the following in mind:

    What kind of underlying network are you using?

    Is the Domino server connected to the Internet?

    What type of communication protocol is being used?

    Are there any users who are not connected to the local area network?

2. Consider a Notes database that holds personnel data along with company policies and procedures. What type of access might different people in the organization have to this database?

Week 1

Day 2

Exploring the Notes Workspace

In this lesson, we are going to open up the Notes workspace for exploration. The workspace is what you see on the screen when you open Lotus Notes. We begin with a quick tour, and then we look at the parts of the workspace that can be customized. For example, you learn how to put database icons on the workspace, how to customize the tabbed folders (workspace pages), how to change your workspace preferences, and how to use SmartIcons, the pull-down menus, and the status bar.

How to Launch Notes

Before you start Notes, a couple of preliminary questions. Are you connected to a network? If you want to use any network services such as printing, you need to log onto the network before starting Notes. The Domino server takes care of many services within Notes, but it depends on the LAN to provide communications protocols and the shared network services such as printing. Therefore, you should log onto the network before starting Notes if you need these services.

Another question. Has Notes already been set up on your workstation? If the software has been installed but you are starting Notes for the first time, you have to provide certain information via dialog boxes while Notes is busy building its background environment. For example, you need to know what type of Notes license you have, how you are connected to the Domino server (or Notes server, if you are working with a version of Notes earlier than Notes 4.5), and where your Notes UserID file is located. For details on how to install and set up Notes, please refer to the documentation that is shipped with Notes, or consult your system administrator.

You start Notes by running NOTES.EXE from your desktop. Whichever operating system you are using, OS/2 Warp, Windows 3.1, Windows 95, Macintosh, you will probably want to place a shortcut icon on your desktop if one is not already showing. The Notes icon, shown in Figure 2.1, displays three people (a workgroup) standing on a platform.

Click on the icon to start Notes.

Figure 2.1.
The Notes 4.5 icon launches the Notes workspace.

Layout of Notes Workspace

After Notes starts up, it displays the Notes workspace, as shown in Figure 2.2. The various elements of the workspace have been highlighted to help you locate them. Each element is described in detail in today's lesson.

Figure 2.2.
The Notes workspace and its basic components.

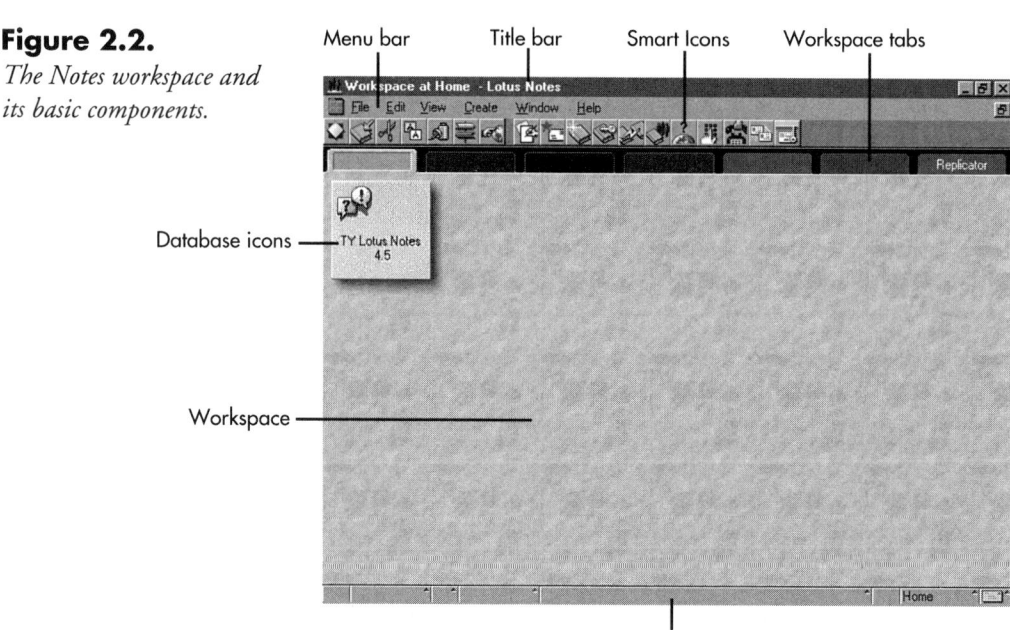

The workspace elements include:

- *Title bar*, which displays the title of the current screen.
- *Menu bar*, which displays pull-down menus.
- *SmartIcon bar*, which contains SmartIcons that can be used as shortcuts to common functions.
- *Workspace page tabs*, which display different workspace pages from which you can access Notes databases.
- *Workspace pages*, where you work with Notes data.
- *Database icons*, which are used to access Notes databases.
- *Status bar*, which provides a summary of your current environment and provides shortcuts to some common functions.

This is your workspace while you are working with Notes.

>  **NOTE** In this book, it is assumed that you are using Notes as it is installed out of the box. If Notes has been customized for your organization, you may not see the standard Notes workspace.
>
> Also be aware that Notes can incorporate Java components that enable you to access data in Notes databases using interfaces other than the Notes workspace.

Now we will look at the parts of the Notes workspace in greater detail.

Title Bar

The title bar is context sensitive, meaning that it changes as you move about within Notes databases. You will be able to see changes in the displayed data as you open new views within Notes databases, and as you open documents.

In some databases, you may notice additional information displayed on the title bar. For example, a Notes application developer can create a formula that displays the date on which the currently selected document was created, and how many documents have been created in response to the document.

The title bar is only informational.

Menu Bar

The menu bar is like the menu bar in any other application. You click on the topic you want, and a menu of available options drops down. To select an option, point to it with the mouse pointer and click the left mouse button.

If a menu option is followed by a small arrow, you can expand the option by sliding the mouse pointer over the arrow. Alternatively, you can click on the arrow to see a nested menu. Also, notice that many of the menu options are followed by keyboard shortcuts. You can see these in Figure 2.3.

As you look at menus, you will also notice that many of the options are grayed out. You can only use options that are displayed in black.

The menu options and the menus themselves are context sensitive. For example, if you have Designer access to a database, you will have more options available to you than if you are restricted to Reader rights in the ACL.

Figure 2.3.
A drop-down menu showing grayed out options and expandable submenus.

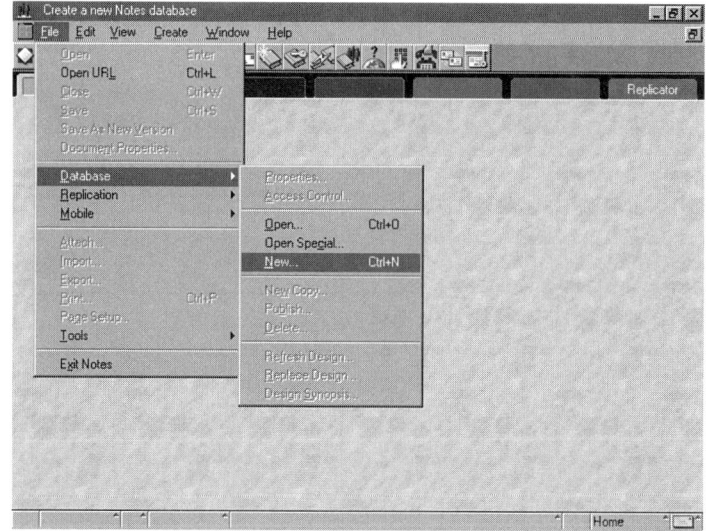

 **NOTE** Remember, too, that a full Notes client will have more menu options available than a Notes desktop client has, because the full Notes client can be used as an application development tool.

Many of the menu options are also available from SmartIcons or from options within a specific Notes database.

Working with SmartIcons

Notes has over 150 context-sensitive SmartIcons that can be displayed on the SmartIcon bar, just beneath the menu bar at the top of the screen. By default, the specific SmartIcons in the set change depending on what you are doing within Notes.

You can place the mouse pointer on a SmartIcon or right-click on it and bubble help will display a description of the SmartIcon's function.

You can modify how SmartIcons are displayed, and you can build custom SmartIcons and sets of SmartIcons. Let's take a look at how to customize the SmartIcons. As we work with the SmartIcons, we use the SmartIcon dialog box. Select File | Tools | SmartIcons to display the SmartIcon dialog box shown in Figure 2.4.

Figure 2.4.
The SmartIcons dialog box is used to customize SmartIcons on your Notes workspace.

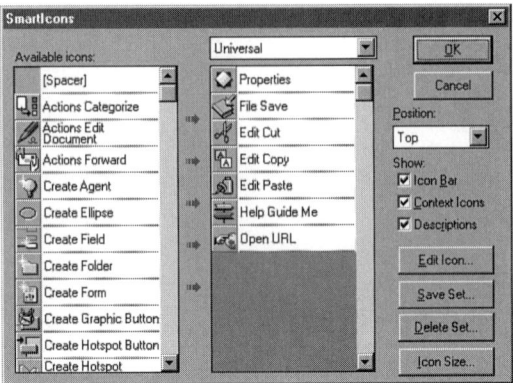

Customizing the Display of SmartIcons

There are several options for customizing the display of SmartIcons, described below.

In the right center of the SmartIcons dialog box, there are three check boxes under the heading "Show:." By default, all three boxes are checked. If you click on a checked box to turn it off, it has the following effect:

- ☐ *Icon Bar.* If you uncheck this box, you will no longer be able to see any SmartIcons.
- ☐ *Context Icons.* There is a basic set of seven SmartIcons that are displayed as long as the Icon Bar is not turned off. Additional SmartIcons are displayed based on your current context. If you uncheck the Context Icons box, only the basic set of SmartIcons, called the Universal set, is displayed.
- ☐ *Descriptions.* If you uncheck Descriptions, you will not see the bubble help that is available when you rest the mouse pointer or right-click on a SmartIcon.
- ☐ *Position.* This allows you to move the SmartIcon Bar to a different part of the workspace. Click on the drop-down arrow and select the top, bottom, left, or right side of the screen.
- ☐ *Icon Size.* You can change the size of the SmartIcons if you prefer larger icons.

WARNING

If you elect to show larger SmartIcons, some context icons may not fit on the screen. Note, however, that you can fit more SmartIcons on the SmartIcon bar if you have an SVGA monitor.

The other buttons are on the SmartIcon dialog box are described in the following sections.

Creating and Displaying a Custom Set of SmartIcons

The default set of SmartIcons is called "Universal." In the SmartIcons dialog box shown in Figure 2.4, there are two columns of SmartIcons. The column on the right is the Universal set, as you can see from the name at the top of the column.

To create a new set of SmartIcons, you have to add and delete icons from the Universal set that is displayed. You can add icons from the column on the left by dragging them to the right column. To drag an icon means that you point with the mouse pointer at an icon and hold down the left mouse button while you drag the icon to its new location. You can remove icons from the set by dragging them from the right column to the left column.

You can reposition icons in the set you are building by dragging them to the position you want, and then dropping them.

You can also insert a spacer, if desired, as a way of visually grouping SmartIcons with related functions.

When the new set is completed, click the Save Set... button to display the dialog box shown in Figure 2.5.

Figure 2.5.
New SmartIcon sets are given an .SMI file extension and saved in your default SmartIcon directory.

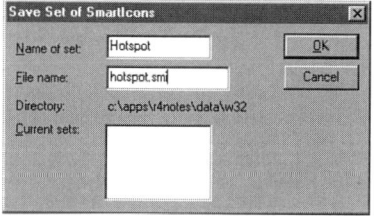

Enter the name of the set to be saved, and a file name. The extension .SMI is used to identify SmartIcon sets. On a Macintosh, the name of the SmartIcon set is the same as the file name. The SmartIcon set you created is saved in your default SmartIcon directory.

After you create a new set, click the drop-down arrow at the top of the column displaying the SmartIcon set. Select the new set. This will now be your default set of SmartIcons, rather than the Universal set. You still have the option of showing or hiding context icons.

Deleting a Set of SmartIcons

Any set of SmartIcons created by you can also be deleted by you. To delete a set:

1. Click the Delete Set... button. A list of user-created sets appears.
2. Click the name of the set you want to delete.
3. Click OK to delete the set.

 **NOTE** You cannot modify or delete the Universal set of SmartIcons. You can only create new sets, and can only delete sets that you have created.

Creating Custom SmartIcons

You can create a custom SmartIcon or edit certain SmartIcons by clicking on the Edit Icon button. Notes displays a list of those icons that can be edited.

Editable icons include those that launch other applications within Notes, along with several icons that can be used to launch your own macros.

 **TIP** You can create your own graphics for an icon. Save the graphic in your default SmartIcon directory as a bitmap (bmp or mac) no more than 22 pixels by 22 pixels. The graphic will then be available when you click on the Edit Icon button.

Click on the icon that you want to edit, and then click on the Formula... button. Notes displays a Formula dialog box, shown in Figure 2.6.

Figure 2.6.
Modify the existing formula to point to the desired application, or create your own formula.

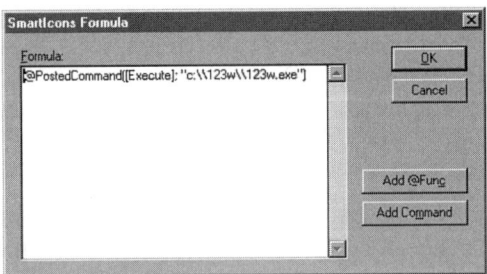

You can modify the existing formula for an icon or create your own formula, for example, to run a Notes macro.

 **TIP** To change a formula so that it points to the correct directory, all you have to do is modify the path in the formula. Backslashes used to indicate the directory structure in the formula are not recognized unless they are doubled, like this "\\," because a single backslash is recognized by the system as an escape character.

NOTE If you want to create a custom icon, you can modify one of the editable icons, copy a valid Notes formula from elsewhere, or experiment by adding formulas and/or commands using Notes Help to guide you on the proper context. Do not test your formulas on live data.

Placing Database Icons on the Workspace

Before we work with pages, let's put a Notes database on the workspace. It will put the workspace in perspective, and illustrate the real purpose of workspace pages.

Using a Template to Create a New Database

Because you are going to be working with Notes databases, you are about to learn one of the essential functions of Notes. In this section you are going learn the basics of creating a Notes database using a template. The workspace environment should make more sense to you with databases on it.

From the menu bar, select File | Database | New. Notes displays the New Database dialog box, as shown in Figure 2.7.

Figure 2.7.
The New Database dialog box is used to create a new database from a template.

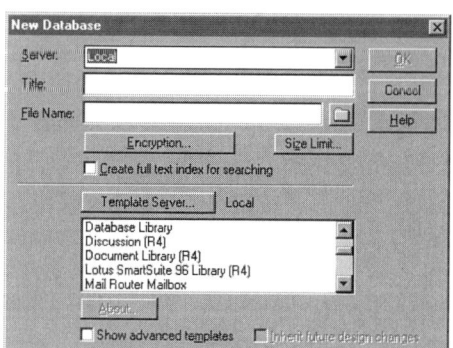

In this dialog box, accept the default location for the database, and give the database a title and a file name. Go ahead and accept the default settings for encryption and size, and ignore the Full Text Index option. All of these are covered in greater detail when we examine databases on Day 4 and Day 5.

For now, follow along and create a single database on your workspace.

1. If you are not already there, select File | Database | New.
2. Leave the location of the database (the "Server" field) as Local. If you had sufficient access, you could create a database on a Domino server from here by selecting the name of a server.
3. Give the database a title, such as "TY Lotus Notes 4.5," and notice as you type how Notes creates a file name that is identical to the title. Change the file name to TYLN45.NSF, keeping in mind that DOS file naming conventions are the lowest common denominator for file names. A Macintosh or a Windows 95 system, for example, would recognize a longer file name, but the name would be truncated in DOS, which only recognizes eight characters plus a three character extension. The NSF extension indicates to Notes that the file is a Notes database.
4. Click on the Size Limit button just to get an idea of how much data can fit into a Notes database. The default maximum amount of space that a single Notes database can occupy is one gigabyte. This can be changed in one gigabyte increments up to four gigabytes. The only time the database size limit can be defined is now, when the database is created. Click on Cancel to return to the New Database dialog box.
5. Skip the Create Full Text Index for Searching check box. This can be set up later, and is discussed in detail on Day 8.
6. Move down to the list box at the bottom of the dialog box. In this list box are the names of Notes templates that reside on your local workstation. Unless you did a very minimal installation to save space, you should have at least a few basic templates. You can change where Notes looks for templates by clicking on the Template Server button, but we are going to use local templates. You can also show additional templates, if they are available, by clicking on the Show Advanced Templates check box. Locate and click once on the Discussion template to select it.

Click on the About... button. Notes displays an "About this database" document so you can get an idea in advance about the purpose of the database. When you are done looking at the "About..." document, click on the Done button to return to the New Database dialog box.

Click on the OK button when you are done, and Notes creates the new database and displays the "About" document. Close the database by pressing the Esc key twice, or select File | Close until you are back at the Notes workspace and can see the icon on the workspace, as shown in Figure 2.8.

When teaching a class of Notes novices, I always like to tell the students at this moment, "Ok, now you are Notes application developers." You have just created your first Notes database, and it is a reasonably sophisticated one, even if it is empty. Don't worry, you will get to fill it with information later on.

Figure 2.8.
The newly created TY Lotus Notes 4.5 database icon on the Notes workspace.

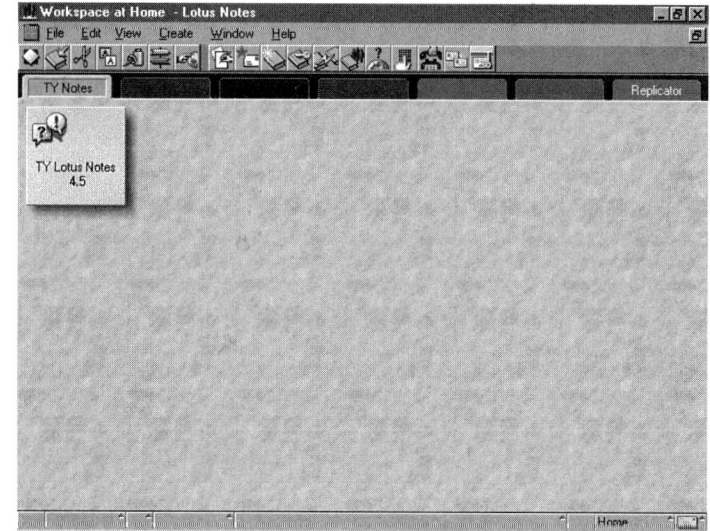

NOTE For now, we will skip any discussion of database encryption. This is covered on Day 12, "Mobile Notes: Using Notes When You're Out of the Office."

Putting an Existing Database on the Workspace

Depending on your Notes environment, you may have existing databases that can be put on your workspace...especially if others in your organization are already using Notes.

To place an existing Notes database on your workspace, select File | Database | Open from the menu bar. Notes displays the Open Database dialog box shown in Figure 2.9.

Figure 2.9.
The Open Database dialog box is used to add an existing database to the workspace.

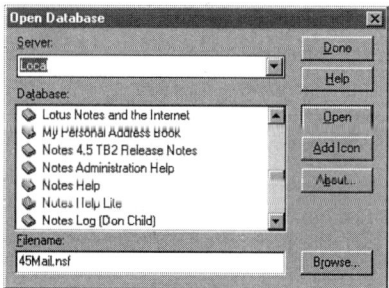

In this dialog box, you can select the Server on which the database resides. If you select Local, you are not opening a database from a Domino server. Instead, the database will be found in the default data directory on your local hard drive. If you are attached to a Notes network, you can click on the drop-down arrow to see a list of available Domino servers. Select the server from which you want to retrieve an existing Notes database.

Beneath the Server selection box is a Database selection box. In this box are listed all Notes databases (that is, all files with an extension of NSF) in the default data directory. As you scroll down the list of databases, you will also come across any subdirectories that are beneath the Notes default data directory. You can also click on the Browse button to look for Notes databases that are stored elsewhere in your "local" directory structure. "Local" is in quotes because it could be anywhere that you can access within the network file server directory structure. Databases that are kept on network directories other than the default Notes data directory cannot normally be opened up through a Domino server.

You can also type an explicit path and file name in the Filename field. The file does not have to have an NSF extension if you know the correct name, but of course it does have to be a Notes database. For example, you could have a Notes database stored as `D:\\HOME\\MYDOCS\\DIARY.PVT`.

NOTE The Domino server is not the same thing as a file server, even though it provides access to Notes database files. The Domino server is just another node on the network. It can only provide Domino server security to Notes databases that are in the default data directory or that have special pointers (defined by the Notes Administrator) to other directories.

Navigate through the databases in the Open Database dialog box until you find the database title you are looking for. Click on the database title once so it is highlighted. You can now click on the "About..." button to view information about the selected database. When you are done reading the "About this database" document, you can return to the Add Database dialog box by clicking on the "Close" button.

You have three options for placing the selected database on the workspace:

- ☐ You can highlight the database title and click Add Icon. The icon is placed on the workspace, and the Open Database dialog box remains open.
- ☐ You can highlight the database title and click Open. The dialog box closes and the selected database is opened. When you close the database (try pressing Esc a couple of times if you need to close the database and don't know how), the database icon will be on your workspace.

☐ You can double-click a database title to open it. When you close the database, the icon will remain on your workspace.

If you decide to close the Open Database dialog box without adding a database to your workspace, click Done.

Moving a Database Icon to a New Location on the Workspace

The database is now sitting on one of your workspace pages. You may have other databases already on your workspace; for example, your mail database and a help database. But we will work for the moment with the TY Lotus Notes database we just created.

First, lets move it to another location on the current workspace page.

Point to the database with the mouse pointer, and hold down (don't click) the left mouse button. While holding the button, drag the icon around on the workspace page. More accurately, drag an outline of the icon. Let go of the mouse button when the outline is where you want to place it. The icon will move more or less to where you dropped it. I say more or less because database icons snap to rows and columns so they are always aligned. You can move an icon to anywhere you want on the current page. If you place the icon on top of an existing icon, your icon will take the position you chose, pushing the other icon farther down the page.

Moving Database Icons to a New Page

Now let's look at how to move the database to a new workspace page.

Notice that the tab for the page you are on has a gray border around it. Pick up the database icon again by holding down the left mouse button while pointing at the icon. This time, drag the outline of the icon up to one of the other colored tabs at the top of the workspace. As you drag the icon over a tab, you will notice that a single-lined box appears on the tab, as shown in Figure 2.10. This indicates that the tab is selected. Drop the database icon on the selected tab and poof! The icon disappears to the new page.

Now click on the tab where you dropped the icon. The new workspace page moves to the top, and if you selected the correct tab, your database icon will be on the page.

You can move any database icon to any workspace page except the Replicator page. The Replicator page has a special function, as you will see when you study mobile Notes.

You can also move multiple icons to a new page with a single move. To select multiple icons, hold down the Shift key while clicking on the icons you want to move. Click and hold down the left mouse key on the last icon you want to select, and then release the Shift key. Now when you slide the mouse pointer around the workspace, all of the selected icons move at once. Point to the tab where you want to move the icons, and release the icons when the single-lined box appears on the tab. All of the database icons move to the new tab.

Figure 2.10.

Dropping a database icon onto another workspace page.

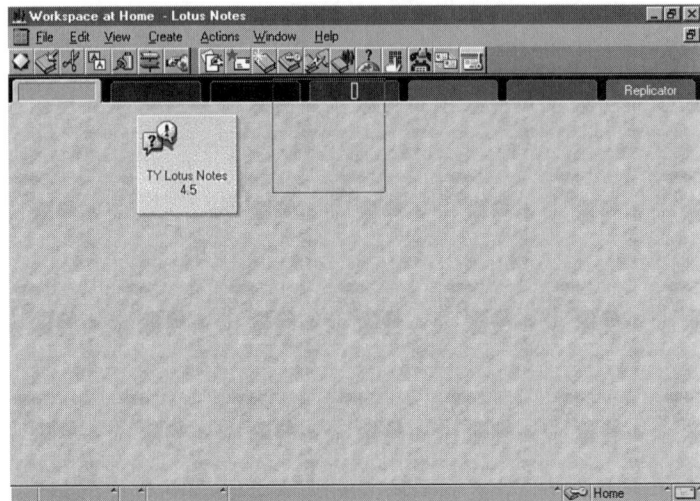

Changing the Information on Database Icons

The database icon always shows a small graphic in the top left corner of the icon and the database title. There are two other pieces of information that can optionally be displayed on the icon, as shown in Figure 2.11.

Figure 2.11.

Database icon showing unread documents and server name.

You display additional information on the icon in the following way:

- *Unread documents.* The icon can display the number of unread documents in the database. An unread document is one that you have not opened to look at. To display unread documents on the icon, select View | Show Unread from the menu bar. Then, when you click on the icon, the number of unread documents will be displayed.

- *Server names.* The icon can show the name of the server (or local hard drive) through which the database is being accessed. Many times it is important to know whether a database is being served up by your local Notes client or by a Domino server. To display the location of a database on the icon, select View | Show Server Names from the menu bar.

NOTE Showing the unread documents and server names will slightly increase the size of the icon. This means that you can display fewer icons on your workspace at one time. However, you can still add up to (at least) 250 icons on a single workspace page. Obviously, you have to do a lot of scrolling up and down and left to right in order to see all of the icons.

Deleting Database Icons

If you click on a database icon and press the Delete key, the database icon is removed from your Notes workspace. The icon is only a pointer to the database, so the database itself is not deleted. A database can only be deleted from the system by the person listed as a Manager in the database ACL, or a local database that does not have ACL security enforced.

Working with Tabbed Workspace Pages

You can customize the workspace pages by adding a label to describe the contents of the page, and by changing the color of each tab. You can also add more pages or delete pages as needed.

Labeling Workspace Pages

You can type a label on the tab of each Workspace page. For example, you can name a workspace page Reference, and keep all of your reference databases on that page. Someone else on your project team might keep the same databases on entirely different pages. The Notes workspace is your personal workspace, and you can organize it in any way that makes sense to you. Of course, there are exceptions. You may have a corporate policy that dictates a specific way of organizing your workspace, or you may share your workspace with other Notes users, in which case you are not entirely free to customize the workspace.

You can label workspace pages and change the color that is displayed on the Workspace Page tabs by using a Workspace Properties dialog box. This dialog box can be displayed in any of three ways:

- Double-click on a tab to display the Workspace Properties InfoBox for that page.
- Right-click on a blank part of the page, and select Workspace Properties from the floating menu that is displayed.
- Click on the Properties SmartIcon at the far left of the SmartIcon Bar.

The Workspace Properties dialog box is shown in Figure 2.12.

Figure 2.12.
The first page of the Workspace Properties box is used to label workspace pages.

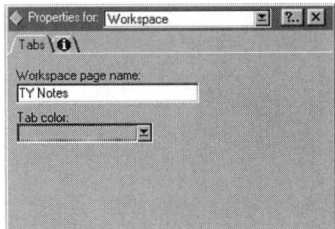

NOTE

A Properties dialog box is available for many elements within Notes, including databases, forms and views, navigators, fields, and individual elements within documents such as text and objects.

The Properties dialog box consolidates in one location most of the things that can be changed for an individual item. Multiple tabbed pages make the Properties box flexible. You will see Properties boxes throughout this book as you learn about different elements in Notes.

Type the name you want to appear on the tab at the top of the page. The tab expands for longer names, and gets smaller for shorter names.

After changing the name, you can also change the color of the tab, if desired. As you click on the different tabs, notice that the tab for the page you are currently on displays a gray border around it, so you can quickly identify which page you are on.

Looking at Workspace Information

While on the topic of Workspace Properties, open the Workspace Properties box again, and click on the second tab, which has workspace information on it. This page, shown in Figure 2.13, summarizes the amount of space being taken up on your computer by the Notes workspace.

Figure 2.13.
Workspace Information lets you manage the space taken up by workspace design elements.

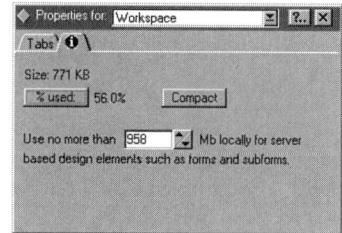

Click on % used to see how much of the total workspace storage is actually being used by design elements.

As you add and delete database icons on your workspace and make other design changes, you may end up with a lot of unused white space that you can reclaim for other uses. To reclaim unused space, click on Compact. Notes takes a minute to compress your workspace and reclaim any unused white space. You will notice the percentage and the size of the workspace change after you compact the workspace. If you are short of disk space, this is one place that you may be able to squeeze out a few more kilobytes of storage.

Adding and Deleting Workspace Pages

You are not limited to the six workspace pages that were on your workspace when you first started up Notes. You can add up to 32 workspace pages on your workspace, or you can delete workspace pages until you only have one remaining.

This lets you re-create a familiar environment, if you want to. For example, you could label pages from A to Z, making your Notes workspace into a filing cabinet. Or name one page Admin, and name other pages after projects you are working on. It is entirely up to you.

You can insert a tab for a new workspace page to the right of any existing page. To create a new workspace page:

1. Click on a tab. The new page will be inserted to the right of the page you select.
2. Select Create | Workspace Page from the drop-down menu, or right-click on a blank part of the page, and select Create Workspace Page from the floating menu. A new page will be inserted.

Click on the tab for the new page and add a label for the page, if desired.

WARNING

There is some inconsistency between different versions of Notes as to how pages are inserted. In Notes, an inserted page pushes all tabs' colors one tab to the right, and recolors the last colored tab gray. In

> other versions, the inserted tab was gray and other tabs retained their color. If the color coding on the tabs is significant to you, you should be aware of this anomaly.

Occasionally, you may want to delete a workspace page after it has ceased to serve its purpose. For example, if you set up tabs on a project-by-project basis, you can delete the page for a project after the project is finished.

To delete a workspace page:

1. Move any database icons that you want to keep on your Notes workspace to another page.
2. Click anywhere on the workspace page that you want to delete to verify that you are on the correct page.
3. Press the Delete key or right-click in a blank part of the workspace page and select Remove Workspace Page from the floating menu.
4. A warning message will be displayed: `This operation will delete the selected workspace page. Are you sure that you would like to proceed?`
5. Click on Yes to delete the page, or No to cancel the operation.

TIP Now would be a good time to compact your workspace, after deleting databases and removing a workspace page.

NOTE Don't panic if you unintentionally delete database icons when removing a workspace page. As you will find out in tomorrow's lesson, the database icon is merely a pointer to the database file. Deleting the icon does not affect the database itself. At the most, accidentally deleting a database icon may cause you the inconvenience of having to locate the database and put the icon back onto your workspace.

Using the Status Bar

The status bar at the bottom of the Notes workspace provides information about your current environment, as well as shortcuts for commonly used functions.

If you just set up Notes on your workspace, you will not be able to see a great deal of information on the status bar; but as you begin to use Notes, you can make good use of the information.

Figure 2.14 shows the elements of a status bar.

Figure 2.14.
The status bar at the bottom of the workspace provides current information and shortcuts.

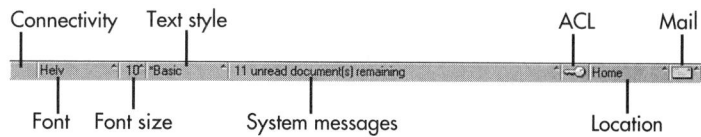

From left to right, the status bar provides the following information:

- *Connectivity.* A small icon is visible when you are actively connected to the Domino server. On a LAN, it looks like a flashing lightning bolt. On a dial-up connection, it looks like a modem.

- *Font.* When you are editing a Notes document and the cursor is in a Rich Text field, the name of the currently selected font is displayed. Click on the font name to display a list of available fonts. You can change the font at the cursor location or change the font for selected text by highlighting another font from the status bar.

- *Font size.* The font size is similar to the font name. If you are editing a Rich Text field, the size of the currently selected text is displayed. You can change the font size by clicking on the status bar and selecting a new font size.

- *Text style.* If you are editing a Rich Text field, you can use predefined styles to define text. The currently selected style is shown on the status bar, and can be changed from there.

- *System messages.* The system displays status messages on the status bar. You can see the current message on the bar, or click on the status bar to see the last several system messages. For example, Checking for new mail... or No matching documents were found... after an unsuccessful search.

- *ACL.* If you are currently in a Notes database or have one selected on the workspace, then an icon representing your access level for the database is displayed.

- *Location.* You can easily switch settings on your Notes client workstation by switching to a new Location. Locations are described on Day 12 when we talk about using Mobile Notes.

- *Mail.* An envelope icon represents your mailbox. When you have unopened mail, the icon changes to an in-box, and a "New Mail" tone sounds. By clicking on the Mail icon, you can create mail memos, read your unread mail, receive mail from the server if you have a local mail database, send mail to the server, receive and send mail, or open your mail database.

Setting Up User Preferences

You have now looked at the Notes workspace in which you will be working. Now let's look at how you will be working. If you have a sufficiently sophisticated understanding of network computing and Internet computing, there is a lot that can be done in Notes.

Also, you need to understand a little about what your specific use of Notes will entail. For example, if you work with Notes in a fulfillment department, you may want to have your Notes workspace open up directly to a Notes database that contains orders sent in from sales reps in the field. If you work for an Internet development company that has decided to take advantage of the Domino server, you may want to take extra security precautions because you may be picking up a lot of Java applets from the Web.

These and other variables are grouped in a complex dialog box called User Preferences, which can be opened by selecting File | Tools | User Preferences. This displays the dialog box shown in Figure 2.15. After setting these preferences, you may need to close and restart Notes before your changes take effect.

Figure 2.15.
The User Preferences dialog box is used to customize the Notes environment.

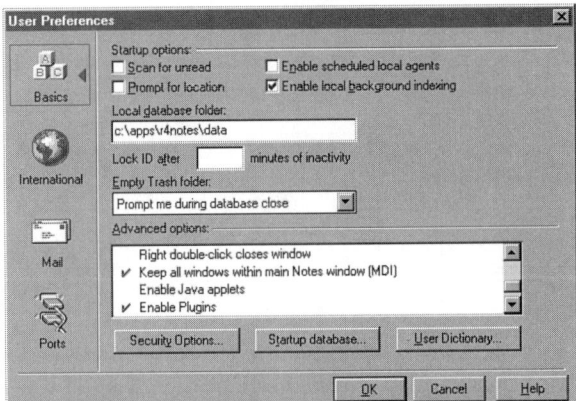

Setting Preferences on the Basics Page

Notice that the User Preferences dialog box has four pages that can be displayed by clicking on buttons down the left side of the dialog box. The first page is the Basics page, and there are several important sections on that page.

Defining Startup Options

Startup Options determine what Notes will do every time it is started. There are four check boxes, which when checked, have the following effect:

- *Scan for Unread.* For database icons, there is an option to display the number of unread documents in the database. If it is important for you to know the number of documents you need to deal with as soon as you open Notes, select this option. The number of unread documents is updated for every database on every page of your workspace. When unread documents are found, a Scan Unread dialog box lets you view the first unread document encountered, or you can mark all documents in the database as Read and continue to the next database, choose preferred databases—ones that are a priority for you—cancel, or get help.

  This will slow down the process of opening Notes, and may cause some delay if every database is checked. If the unread document totals are not important for most databases, you may want to leave this unchecked. You can update the number of unread documents for a single workspace page by clicking on a blank part of the page and pressing the F9 key, or you can select View | Refresh Unread Marks. You can refresh a single database by clicking on the database to select it, and then pressing F9 or selecting View | Refresh Unread Marks. The number of unread marks in a database is also updated automatically when you open the database.

- *Prompt for Location.* If you are running Notes on a laptop computer and move around frequently, or if you have a desktop computer but use different Notes environments (for example, one configuration that is behind a firewall, and another that is exposed to the Internet), then you may want to make sure you set the correct Location when you start up Notes. You will be prompted for your current location if you select this option. Otherwise, Notes opens to the Location that was open at the time Notes was shut down.

- *Enable Scheduled Local Agents.* If you use workflow applications that depend on scheduled agents, you can have those schedules initiated automatically when Notes starts up. This ensures that documents are mailed and all databases are current on startup. There are performance issues to consider, however, because running the agents does require system resources.

- *Enable Local Background Indexing.* When you create full text indexes for databases, you must wait until the index has been created before you can continue working. Also, you may experience noticeable pauses when you open a new view, which must be reindexed before it can be opened. You can avoid this delay by enabling background indexing. This does slow down your system while indexes are being built, but you will be able to continue working, and indexes will be kept up-to-date as documents are added to the database. This includes documents that are added to a local database through replication, and are then automatically indexed if you have a full text index for the database, and you have enabled background indexing.

Defining a Local Database Folder

When you create new databases from a template, or when you place a database icon on your workspace, Notes looks in its default database folder. When Notes is installed, this folder is created as DATA and is placed directly beneath the Notes directory. You can change this default directory by naming a new directory on the User Preferences Basics page, or by changing it in the NOTES.INI file.

WARNING

> If you modify your NOTES.INI file directly, you run the risk of corrupting your Notes setup. Whenever possible, make changes from within the Notes user interface.

Locking Your UserID Automatically

As far as Notes is concerned, if somebody is using your Notes UserID to access data, that somebody is you. If you walk away from your Notes workstation without locking your UserID (that is, logging off), then anyone with access to your workstation can send e-mail in your name, open databases using your access, edit documents for which you are listed as an author and so on.

Someone else using your Notes UserID may not be a problem if it's your friend playing a prank and posting something nonoffensive in the company water cooler. But what if they post something offensive that will get you in trouble? What if someone tries to sabotage a corporate project and uses your name to do it? What if someone uses your ID to access a database that they are not supposed to have access to? You are then unintentionally abetting corporate espionage.

You have a choice of how to handle such a situation.

- ☐ You can lock your UserID by pressing the F5 key every time you leave your workstation.
- ☐ You can select File | Tools | Lock ID from the menu.
- ☐ Or you can use the User Preferences page to set the number of minutes of inactivity before the UserID is automatically locked.

The final option leaves little to chance. If you forget to lock your Notes UserID, it will lock itself within five minutes, if that is the length of time you entered on the User Preferences page. That narrows the window of opportunity for someone to misuse your UserID, thus increasing the security of your Notes environment. If you are busy using other applications for longer than five minutes and toggle back to use Notes, you will be asked for your password before you can access the server.

Options for Emptying Your Mail's Trash Folder

On the User Preferences page, you can determine when the trash folder in your mail database is emptied. When you delete mail documents, they are held in a trash folder until the database is closed. At that time, you can have Notes prompt you so you can undelete documents, if you change your mind, before closing your mail. You can choose to have the documents deleted automatically when the database is closed. Alternatively, you can choose to delete the documents from the trash folder manually by selecting Actions | Empty Trash.

Setting Advanced Options

In the Advanced Options section of the Basics page, there are a number of options that can be checked by clicking on them. These include:

- ☐ Options that deal with how information is displayed on the screen, such as Typewriter fonts only, Large Fonts, Textured Workspace (gives the background of workspace pages a marbled appearance), Monochrome display, and Dither images in documents.

- ☐ Options that determine how the environment handles windows, including Mark documents read when opened in preview pane, Keep Workspace in back when maximized (displays the workspace rather than a gray background when you minimize windows), Right double-click closes window, and Keep all windows within main Notes window (MDI), which allows you to toggle between applications in Windows 95 using Alt + Tab.

- ☐ Options that determine how Internet elements are handled, including Make Internet URLs into Hotspots, Enable Java applets, and Enable Plugins.

Many of these elements are discussed in later lessons when they effect functionality, but others have no effect beyond controlling your workspace environment. Try experimenting with different options to see what effect they have.

NOTE Many of the options do not take effect until you exit and restart Notes.

What Is Execution Control List Security?

When you click on the Security Options... button at the bottom of the Basics page in the User Preferences dialog box, you see the Execution Control List (ECL) screen shown in Figure 2.16.

Figure 2.16.
The Execution Control List controls what actions can be performed on your system.

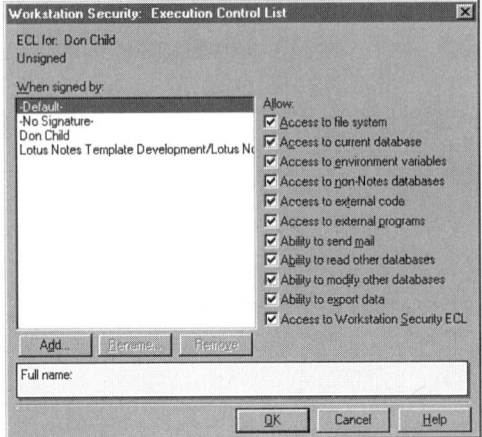

In Lotus Notes versions beginning with 4.0, application developers can create programs using the LotusScript programming language. With this language, they can work with elements of your system environment outside of Notes, and with elements of the Notes environment beyond the scope of a simple database application. The ECL simply gives you control over what can be done by programs that reach beyond the normal Notes development environment.

If you use a Web browser, you are probably familiar with security alerts that are displayed whenever an embedded program attempts to run on your workstation. You have the option of allowing the program to run or halting the operation. The same thing happens in Notes.

If Notes comes across a function that was created by a developer not recognized in your ECL, a dialog box is displayed giving you the option of canceling the execution, letting it run one time, or trusting the signer (the person who created the function) for all executions in the future. If you decide to trust the signer, your ECL is updated. You can refine the ECL in this Security dialog box by making sure only those functions you want executed are checked. You can also add new signers to your ECL, or give full ECL rights to a default user if you are not concerned with what the execution of outside programs can do on your computer.

Defining a Startup Database

I'm going to assume, for the moment, that you are using Windows 95, because that is the environment I'm most familiar with. You could be using any of the platforms on which Notes runs, and what I'm about to say will still hold true. When you start up your computer, chances are pretty good that you have Windows start up automatically. And if you have an application that you use all the time, you may have a pointer in your startup directory so that the application is launched automatically.

You can do the same thing with Notes 4.5. When Notes is launched, you can have it open a specific database that you use all the time, and within the database, you can even have the application designer define which view you will see.

So imagine this scenario. Your job is to take telephone orders. You have access to an online catalog, a customer list, and other related information, but you always start out with a screen, a graphical view within Notes, that gives you an option of looking up customers, looking up inventory, placing a new order, or following up on an order. That is your home page.

First thing in the morning, you go to your desk and turn on the computer. It takes a few minutes to warm up and go through all of its system tests and so forth. So you take a minute to get organized. Get a cup of coffee. Read the new notices on the bulletin board. Whatever your morning routine is. By the time you get back to your desk, your home page is waiting for you.

In this scenario, I'm assuming that the home page is a local navigation database without no local security. The first time you click on a button and try to get any data from the system, Notes will prompt you for your password because it has to open another database that resides on the Domino server. Other than that, everything is handled automatically.

You can determine which database is opened automatically by doing the following:

1. Open up the User Preference dialog box (File | Tools | User Preferences).
2. Click on the Startup Database... button at the bottom of the dialog box.
3. Scroll through the list of database icons on your workspace until you find the database you want to be opened on startup.
4. Click once on the database title to select it, and then click on OK.

The next time you start Notes, the selected database will be opened automatically. In the scenario described above, Notes was in the Windows startup directory, and the graphical navigator database was selected as the startup database.

Managing Your User Dictionary

Later on, you will get to work with text editing functions such as spell-checking. While we are here looking at the User Preferences, take a look at how easy it is to manage your customized spelling dictionary.

When you do a spell check and an unrecognized word is found, you can click on a button to add the word to the dictionary. There is a lot of computer jargon, for example, that hasn't yet made it into the online dictionary—words like "online." Or you may want to add the last names of colleagues, or street names, anything that is frequently referred to in Notes documents. These words find their way into your user dictionary, which you can then open up and edit if necessary. The User Spell Dictionary dialog box is shown in Figure 2.17.

Figure 2.17.
Adding and updating words in the user dictionary.

To edit the user dictionary:

1. Open up the User Preference dialog box (File | Tools | User Preferences).
2. Click on the User Dictionary... button at the bottom of the dialog box.
3. To add a new word to the dictionary, type the word in the single line input field at the bottom of the User Spell Dictionary dialog box, and then click on the Add button. The word will be inserted at the bottom of the list, and will be alphabetized the next time the dialog box is opened. Adding words through the User Spell Dictionary dialog box is an alternative to having the words added during a spell check.
4. To update a word that is misspelled, locate the word in the list and click on it so it appears in the single line input field. Correct the spelling and then click on the Update button.
5. To delete a word, click on the word to highlight it, and then click on the Delete button.

Setting the Environment for International Users

International users can set a number of environmental variables, such as how words are sorted and which spelling directory should be used.

Click on the International button to display the International page of the User Preferences dialog box, shown in Figure 2.18.

On this page of the User Preferences box, you can set the following parameters:

- *Scandinavian Collation* sorts some accented characters last in lists.
- *Numbers Last Collation* sorts numbers after alphabet characters in lists.
- *French Casing* removes certain accent marks when characters are converted from lower- to uppercase.
- *Imperial* (inches and feet) or *Metric* measurements.
- *Import/Export Character Set* identifies which file to use for translating from the Roman alphabet to another during import/export.

- *Spelling Dictionary* lets you select which international dictionary should be used during spell checks.
- *Week Starts On...* lets you set the first day of the week for calendar functions.

Figure 2.18.
Setting International options in the User Preferences dialog box.

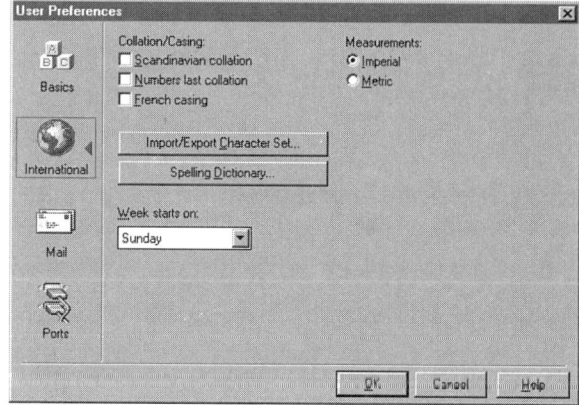

Setting Mail Preferences

Although there is a lot more that goes into setting up your e-mail than setting preferences, we assume in this book that you are using Notes mail. There are several settings on the Mail page of the User Preferences dialog box, that let you determine how your mail is handled.

In this dialog box, you can set the following:

- *Mail Program.* Choose between Notes mail or you can use, from within Notes, another mail system that supports Vendor Independent Mail (VIM) standards. If you use another VIM-standard mail system, you also have to enter the name of the file that runs the mail system.
- *Save Sent Mail.* You have the option of always saving a copy of mail messages that you send out, never saving them, or being prompted each time so you can decide whether to save the message.
- *Local Address Books.* You can browse to locate one or more local address books to use for checking addresses when sending out mail. Mobile users can use this to their advantage by setting up different address books to be used from different locations.
- *Check for New Mail Every 15 Minutes.* You can determine how often your local workstation looks in your mail box to see if there is any new mail. If there is new mail, an in-box is shown on the status bar, and you can have either audible or visible notification.

- *Audible Notification.* If you set this and your workstation finds new mail, Notes chimes to inform you that you have new mail.
- *Visible Notification.* If you set this, Notes displays a message in the middle of your screen when new mail messages are received.
- *Sign Sent Mail.* If you select this, all outgoing memos will have a digital signature attached to them. The digital signature verifies that the memo was created using your Notes user ID.
- *Encrypt Saved Mail.* If you select this, all mail sent to you will be encrypted in your mail file, which means that others cannot read your mail unless they have your Notes UserID and password.
- *Encrypt Sent Mail.* If you select this, the person to whom mail is addressed is the only one who can open and read the message. The recipient must have access to your public key, which is stored in the Notes Public Address Book. A recipient in a foreign domain (for all practical purposes, someone outside of your organization) must have a copy of your public key available to them before they can read encrypted mail you send them.

Setting Port Preferences

If your workstation is attached to a LAN and that is the only place you ever use Notes, then you probably will not have to deal with Ports. In some instances, however, you may have multiple ports set up, and use different protocols for the different ports. For example, you may have a mobile or home computer set up to dial in directly to a Notes server using a COM1 port, but also have a TCP connection for communicating with a server that is attached to the Internet.

Look briefly at the Ports page of the User Preferences dialog box. You will revisit this page on Day 12 when you learn about mobile Notes, but there are one or two things to be aware of at this point.

- *Communication Ports.* Ports that you have set up and enabled have a checkmark next to them. Assuming the ports have been correctly set up, you can use any enabled port.
- *Reorder.* Notes tries to use the first port in the list. If that port cannot be used for some reason, it moves on to the next port in the list. If you have a preferred port, you can move it to the top of the list. To change the order of the ports, highlight a port and click on the up and down arrows to change its position on the list.
- *Port Enabled.* Highlight a port on the list and click on this check box to enable the port.

☐ *Encrypt Network Data.* If you select this, all communication through the selected port will be encrypted as it travels between you and the Domino server. This does slow down communications as data is encrypted and decrypted, but you can use this if you are working in an environment where all data must be kept secure.

WARNING

Do not play around with the ports unless you understand what you are doing. You could accidentally disable your workstation so it can no longer communicate with the Domino server. The Notes administrator shows a distinct lack of amusement at having to troubleshoot your workstation communications.

How to Close Notes

Now that you are familiar with the elements of the Notes workspace, you need to know how to close Notes.

When you close Notes, everything that you have changed on the workspace—the SmartIcons, the database icons, the workspace folders, and changes to the environment itself—is saved in a file called DESKTOP.DSK. This file is your workspace. Whenever Notes is reopened on your Notes workstation, it will use this file to determine what the workspace should look like.

To exit from Notes, you have several options, most of them standard Windows functions.

☐ Select File | Exit Notes from the menu bar.
☐ Double-click on the system icon in the top-left corner of the Notes workspace, or click once and select Close.
☐ Press Alt+F4.
☐ Click on the X icon in the top-right corner of the Notes workspace.

Summary

In today's lesson, we considered the Notes environment from your perspective as an end user. We started up Notes and looked at the Notes workspace, including the title bar, the menu bar, the SmartIcons, the workspace, and the status bar. Before looking at the workspace, we made a very important side trip to learn how to put database icons on the workspace. Then we looked at many of the user preferences that determine how information is displayed by Notes. Some of the highlights:

- ☐ The title bar tells you what screen you are on.
- ☐ The menu bar and menu options change according to where you are and what your role is in the Notes system.
- ☐ The SmartIcons provide one-click shortcuts to common Notes functions. You can create customized SmartIcons.
- ☐ The workspace pages are home to Notes databases. You can name the individual workspace pages, change the color of the tabs, and you can add or remove workspace pages.
- ☐ The Database Icons that go on the workspace page can be placed there by creating a new database from a template, or by opening up an existing database that resides on your local system or on a Domino server.
- ☐ The status bar provides information about what is happening within the Notes environment, and provides key shortcuts.
- ☐ The User Preferences can be used to set up how Notes handles data on your workspace. The preferences that you set will apply for all work you do within Notes.

Workshop

The Workshop section presents quiz questions to help you cement your new knowledge and exercises to give you experience using what you have learned. Try to understand the questions and exercises before moving on to the next lesson. Answers are in Appendix A.

Q&A

Q Do I really need to do all of that User Preferences setup just to use Notes?

A No. You can just accept Notes defaults for most settings. As you become more accustomed to Notes, you can return to the User Preferences to customize the Notes environment.

Q Is there any way to create new Notes databases besides using a template?

A Yes, there are other options. You can copy and rename an existing database. You can create a new database from scratch if you are an application developer. But using a template is one of the easier ways to create an instant Notes application. In this lesson, you learned how to use a template so you could create databases to use in later lessons.

Q I don't use an IBM PC with Windows 95. Is everything I'm learning in this book still valid?

A The Notes environment is virtually the same on all platforms. The only significant difference you might notice is how files are named. If you use a file name eight characters or shorter, the name can be used across all platforms.

Quiz

1. Why are most of the fields on the status bar empty when you are looking at the Notes workspace?
2. Can you work with a Notes database if it is not kept in the Notes data directory?
3. How do you open a Notes database that does not have an NSF file extension?
4. How many workspace pages are there in Notes?
5. If you accidentally delete a database icon, how do you get it back?

Exercises

1. Create a Document Library database on your local hard drive. Figure out how to make a copy of the database from within Notes. Give the copy a new name, and then delete the original database—not the icon, but the entire database.
2. Create a SmartIcon that launches your word processor from within Notes.

Week 1

Day 3

Using Notes Help

In today's lesson, we are going to be looking at the general topic of help, and how to obtain it while using Notes. This goes beyond "read the manual" and "use the online help" by showing you how to make the most out of the various help resources that are available to you. Many of the resources are built right into Notes documents via pop-ups, DocLinks, and field-level help. In addition, the online help can be navigated in a variety of ways that you can adapt to your use of Notes. The intent is to make you self-sufficient in your use of Notes. And of course, if all else fails, you can always refer back to this book.

The lesson is organized so you can begin by opening up Notes online help and learning to navigate within Help. The navigation applies to all Notes databases, so it will serve as a prelude to using Notes databases, which is really what this entire book is about.

The levels of help that are available within Notes include:

- ☐ Printed documentation that comes with Notes.
- ☐ Third-party books such as this one. You can find this and several other excellent Notes titles from Macmillan Publishing at http://www.mcp.com.

- Online help databases, including an online version of printed documentation, and context-sensitive help
- Database-specific help
- View and document help
- Help that is embedded in documents
- Field-level help

This lesson does not include a review of the printed Notes documentation. Instead, it provides a tour of the various types of online documentation.

Putting the Help Database on Your Workspace

There are several help databases that are shipped with Notes, including help for the Domino server, help for network management, and so forth. And there are two help databases that you can use as an end user of Notes. The only differences between the two are the level of complexity and the size of the two databases.

- *Notes Help* is a comprehensive database (a very healthy 34MB) that can be either local- or server-based. It includes help for the application developer and the system administrator in addition to help for the end user. The database can be placed on your local Notes client if you have space for it, or you can open it from the Domino server if you are constantly attached via a LAN.
- *Notes Help Lite* is a trimmed down version of Notes Help (less than one megabyte), and includes just about everything you will need as an end user of Notes, including help for the mobile user. Notes Help Lite can be placed on your local system as a backup in case you cannot get to the server, for example if you are on the road. Notes Help Lite is also the only version of Help available to you if you use a Notes Mail license.

There is an easy way to put Notes Help on your workspace, whichever version you have. To place the Help database on your workspace:

- Press the F1 key.
- Select Help | Help Topics (or Guide Me or Shortcuts) from the menu bar.

The Notes Help icon (whichever one Notes finds) will be placed on your workspace, as shown in Figure 3.1.

Figure 3.1.
The Notes Help and Notes Help Lite icons on the Notes workspace.

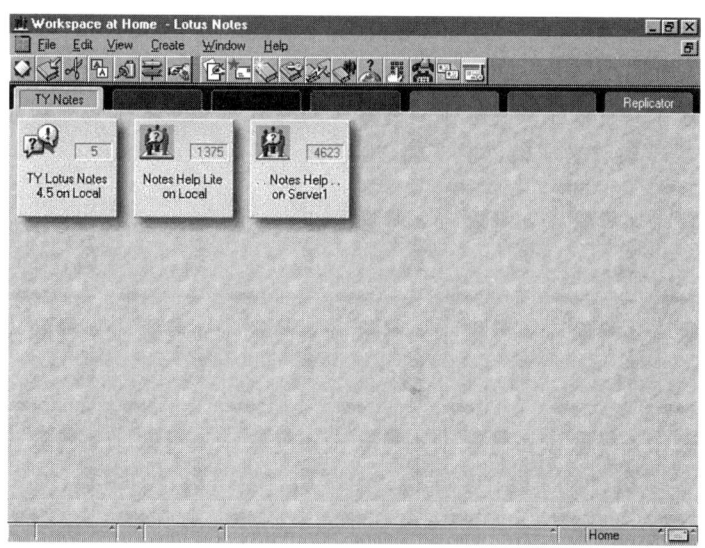

If Notes fails to find a Help database, you may have to search for it in another directory on your local drive or on the Domino server. You learned in yesterday's lesson how to search for a database and place it on your workspace. In case you forgot, the steps are described below.

1. Select File | Database | Open from the menu bar to show the Open Database dialog box shown in Figure 3.2.

Figure 3.2.
You can add a Help database from the Open Database dialog box.

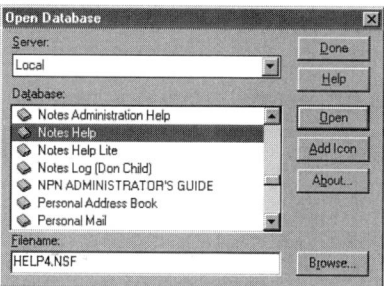

2. Accept the default Local if the Help database is on your local hard drive, or select the server from which you want to retrieve the database.
3. Locate the Help database in the lower part of the dialog box, switching directories if necessary. Notes Help has the file name HELP4.NSF. Notes Help Lite is HELPLT4.NSF. If you have it available, select the full version of Notes Help. If not, then Notes Help Lite contains all the end-user help.

4. Click once on the Help database to highlight it.
5. Click on Add Icon to add the Help database icon to your workspace, or click on Open to open the database immediately.

In this lesson, you will be looking at the Notes Help database, not Notes Help Lite.

Opening Help

You can open Help in one of three different ways:

- ☐ Double-click on the Help database icon.
- ☐ Select Help | Help Topics from the menu bar.
- ☐ Press the F1 key.

The third option is discussed later in the section "Using Context-Sensitive Help." The other two options display the Notes Help Index view, as shown in Figure 3.3.

Figure 3.3.
The Notes Help Index view is used to navigate to Notes help topics.

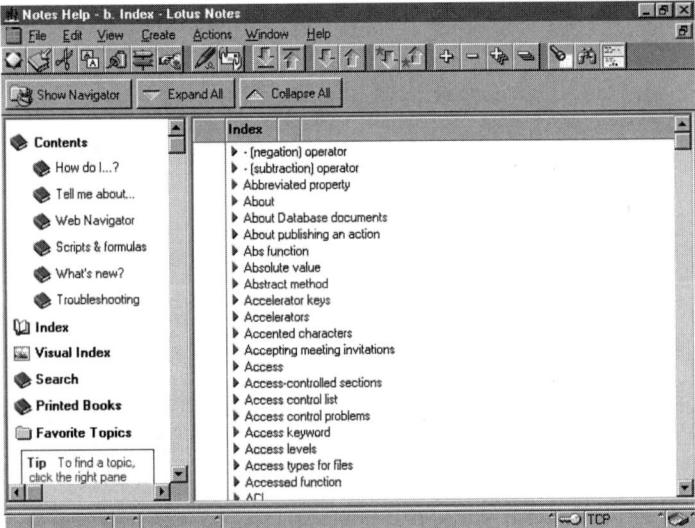

Exploring the Help Index View

Before actually getting into using Help, let's look for a minute at some of the elements on the screen. This may the first time you have seen a Notes database.

What is shown in Figure 3.3 is a Notes view. A *view* is a collection of Notes documents. A Notes database can have many different views, each showing a different subset of the documents in the database.

The screen is divided into two panes. If you do a lot of work on the Internet, you have probably seen panes referred to as "frames" on the World Wide Web. The left pane is used to navigate between different views and folders in the database. The pane on the right shows a list of documents, and is referred to as the *view pane*. Later on, you will be able to change the panes to other configurations, but for now, you will be using the default configuration.

Displaying the Preview Pane

There is a third hidden pane that is used to preview documents. With this pane open, you can highlight a document and see it from the view screen without actually opening the document.

There are two ways to open the preview pane:

- ☐ Click on the Show/Hide Preview Pane SmartIcon. It should be the far right SmartIcon, showing a horizontally split screen.
- ☐ Point to the edge of a pane and drag it to resize it. At the bottom of the view screen, you can actually see the top edge of the preview pane. Point to the edge of the pane with the mouse pointer, hold down the left mouse button, and drag the edge to resize the frame. If you point directly at the intersection of the navigation pane, the view pane, and the preview pane, you can resize all panes at the same time.

Figure 3.4 shows the Index view with the preview pane open. In this view, a document has been selected to illustrate how it appears in the preview pane.

Figure 3.4.
The Index view showing the preview pane with a document selected.

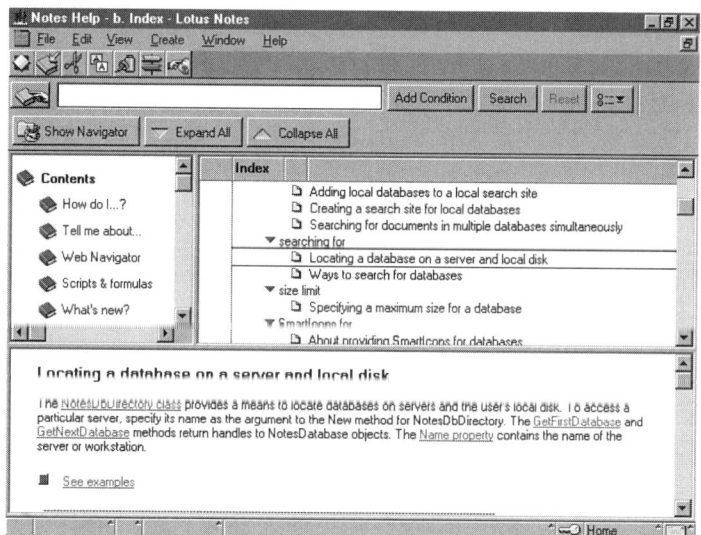

> **TIP** Using the preview pane is a matter of personal preference, but be aware that there are performance considerations. Applications that were not designed with previewing in mind can slow down navigation in the view pane. For example, if the preview pane is displaying graphics for each document, it will take you longer to move from document to document in the view pane. Therefore, you may want to use the preview pane judiciously.

Expanding Categories

You may have noticed a difference in the view pane in Figure 3.4. In order to select a document, a category in the view had to be expanded.

Notes views are usually organized so that related documents are grouped into categories that can be collapsed or expanded to display all the documents contained in the category.

Documents in views get categorized because that makes it easier locate related documents. Although application developers are not required to, they usually indicate categories in views by using what is referred to as a *twistie*, a small triangle to left of the category name. If the twistie points to the right, it means the category is collapsed so you cannot see any documents. If the twistie is pointing down, it means that the category is expanded so you can see what it contains—documents, or other categories nested within it.

To expand a category, click on the twistie while it is pointing to the right.

To collapse a category, click on the twistie while it is pointing downward.

Figure 3.5 shows part of a view with all categories collapsed. Figure 3.6 shows the same view with a category expanded so you can see the documents.

Notice that the documents within this view of the Help database are denoted by a small document icon. This is an option available to the database designer, but is not necessarily done in all databases.

Figure 3.5.
Twisties pointing to the right indicate collapsed categories.

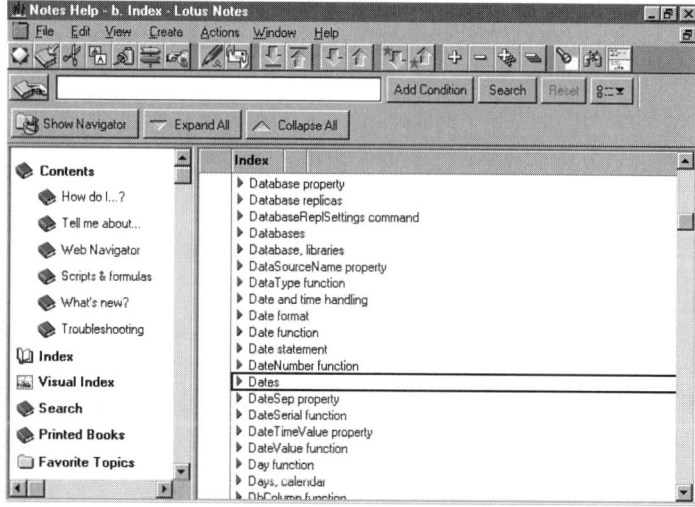

Figure 3.6.
Twisties pointing down let you access categorized documents.

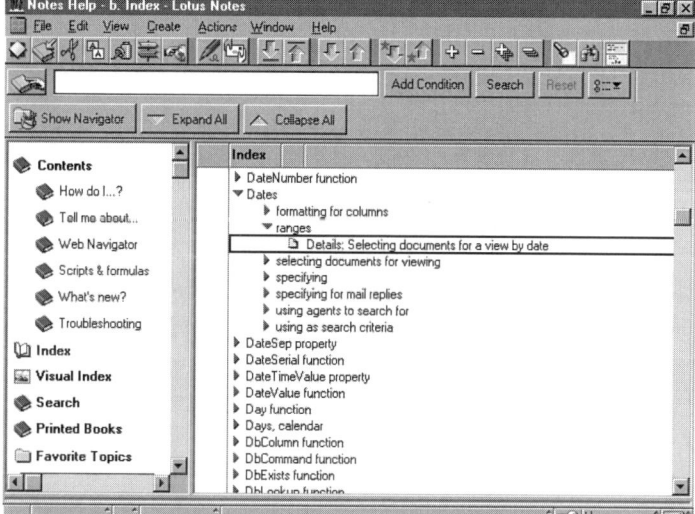

Looking for Help on a Topic Using the Index View

The Index view contains literally hundreds of documents. Finding the specific information you need from among all these documents could be a daunting task. If nothing else, you would at least need to scroll through a long list of documents.

The view has a Quick Search function that lets you move immediately to a specific location within the Help database. To activate the Quick Search function, just begin typing the word you want to find. The Quick Search dialog box will pop up. Type enough characters to identify where you want to go, and then press Enter or click on OK. You don't have to use the SmartIcons, the menu bar, or the Search Bar (which you will learn about later in today's lesson).

For example, in Figure 3.7, I am looking for more information on "views." The Quick Search dialog box appears as soon as I type "v," but a search would only take me as far as "V2If function" at the start of the "v" listings. If I continue typing and enter "view," I will be taken close to what I want, and with a few keystrokes, I can view the document.

Figure 3.7.
Do a Quick Search to move the search focus near to what you want to find.

TIP Enter as few characters as possible to make your search quicker. The object is not necessarily to find an exact match, but to move the focus of your search close to what you are searching for. If you try to get too exact a match, your search may not find any matches.

Reading a Help Document

After you locate the document you want, you can, of course, read it in the preview pane. But you may prefer to open the document so you can see it on the full screen.

To open a document for reading, do one of the following:

- Double-click on the document title in the view.
- Click once on the document to highlight it, and then press the Enter key.
- Click once on the document to highlight it, and then select File | Open from the menu bar.

Following a Link to Another Document

When reading a Help document, or any other Notes document for that matter, you can frequently navigate directly to related documents without having to return to the view. For

example, the document shown in Figure 3.8 is about views, but you can navigate to related documents by clicking (or double-clicking, depending on what platform you are using) on underlined words. This is essentially the same thing as the hypertext links you may be familiar with when navigating the Web.

Figure 3.8.
Navigate to related documents by using underlined links or Action buttons.

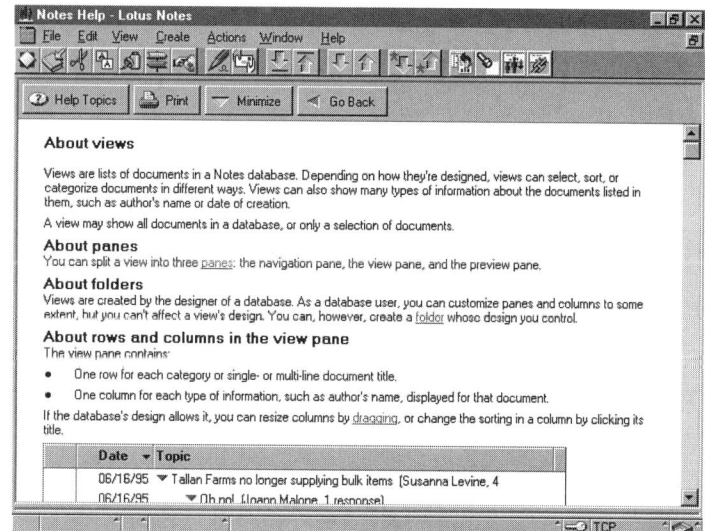

In the example shown in Figure 3.8, you can click on pane to navigate to a document about panes, and you can click on folders to go to a Help document that describes how to use folders.

You can also navigate or print help topics by clicking on the following buttons at the top of the document:

- ☐ *Help Topics.* This takes you back to the Index view in the Help database, but leaves the Help document open in the background.
- ☐ *Print.* This sends the current document to whatever printer you have selected for your workstation.
- ☐ *Minimize.* This shrinks the Help document so you can see other documents at the same time.
- ☐ *Go Back.* This takes you back to the document you were on before you followed a link to the current document.

TIP If a document or view is open in the background, you can move to it directly by selecting it from the Window menu on the menu bar.

Closing a Help Document

You can close a document by using any of the following techniques:

- ☐ Press the Esc key.
- ☐ Select File | Close from the menu bar.
- ☐ Press Ctrl+W (hold down the Control key while pressing W).

NOTE These steps close any Notes document or view. You can close help by successively closing documents and views until you reach the workspace.

Saving Commonly Used Help Documents in a Folder

Refer back to Figure 3.3, which showed the navigation pane for the Index view. At the bottom of the navigation pane is a Folder called Favorite Topics. A folder can be used to hold documents of your choice, as opposed to views, which hold documents selected by a formula.

To save a document in the folder, do the following:

1. Locate the document in the view pane.
2. Point to the document and hold down the left mouse button. A small document icon appears.
3. Holding down the mouse button, drag the icon until it is on top of the folder in the navigation pane, as shown in Figure 3.9.
4. Drop it on top of the folder.

To view the documents you have stored in your Favorite Topics folder, click on the folder to select it. The Favorite Topics will be displayed in the view pane, which will show only documents you have dropped onto the folder or placed into the folder from views.

Figure 3.9.
Dragging and dropping a help topic onto the Favorite Topics folder.

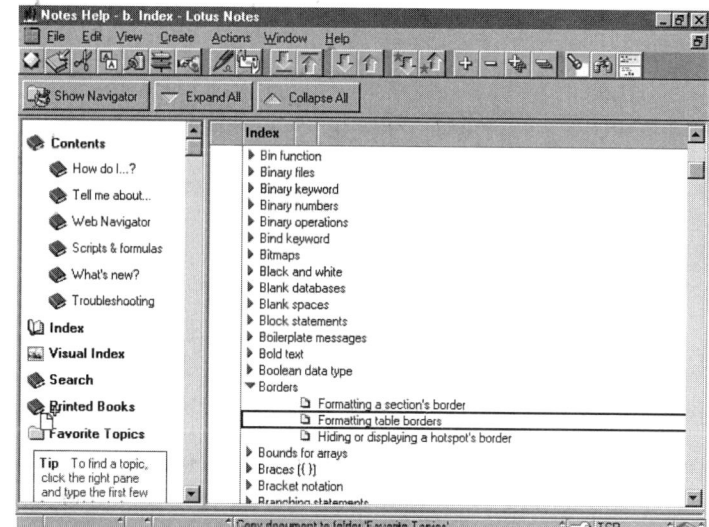

Looking at the Contents Views of the Help Database

There are a lot of different ways to access help. The type of help you need depends a lot on how experienced you are at working with Lotus Notes, and what tasks you are trying to accomplish.

Help documents are categorized in six different ways in the views grouped under Contents on the Help navigator pane. Each category presents a different way of looking at the documents. Within Notes, each method of categorizing the documents within a database is called a view.

These six views are described in the following paragraphs.

How Do I...?

The How Do I...? view is just what it sounds like. If you have a specific task that you want to accomplish and you don't know how to find the information you need in the Index view, you can look in here.

Figure 3.10 shows the expanded contents of the Do Everyday Tasks category. Notice that a lot of the tasks shown in this view are the same sort of tasks you are learning in this book. The other categories within this view are for more advanced users. Everyone can quickly learn the specific information needed for their jobs.

Figure 3.10.
How do I... ? view gives quick access to help directed toward specific tasks.

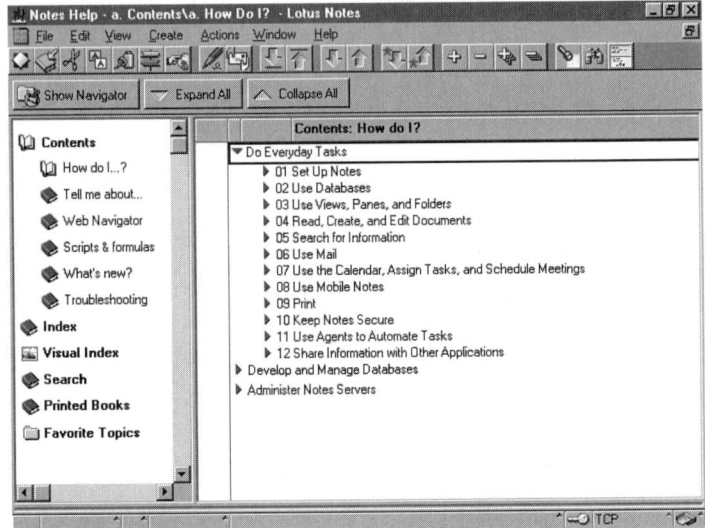

Tell Me About...

The Tell Me About... view shows many of the same documents that were in the previous view, but they are structured differently. For the novice, the How Do I...? topics are categorized under General Notes Concepts. For the application developer, there is a wealth of information about formulas and commands and the LotusScript programming language.

For you, the end user, there is a bonanza in this view, especially if you prefer to use a keyboard rather than the mouse. The Shortcuts category contains tables of keyboard shortcuts to many common functions throughout the Notes workspace.

Web Navigator

The Web Navigator provides information about using the Web Navigator, the Web browser built into Notes.

 **NOTE** On Day 14, "Notes and the Internet," you will learn about Notes and the Internet, including a tutorial on how to use the Notes Web Navigator.

Scripts and Formulas

Scripts and Formulas is a view specially designed with the Notes application developer in mind. It groups all help about the programming functions in Notes into a single view so that the developer can have quick access to the information. As an end user, you will not need to concern yourself with scripts and formulas.

What's New?

This is a specialized view that contains information for people who have been using earlier versions of Notes. It provides information on how to find functions that have been moved or renamed, and an itemization of what is new in the latest releases of Notes.

Troubleshooting

The Troubleshooting view provides suggestions to overcome common hurdles within Notes. It also contains documents explaining error messages that you may encounter.

Each of these views serves a specific audience, and each one shows just some of the documents that were in the comprehensive Index view. You can see how a simple view selection formula, written by the database designer to select documents based on the content of a certain field or fields, can alter the appearance of a database. In the remaining two views, you will see other ways of approaching Notes data.

Using the Visual Index View

What you have seen so far would accurately lead you to believe that Notes is primarily a document- and text-oriented application. But from all of the icons you have seen—such as the closed and open book icons on the Help navigator—you can see that Notes also has graphical capabilities.

When you select the Visual Index, you see a single navigator screen. There is no view pane filled with documents. There is little text. The screen is dominated by large icons that give access to specific categories of help. And when you click on the category icons, you may be confronted with an entirely graphical way to navigate to Help documents. For example, Figure 3.11 shows the screen used to navigate to Help documents about the User Workspace—the same information you learned about on Day 2, "Exploring the Notes Database."

Figure 3.11.
Using a graphical navigator to access Help documents about the Notes workspace.

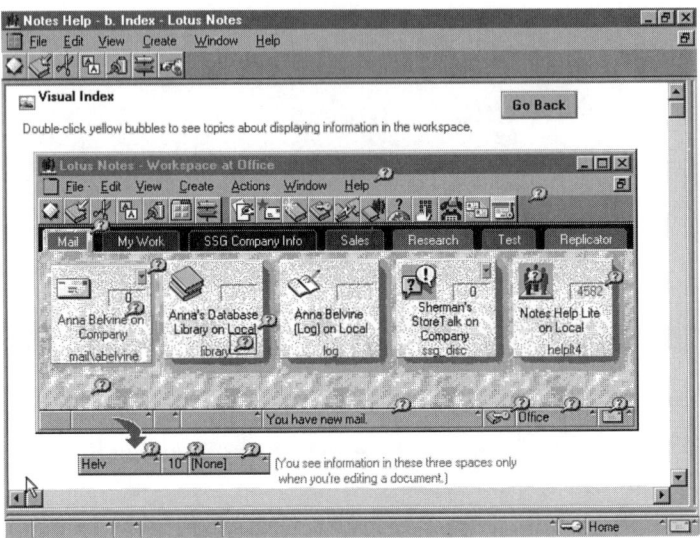

If you are familiar with navigating the World Wide Web, you will recognize the graphical navigators as imagemaps. Specific parts of the image are defined as "hotspots." When you click on them, you are taken to a Notes document. In the example shown in Figure 3.11, the question mark balloons take you to the same documents you would see if you navigated in another Notes Help view.

Using the Search View

In the Index view, you learned how to find help using the Quick Search function. Quick Search lets you move quickly to the vicinity of a document in the view pane, as long as you type the right search string and the search text is used at the start of a help topic.

Quick Search is obviously limited in what it can do. You can only use it to locate documents that start with the exact search string you enter. If the document starts with anything else, you may not find it.

The Search view offers a different and far more effective method of finding documents. Using a *full-text search* (a search that can sift through all the text in all documents and attachments in a Notes database), Notes looks for a search string anywhere within any document in the view. The search string (or its variants) can be in the title of a document or in the body.

Although full-text searching is covered in detail on Day 8, "Searching for Information in Notes Databases," today you learn to do a simple search using the Search view, shown in Figure 3.12.

Figure 3.12.
Using the full-text search function in the Search view.

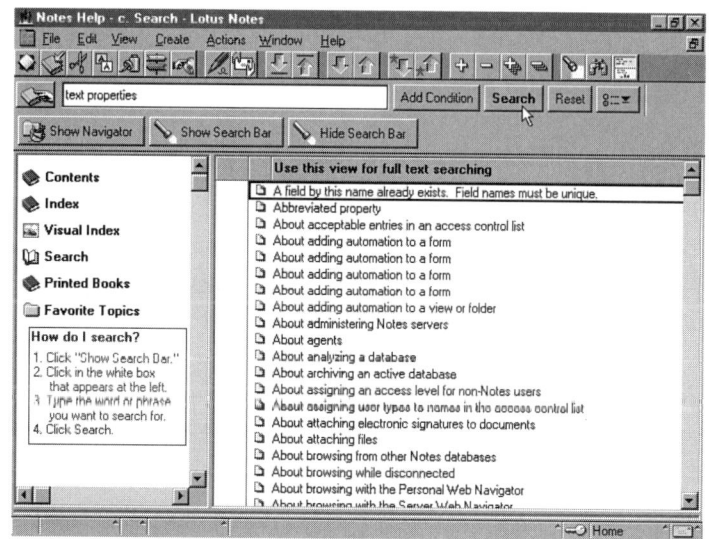

There are a couple of things that you need to do in order to search for a word or string:

1. Open the Search view. It is optimized for full-text searching.
2. Display the Search Bar at the top of the screen. If it is not already showing, click on the Display Search Bar button to display it, or select View | Search Bar from the menu bar.
3. Enter the word or string you want to find. In the example shown above, the phrase "text properties" is entered in the search bar.
4. Click on the Search button.

Notes will generate a new view that contains only the results of your search.

 **Tip** If you search for a long phrase, Notes only finds a document if it contains that exact phrase. Therefore, you should use search phrases judiciously.

In Figure 3.12, the phrase "text properties" is entered in the search bar. The results of that search are shown in Figure 3.13.

Figure 3.13.
The results of a search, with documents ranked by relevance.

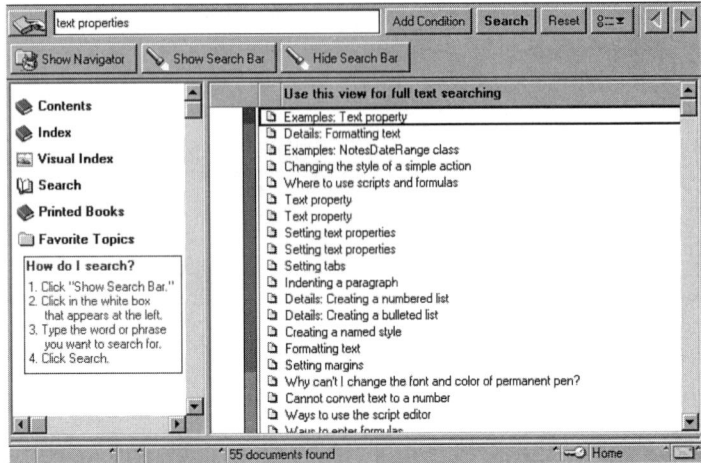

Note the gray bar to the left of the documents found by the search. This bar gets gradually lighter for documents that have fewer instances of the word or phrase being searched for. They are less likely to be relevant to the person doing the search, because the documents have fewer mentions of the search term.

There are a lot of documents that were selected by the phrase "text properties." I could now use the search results as a view, and narrow my search further by searching for another word or phrase, such as "dialog box."

If you want to do another search, you can clear the results of the first search by clicking on the Reset button on the Search bar.

You can play with the search function if you want, or wait until Day 8 when we take a much closer look at doing a full-text search.

Using the Printed Books View

The Printed Books view delivers the printed Notes documentation in online form. If you do not have a printed copy of the documentation and you desperately want one, hook your help database to a printer and print it yourself.

Actually, the Printed Books view includes several books. The first one is the User's Guide, which will be the most relevant to your current needs. As you become more experienced, you may be interested in some of the other books. The books in the Printed Books view include:

- ☐ User's Guide
- ☐ Application Developer's Guide

- Database Manager's Guide
- Programmer's Guide
- LotusScript Language Reference

You can print the books by clicking on a Print button at the top of the view. Print all help documents in the Printed Books view, or select specific documents to print. In Figure 3.14, three documents have been selected by clicking once in the column beside the document titles (called the View Marker column). Click on Print Selected Topics to print the selected documents.

Figure 3.14.
Topics selected for printing from the User's Guide in the Printed Books view.

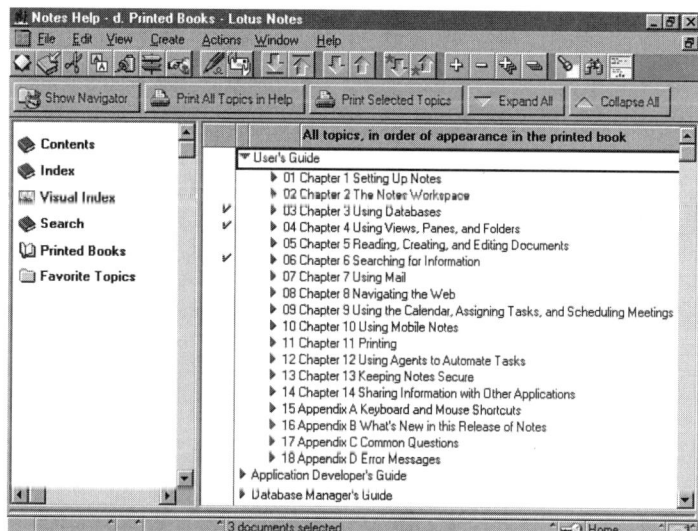

Other Ways to Access Help

Notes has other types of online help available besides what you saw in the Help database. We will discuss these in a minute, but first, one more way to get at the Help database.

Using Context-Sensitive Help

Notes has context-sensitive help, which is help that displays different documents depending on where you are within Notes, and what task you are trying to accomplish.

Obviously, Notes is not intelligent enough to second guess you. But what it does is provide a short list of help topics that are likely to help you in your current situation. For example, if you are editing a document, context-sensitive help will present help topics on tasks such as adding text and graphics, adding a hotspot, or checking the spelling of the document. On the other hand, if you were on the workspace when you accessed context-sensitive help, Notes would show help topics such as how to work with the tabbed workspace pages, and how to add new databases to the workspace. A sample of the Guide Me view is shown in Figure 3.15.

Figure 3.15.
The context-sensitive Guide Me view accessed from a workspace page.

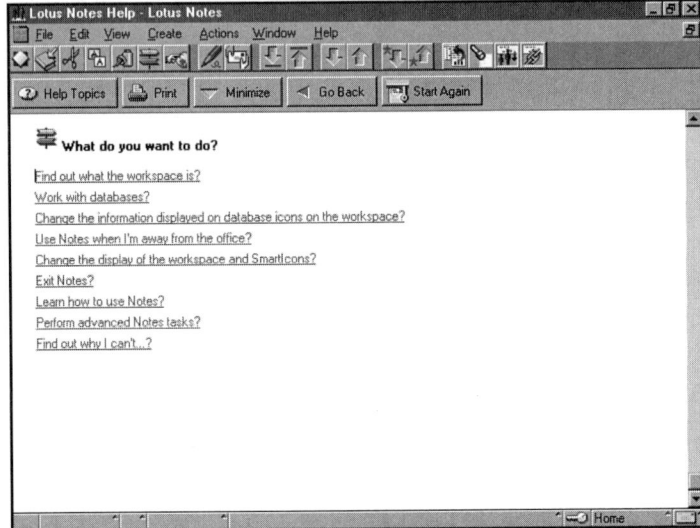

There are three ways to access the context-sensitive help, referred to within Notes as the Guide Me help view:

- Press the F1 key.
- Click on the Guideposts SmartIcon.
- Select Help | Guide Me from the menu bar.

The context-sensitive help is another subset of the Notes Help database. Once you get beyond the navigation, you will see some of the same documents you saw when opening the Help database directly.

Accessing Help from Buttons

If you refer back to the picture of the Guide Me screen in Figure 3.15, you will notice several buttons whose sole purpose is navigation within the Help database. These buttons can point to a view within the Help database, like the Help Topics and Start Again buttons that point back to the Index view. Or they can point directly to a document, as the Go Back button sometimes does, returning you to the previously open document. If you accessed the Guide

Me page directly from the Notes workspace, you are returned to the workspace, but if you were in another Help document, it will take you back to that document.

Buttons are design elements put there at the discretion of the application designer. Not all Notes databases have navigation buttons, and even if they do have them, they may not lead directly to online help documents. But do keep your eye out for them.

Database Level Help

Remember on Day 2 when we put a database on the workspace? One step was to click on an About... button that displayed an information screen that described the database. Database designers can take advantage of two special design documents that describe the purpose of the database and how to use the database. About and Using documents can be accessed from Help on the menu bar.

About This Database is the document that you see when you click on About... in the Open Database dialog box. The information in this document usually describes the overall purpose of the database, who should be using it, what level of access they should have, and additional information such as copyright information.

Using This Database is a Help document for the database. If you click on a Help button on the Action Bar at the top of a document and then see a Help document, you are probably seeing the Using document. It usually has information about how to use the application, including a description of workflow, special forms, and so on, and may even provide information about how to contact the developer for additional help.

Document Level Help

There is nothing within Notes that is specifically document level help, but there are a few types of help that you can look at that are specific to documents, or to the forms that are used to display documents. These are described below.

Screen Titles

On Day 2, you learned about the elements of the Notes workspace. One of those elements was the title bar at the very top of the screen.

The screen title can provide you with a lot of information, depending on how an application was designed.

The title bar usually tells you which form or view you are currently using. If you are in an application where forms and views tend to look like one another, you can use the title bar to identify your location.

The title bar can also display information based on a formula. For example, the title bar at the top of a customer document could display information such as the name of the account manager and the number of orders the customer has placed in the past year. In a discussion database, the title bar is likely to show the main topic and the number of responses that have been posted to it.

Buttons

You saw in the Help database how buttons can be used for navigation within a database. The same type of navigation is sometimes put to good use within Notes applications to display form-specific Help documents that are otherwise hidden.

For example, if you are working with a particularly complex form, there may be a help document that can be displayed by clicking on a Help button. When the help screen is closed, you are returned to the task of filling out the form. It is a quick and easy way for an application designer to create online, context-sensitive help.

Buttons can be displayed on the Action Bar at the top of forms and views, or they can be embedded within a document. With Notes, you will usually find buttons on the Action Bar for a couple of reasons.

- ☐ The Action Bar remains in view, even though the document you are looking at may scroll off the screen. If a button were included within the document, the button could scroll off the screen with the remainder of the document.
- ☐ Probably a more important consideration for application designers is that the Domino server can publish Notes documents directly to the Internet, but it does not translate buttons. Only the first button in a document is used, and it becomes a Submit button on the Web, no matter what its purpose was in Notes. In contrast, buttons on the Action Bar can also work on the Web, depending on what actions they are designed to perform. A button that displays a hidden Help document in Notes will also work on the Web.

Links

Buttons are not the only way to get from one Notes document to another. Links can be placed in a Notes document. When a user clicks on the link, he is taken to another document, to a view, or to another database. If he has a connection to the Internet, then links in a Notes document can even be used to launch a Web browser and display a Web page.

The linked document, view, database, or Web site can obviously contain Help documents.

What does a link look like? It can look like a small icon, underlined text, a button.... Figure 3.16 shows several types of link.

Figure 3.16.
Several examples of the types of links that could lead to document level help.

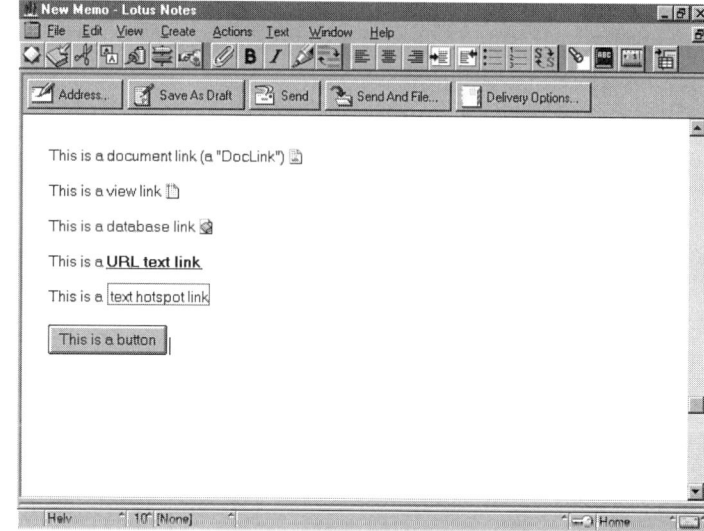

 **NOTE**
You will be learning how to create all of these links in your own documents on Day 6, "Working with Objects."

Pop-ups

Pop-ups are similar to what is commonly called "bubble help," help that pops up when you point to a word or icon. But with pop-ups, you have to point at the pop-up and hold down the left mouse button to see the text that annotates part of a document.

Field-Level Help

On Day 4, "Creating Notes Documents," you will learn how to create documents in Notes databases. When you move from field to field, the database designer has the option of showing help for the field at the bottom of the screen. This is covered in tomorrow's lesson.

What to Do If You Still Need Help

If you still need help after reading this book and going through the online help, there are other help resources available. The most notable resources come from Lotus and its large community of business partners and Lotus Authorized Education Centers (LAEC). You can contact the Lotus Education Helpline by calling 1-800-346-6409 to find out about LAECs. You can also look on the Lotus Web site at http://www.lotus.com for information and the name of a Lotus business partner in your locale.

Summary

Today's lesson was ostensibly about using Notes Help. The Help databases were put on the Notes workspace. Then we explored the database, looking at several different ways to access help, including:

- Context-sensitive help using the F1 key
- Guide Me help
- Opening help views from the menu bar
- Opening the Help database directly

You also learned about the other sources for Notes Help, such as database, document and field-level help.

Although accessing help was the main topic in this lesson, there was a definite subtext. You learned how to navigate in a Notes database, and you learned how to open and close documents. You learned what a Notes database looks like when it is open. As a user of Notes, this knowledge is fundamental, and will soon become second nature.

Workshop

The Workshop section presents quiz questions to help you cement your new knowledge and exercises to give you experience using what you have learned. Try to understand the questions and exercises before moving on to the next lesson. Answers are in Appendix A.

Q&A

Q Sometimes I follow along in Notes, but what I see on my screen is not the same as what is shown in the book. What's happening.

A Three things are possible. First, you might have a different version of the Notes Help database. Lotus is constantly updating the online help, so different point releases might have slightly different help databases. Second, you may have your environment set up differently, which can account for some differences. Third, the full text searching that was shown has to be set up in advance to show relevance ranking. You will learn how to set up relevance ranking on Day 8.

Q Do I have to use the Notes Help Lite database if I'm using a laptop computer?

A No. The Notes Help Lite database is much smaller, and contains help for end users and mobile users. If you have sufficient disk space and require some of the more advanced Help topics, you can place the full Notes Help database on your laptop computer.

Q I use a Macintosh. Is there help for Macintosh users?

A Because the user interface is virtually the same for all platforms, most of what you learn is universal. When relevant, the platform-specific information for a Help topic can be found in a collapsed section of the help document for that topic.

Quiz

1. How do you print out a copy of the Notes User's Guide?
2. Using online help, what is the best way to find out if you can change the default font in Notes?
3. Open up the Index view in the Help database. Using this view, how do you navigate to a help topic on how to display a horizontal scroll bar?

Exercises

1. Pick out a function that interests you, then use the Index view to find a detailed document describing how to perform that function. Then close the help document, change to the Search view, and try to locate the same document by performing a full text search.
2. Plan a business trip on which you will need to take Lotus Notes on a laptop computer. For which functions are you likely to need online help? Can you get this help from the Notes Help Lite database, or do you need the full Notes Help?

Week 1

Day 4

Creating Notes Documents

In today's lesson, you get to the heart of the matter—creating documents in Notes. But first, we have to define what a document is.

A *document* can take many forms. It can be a letter, a report, or a proposal. But it can also be a complex document with various types of data, as well as collapsible sections and links to other documents, and even links to other applications outside of Notes.

The skeleton for a document is a form. The *form* is a template that defines the format of the document and how it will be handled by the system.

To understand how the form is used, think in terms of filling in a loan application at the bank. You start with a blank, generic application form. You fill in all of the required blanks on the form, and you fill in as many of the optional blanks as are needed. It still is not a document. First you have to sign it and hand it to the loan officer. Only then can you really call it a document. Before that, it is just a worksheet.

We will be creating documents, but first we need the prerequisites: forms. That will require a quick review of how to put databases on your desktop.

Putting Databases on the Desktop

In this book, we are going to use only databases that I know you have access to. That includes only databases that come with Notes or that you can create from standard Notes templates.

On Day 2, "Exploring the Notes Workspace," we created a database from a Discussion template. On Day 3, "Using Notes Help," we put the Notes Help database on your desktop. In addition to that, you should have on your desktop a Public Address Book, to which you are likely to have limited access privileges, and a Mail database.

NOTE The Notes Public Address Book and your Mail database are created automatically when you connect to the Domino server during setup. The Mail database is one of the databases we will use in this book, along with a personal version of the address book that we will be creating from a template. If you connected to the server during setup, then the Mail database should already be on your desktop. If not, you will have to open your Mail database from the server or create a local version from a template so you can follow along.

We will be putting a Personal Address Book on the desktop as well. That will make at least three databases that you can use to create documents and to see the different types of data that can be entered into Notes documents: a Discussion database, a Personal Address Book, and a Mail database.

To review from Day 2, this is how you create a database from a template:

1. Select File | Database | New from the menu bar, or press CTRL+N .
2. Leave the Server field as Local if you want the database stored locally (which in this case we want to do).
3. Enter a descriptive title for the database you are creating.
4. Enter a file name for the database you are creating. The database will be stored in your default Notes data directory.

    Select a template to use for creating the new database. If the template you want is not on your local drive, select the name of the template server before selecting a template. The templates that you may need, for now, include Discussion (R4), Mail (R4.5), and Personal Address Book.

NOTE Other commonly used templates that you might want to explore on your own include a document library, a personal journal, and the Personal Web Navigator, which you will work with on Day 14, "Notes and the Internet."

If these or similar databases that you want to use are already on your computer, you can put them on your desktop instead of creating new databases from templates.

To put a database on your desktop:

1. Select File | Database | Open from the menu bar, or CTRL+O.
2. Accept the default of Local as the Server if the database is on your local workstation. Otherwise, select the name of the Server from which you want to open a database.
3. Locate the name of the database you want to open. Click once on the database name to highlight it.
4. Click on Add Icon to put the database icon on your desktop, or click on Open to open the database immediately (which also places the database icon on the desktop).
5. If you selected Add Icon, you can close the dialog box by clicking on Done when you are through adding icons.

Creating a Simple Document

To learn how to create documents, we begin with the Discussion database. The forms in a discussion database are simple, and discussions are one of the most commonly used Notes applications. A Discussion database can be used by a workgroup to develop an idea, or it can be used as a bulletin board where people with common interests can congregate in cyberspace. For our purposes, the database will be used to discuss what you hope to accomplish by using Lotus Notes in your organization.

NOTE You can create and work with a Discussion database on your local Notes client workstation, but other Notes users will be unable to share in your discussions unless the database is stored on a Domino server.

Getting Started

To create a Notes document, you begin by opening a form in a Notes database. That should be obvious, if you have used templates in other computer applications. What you need to do is locate the correct form in the correct database, and then fill in the blanks and save it.

Locating and Opening the Correct Database

You must first locate and open the database in which you want to create a document. In this case, we are going to use the Discussion database that we created.

To locate the Discussion database, click the tab that moves you to the correct workspace page.

NOTE Locating the database on a workspace page assumes that you already have the database icon on your desktop. If you followed the directions on Day 2 and at the beginning of this lesson (repeated in the Exercises section at the end of the lesson), you already have the databases on your desktop.

I am going to use the database I named "TY Lotus Notes 4.5" when the database was created on Day 2. You may have given your database a different name, or you may want to use a Discussion database that is already in use in your organization.

Double-click the database icon to open the database to the default All Documents view.

TIP If you see the About This Database document, take a minute to read about the database, and then press the Escape key once to close the About document.

If you see the view, but the navigator is in text and you want to see a graphical navigator, you can toggle between the two by clicking on the Navigator button.

What to Look for in the View

There are a couple of things visible in the view window that you should be aware of before you continue. From the view shown in Figure 4.1, you can tell whether you are authorized to create documents in this database, and what types of document you are able to create.

Figure 4.1.
All Documents view of a Discussion database.

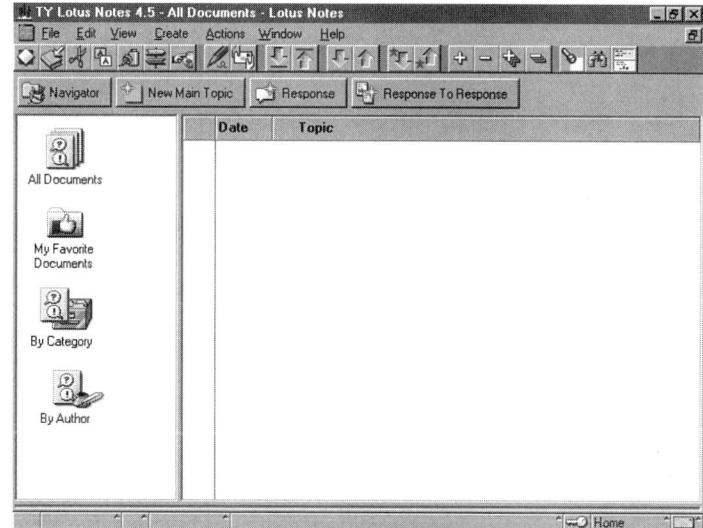

Are You Authorized to Create Documents?

On Day 1, "Understanding Notes," you learned about the Access Control List (ACL), which determines what you are able to do within a database. On Day 2, you learned that the status bar shows your level of access for the database that is open on your desktop. Now, let's put that knowledge to use.

The third icon from the right on the status bar in Figure 4.1 shows a golden key. That icon represents your level of access to this database.

To find out what the icon represents, click on the key icon. Notes displays the dialog box shown in Figure 4.2.

Figure 4.2.
The Groups and Roles box shows what your access rights are for the currently open database.

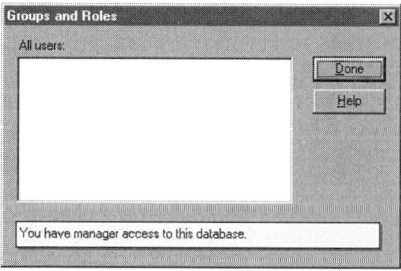

Your role in the ACL is listed at the bottom of the dialog box. If you are a member of a group that has access, or if you have specific roles within the database, these will also be listed in dialog box. Because this is a local database and you have not modified the ACL, you should be listed as a Manager, and there should be no other roles or groups listed.

>  **NOTE** When you create a new database, you are automatically made Manager for that database. You also have Manager access for any database that you *copy* to your local Notes client workstation. However, if you make a *replica copy* of a database that has the ACL consistently enforced across all replicas, or if you open a database from a Domino server, then you may have a more restrictive level of access.

What Types of Document Can You Create?

If you look at the top of the All Documents view, you will see four buttons. The first button switches between a graphical navigator and text navigator. The other three buttons are used to create documents in this particular database. However, the three document types—main documents, response documents, and response to response documents—are applicable to all Notes databases.

Main Document Type

If you encounter a Notes database with only one type of document, then that document will be defined by the application designer as a main document type. The main document type, as the name implies, is a primary document. You cannot create secondary documents unless there is a main document already in place.

One analogy that everyone will understand is the 1040 tax form. You might have a Schedule A and a Schedule C form that you also need to file with your taxes, but you cannot file them unless they are attached to a 1040 form. The other documents are dependent on the main document for their identity.

Every Notes database has at least one main document type. In the Discussion database, the Main Topic is a main document type.

Response Document Types

There is a parent-child relationship between the main document type and the response document type. The response is the child of the main document.

This sort of relationship exists in many applications. For example, when you visit the doctor's office, there is a main medical record that has your vital statistics on it. That main record acts as a binder that holds secondary records, the records of individual visits to the doctor. Those secondary records are considered response document types in Notes.

Response to Response Document Types

Keeping with the same analogy, suppose the doctor orders some lab tests or x-rays as a result of an office visit. The results of these tests go in your medical record, but they are attached to one particular visit record. They could just as easily be attached directly to the general medical record, for example, as part of your annual physical. These are the same as response to response document types in Notes. They can be subsidiary to any document type, including another response to response document.

Creating a Main Topic

Now that you have learned about the document types, it is time to create your first document. The documents that you will be creating can be created by displaying a form in one of two ways:

- Select Create | Main Topic from the menu bar.
- Click on the New Main Topic button on the Action Bar at the top of a view window.

Notes displays the Main Topic form shown in Figure 4.3.

Figure 4.3.
The Main Topic form is used to create a document in the Discussion database.

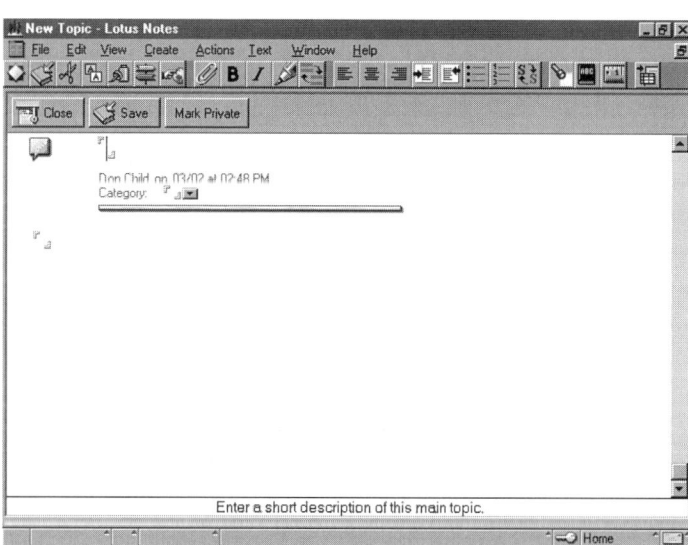

The form has three editable fields, and at least two visible fields that cannot be edited.

The fields that cannot be edited are the Author Name field, which shows who created the document, and a Time field, which shows when the document was created. You have very little control over these fields. The author name comes from your Notes UserID, and the time and date come from your system clock.

The cursor is in the first editable field, which is marked by corner brackets. To fill out the form, do the following:

1. Look at the bottom of the form. There should be a line of field-level help that says `Enter a short description of this main topic`. If you do not see this field-level help, you may want to display it by selecting View | Show | Field Help.
2. In the first field, type a document title, for example **Ways Notes will help me do my job.** The document title will be used to identify the document in views.
3. Press the Tab key or use the arrow keys to move to the Category field, or click in the Category field to move there. The Category field is a keyword field, indicated by the expander button, and by the field-level help, which tells you to `Press ENTER for list of keywords or to add new keyword`. You can accomplish the same thing by clicking on the entry helper button (the drop-down arrow) to show a keyword dialog box similar to the one shown in Figure 4.4. The keywords you select will be used to categorize documents in views.

Figure 4.4.
The Select Keywords dialog box is used to enter select an entry in a keyword field.

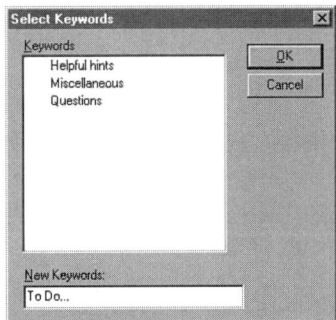

In this example, a few keywords have already been added to show what it might look like in a real situation, but the box will be empty the first time it is opened. You will need to enter keywords through the New Keywords field. Any keywords that you use will be added to the list of keywords from which you can select for subsequent documents. Keywords are complex and are described in more detail later in this lesson.

4. Press the Tab key or use the arrows to move to the next field. Again notice the field-level help. This is a Rich Text field in which you can enter the body of your document.

5. When you are done entering data, click on one of the buttons under the Icon bar to indicate how the document should be handled by the system. "Mark Private" means that when it is saved, only you will be able to view the document. "Save" means that the document will be saved, but will remain open so you can continue editing it. "Close" will display a dialog box that gives you the option of saving the document (Yes), closing it without saving (No), or canceling and returning to the document.

The completed document is shown in Figure 4.5.

Figure 4.5.
The completed main document, ready to be closed and saved.

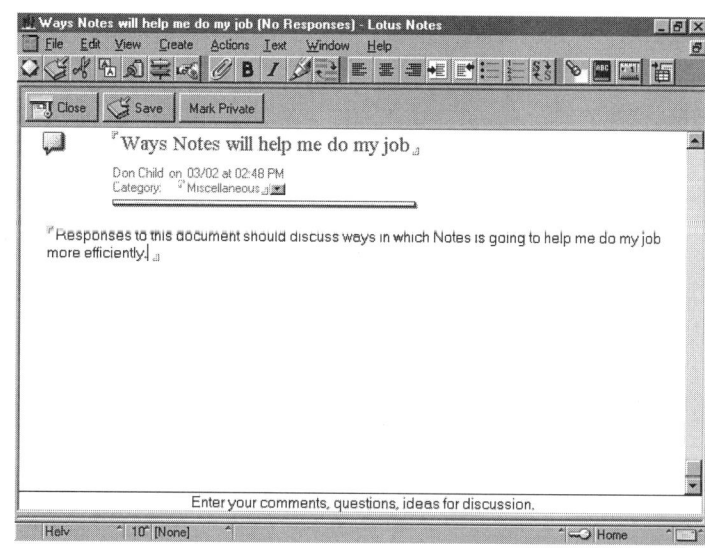

Responding to a Document

You have now seen how a document is created in a Discussion database. The other part of a discussion is a response. And with the response to response capabilities, you can get some very dynamic dialogs going in Notes. Notes has a tendency to flatten an organization. People are empowered by the ability to respond to issues where they can contribute vital information, even though they might not normally be asked because of their position in the organizational hierarchy.

You can respond to any main topic by creating a Response document, or you can respond to any document in the database by creating a Response to Response document.

Think of the relationship between documents as a parent/child relationship. There is always a Main document, which is always a parent. The Main document can have one or more

Responses, which are children of the parent. In addition, there are Response to Response documents, which can attach themselves as a child of any other document—Main documents, Response documents, or other Response to Response documents. They are like foster children, who end up wherever you place them.

To create a Response or a Response to Response document, follow these steps:

1. Use any view to locate the document to which you want to respond.
2. Highlight the document.
3. Click on the Response or the Response to Response button, or select the type of document you want to create from Create on the menu bar.
4. Alternatively, double-click on the document to which you want to respond, and when it is open, click on the Response button.
5. Enter a brief title for your response, and enter the body of your response. If necessary, you can click on a button to show the parent document in a Preview pane as you edit your response.
6. Save your response. When you close the document and return to the All Documents view, your document will be indented under the document to which you responded.

Notice the similarity. You display a form. You fill in some fields. You close and save the document. Beyond that simple process, the primary differences between Notes applications arises from security constraints, background processing, and the complexity of forms.

What Types of Data Do Notes Documents Accept?

Even on the simple forms in the Discussion database, you were introduced to five different data types. The different data types have specific properties that determine what you can do in a particular field. The following section should help you gain some understanding of data types.

Text

Most fields you see on Notes forms are text fields. They are versatile, but at the same time they have limitations. For example, you can enter numbers, dates, names, and assorted information in text fields, but you cannot format the text with attributes such as bold, underline, and italic, and you cannot use rich text tools such as tables, graphics, links, and so forth.

A text field can contain letters, punctuation, space, and numbers that are not used mathematically. Examples of the type of information you might enter in a text field using these characters include telephone numbers, social security numbers, street addresses, or even the text of a corporate brochure. In other words, a text field is pretty much like an ASCII text file, which can contain only the sorts of letters, numbers and characters you would find on a typewriter keyboard.

Rich Text

Two lessons in this book are dedicated to a discussion of Rich Text. On Day 5, "Working with Rich Text in Documents," you will learn about all the text editing features of Notes, the word processing functions. Some Notes users become so involved in the Notes environment that they use Notes as their preferred word processor. On Day 6, "Working with Objects," you will learn about Notes Rich Text fields as multimedia containers. There is almost no limit to what you can put into a Rich Text field, including graphics, embedded sound and video files, spreadsheets, tables, and links to other applications.

There are limits to the Rich Text field format, though. For one thing, you cannot display information from a Rich Text field in a Notes view. You can reference most other fields in a view, but the application developer cannot do much more with an RTF field except to verify that the field is blank or not blank. For another thing, one form cannot inherit Rich Text data from another Notes form using simple application development techniques.

Keywords

There are three types of keyword field—radio buttons, check boxes, and dialog lists—and all three have one thing in common: They let the user pick from a set of predefined input options. Once a keyword has been selected, the rest of the form can change dynamically to reflect the user's input.

Radio Button Keywords

Younger readers might not remember, but until a few years ago, car radios had manual push buttons that changed the channels, rather than the electronic touch buttons that are available today. With the old buttons, you would push in one button, and whichever button was previously selected would pop out. Only one button could be depressed at a time.

The radio button keywords look just like that old radio. You push buttons by clicking on them. And the only way to deselect one button is to select another. If there is no default setting, then you may see a set of radio buttons where no button is selected. But as soon as one is selected, you cannot unselect that button. Radio buttons are illustrated in Figure 4.6.

Figure 4.6.
Radio buttons let you select one mutually exclusive keyword.

Radio buttons are used whenever keyword choices are mutually exclusive, such as yes/no choices, or status changes.

Check Box Keywords

Check boxes provide a way of selecting or deselecting keyword choices. To turn a selection on, click in the check box. To turn an option off that is already selected, click in the check box. You are probably familiar with forms that have the check boxes, and some sort of instruction that says "Check all that apply." That is what a check box is. Figure 4.7 shows a series of check boxes.

Figure 4.7.
Check boxes let you select multiple keywords.

The list of allowable check box keywords is usually hardcoded into the form, but the list can be generated on-the-fly using a formula that looks up information from elsewhere. Using such a technique, envision an application where someone is ordering supplies. Instead of letting them order something that is out of stock, Notes can generate a list of check boxes based on a lookup in an inventory database. The list only shows items that are currently in stock, thus helping your company with its customer connection.

Dialog List Keywords

In the Discussion database, you saw an example of dialog list keywords. Keywords are not displayed on the screen until you place the cursor in the field and press Enter, or click on the entry helper button beside the field. When you launch the dialog list, a box pops open on the screen with a list of keywords, as shown in Figure 4.8.

In this dialog list, highlight the keyword you want to select, and then click on OK.

You can also enter keywords into a field using type-ahead, where Notes will insert the keyword as soon as you type enough characters to distinguish the selection from other keywords. You can also toggle through all keywords in a field by placing the cursor in the field and pressing the spacebar each time you want to toggle.

Figure 4.8.
A dialog list box lets you select keywords from a pop-up list.

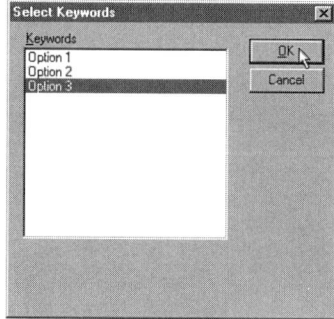

Dialog list keywords are more flexible than the other two options. For example, dialog lists can be defined with the following options:

- ☐ Limit keywords to a single specific choice, as with radio buttons.
- ☐ Allow multiple choices to be made, as with check boxes, and then display the multiple choices separated by commas, semicolons, or by new lines.
- ☐ Allow the user to select from a list, or add his own new keywords.

The keyword list can be created by user input, hard-coded, or generated by a lookup in a view in the same database or in another database.

Another more complex version of the dialog list uses a Notes Address Book to look up entries. You can select entries from an address book on one side of the dialog list, and add them to a list on the other side. You will see this dialog list later.

Other Keyword Options

Keywords may be displayed using variants of list boxes. Notes 4.5 developers may make use of a design element known as a layout region, which allows fields to be embedded in a graphical background that pops up on the screen. In these graphical layout regions, keyword lists may be displayed in scrolling list boxes or in drop-down combo boxes. These layout regions can be hidden by the application developer until specific information is needed from the user. At that time, they can be displayed so the needed information can be entered. A common use of layout regions is to help the user define routing information when a document is ready to be reviewed by other Notes users in a workflow application.

Numbers

Number fields are used whenever the information needs to be used mathematically. The only acceptable information that can be entered into the field are numbers (0 – 9), a decimal point (.), and mathematical operators (+ - E e).

A common error with number fields is to combine numbers with text. For example, if you have a field that asks for total sales in dollars, you cannot enter "5 million." If you do, an error message will be displayed that says "unrecognized characters after number." If a number is formatted as a currency field, all you have to enter is a number, for example, "15" for $15.00".

Number fields are often used for simple mathematical calculations, for example, calculating a purchase order total, including tax, on a multiple item order form.

Number fields may be formatted as integers, decimals, scientific notation, or as currency.

NOTE At the very beginning of Day 1, you learned, if you didn't already know, that Lotus Notes is not the same thing as Lotus 1-2-3. Although number fields can be used in calculations, Notes is not meant to function as a powerful spreadsheet. If you want to use Notes to share spreadsheet data, there are several ways to do so, including embedding a spreadsheet or attaching a spreadsheet file in a Rich Text field, or using Lotus Components or JavaBean applets. These alternatives are covered later in this book.

Time

Time fields are used for date and time information. You saw in the Discussion database how Notes was able to use a formula to display the date and time that a document was created.

Dates are entered into Notes numerically, for example "03/21/97" rather than spelling out the date. If dates are spelled out on Notes documents, it is the result of a translation formula created by the application designer. If you enter a two-digit date, Notes assumes the date is in the 20th century. If you want to enter a date in the 21st century, you must enter all four digits of the date, for example "03/21/2007." Date fields also recognize "Today" and "Yesterday."

Time is entered in either 12-hour or 24-hour format, for example "04:20 PM" or "16:20." Depending on how a field is defined, time may be shown in seconds as well as hours and minutes.

Authors

Authors fields hold a list of user names of individual users (or group names or access roles) who are allowed to edit a document even though they have only Author access to the database.

In most applications where you can create and edit documents, there is a hidden (or at least non-editable) field that holds the name of the person who created the document. Other users with Author access to the database cannot edit the document unless their name is somehow entered into the Authors field.

In an environment where you have flexible teams, but you do not want to give people a level of access higher than Author, the Authors field may be editable, with a lookup in the Notes Public Address Book so you can add new names as needed.

Readers

A Readers field is used to restrict who can read a document or a section within a document. The Readers field is only applicable to those who may be able to read the document because of their role in the ACL, that is, Managers, Designers, Editors, and Readers. If a document has a blank Readers field, then anyone with at least Reader access to the database will be able to see the document. However, if the field is not blank, then only those who are included in the field will be able to view the document.

Names

Names fields display user or server names the way they appear on the Notes ID. Names fields are generally multi-value, and are used whenever you need to enter a valid user name but do not need to restrict access or assign an author to a document.

Depending on the design, a Names field can be populated from an address book, a view, or the ACL for the database. If you add multiple names from an address book, Notes will display the dialog box shown in Figure 4.9.

Figure 4.9.
Dialog box used to enter names from a Notes address book into a Names field.

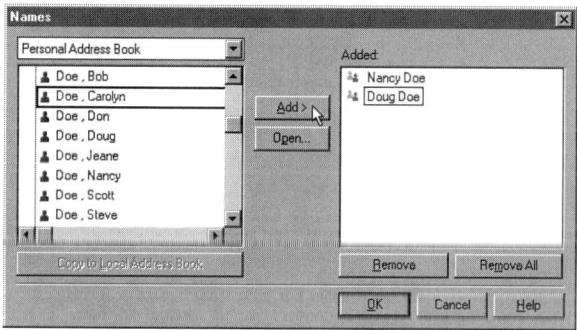

In this dialog box, you select the address book from which to select names, then click on a name to highlight it, and then click on Add to copy the name to the right column. When you close the dialog box, the names in the right column are placed into the Names field. If names come from a public address book, you can copy them to your private address book by clicking on the Copy to Local Address Book button. If you need to look up or change information about a person in the address book, highlight his name and click on Open. If you need to remove a name from the list, highlight the name on the right side of the dialog box and click on Remove.

You might find a Names field in an application where you are assigning individuals to various roles within a project or account, such as the Account Manager, the Sales Manager, and so forth. These names are then available to Notes for workflow routing and wherever names might be required, such as approvals, status changes, notifications, and audit trails.

For the Names field, the Readers field, and the Authors field, you can select names directly from a Notes Address Book.

Which Fields Can You Edit?

Now that you are familiar with the data types, and you have seen how you enter data in the bracketed fields, how can you determine which fields you can edit and which ones you cannot? If the system puts data into a field, can you change it? And where does the data come from when the system populates a field?

Computed, Computed When Composed, Computed for Display, and Editable Fields

All fields in the Notes database are either Computed, Computed When Composed, Computed for Display, or Editable. Here is how Notes handles those three types of data:

- ☐ *Computed data* is displayed in a field based on the contents of other Notes fields. If the data in the other field or fields changes, then the computed data will change the next time the document is recomputed. Many Notes applications have one appearance for data entry, and an entirely different appearance when data is displayed. One of the ways this is accomplished is to create a display-only field that is computed. The computation is simple: Get the data that is in the data entry field, and display it in a different format. Another common use of computed data is to consolidate other data. For example, a net profit field might be computed based on data in a number of other fields, such as total sales in dollars, cost of goods, sales-related expenses, and so forth. If any of the data used in the calculation changes, then the computed result also changes next time the document is recomputed or refreshed (by pressing F9 or selecting View | Refresh from the menu bar, by saving the document, or by opening the document, for example).

- *Computed When Composed* fields are similar to Computed fields, but they are computed only one time, at the moment when the document is first created. That means that they can only be computed using data that already exist somewhere on the system. Common examples of these data are the date and time of creation, which are taken from the system clock; the Username on the Notes userID being used by the person who is creating the document; the name of the form being used to create the document; and the number of sibling documents at the moment of creation.
- *Computed for Display* fields are computed at the very moment a document is opened for viewing or opened for previewing. The content of the field is calculated every time the document gets opened, but the data does not get stored with the document. The field cannot be referenced in views or formulas, since there is no information stored in the field. This type of field is commonly used to display information in a special format when a document is opened for viewing, using data that gets entered in another format when the document is opened for editing.
- *Editable* fields can be edited at any time. If there is data in the field, you can delete the data and enter new information if it is a text field, or change the selected keyword if it is a keyword field. In fields that allow multiple values, you can delete part of the contents, or add new data. One caveat, however. If you delete a name from a Readers or Authors field, that person can no longer read or edit the document. If you are the only authorized author and you remove your own name, then nobody with Author access will be able to modify the document.

Inherited Versus Default Data

Earlier, when talking about main documents and response documents, a medical records environment was used as an example. Going back to that same example, consider what happens when you make an office visit. The doctor or nurse will fill in a visit record, and on that record, they have to put your name, your medical record number, and they probably weigh you and check your temperature as part of a standard screening procedure. If records are being kept manually, there is a lot of duplication of effort. With computerized records, that duplication does not have to take place.

When a new visit record (a Response document) is created, data is copied from your main medical record, or possibly from your most recent visit record. Some fields, such as name and medical record number, are not going to change. This information can be inherited into a Computed When Composed field.

Other data may change over time, such as your height and weight, but this information is likely to be pretty close to the same as it was during your last visit. This type of data can be inherited into an Editable field as default data. Default data can be changed if necessary, but the most likely information is filled in. Another example where default data might be useful is the time of your visit. You had an appointment to be there at a specific time. Your appointment time can be copied into the time-of-visit field, and then modified in case you got in early or were delayed. Default data is a way for the application designer to anticipate your likely responses to specific fields, and maybe save you a little bit of time.

NOTE One of the shortcomings of a Rich Text field is that data from it cannot be inherited into another field. However, the Rich Text field can inherit default data.

How Notes Checks for Required Data

You may be required to enter data in certain fields when creating a Notes document, while other fields are optional.

A good database design should have some way to signal when a field is required, but there is no standard indicator in Notes. You may see some conventions used such as an asterisk next to required fields, or all required fields grouped together. And don't forget to look at the field-level help at the bottom of the screen. This field help will frequently tell you when the field is required.

Notes performs a validity check on all fields to ensure that they have the correct type of data. In a required field, that validity check includes determining that the field is not blank, in addition to checking for a valid data format.

The one thing Notes cannot check is whether the data makes any sense. That is left to the user, although many designers make required fields into keyword fields. Another strategy is to make the required field a Computed When Composed field when possible, or place default data into the field to ensure that it is not left blank.

Notes performs a validation check whenever the document is refreshed, or when the entire document is saved. The designer has the option of refreshing the document when certain keyword fields are exited, or refreshing the document every time you move from field to field. This slows down processing, so it is rarely used unless it is vital for Computed fields to stay current.

When the document is saved, all fields are validated. If an error is discovered, the cursor moves to the field where the error was found and an error message is displayed. If there are multiple errors, you have the opportunity to correct them one field at a time. The document cannot be saved and closed until all errors are corrected.

Looking at a Complex Document

You learned how to create a simple Notes document, and you learned about the different types of data that can go into a Notes document. For the moment, you are not going to create a complex document, but you can at least look at one to see how the different field types can work together.

Figure 4.10 shows part of the Location document in the Personal Address Book. If you placed a Personal Address Book on your desktop, you can follow along by highlighting the database icon, and selecting Create | Location from the menu bar. Scroll down until you locate the Mail section and, below it, the collapsed Advanced section.

Figure 4.10.
Part of the Location document in the Personal Address Book showing many field types.

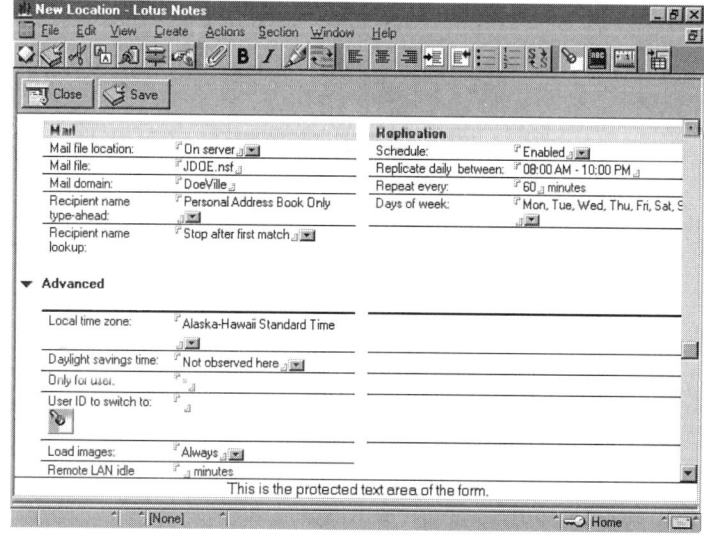

The field types shown in Figure 4.10 include:

- [ ] Keyword fields, including Mail File Location, Daylight savings time, Recipient name type-ahead, Recipient name lookup, Local time zone, Load images, Schedule, and Days of Week. The Replication fields are only displayed after you select the "enable" keyword in the Schedule field.
- [ ] Text fields, including Mail file, Mail domain, and User ID to switch to.
- [ ] Names field, where Only for user: has a default asterisk (*), which means that all users can use this Location document. If any name is entered in the field, then only those who are explicitly included in the field will be able to use this Location document.

- Number fields, including Remote LAN idle (blank) minutes, and Repeat every (blank) minutes.
- A Time field in Replicate daily between, which is a time range when automatic replication will take place.

Note also that there was a collapsible section. The information in the collapsed section is not needed for Notes to function properly, so it can be hidden from the casual user. A collapsible section is similar to a collapsed category in a view, where the section can be collapsed so only the section title is visible or expanded so all of the content is visible by clicking on a "twistie."

Not illustrated are the Readers and Authors field types. Also, there is no Rich Text field in the selection shown.

The purpose of showing part of this document in this lesson is not to attempt to define the fields and describe how they are used. It is simply included to illustrate the data types.

Closing a Notes Document

When you are done entering data in a Notes document, you need to save it and close it.

You can save a document at any time during the editing process in any of the following ways:

- Click on the Save Document SmartIcon (use bubble help to locate the Save Document SmartIcon).
- Click on a Save button, if there is one in the document or on the Action Bar.
- Select File | Save from the menu bar.
- Press Ctrl + S.

You also have the option of saving the document when the document is closed.

What happens when the document is saved? All fields are validated, as already mentioned. Computed fields are recomputed. If the form is mail enabled, the document is mailed or a memo is automatically generated. And the document appears in views and becomes available to other people using the database.

As with many functions in Notes, there are several ways to close a document:

- Click on a Close button, if there is one on the Action Bar or embedded in the document.
- Press the Escape key.
- Select File | Close from the menu bar.
- Press Ctrl+W (Close Window).

If changes have been made to the document since it was last saved, Notes displays a dialog box, as shown in Figure 4.11. Click on Yes to save the document. Click on No if you want

to abandon your changes. Click Cancel if you want to return to the document and continue editing.

Figure 4.11.
You have the option of saving your changes before closing a document.

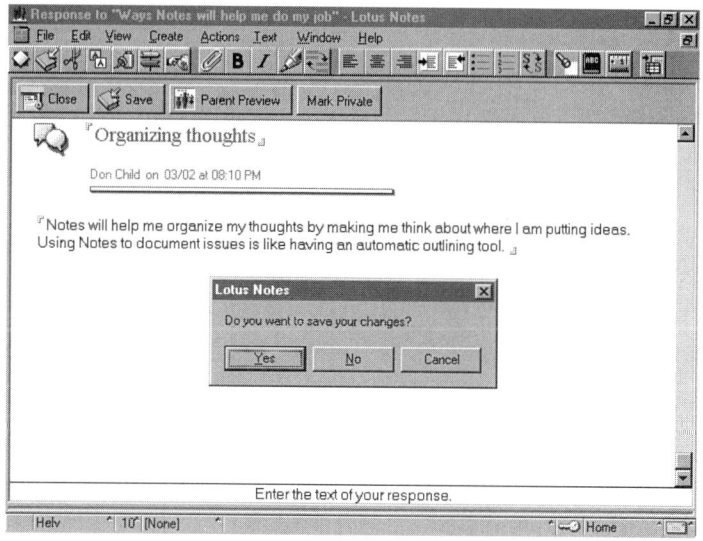

Editing Existing Documents

To edit an existing document, you have to access the document from a Notes view, as shown in Figure 4.12.

Figure 4.12.
Select a document from a Notes view to open it for editing.

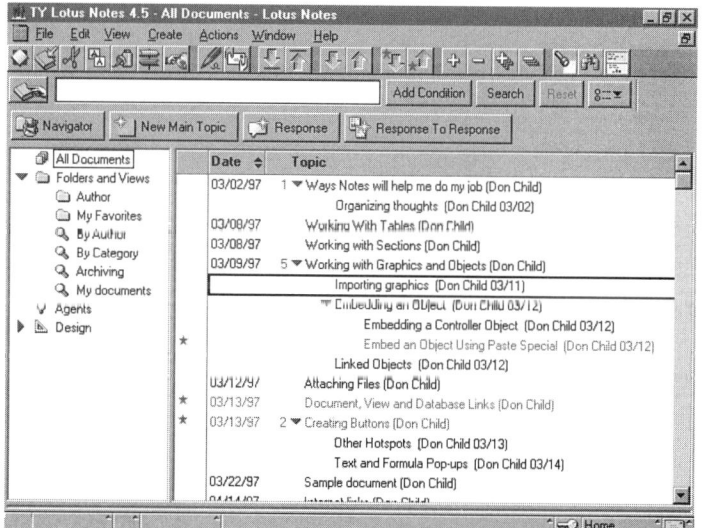

Once you have located the document, there are a number of ways that you can open it and put it into the Edit mode. You can do any of the following:

- [ ] Highlight the document and select Actions | Edit Document to open the document in the Edit mode.
- [ ] Highlight the document and press Ctrl+E to open the document in the Edit mode.
- [ ] Open the document in the Read mode, and then press Ctrl+E to toggle it into and out of the Edit mode.
- [ ] Open the document in the Read mode, and then click on the Edit Document button on the Action Bar, if the application has an Edit Document button.
- [ ] Open the document in the Read mode, then select Actions | Edit Document to put the document into the Edit mode.

NOTE Remember, you must have Editor access to the document before you can put it into Edit mode. That means that your name must be in an Authors field, or you must have at least Editor access.

Modify data while in the Edit mode, and then save the document in the same way you would save a new document. All validations take place just as they do with a new document, so required fields must still contain valid data.

Summary

In today's lesson, you learned what is probably the most fundamental function in all of Notes: how to create and edit documents. The lesson began by ensuring that there were some usable databases on the desktop.

We walked through the creation of a Main Topic document in the Discussion database, learning how to fill in fields and save the document. Then a Response document was created.

What was perhaps as important to learn, though, was the type of data that goes into a Notes document. There are several field types, including Text, Rich Text, Numbers, Time, Keywords, Authors, Readers, and Names field types. Layered on top the field types were Computed fields, Computed When Composed fields, and Editable fields. This creates the texture, the richness, and complexity of Notes documents.

This complexity was demonstrated in the Person document in the Personal Address Book.

To conclude the lesson, you learned about validation and what happens to a Notes document when you save it. You also learned how to reopen the document in case you have to modify it after it was saved.

Workshop

The Workshop section presents quiz questions to help you cement your new knowledge and exercises to give you experience using what you have learned. Try to understand the questions and exercises before moving on to the next lesson. Answers are in Appendix A.

Q&A

Q I access Notes from a Domino server using a Web browser. Can Notes do all of that validation for a Web page?

A When you use a Web browser, you make all the changes to a document locally, and then submit the document back to the Domino server. In this sort of an environment, there are some functions, such as a keyword list that does a live lookup of another database, that just will not work. Most Domino-published applications have been designed to avoid these shortcomings, so you can do almost everything on the Web that you can do in a native Notes environment. For a full discussion of this, see the lesson on Day 14.

Q I created a document in a database that had an "Authorized Authors" field on it. I added somebody's name to the field, but he still can't edit the document. What am I doing wrong?

A There are a couple of possibilities. First, the person must already have at least Author access to the database before he can be made the Author of a document. You cannot grant any rights that are greater than those already granted in the ACL. Second, you may have the name entered incorrectly. The name has to be recognized by the Notes Public Address Book, so a misspelling or the wrong punctuation would be enough to cause Notes to not recognize the name. The safest way to enter a name is to pick it from the address book.

Q I keep getting error messages when I try to save the document. Is there a way to save it until I figure out where the problem is?

A Unfortunately, the answer to this one is no. Look for the field where the cursor is after the error message. If you can't find anything wrong, you may have to delete the data from that one field, and then try again to save the document. If you have questions about data format, check the online help for hints.

Quiz

1. What are the three field types that involve user names, and how are they used?
2. Name four different types of Keyword fields.
3. You created a document and saved it. When you open it, the document looks almost completely different. Why?
4. Name the three document types and their hierarchy.
5. What is the difference between a Text field and a Rich Text field?

Exercises

1. Using the Discussion database, create at least three main topics, each under a different category. Then create response documents and response to response documents under each main document.
2. Open up several different Notes databases and try to create documents in them. If you cannot create documents, at least try to read documents in them. Look at each data element and determine which Notes data type was used for that field.

Week 1

Day 5

Working with Rich Text in Documents

In today's lesson, you learn some of the advanced text-editing features available in Notes. The features you will learn about are only available in a Rich Text field. To try out these features as you go along, you have to create or edit a document that has a Rich Text field, and then place the document in the Edit mode. Then move to the Rich Text field.

How do you know if you are in a Rich Text field? There are a couple of indicators that are always present. Look at the status bar at the bottom of the Notes workspace. From the left, the second, third, and fourth status bar fields have data in them if you are in a Rich Text field. They show you which font is currently selected, what type size is selected, and which style is selected, if any. These Rich Text status fields also allow you to change the font, size and style settings.

Working with Text in a Rich Text Field

Tomorrow, you will be working with graphics and objects in a Rich Text field. Today, you work primarily with text-editing and formatting functions.

NOTE As you work your way through today's lesson, bear this in mind: You can always undo the last text editing changes you made by selecting Edit | Undo from the menu bar.

In yesterday's lesson, you learned how to enter text in a document. Most plain text fields will probably only require that you enter a few words at the most, but there are occasions where you might want to enter more extensive text. For example, if a field in a Customer Tracking database says something like "Company Background," you could probably write a book about some of the customers you deal with. In a field that is defined as text, you would have to settle for uniform fonts, with no formatting except line breaks between paragraphs, and maybe indents created the same way you first learned on a typewriter—five spaces.

But what you probably want to do is to spice up the Company Background. Put in some bold headings using a larger font. Identify key selling points by italicizing them, or maybe showing them in a green font. Create bulleted or numbered paragraphs to create emphasis. Later, you can include a table that shows what purchases the customer has made in the past, and put in a graph that illustrates buying trends, but first, make that text look good. What you want is a *Rich Text field*, because in a rich text field, you can include almost anything you can imagine.

You can spice up plain text, as long as it is in a Rich Text field, by changing the formatting and text characteristics from the following places on the Notes desktop:

- [ ] From the status bar at the bottom of the screen, where you can change the font, the size of the text, and you can pick a pre-defined text style.
- [ ] From the Text menu on the menu bar, or using keyboard shortcuts that are identified on the drop-down menu.
- [ ] From the SmartIcon bar, where context-sensitive SmartIcons give quick access to many formatting functions.
- [ ] From the floating menu displayed when you right-click in the Rich Text field.
- [ ] From the Text Properties InfoBox, where all of the text formatting functions are consolidated.

You will learn to access these features from the Text Properties InfoBox, but in some circumstances, you may find that the other methods provide a quicker alternative.

Displaying the Text Properties InfoBox

Display the Text Properties InfoBox the same way you display any Properties InfoBox within Notes:

- From a SmartIcon (Hint: far left side of the icon bar).
- From the menu bar (Text | Text Properties).
- From the desktop. Right-click in a rich text field and select Text Properties.

NOTE If you cannot display the Text Properties InfoBox, then you are probably not in a Rich Text field. You are in a Rich Text field only if you can see a font name in the second field on the status bar.

The first page of the Text Properties InfoBox is shown in Figure 5.1. Notice the five tabbed pages in the dialog box that give you access to different text formatting functions.

Figure 5.1.
The Text Properties InfoBox consolidates all text formatting functions in a single location.

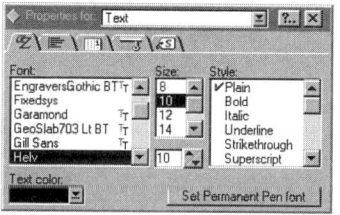

NOTE The ubiquitous Properties InfoBox remains on the screen as you move around in Notes, and reflects the properties in the current context. You can view any available properties using the drop-down arrow beside the Properties InfoBox title bar. For example, while working with text properties, you can also access field, document, and database properties from the Properties InfoBox title bar.

You can minimize the Properties InfoBox by double-clicking on the top bar beside the title. You can get context-sensitive help by clicking on the "?" button. You can close the Properties InfoBox by clicking on the X button in the upper right corner, by double clicking on the diamond icon in the upper-left corner of the InfoBox, or by selecting Close from the menu that is displayed when you click on the diamond icon.

Setting Text Characteristics

Text characteristics define the appearance of type on the page. The default typeface in the Notes environment is 10-point helvetica with no style—in other words, plain text. You can change the typeface (the font), the size of the type, the style of the text (underlined, bold, and so on), and the color of the text. This is just like using any of the popular word processors (such as Lotus WordPro or Microsoft Word) that have a graphical user interface.

When you change the characteristics of text, you do it one of two ways:

- ☐ Highlight the text, then select the characteristics for that highlighted text.
- ☐ Select text characteristics and then start typing. The selected text characteristics will be in effect from the cursor position forward.

The available fonts on your desktop are in large part dependent on your system and the printer you have defined. Notes does have some display fonts that are available to all users.

To select a new font, scroll through the font list and click on the font that you want.

To change the size of your typeface, click on a new size from the scroll box, or type in/select a size at the bottom of the list box.

To change the type style, click on a new style from the list box on the right side of the first page of the Properties InfoBox so a checkmark appears next to the selected style. You can select multiple styles such as underlined and bold, or select Plain to reset everything back to plain text. To deselect one style, click on it so the checkmark is removed.

To change the color of text, click on the expander box next to the Text Color field, and select a color from the palette that is displayed.

In the next section, you will learn how to use the Permanent Pen button.

Setting a Permanent Pen

A *Permanent Pen* is handy for editing a document in another text color so your edits stand out. Remember your seventh grade English teacher, and his or her red pencil? With a permanent pen in Notes, you get your revenge.

You can select or deselect your permanent pen by clicking on a SmartIcon or by choosing from the Text menu on the menu bar. As you toggle back and forth between the Permanent Pen and regular text, the message on the status bar will say `Permanent Pen Enabled/Disabled`. When the Permanent Pen is selected, everything that you type is in the Permanent Pen type characteristics. So if you select a bold, red font, your words will be bold and red, no matter where in the Rich Text field you put the cursor to start typing.

To set the Permanent Pen characteristics, open the first page of the Text Properties InfoBox and set the text properties you want for your Permanent Pen. Then click on the Set Permanent Pen Font button. The selected characteristics will be your Permanent Pen type style until you set it again with other characteristics.

TIP Remember that you can activate your Permanent Pen font at any time in any Rich Text field within Notes. You might want to have a different Permanent Pen color for each member of your workgroup so you can recognize each other's edits to shared documents.

Formatting Paragraphs

Click on the second page of the Text Properties InfoBox to access paragraph formatting functions. On this page, you can set alignment, first line indent, bullet and numbering styles, the left margin, and paragraph spacing. The second page of the Text Properties InfoBox is shown in Figure 5.2.

Figure 5.2.
The second page of the Text Properties InfoBox is used for paragraph formatting.

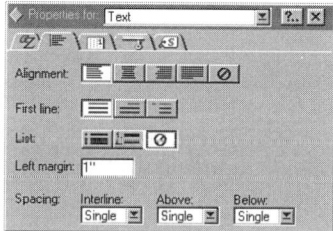

To set formatting for a single paragraph, click anywhere in the paragraph, and then select the desired formatting options. To set formatting for multiple paragraphs, highlight the paragraphs and select the formatting. If any part of a paragraph is highlighted, that paragraph will be formatted with your new selections. The functions that can be selected from this page work as follows:

- Alignment can be set by clicking on buttons for ragged right, centered, ragged left, full justification, or no right margin, which turns off text wrapping.
- The first line of paragraphs can be set by clicking on buttons for no indent, an automatic indent, or a hanging indent, where all lines are indented except for the first line.
- Lists can be set by clicking on buttons to display bullets, numbers, or neither.

- ☐ The left margin can be changed by deleting the current setting and typing in a new number. Whether the margin is in inches or centimeters is determined on the International page of the User Preferences dialog box that you explored on Day 2, "Exploring the Notes Database."
- ☐ Spacing can be set for interline, above, and below a paragraph by selecting single, one and a half, or double spacing by clicking on drop-down boxes beside the fields.

Besides using the Text Properties InfoBox, you can toggle through paragraph spacing using a SmartIcon. You can set the paragraph alignment, you can select bullets and numbered lists, and you can move the left margin in or out using SmartIcons. When you are in a Rich Text field, use bubble help to determine which SmartIcons to use.

Using the Ruler to Set the Left Margin and Tabs

You can also set the left margin using a ruler bar, which is displayed by clicking on a SmartIcon or by selecting View | Ruler from the menu bar. Figure 5.3 shows the ruler bar.

Figure 5.3.
The ruler bar can be used to set the left margin, indents, and tabs.

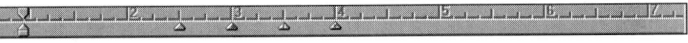

On the left side of the ruler bar is the left margin marker. You can reset the margin by dragging the marker to a new location.

You can drag the top half of the margin marker independently to set either a regular indent or a hanging indent.

Set tabs by clicking on the ruler at the location where you want a tab. If you click with the left mouse button, a left tab is set. If you click with the right mouse button, a right tab is set.

Set centered tabs (for centering text around the tab setting) and decimal tabs (which align on the decimal point, for example, when aligning currency in a column) by right-clicking on an existing tab, and selecting Center or Decimal from the drop-down menu.

NOTE By default, Notes has tabs set every .5 inches. If you set any tabs, then the .5 inch tabs take effect to the right of the last tab you set.

Pagination and Printing a Rich Text Field

Printing is not one of the strong points of Notes. That being said, you can set properties for rich text that give you quite a bit of control over printing—more control than most give Notes credit for.

Think about one of the strengths of Notes. You may not have noticed yet, but Notes wraps text to the next line based on the width of your display window, assuming you have your text justified. For example, the default text in Notes is Helvetica 10 point. If you resize the window so it is only 20 characters wide, then Notes will wrap words at 20 characters, leaving them at a readable 10 points. Try that with a word processor. You either get unreadable text, or you see only a small portion of a line of text in the window. That is because word processors are formatted for paper, not for online display. So naturally, the page formatting for a word processor is more sophisticated. But you can control printing with a little bit of foresight.

The third page of the Text Properties InfoBox, shown in Figure 5.4, controls pagination, the width of a page for printing, and Tab settings.

Figure 5.4.
The third page of the Text Properties InfoBox is used to set page properties for rich text.

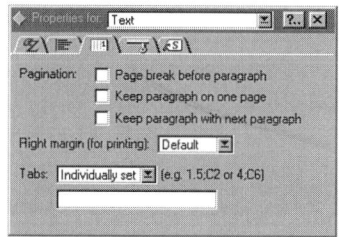

On this page, you can do the following:

- ☐ *Pagination: Page Break Before Paragraph.* Force a paragraph to print at the top of a page by highlighting the paragraph and clicking in the check box.
- ☐ *Keep Paragraph on One Page.* This keeps a paragraph from being broken by printer page breaks. There are no automatic page breaks shown on-screen, so this only effects printed documents.
- ☐ *Keep Paragraph with Next Paragraph.* Ensure that paragraphs are printed on the same page by highlighting the first paragraph and clicking in the check box.
- ☐ *Right Margin (for Printing).* If you do not want the default right margin settings, you can set the right margin for a paragraph (or group of paragraphs) by selecting Other, and then enter the right margin you want. The margin is set relative to the width of the paper, so if you are printing on paper that is 8.5 inches wide and you want a 2-inch right margin, set the margin as 6.5.

> **Tip**
>
> Remember, you can also change the unit of measure from inches to centimeters on the International settings page in the User Preferences dialog box. You can also set print parameters for an entire print job using File | Page Setup from the menu bar.

- *Tabs.* You can set tabs for highlighted paragraphs by selecting "Evenly spaced" and typing in the distance between tabs (for example, .5). If you want to set specific tab settings, select "Individually set" and type in the number of inches (or centimeters if you specified that as your unit of measurement) from the left side of the page. Separate individual tabs with semicolons, and specify whether they are left (L), centered (C), right (R), or decimal (D). For example, if you enter "L2;C3;R4;D5," then you would have a left tab at 2 inches, a centered tab at 3 inches, a right tab at 4 four, and a decimal tab at 5 inches.

> **Note**
>
> You can also work with tabs on the ruler bar at the top of the screen. Display the ruler bar by selecting View | Ruler, or click on the Ruler SmartIcon. Set the location of a tab by clicking on the ruler where you want the tab. Move a tab by holding down the left mouse button on the tab and dragging it to a new location on the ruler. Delete a tab by clicking on it. Change the type of tab by clicking on it with the right mouse button and selecting Left, Right, Center, or Decimal.

Selectively Hiding Paragraphs

Do you know the 80 / 20 rule? Eighty percent of the time, people are only going to need to use 20 percent of the information in a document.

For example, you are working on a proposal. You have included a paragraph that illustrates to anyone editing your document how you reached the final figures you quote in a proposal. But if someone is reading the proposal online, you just want them to see the final figures, without bothering them about the process you used to reach those figures. You can hide your worksheet paragraph from users when the document is open in the Read mode, but display the paragraph when the document is open in the Edit mode. This is not a security measure, just a way to make the document more usable.

You can control when and under what conditions information in a Rich Text field is displayed by using the Hide When... page (the "windowshade" icon on the tab) in the Text Properties InfoBox, shown in Figure 5.5.

Figure 5.5.
Selectively hide text using the Text Properties InfoBox.

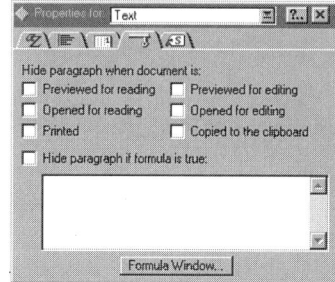

Use the check boxes to hide paragraphs under the following circumstances:

- *Previewed for Reading.* When readers have the preview pane open in a view so they can read documents without opening them, you can hide certain information from them. For example, suppose you have a large graphic at the top of a document. Anyone previewing documents will have to wait for the graphic to be displayed, unless the graphic is hidden when the document is previewed for reading.

- *Opened for Reading.* If a paragraph is hidden when a document is open for reading, nobody will be able to see the paragraph in the Read mode. This implies that people with Reader access to the database will not be able to see the information under any circumstances. This is frequently used to hide data input or administrative fields from readers so they only see what is of interest or of use to them. When you mark a paragraph as hidden when opened for reading, it is automatically hidden when the user prints the document, as well.

- *Printed.* If a paragraph is hidden when printed, the paragraph may be visible while being read or edited, but it will not appear on a printed copy of the document. For example, you may have a note for online readers telling them how to navigate to a related online document, but the same information would not be relevant to someone reading a printed copy of the document.

- *Previewed for Editing.* If you have Editor access to a document, you can put the document into Edit mode from the preview pane by double clicking on the document, or by pressing Ctrl+E. You can prevent paragraphs from displaying during this form of preview editing, even though the paragraph will be visible if it is edited with the document opened on the desktop.

- *Opened for Editing.* You might use a document in multiple styles. You could display one style when users are reading the document in the preview pane (for example, only show a document summary paragraph, and show it in a bold red typeface), and have another style displayed when the document is opened for editing. If an editor needs to access the hidden paragraph, she can uncheck the Hide When Open for Editing check box.
- *Copied to the Clipboard.* You can hide information to prevent it from being copied to another document or to another Windows-based application, and you can prevent users from forwarding some information within Notes by hiding it when it is copied to the Clipboard. For example, you could hide location-specific information so that users in other locations can copy the document and not have to delete extraneous information.

Hiding a Paragraph Conditionally

Paragraphs can be hidden conditionally using simple Notes formulas. This book isn't intended as a tutorial on writing Notes formulas, but you can do simple selection formulas without too much pain. You learn one simple formula here that lets you hide a paragraph from an individual user, or from all users except one.

The formula to hide a paragraph from a specific user is:

```
@Name([CN];@UserName)= "John Doe"
```

The formula basically says this: Hide the paragraph from the person whose common name ([CN]), derived from the Notes hierarchical name (@UserName), is John Doe.

This excludes the person whose name you enter.

The formula to only include the person named is:

```
@Name([CN];@UserName )!="John Doe"
```

This formula excludes everyone whose name is not John Doe.

NOTE In both formulas, include every character including the quotation marks and the semicolon. If you want to know more about using Notes formulas, refer to the Notes online help and to the Notes Application Developer's Guide.

To activate the formula, you must click in the check box Hide Paragraph If Formula Is True:, and you must save the document.

TIP A stupid human trick: Do not put your own name in the first formula, or you will no longer be able to view or edit the selected paragraphs yourself.

Actually, there is a way to access data you have accidentally hidden from yourself. The Hide-When function should not be considered a security function, it is only used to make the information in a document more readable to users by selectively displaying the information the reader or editor needs. All data (with the exception of data stored in encrypted fields) can be viewed from the Document Properties InfoBox on the Fields tab. This page of the InfoBox lists all visible and hidden fields on the document, and displays the stored contents of the field on the right. You can copy hidden information from this box and paste it back into the document if you accidentally lock yourself out of a paragraph.

Using Named Styles

Notes has four predefined styles: Outline, Basic, Bullet, and Headline. You can apply these styles to paragraphs, and you can redefine the styles or define your own styles. When a style is redefined, all paragraphs within the current document tagged with that style are changed to the new definition.

Defining Named Styles Using the Text Properties InfoBox

Styles are defined by formatting text in a Rich Text field until it matches what you want the style to look like, and then using the last page of the Text Properties InfoBox, the page that shows a style "tag" (see Figure 5.6).

Figure 5.6.
Define paragraph styles using the last page of the Text Properties InfoBox.

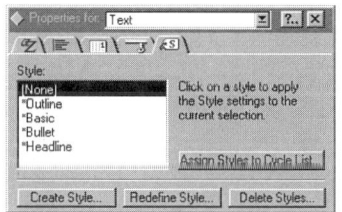

To define a new style, do the following:

1. Format a paragraph so it matches the style you want to define.
2. Display the last page of the Text Properties InfoBox.
3. Click on the Create Style button. The Create Named Style dialog box, shown in Figure 5.7, appears.

Figure 5.7.
The Create Named Style dialog box is used to name and specify a new style.

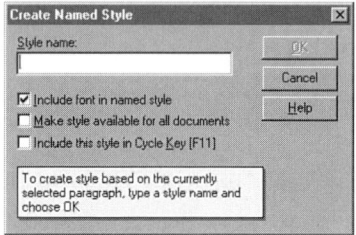

4. In the Create Named Style dialog box, do the following:

   - *Enter a name for your new style.* You will use the name to identify the style in the style menu.
   - *Include Font in Named Style.* Check the box to indicate that you want the font to match the one used in the named style.
   - *Make Style Available for All Documents.* Click on this check box if you want your new style to be made available to other Notes documents in the same database. If the box is unchecked, the style will only be applicable within the current document.
   - *Include This Style in Cycle Key [F11].* If you select this, you can apply the style by pressing the F11 key in addition to other methods of applying styles.

Redefining Existing Named Styles

Redefining an existing style is similar in concept to creating a new style from scratch.

1. You format a paragraph the way you want the redefined style to appear, and then select the paragraph.
2. On the last page of the Text Properties InfoBox, you click on the Redefine Style button.
3. A list of existing styles is displayed in a Redefine dialog box.
4. Click on the style you want to redefine, and click on the OK button.

The redefined style will have the same options as the style that is being replaced. For example, if you renamed the Basic style, your new definition would be applied to all documents in the database.

NOTE You can also redefine a style by deleting the original style (click on the Delete Style button and select the style to delete from a dialog box), and then defining a new style with the same name. You can then redefine the optional settings for the style.

Applying Named Styles

Refer back to Figure 5.6, which shows the Styles page of the Text Properties InfoBox. There is a list of all available named styles. Default styles are marked with an asterisk (*), while styles you defined do not have the asterisk.

You can apply any of these named styles to a paragraph by clicking anywhere within the paragraph, and then clicking on the named style in the Text Properties InfoBox. You can also select any style from the status bar at the bottom of the screen, as shown in Figure 5.8.

Figure 5.8.
Applying a Named Style to paragraphs from the status bar.

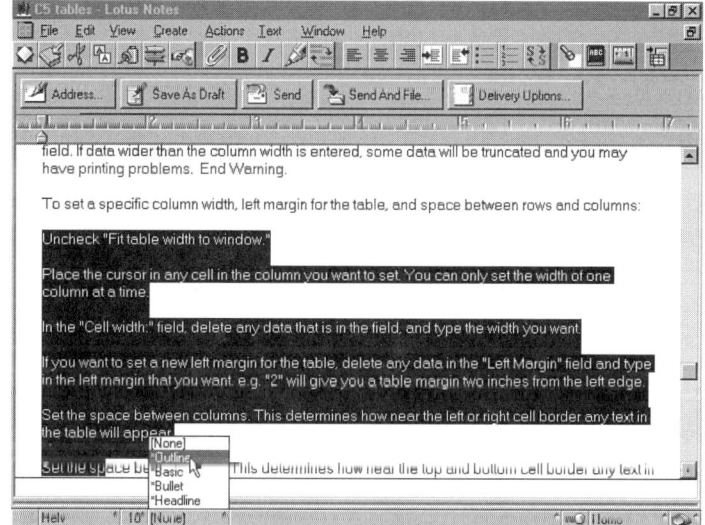

In addition, you can apply selected styles by highlighting text and clicking on the Text Style Cycle Key SmartIcon (which looks like a red and a green "S" replacing each other) until you locate the style you want. Whew! Say that three times quickly. It sounds like an industrial washing machine!

You can also cycle through selected styles by highlighting the text to which you want to apply a style, and then pressing the F11 key until you find the style you want.

Think back to when you were defining a new style. One of the options you could check in the Create Named Style dialog box said Include This Style in Cycle Key [F11]. If you checked a style in that dialog box, then it is available from the Text Style Cycle Key.

You can add styles to the Cycle Key list, and you can remove styles from the list. On the Styles page of the Text Properties InfoBox shown in Figure 5.6, click on the Assign Styles to Cycle List button.

The Manage Cycle Keys dialog box (as shown Figure 5.9) will appear.

Figure 5.9.
The Manage Cycle Keys dialog box is used to define which styles can be accessed using the F11 or the Cycle Key SmartIcon.

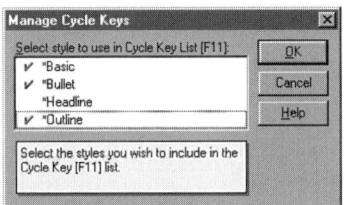

Click on a style to make it available for the cycle list. In the example shown above, the Headline style will not be available from the cycle key because there is no checkmark next to it.

Text styles provide a quick shortcut when you want to format text, and make it easier to achieve a consistent appearance in long and complex documents. If you take advantage of text styles, you also have the benefit of being able to modify the design of a document with a simple redefinition of a text style.

Working with Tables in a Rich Text Field

You can use the Notes editor to build tables in most Rich Text fields in Notes. These tables are simple tables, not embedded spreadsheets, Lotus Components, or Java applets. They are just rows and columns that can be formatted to enhance the display of tabular material in a Rich Text field.

You will learn how to create a table, and how to format it using these characteristics:

- ☐ Cell borders
- ☐ Cell shading
- ☐ Combining cells
- ☐ Resizing columns
- ☐ Adding, appending, and deleting rows and columns

NOTE There is one notable exception to tables in Rich Text fields. Notes does not allow nested tables. If a database design uses hidden tables to align fields, then a Rich Text field in that hidden table will not allow you to create another table, because your table would be nested in the first table. This is a limitation that Lotus is reported to be working on, so this caveat might not apply to later releases.

Creating a Table

There is only one way to create a table in Notes—one of the few functions in Notes for which there are not alternative techniques. To create a table:

1. Position the cursor in a Rich Text field.
2. Select Create | Table from the menu bar to display the Create Table dialog box.
3. Enter the number of rows and columns you want for your initial table.
4. Click on OK.

The basic table will be inserted at the cursor.

Using the Table Properties InfoBox to Format the Table

All table formatting can be handled from the Table Properties InfoBox. To display the InfoBox, do one of the following:

- ☐ Click once in the table, and then click on the Properties SmartIcon on the left end of the icon bar.
- ☐ Click once in the table, and then select Table | Table Properties from the menu bar.
- ☐ Right-click on the table and select Table Properties.

The first page of the Table Properties InfoBox is displayed, as shown in Figure 5.10.

Figure 5.10.
The Table Properties InfoBox is used to format tables in Rich Text fields.

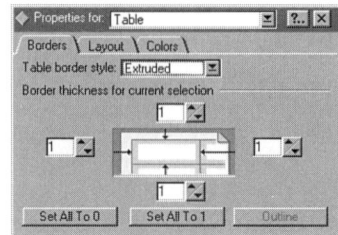

Defining Table and Cell Borders

On the first page of the InfoBox, you determine what the borders will look like for your table. First you pick a border style, then define border thickness for specific cells, rows or columns, or for the entire table.

The table border style is set using a drop-down list. Click on the drop-down button and select Single, Extruded (raised), or Embossed. All visible borders will have whichever style you select.

The border thickness can be set for an individual cell by clicking in the cell before selecting the border thickness, or you can set the thickness for multiple cells by holding down the left mouse button and dragging to highlight the cells you want to change. Then click on the spinner controls to change left, right, top, and bottom borders individually in thickness increments from 0 to 10.

If you want to reset all borders for the selected cell(s) to single thickness, click the Set All To 1 button.

If you want to make all borders invisible for the selected cells, click the Set All To 0 button.

If you want to show only the outside borders for selected cells, click the Outline button. This button is only active if you have multiple cells selected. To undo the outline, set the selected cells back to single thickness.

Figure 5.11 shows a table with an extruded, single line style. Rows two and three in the right column have the border set to Outline so that interior lines cannot be seen.

Figure 5.11.
A table with extruded lines and two cells with no interior lines showing.

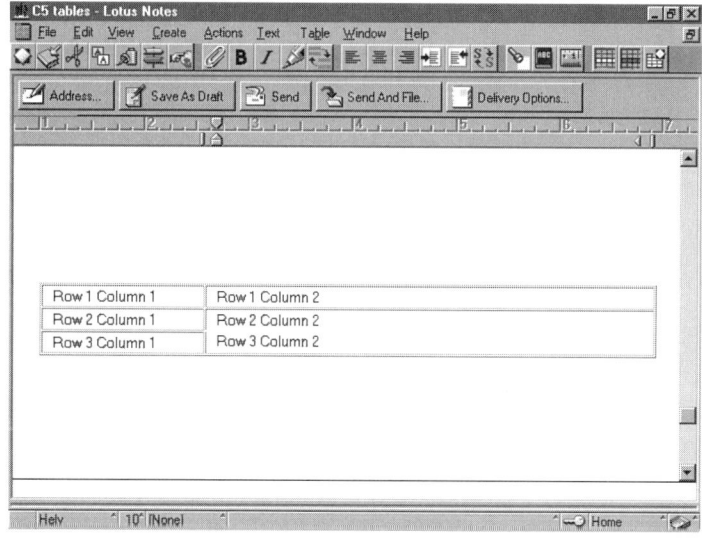

TIP As you work with the InfoBox, you will discover that the InfoBox stays on the desktop, even while you are working with the document in the background. However, the InfoBox may change context from Table to Text as you work. You can reset the context to Table from the InfoBox title bar as long as the cursor is somewhere inside the table.

Setting the Column Width, Left Margin, and Space Between Rows and Columns

Sizing columns on tables can be a little bit tricky if you do not understand the settings on the Layout page of the Table Properties InfoBox. You have to decide first whether you want the table to be resized automatically to fit in a resized window.

A check box determines whether a table is resized to fit the width of the table to the window. If you have a checkmark next to Fit Table Width to Window, the table will be resized whenever the window is resized. If you want to set absolute column widths, make sure that this option is not checked. This is done on the second page of the Table Properties InfoBox, shown in Figure 5.12.

Figure 5.12.
The second page of the Table Properties InfoBox is used to define the width of a table.

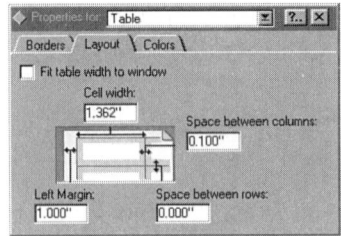

Warning

If you use Fit Table Width to Window, be prepared for some possible quirks. For example, if you change the left margin from 1 inch to .5 inch, the entire table will shift to the left half an inch, but the right margin will not resize to the edge of the window.

If you are planning to expand your Notes knowledge to include application development, then you should be aware that tables with fixed column widths limit the amount of data that can fit into a field. If data wider than the column width is entered, some data will be truncated and you may have printing problems.

To set a specific column width, left margin for the table, and space between rows and columns, follow these steps:

1. Uncheck Fit Table Width to Window.
2. Place the cursor in any cell in the column you want to set. You can only set the width of one column at a time.
3. In the Cell Width: field, delete any data that is in the field, and type the width you want.
4. If you want to set a new left margin for the table, delete any data in the Left Margin field and type in the left margin that you want; for example, typing 2 will give you a table margin two inches from the left edge.
5. Optionally set the space between columns. This determines how near the left or right cell border any text in the table will appear.
6. Optionally set the space between rows. This determines how near the top and bottom cell border any text in the table will appear.

Note

You do not have to worry about resizing rows. They expand automatically to hold the data entered into them.

Using the Ruler Bar to Resize Columns in Tables

You can also resize columns from the ruler bar. This lets you see your changes immediately. The process of resizing a table is similar to what you learned earlier about changing margins and indents from the ruler bar.

Take a close look at Figure 5.13, which shows the ruler bar being used to resize the left column of a table. The mouse pointer is pointing at a vertical bar that marks the right border of the column. Text markers indicate where text will be displayed in the column.

Figure 5.13.
Using the ruler bar to resize columns in a table.

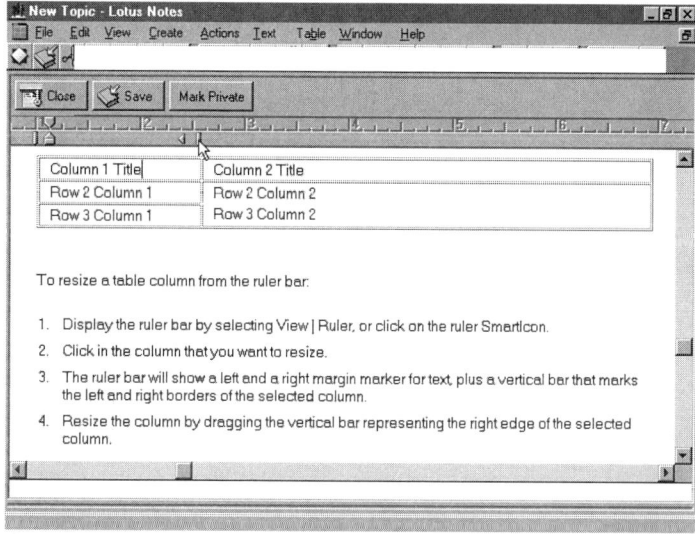

To resize a table column from the ruler bar:

1. Display the ruler bar by selecting View | Ruler, or click on the ruler SmartIcon.
2. Click in the column that you want to resize.
3. The ruler bar will show a left and a right margin marker for text, plus a vertical bar that marks the left and right borders of the selected column.
4. Resize the column by dragging the bar that marks the right border of the column to a new location on the ruler.
5. If necessary, change the text margins within the column by dragging the text margin markers along the ruler.

Click in the next column and repeat steps 3, 4, and 5.

 **NOTE** When you click in a column, the left side of the column is fixed. You can only resize a column by dragging the right edge.

Shading Table Cells

You can enhance the display of tables by selectively shading cells. On the third page of the Table Properties InfoBox, you can display a palette of colors that can be used for shading. Figure 5.14 shows a table with the top row shaded, and the InfoBox still open.

Figure 5.14.
Selectively shade cells in a table using the Table Properties InfoBox.

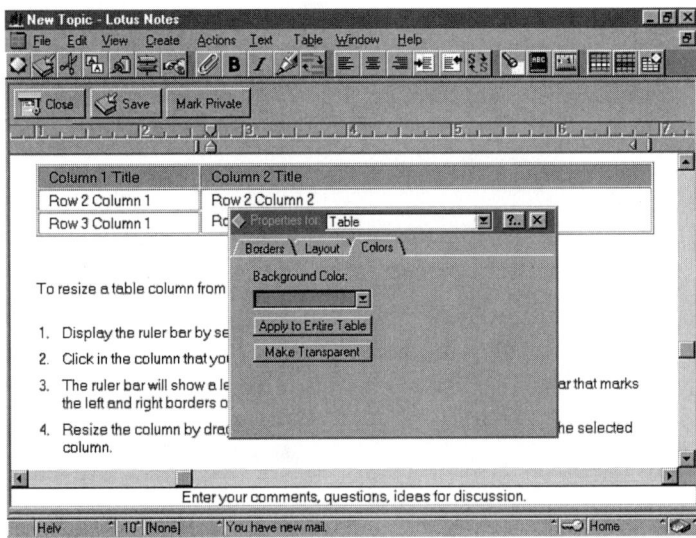

To shade cells, do the following:

1. Right-click on the table and display the Table Properties InfoBox. Move to the Colors tab.
2. Left-click in the table and drag the mouse pointer to highlight the cells you want to color.
3. Click on the drop-down arrow in the Background Color field and select a color from the pop-up palette. The selected color will be applied to the selected cells in the table.

You can apply the selected color to the remainder of the table by clicking on the Apply to Entire Table button.

You can make selected cells transparent by highlighting the cells and clicking on the Make Transparent button. A transparent cell is the same color as the background color for the document.

To make an entire table transparent, place the cursor in a transparent cell and click on the Apply to Entire Table button. This technique is commonly used to display information in columns, because Lotus Notes does not have a column function, per se.

Formatting Tables from Menus and SmartIcons

Limited table formatting functions are available from the menu bar and from a floating menu. You can also insert and delete rows and display the Table Properties InfoBox using SmartIcons.

Inserting or Appending a Single Row

To insert a single row above the cursor position in a table, do any of the following:

- Click on the Insert Row SmartIcon.
- Right-click on the table to display a floating menu and select Insert Row from near the bottom of the menu.
- Select Table | Insert Row from the menu bar to insert a single row.

To append a single row at the bottom of the table, do the following:

- Select Table | Append Row from the menu bar.

Inserting or Appending a Single Column

To insert a single column to the left of the cursor position, do the following:

- Select Table | Insert Column from the menu bar.

To append a single column on the right side of the table, do the following:

- Select Table | Append Column from the menu bar.

NOTE The behavior of tables when you add or append columns depends on whether you elected to fit the table to the page (on the second page of the Table Properties InfoBox). If the table is fit to the page, then inserting or appending a column will cause the other columns to be resized so that the table still fits. If the table is not fit to the page, then inserting or appending a row may cause the table to exceed the width of the screen, and part of the table may not be visible if you print the document.

Inserting or Appending Multiple Rows or Columns

You can insert or append multiple rows or columns by selecting File | Insert Special from the menu bar. Notes will display the Insert Row/Column dialog box shown in Figure 5.15.

Figure 5.15.
You can insert or append multiple rows or columns from the same dialog box.

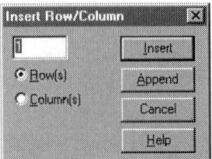

You have the following options in this dialog box:

- Enter the number of rows or columns you want to add to the table.
- Use the radio buttons to determine whether you are adding rows or columns.
- Click on the Insert button to insert rows above the cursor position in the table or to insert columns to the left of the cursor position in the table.
- Click on the Append button to add rows to the bottom of the table or to add columns to the right of the table.

Deleting Rows or Columns

You can delete rows or columns using similar techniques to what you just learned for adding rows and columns. When you delete a row or column, all data in the deleted cells is also deleted. You cannot undo a row or column deletion.

To delete rows, place the cursor in the row you want to delete or highlight cells in multiple rows, and then click on the Delete Row SmartIcon. You can also select Delete Selected Row(s) from the floating menu or from the Table menu on the menu bar.

To delete columns, place the cursor in the column you want to delete or highlight cells in multiple columns, and then select Table | Delete Selected Column(s) from the menu bar.

You can also select Table | Delete Special... from the menu bar. In the dialog box, specify how many rows or columns you want to delete. Select whether you want to delete rows or columns. Click on the Delete button. If you are deleting rows, then the specified number of rows (n) will be deleted, beginning with the row where the cursor is positioned and n-1 rows beneath it moving toward the bottom of the table. If you are deleting columns, the specified number of columns (n) will be deleted, beginning with the column where the cursor is positioned and n-1 columns to the right of the cursor.

Combining and Splitting Cells in a Table

You can combine two or more adjacent cells into a single cell. To combine cells, do the following:

1. Highlight the cells you want to combine into a single cell.
2. Select Table | Merge Cells from the menu bar.

The selected cells will be merged into a single cell, and all data from the original cells will be kept in the single merged cell.

You can split a cell that was previously merged as long as the original rows or columns have not been deleted from the table. To split a cell:

1. Place the cursor in the cell you want to split.
2. Select Table | Split Cell from the menu bar.

If the cell can be split (that is, if the menu option was not grayed out), the cell will be split into its original rows and/or columns. All data will be displayed in the top-left cell of the newly formed cells.

TIP Before playing with functions such as merging and splitting cells, you should save your data if it is important to you. You can then close the document without saving it if you get into trouble, and you can then retrieve your original data in its original format.

WARNING Table printing can be a little unpredictable. Cells that fall in the middle of a page break are not automatically kept together on the same page as with many programs that have table functions. If the cell that falls on a page break is a merged cell, the table may appear even more disjointed than with unmerged cells.

Creating Page Breaks

It is rather appropriate that this short lesson follows immediately on the heels of creating tables, because putting a page break immediately before a table ensures that it will print at the top of a page, making it less likely that you will have any of the printing problems just described.

A page break in an online document appears as a single line across the screen. When printing a document, the page break will force a new page in the printed document.

To insert a page break, follow these steps:

1. Place the cursor anywhere within a Rich Text field.
2. Select Create | Page Break from the menu bar.

If the cursor is on a blank line, a page break will be inserted at that point. If the cursor is in a paragraph, the page break will be inserted just above the paragraph.

> **NOTE** You cannot insert a page break inside a table. You can place a page break on the blank line above the table. If you want to break a table near the bottom of a page, you will have to create a second table that begins at the top of the next page.

To delete a page break, place the cursor anywhere on the line immediately following the page break, or anywhere in the paragraph that immediately follows the page break. Select Create | Page Break from the menu bar again. The page break will be removed.

You can also place the cursor on the left side of the line just below the page break and press the Backspace key, or place the cursor just above the page break and press the Delete key.

Using Collapsible Sections in Your Document: The 20 Percent Solution

You have already learned how to create a simple document, and now that you have all of the capabilities of the Rich Text field, you can see how a Notes document can be quite complex. To make the document more accessible to anyone who reads it, you can place parts of the document into collapsible sections. The collapsible sections are similar to the collapsible categories you have already seen in views in the Help database.

As mentioned earlier, 80 percent of the time, you only need 20 percent of the information. Put that 20 percent of the document up front, and hide the rest of it in collapsible sections. If someone needs the other 80 percent of the document, he or she can still get at it.

Consider a consulting proposal, for instance. You can build a really good executive summary that tells the entire story. The rest of the proposal is just details. Why not hide those details?

If someone really needs to know about the workplan, he or she can open up that section. Most people would just page through that part of the document anyway, so make it easy for them to page past it.

Creating a Collapsible Section

Collapsible sections can be created in any Rich Text field. You can create a section and then enter data into it, or you can create a section using existing data. We will focus on the second technique.

To create a section in a document, do the following:

1. Highlight the portion of a document you want to place into a collapsible section. This section can contain text, graphics, tables, bullets, outlined text—anything that can go into a Rich Text field. If any part of a paragraph is highlighted, the entire paragraph will be included in the section.
2. Select Create | Section from the menu bar.
3. The section will be created, with the first line of text in the section used as a section title.
4. Refine your section parameters using the Section Properties InfoBox.

Figures 5.16 and 5.17 show part of the same document before and after it was made into a collapsible section. You will recognize the document as part of the text for today's lesson.

Figure 5.16.
A fully expanded document can make it hard to locate information.

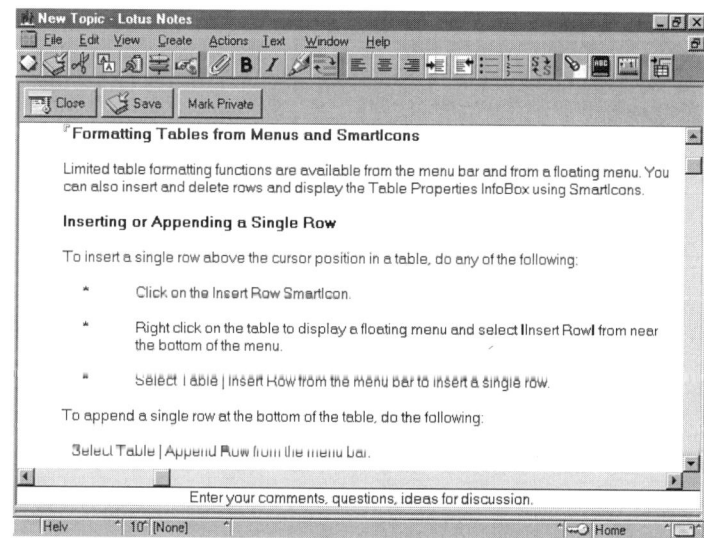

Figure 5.17.
The same document collapsed into sections makes it easy to locate information.

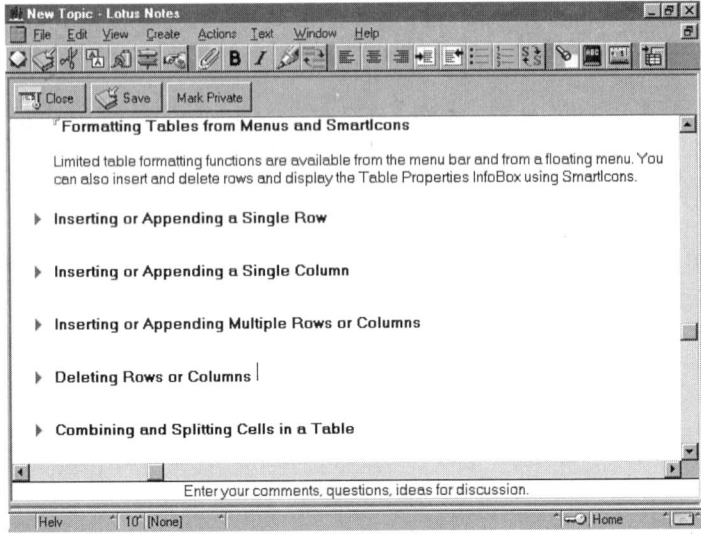

Defining Section Properties

Now that a section has been created, you can work with the section to make it more usable. The first line of text becomes the section title when you highlight a paragraph and make into a section. But when you expand the section, you will discover that the first line is repeated inside the section, as shown in Figure 5.18.

Figure 5.18.
The first line of text in an open section is repeated as the section title.

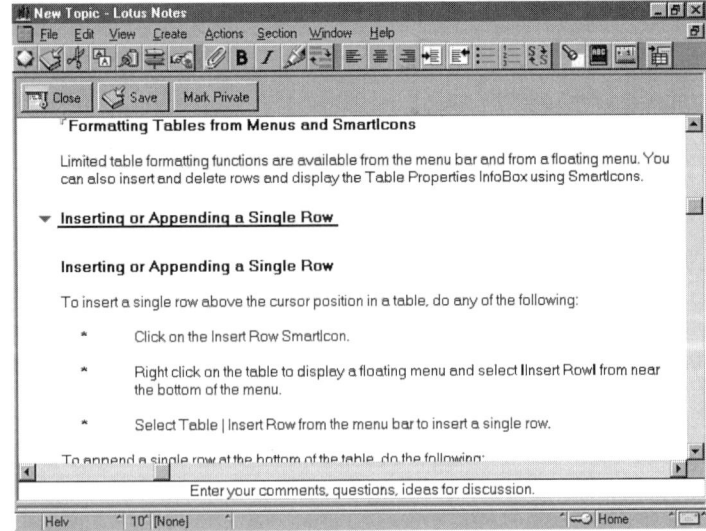

The repetition looks a bit awkward. That can be corrected by deleting the title inside the section, or by changing the title of the section. The first option is the one you would probably use, but for the sake of this lesson, we will change the title.

To change section properties, display the Section Properties InfoBox. This can be displayed by clicking on the section title and then clicking the Properties SmartIcon, or you can right-click on the section title. The first page of the InfoBox is shown in Figure 5.19.

Figure 5.19.
The Section Properties InfoBox is used to define section characteristics.

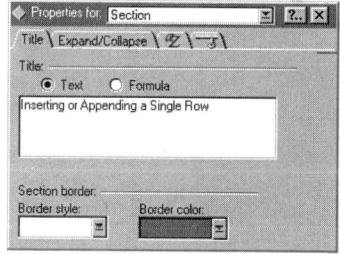

Defining Section Basics

In this InfoBox, enter the following information:

- *Title.* You can change the title or enter your own text title for the section, or you can enter a formula. If you click on the Formula radio button, any text in the Title field will be lost. A simple type of formula to use combines text and a field name or a Notes function such as @UserName. You can impress your workmates with a Section Title formula that says something like

  ```
  "For the eyes of " + @Name([CN]@UserName) + " only."
  ```

  No matter who reads the document, he or she will see a section directed to his or her attention.

- *Border Style.* Click on the drop-down arrow in this combo box to see several border styles. The border style will be applied to the section title. For example, you can have section titles underlined, double underlined, or displayed inside a box.

- *Border Color.* You can change the color of the section title border from a pop-up palette.

Defining Section Expand/Collapse Characteristics

On the second page of the Section Properties InfoBox, you define how the section is displayed—expanded or collapsed. The second page is shown in Figure 5.20.

Figure 5.20.
Defining expand/collapse characteristics for a section.

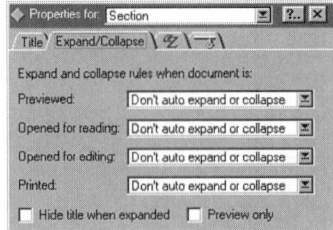

On this page, you determine whether the section should be expanded or collapsed when it is viewed in the preview pane, when it is opened in the Read mode, when it is opened in the Edit mode, and when it is printed.

The choices for each of these modes are:

- *Don't Auto Expand or Collapse.* This turns off automatic collapsing or expanding. If a document is closed while a section is still expanded, it will still be expanded the next time it is opened in that same mode, and vice versa.
- *Auto Expand Section.* Select this to have the section display fully expanded whenever the document is opened in a particular mode.
- *Auto Collapse Section.* Use this to have the section fully collapsed whenever the document is opened in a particular mode.

By selecting one of these options for each mode, you can control when and how other people see particular information in your document.

The Hide Title When Expanded check box is fairly self explanatory. Earlier it was suggested that you could delete the title in your text and keep the section title instead. But you can also do it the other way around by hiding the section title when the section is expanded.

The other check box, Preview Only, is not as clear. You can create a section that is only visible in the preview pane by clicking on this option. You could, for example, create a special notice that appears in the preview pane only, and use it to tell users that they will only be able to access other sections under special circumstances, which you can then define on the Hide When page of the Section Properties InfoBox.

Defining Section Text Characteristics

The third page of the Section Properties InfoBox enables you to define the font used for displaying the section title. The dialog box is identical to the dialog box used to define text in the Text Properties InfoBox, except that the Permanent Pen option is not there because it is not relevant to section titles.

Define the font, font size, font appearance (bold, italic, and so on), and the font color.

Defining Section Hide-When Characteristics

Section hide-when characteristics, shown on the fourth page of the Section Properties InfoBox, are identical to the hide-when characteristics defined for text in yesterday's lesson.

You can hide a section when it is in any of these modes:

- ☐ Previewed for reading
- ☐ Opened for reading or being printed
- ☐ Printed
- ☐ Previewed for editing
- ☐ Opened for editing
- ☐ Copied to Clipboard

In addition, you can hide sections based on a formula. This is commonly used to restrict access to a section, using a formula that says something like "Hide this section when the UserName is not User1, User2, User3," where User1, User2, and User3 are the usernames of the people who are authorized to access this section. More likely, you would use a group name.

NOTE The users and individuals included in groups will only be able to access the section if they have at least Reader access to the document in the database's ACL.

Deleting a Section

When you use the regular delete function to delete a section title, all contents of the section are deleted along with the title, and cannot be recovered. Therefore, if you want to get rid of a section but you still want to keep the contents of that section, you have to do the following:

1. Click on the section title. It doesn't matter whether the section is expanded or collapsed.
2. Select Section | Remove Section from the menu bar.

Alternatively, right-click on the section title and select Remove Section from the floating menu.

The section title will be removed, and the contents of the section will remain as part of the document.

>  **NOTE** You can still edit the contents of a section. If you delete text from within the section, highlight the text and cut or delete it. Just be sure that you do not have the section title selected. If you see a message telling you that this action cannot be undone, cancel and try again, because you accidentally highlighted the section title.

Moving a Section

To move a section:

1. Click the section title to select the entire section.
2. Select Edit | Cut from the menu bar.
3. Place the cursor where you want to move the section.
4. Select Edit | Paste from the menu bar.

Summary

Today, you learned how to work with text in a Rich Text field. Rich text can be formatted by changing the display of your font, including the size and color of the typeface. You learned how to create and use Named Styles as a shortcut for changing type characteristics. You also learned how to create your own type style for use as a Permanent Pen when you are marking up or commenting on documents.

Beyond pure text, you learned how to create tables, which can only be created in Rich Text fields. The table function may be limited compared to some software applications that are dedicated to word processing functionality, but you can use them to make your data more presentable to readers.

Finally, you learned how to use collapsible sections in a Rich Text field to make information more accessible.

Workshop

The Workshop section presents quiz questions to help you cement your new knowledge, and exercises to give you experience using what you have learned. Try to understand the questions and exercises before moving on to the next lesson. Answers are in Appendix A.

Q&A

Q I have some text that I want to format, but all the options are grayed out on the Text menu. What happened?

A You are not in a Rich Text field. The text formatting options are only available in a Rich Text field. The database designer is the only one who can define how text is formatted in a regular text field.

Q I don't have the same fonts in Notes on my home computer as I have in the office. Why not?

A The fonts are printer dependent. If you probably have a different printer defined for your home computer. Try selecting standard fonts so they are accessible to all Notes users.

Q I opened one document, and it looked like it was written in hieroglyphics. Why can't I read it?

A You can. This is a problem related to the previous question. The font used by the document's author is not available to you. Try putting the document into Edit mode (if you only have Reader access, copy the unreadable text into a Rich Text field in another Notes application) and change the font to Helvetica. Then you will be able to read it.

Q I discovered an "Undo" option on the Edit menu. I just deleted a table, but now I need to undo the delete, and the option is no longer there. Where did it go?

A When you delete a table, there is a message saying that you cannot recover the table once it has been deleted. There is no "Undo" for table deletions. The only way you may be able to recover the table is if there is a copy of the document in an earlier version of the document you are editing, or if there is a replica copy of the document in a database that has not yet replicated your changes. Of course, you could always close your document without saving it, if the table is in a previously saved version of the document.

Q I created a section in my document, then closed the document. When I reopen the document, the section is no longer there. Where did it go?

A Uh oh. You used a hide-when formula, didn't you? And you forgot to put your own name in the formula as an authorized reader/editor of the section. The only way you can see the section again is to find someone who is both an authorized editor in the document and is authorized to access that section. Have that authorized section editor change the hide-when formula and include your name.

Q Can I change the appearance of bullets?

A I have not found a way to change the default bullet character that Notes uses, but here is what you can do. Create a new Named Style using the character of your choice as a bullet. The character you use has to be available in the font you use for the rest of the paragraph.

Quiz

1. You have created a Permanent Pen. Now how do you use it?
2. What type of field do you have to be in before you can create a table?
3. If you create a new named style, is it available in all Notes databases on your desktop?
4. How do you hide a section so that it can only be read in the preview pane?
5. Where do you find the function for merging two cells in a table?
6. Can you create a table using tabular text pasted into Notes from another application?

Exercises

1. Using your Discussion database, create one document that uses different fonts, type sizes, and text colors. Create two sections in the document that use the expand/collapse characteristics in different ways.
2. Create another document that uses a table. Include at least one merged cell in your table.
3. Using the same table, create a section that includes text as well as a table. Make the section so it can only be viewed and edited by you, but it can be seen by others if they are in the preview pane.

Week 1

Day 6

Working with Objects

In yesterday's lesson, you learned how to work with text in a Rich Text field. Today, that lesson will continue, but with a difference. Today you are going to work with graphics and other objects that can be pasted or embedded into Rich Text fields. This includes links to external applications on your desktop or on the network. Links to the Internet are discussed on Day 14.

To put this lesson in perspective, imagine that you are working with another Notes user, who happens to be in another location. Together, you are designing your company's home page on the Web. How can you use Notes to collaborate on the graphical design of a Web site? There are several ways, besides sharing your ideas using text:

- [ ] You can paste graphics into a Rich Text field.
- [ ] You can embed a graphic object in a Rich Text field so that the host application is automatically launched when you click on the object.
- [ ] You can link a graphic object so that the original file is launched when you click on an object.
- [ ] You can link to other Notes documents.

- You can link to a site on the Web.
- You can attach a file in a Notes document, so that the other members of your workgroup can launch the host application to view the file, or detach the file to work with it on your own computer.

Each of these options is discussed in today's lesson.

Using Graphics in Rich Text Fields

Any time a Notes document contains anything besides plain text, the container must be a Rich Text field. That means that if you want to share a graphic within a Notes document, you must put the graphic into a Rich Text field.

Because you are developing graphics for a Web site in this scenario, you can paste a graphic into a Rich Text field. Your coworker can then open the document and see the graphic you pasted there. It is a simple way of sharing a graphic.

To share a graphic via a Rich Text field, do the following:

1. Create a graphic using any popular graphics program, such as MS Paint, Adobe Photoshop, Lotus Freelance, and so on.
2. Copy the graphic into the Clipboard.
3. Open a Notes document in the Edit mode.
4. Place the cursor in a Rich Text field and select Edit | Paste from the menu bar. You can also use the Paste SmartIcon, or the Ctrl+V keyboard shortcut to paste the graphic.

The graphic shown in Figure 6.1 is a bitmap pasted from Lotus Freelance Graphics. Notice the outline around the graphic. You can resize the graphic by grabbing the dark square in the lower-right corner of the frame, and dragging the graphic to a new size.

With the document in Edit mode, you can display a Picture Properties InfoBox by right-clicking on the graphic or by selecting it from the Picture menu on the menu bar. The only picture-related information in the Picture Properties InfoBox is an Aspect Ratio page. The aspect ratio defines the horizontal and vertical size of the graphic in relation to its original pasted size. For example, a ratio of 68 percent by 68 percent means that the horizontal and vertical have been shrunk equally to 68 percent of the original size.

Sizing is the only manipulation you can do with a pasted graphic, aside from moving it to another position. The graphic is treated as a text character. It can be positioned using spaces or tabs, and it can be centered or right justified. It can be highlighted and cut from its current location, and then pasted into another location.

Figure 6.1.
A graphic that has been pasted into a Rich Text field.

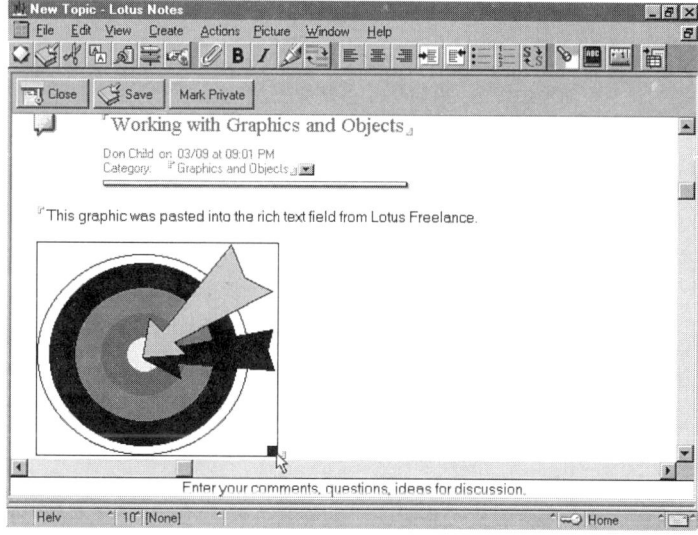

NOTE The color palette on some graphic applications is not fully compatible with the Lotus palette. Therefore, you may see some color shifting when graphics are pasted into a Notes document. Experiment with different formats to see what translates well.

Cutting and pasting is the easiest way to bring data into Notes from another application. And you are not limited to bitmap graphics and text. You can cut cells from a spreadsheet and paste them into a Notes document, and then edit the cell contents as if the spreadsheet were a Notes table. Again, experiment. If you can copy data into the temporary storage area known as the Clipboard, then you can paste it into a Notes Rich Text field.

NOTE You can also paste vector graphics into a Notes document, but the graphics are saved as a single bitmap, and can no longer be manipulated.

As you move through today's lesson, you will learn other techniques.

Importing Data into Notes

You can import data from many other applications using the Notes import filter. Data can be imported directly into a Notes document, but data can also be imported into a Notes view.

Importing Data into a Notes View

You should at least be aware that it is possible to import data into a Notes view, although you are not likely to do it often. It is a process that is sometimes used to populate a Notes database with information that already exists in a spreadsheet or database application.

To import data into a view from a spreadsheet, one of two things has to take place:

- A Notes form has to be created that has fields with the same names as the columns in a spreadsheet.
- The spreadsheet has to be designed so it matches the fields in a Notes form.

In short, there is a lot of setup that goes into importing into a view. As an end user, let it suffice that you know it is possible.

Importing Data into a Document

You are much more likely to import data directly into a Notes document—into a Rich Text field, to be more precise. You can import documents from word processing applications such as WordPerfect or Microsoft Word. You can import spreadsheets from Excel or from Lotus 1-2-3. And you can import graphics.

There are two things you cannot do. You cannot import more than one graphic at a time. And you cannot import graphics as a part of more complex documents. For example, if you import a Microsoft Word file that contains a graphic in addition to text, all you will get is the text, not the graphic.

Aside from that one caveat, there is a lot you can do. Popular formats of word processing documents can be imported with most of their formatting intact. BMP, PCX, and TIFF graphic formats can be imported successfully. Spreadsheet files or ranges from a spreadsheet can also be imported.

To import a file:

1. Make sure your Notes document is in Edit mode, and that the cursor is positioned in a Rich Text field.
2. Select File | Import from the menu bar.
3. Using a standard Windows selection box, define the type of file you want to import (see Figure 6.2).

Figure 6.2.
Selecting a file to import into a Notes Rich Text field.

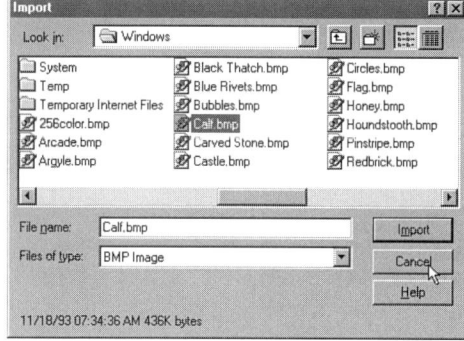

4. Navigate in the Windows selection box until you locate the file you want to import.
5. Click on the Import button.
6. If necessary, resize the image/graphic.
7. Save the document.

Exporting Notes Data to a File

You can export Notes documents or parts of documents to graphics, ASCII text, structured text, or word processing files. To export a document or part of a document, you highlight what is to be exported, and then select File | Export, give the export a file name, and define which format you want the saved file to be.

Exported Notes data have the following characteristics:

- Graphics can be exported only as CGM Images or as TIFF 5.0 Images. These two formats can be used on PCs, Macintosh, and UNIX systems. If a document is exported to a graphic file, only the first graphic in the document gets exported. If you want to export other images, they must be selected explicitly and exported one at a time.
- ASCII text is exported without any formatting aside from line length, which you define when you export the data. Any text longer than the defined line length is automatically put on the next line. There is no text wrapping.
- Structured text can be exported from a Notes view. You highlight the documents you want to export, and select Structured Text as the export format. Notes then displays the dialog box shown in Figure 6.3.

The Notes documents being exported in Figure 6.3 have a line break as a delimiter, and each record will be 75 characters in length. This makes each Notes document into a separate record in the structured text file.

Figure 6.3.
Export documents from a Notes view as structured text.

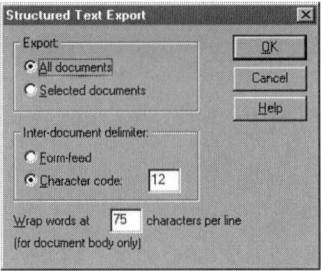

- Word processing export formats include Ami Pro, Microsoft Word RTF, MS Word 6.0, and WordPerfect 5.1, 6.0, and 6.1.

Creating and Using Embedded Objects

Embedded objects in Notes documents are a big step above pasted bitmaps, because embedded objects can be manipulated. The manipulation takes place in the object's native application if the object is an OLE object. If the object was created in an OLE2 application, then you can manipulate the object from within Notes (Notes displays new menu choices that let you edit the object).

An embedded object is an object that is no longer linked to its source. For example, a Notes document that contains an embedded graphic could be opened by a Notes user, and the graphic could be modified. Even though the graphic is changed and the changes are saved in the Notes document, the original source file for the graphic remains untouched.

The absence of links in embedded documents is illustrated in Figure 6.4.

Figure 6.4.
Documents with embedded objects are not linked to the source file.

Embedded Objects
Each user works with a copy of original on their own workstation. Original is not updated.

Embedded objects can be placed into a Notes document in one of two ways:

- You can create an empty application object in Notes, and then create the object from scratch using the application.
- You can copy all or part of an existing application object (a Lotus 1-2-3 spreadsheet, for example), and then paste it into your document using a Paste Special command.

We will walk through these two techniques so you can get a feel for how to do it.

Creating an Embedded Object from Scratch

To create an embedded object from scratch:

1. Position the cursor in a Rich Text field.
2. Select Create | Object... from the menu bar to display the dialog box shown in Figure 6.5.

Figure 6.5.
The Create Object dialog box is used to define objects in rich text fields.

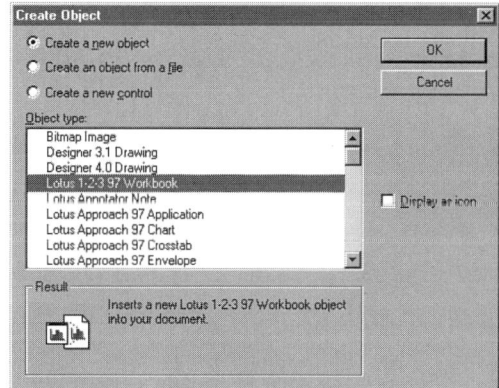

The Create Object dialog box has three significant parts. The first part contains radio buttons, which are used to determine how you want to create your object. Your options are:

- *Create a New Object.* This opens up the source application you select. You can then create an object, which will be saved as an embedded object in the Notes document.
- *Create an Object from a File.* This lets you create an object using an existing file. For example, if you have a bitmap image you want to embed, you can create the embedded object by identifying the file. That way, you do not need to launch the application to create the object.

☐ *Create a New Control.* Controls are applets that can be embedded into documents. For example, you could embed an ActiveXPlugin Object. This book does not discuss OCX controls and applet programming, but if you have experience with these, you may want to embed control objects.

The second part of the Create Object dialog box is a list of available source applications. This list will change as you add or remove applications from your system, and will change if you are creating an object as opposed to creating a control. In this part of the screen, highlight the application you want to use to create the object.

NOTE   An application's behavior depends on whether it is an OLE application or an OLE2 application. If you create an object using an OLE application, the full application will be launched so you can create your object. If you create an object using an OLE2 application, the application's controls are displayed within the Notes window, as shown in Figure 6.6.

Figure 6.6.
Creating a bitmap object with the OLE2 Paint controls showing in the Notes workspace.

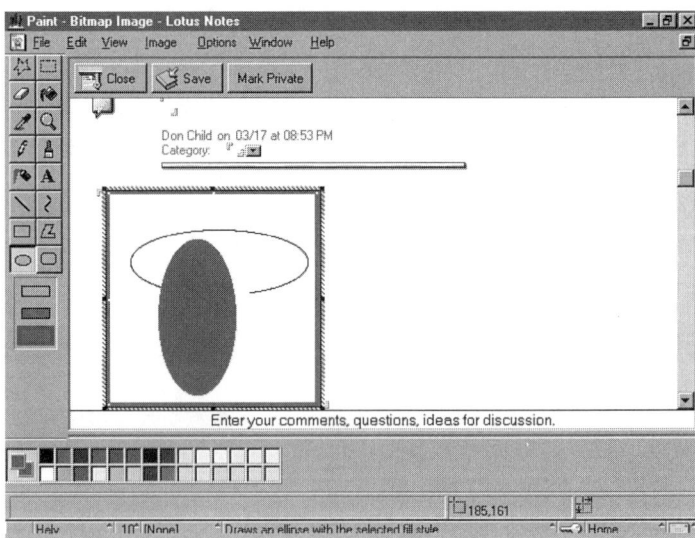

The third part of the Create Object dialog box is the option to display the object as an icon. If you want people reading your document to see the spreadsheet, the bitmap, or the text that you have embedded when they first open the document, then do not display the embedded object as an icon. If you want them to have the option of displaying the object, then you can display the object as an icon. The reader will see an icon for the application that will be used to view and work with the object.

Creating an Embedded Object from a File

The process for creating an embedded object from a file is essentially the same as creating an embedded object from scratch. The only significant difference is that you select a file instead of an application. If your system has an application available that can work with the selected file, then an embedded object is created.

However, there is an interesting alternative technique you can use when working with an existing file—even if that file has not yet been saved!

Creating an Embedded Object Using Paste Special

Suppose you are working with a Lotus 1-2-3 97 workbook that has several pages on it. You do not want to include the entire workbook in your Notes document—only a few select cells from one page of the workbook. In that case, you can copy the selected cells and then do a Paste Special to create an embedded object.

To paste an embedded object into a Notes document:

1. Open the application and the file that contains the data you want to embed in your Notes document.
2. Highlight the portion of the document that you want to embed, and copy it into the Windows Clipboard.
3. Toggle to Notes. In Windows, you can toggle between open applications by pressing Alt+Tab until the icon for the application you want on your desktop is highlighted.
4. Make sure your Notes document is in Edit mode, and that the cursor is positioned in a Rich Text field.
5. Select Edit | Paste Special from the menu bar. The Paste Special dialog box, shown in Figure 6.7, is displayed.
6. Select the Paste option button.
7. Select the type of object you want to create. For example, select Lotus 1-2-3 97 to create an object that launches Lotus 1-2-3 when the object is activated.

Figure 6.7.
The Paste Special dialog box is used to define how the Clipboard contents will be pasted.

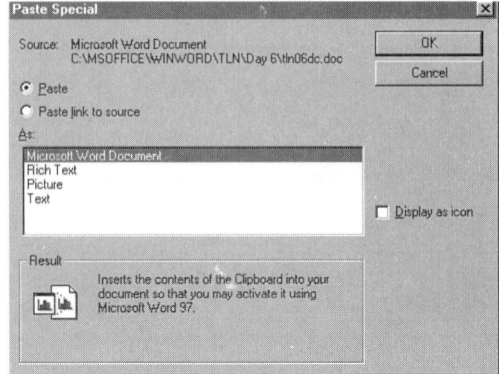

8. Elect whether to display the object as an icon.
9. Click on OK when you're done, and the object will be pasted into your Notes document.

NOTE Keep the source application open in the background when you paste an embedded object. If you have already closed the application, you will have only the option of pasting the object as text or Rich Text.

Figure 6.8 shows what a Lotus 1-2-3 97 worksheet range might look like when embedded in a Notes document.

Editing an Embedded Object

To edit an embedded object, place the Notes document into Edit mode, and then double-click on the object. If an application is available to edit the object, then the application will be launched—on its own if it is OLE, or within the Notes workspace if it is an OLE2 application.

Figure 6.8.
A spreadsheet embedded in a Notes document can be edited using its source application.

 **TIP** Although you can edit an object that is in a read-only document, those changes cannot be saved back to Notes. If you make changes in the object's source application, you can select Save As... to save your edits to a new file.

When you make changes to an object and you want to save the changes back to Notes, look on the File menu for the application. It should have an option that says something like Update Notes... or Update Host Application. Select this option, and then save the Notes document when you are through making changes.

Working with Linked Objects

How the data is stored is the primary difference between embedded and linked objects. With embedded objects, the data is stored within the Notes document. With linked objects, the data is stored in a file that is external to Notes. The file is usually stored on a file server so it can be accessed by multiple users.

Figure 6.9 illustrates the linked relationship between a Notes client workstation and the file server where the linked data is stored. Compare this to Figure 6.4, which shows how embedded objects are not linked.

Figure 6.9.
Data from linked objects are stored in files that are external to Notes.

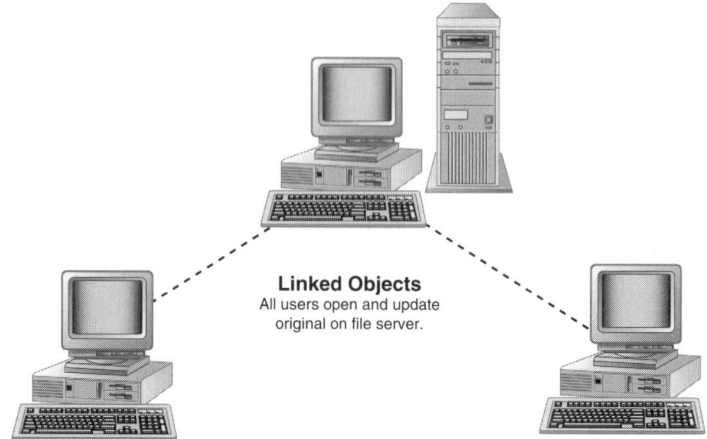

Creating a Linked Object

To create a linked object, follow the same steps you would follow to create an embedded file using Paste Special. The only difference is that you select Paste Link to Source. To review the steps quickly, here is what you do:

1. Open the file you want to link to in its OLE server application.
2. Copy the opened file to the Clipboard.
3. Switch to Notes, and open (in Edit mode) the document where you want to place the link.
4. Position the cursor where you want the link to appear in a Rich Text field.
5. Select Edit | Paste Special.
6. Select Paste Link to Source.
7. Select the format you want to use for the link.
8. Optionally select to have the link appear as an icon.
9. Click on OK to create the link.

Managing Links

When you create a link, it is set to update automatically. That means that if you open up the document, you will be asked whether you want to update the document with the latest data in the source file. When you edit the linked file from within the Notes document, your edits will be reflected immediately. But you have the option of changing the update process to a manual one.

You also can edit the link so it points to a different range within the source document or even to a different source document.

To manage links, display the External Links dialog box (shown in Figure 6.10) as follows:

1. Open the document that contains one or more linked objects.
2. Place the document in Edit mode.
3. Select Edit | External Links from the menu bar.

NOTE Do not select the link before doing this.

Figure 6.10.
The External Links dialog box is used to manage all external links in a Notes document.

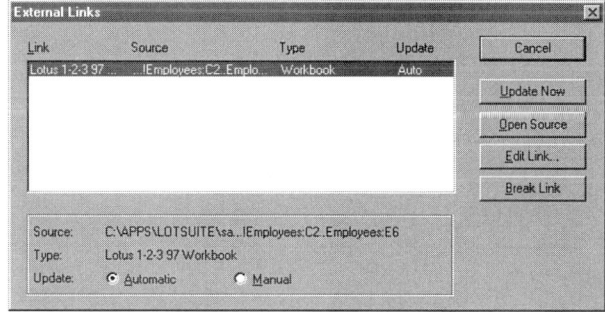

In addition to editing links, you can update the linked object or open up the linked file by clicking on a button from this dialog box.

Updating Linked Objects Manually

You can toggle between automatic and manual updates of linked objects by clicking on radio buttons.

If you select Manual, the only time a linked object gets updated is when you press the F9 key, or select View | Refresh from the menu bar. Even if you edit the linked file from within Notes, the Notes document does not get updated unless you specifically refresh the linked object.

If you leave updates as Automatic, the linked object can optionally be updated every time the document is opened. If you update the linked object, then Notes will reflect any changes that any user might have made to the source file. You do not have to put the document into Edit mode. And as already mentioned, the linked object is updated automatically when you change the linked file from within the Notes document.

Editing Links

Within the External Links dialog box shown in Figure 6.10, you can change the file to which a link points, or change the range of cells within a file to which the link points.

To edit a link, double-click on the link you want to edit, or highlight the link and click on the Edit Link... button. The Edit Link dialog box shown in Figure 6.11 will be displayed.

Figure 6.11.
The Edit Link dialog box lets you point a link to a new file or range of cells.

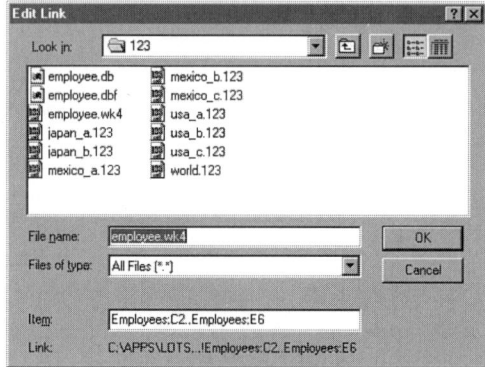

If you want to point the link to a new file, select the new file to which the link should point.

If you want to change the range of cells to which the link points, modify the Item field to reflect the new range.

NOTE A range of cells is used only as an example. Obviously, the type of data is dependent on the type of file to which you are linked.

When you are done editing a link, save your links and refresh the link, if necessary, so your Notes document reflects the changes.

Breaking a Link

To break a link, highlight the link you want to break, and click on the Break Link button.

A warning box will inform you that the link will be broken and you no longer will be able to edit the data.

Depending on the type of data, you may be able to edit it as text within the Notes document, but the data will no longer be linked or embedded.

Editing a Linked Object

To edit a linked object:

1. Put the Notes document into Edit mode.
2. Double-click on the object to launch the OLE server application.
3. Edit and save the document in the OLE server application.
4. Return to the Notes document. Refresh the document if you have Manual refreshing selected.

Working with Attached Files

So far, you have learned about pasted, imported, embedded, and linked files. There is a common limitation to all of these methods of sharing data in Notes. You can use these techniques only if the data is in a format that allows you to edit it in an application that is OLE compliant, or that you can import or paste into Notes.

By attaching files in a Rich Text field, you can share virtually any type of data—multimedia files, Macintosh and UNIX files, any type of file that you have access to through your computer.

Attaching Files

Attached files can be attached only in a Rich Text field. To attach a file:

1. Open a Notes document in Edit mode.
2. Position the cursor where you want to place the attached file.
3. Select File | Attach from the menu bar to display the Create Attachment(s) dialog box shown in Figure 6.12.

Figure 6.12.
If you can navigate to a file in the Create Attachment(s) dialog box, you can attach it.

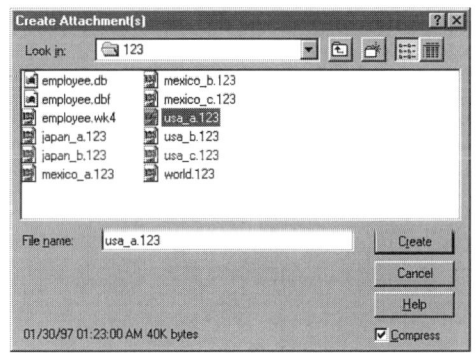

4. Locate and highlight the file you want to attach.
5. Click on the Create button to create the file attachment.

NOTE A file attachment is actually just a copy of the original file. If you look on the drive where the original file is located, you will see that it is unchanged. There is no link between the original file and the attachment.

Figure 6.13 shows two file attachments in a document. The first attachment is an Adobe Acrobat file. Because there is no application available on the system to edit this file, it shows up as a gray document icon. The second attachment is a Lotus 1-2-3 97 file. Because the application is available on the system, the Lotus 1-2-3 icon is displayed.

Figure 6.13.
Attached files appear as application icons if an application is locally available.

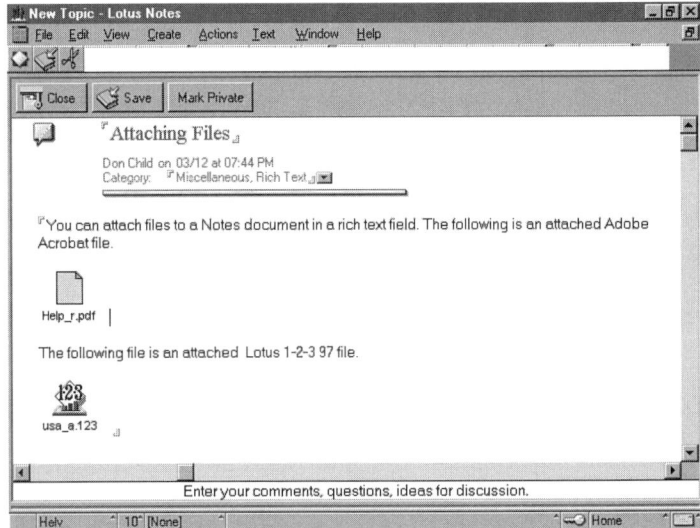

Linking to Other Notes Documents, Views, and Databases

So far, you have been learning how to incorporate elements from external applications in your Notes document. You also can include internal elements, including:

- DocLinks to other Notes documents.
- View links that take you immediately from a document to a specific Notes view.
- Database links that let you open another Notes database from within a Notes document.

All three types of links are created in the same way:

1. Locate and highlight or open the Document, View, or Database you want the link to lead to.
2. Select Edit | Copy as Link | Document Link, View Link, or Database Link.
3. Go to the document where you want the link to appear.
4. Make sure the document is in Edit mode, and position the cursor where you want the link to be placed. It must be in a Rich Text field.
5. Select Edit | Paste from the menu bar, click on the Paste SmartIcon, or press Ctrl+V.
6. The link will appear as a small document, view, or database icon.

NOTE If you are linking to a newly created document, the document must be saved before you can copy it as a link. If a link cannot be created in the current state—for example, if you have the Notes desktop displayed, but no database icon is selected—then the Edit | Create Link options on the menu will be grayed out.

Figure 6.14 shows the three link types.

You can click on a Document Link like the one shown in Figure 6.14 and the linked document will open. When the linked document is closed after you read it, you will be returned to the document where you clicked on the DocLink icon.

Figure 6.14.
Document, View, and Database links are displayed in a Rich Text field.

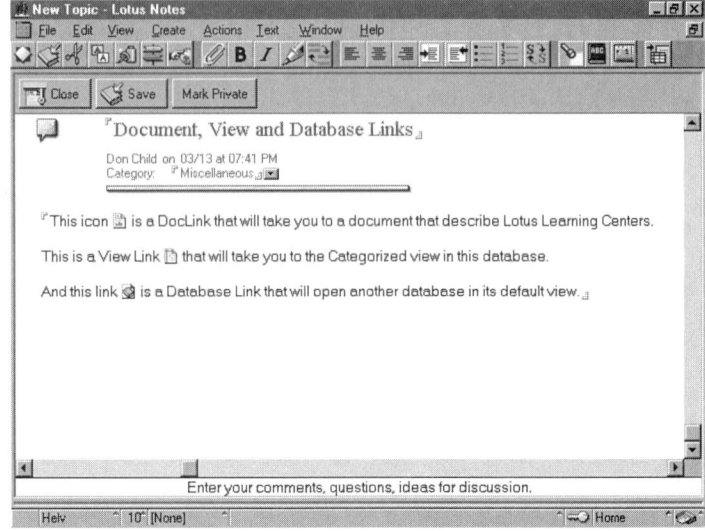

You can click on a View Link like the one shown above, and you will be taken to the linked view.

TIP The document or the view you are linking to does not have to be in the same database. You can use links to open up other databases to display related data, for example.

The Database Link is frequently used to provide access to a database, making it easy for others to locate and open a database without having to navigate through the menu structure on the Domino server.

NOTE Regardless of links, the ACL still determines whether another Notes user will be able to open a document, view, or database. All the link does is provide an easy way to navigate to another location within Notes.

Other Ways to Link within Notes Documents

So far, you have seen ways to access data from other applications on your local workstation or from somewhere on your organization's network. And, of course, you saw how to share data in a limited way with other Notes databases. There are still more ways to share data in a Rich Text field. In this section, you learn three other techniques for embedding or linking data. You learn how to work with buttons, pop-ups, and finally, you get your first taste of how Notes thrives on the Internet.

Buttons

You may have noticed as you moved through Notes that many Notes views and documents have a button bar across the top of the workspace. The buttons on this button bar are controlled by the application developer. You, as an end user, cannot change the buttons on the button bar unless you also happen to have Manager or Designer access to the database. What you can do, though, is create buttons in a Rich Text field.

You have seen some things that a button can do. It can close a document or put it into the Edit mode. It can create a new document or delete a document. These are all functions within Notes.

You are not limited to Notes functions, however. You can also run external programs using a button. For example, you may have a button that starts a backup program, or you might want to run a batch file. By running a program from a button embedded in a document, you can control when the person reading the document runs the external program.

Creating a Button

Let's look at how to create a button. We will do it in the TY Notes 4.5 database that by now is getting populated with several documents.

1. Create a new document by clicking on the New Main Topic button.
2. Give the new document a title and categorize it, and then place the cursor in the Rich Text field.
3. Select Create | Hot Spot | Button from the menu bar.
4. A button is created, and Notes opens a Design pane in the bottom half of the screen, and the Button Properties InfoBox is displayed.
5. Enter the label to be displayed on the button in the InfoBox, as shown in Figure 6.15. When done entering text, either click outside the InfoBox or click on the checkmark to update the button label.

Figure 6.15.
Define button properties in the Button Properties InfoBox.

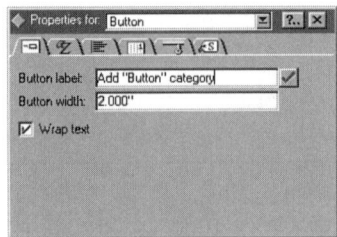

NOTE Note that you can also define a set width for the button, and make the text on the button wrap within that set width. You can also use text editing functions on the other pages within the InfoBox.

6. Now look at the Design pane at the bottom of the screen. There are three radio buttons. Select Simple Action.
7. Click on the Add Action button to select an action for the button. The Add Action dialog box is displayed as shown in Figure 6.16.

Figure 6.16.
Define a simple action for the button to perform in the "Add Action" dialog box.

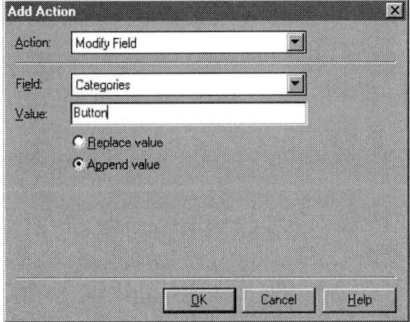

8. Select the action you want the button to perform. In this example, Modify Field is selected. Depending on the action you select, different fields are displayed to prompt you for needed information.
9. Fill in the fields to define how the button will behave. In the example, the Categories field will have a new value appended to existing values when the button is clicked.
10. Click on OK in the dialog box, and a simple formula will be created for you in the Design pane.

11. Click anywhere on the document at the top of the screen, and the Design pane will be closed. Close the InfoBox if you want to.
12. Close and save the document.

When any user who has Author access or higher clicks on the button while the document is in the Edit mode, the button's action will be performed.

NOTE Because the button changes the document, it can be used only in the Edit mode, and only by a user who is authorized to change the document. On the other hand, a button that places the document into the Edit mode would work only when the document is not in the Edit mode. The button provides a shortcut to functions that you already have the right to perform, but it cannot extend your rights beyond what is already defined in the database ACL.

The example shown above describes how to create a button that performs a simple action. If you walked through the process of creating a button, you will have noticed that you can also define a button's action using a formula or LotusScript, if you are familiar with application development.

Editing a Button

To edit a button, put the document into the Edit mode, and then do one of the following:

- Right-click on the button and select Edit Button.
- Select Button | Edit Button from the menu bar.

Proceed as described in the previous section, "Creating a Button."

Deleting a Button

To delete a button, place the cursor in front of the button in Edit mode. Press the Delete key. Alternatively, highlight the button by dragging the mouse pointer across it, and then press the Delete key.

If you delete a button by mistake, you can restore it by selecting Edit | Undo Delete from the menu bar.

Other Hotspots

Buttons are one type of hotspot. A *hotspot* is simply part of the screen that you can click on to make something happen.

The hotspot can be exactly what you just learned to do with a button—a simple action or a formula launched from text or from a pasted bitmap graphic instead of a button.

The hotspot can be a text or graphic link to a Notes document, view, or database—the way you just learned with DocLinks.

Or the hotspot can be a link to a site on the Internet.

Creating a Link Hotspot

A link hotspot does the same thing a document, view, or database link does. When you click on the link, you are taken directly to the new location within Notes. The link hotspot is created in essentially the same way, too.

1. Navigate to the document, view, or database that you want to link to.
2. Select Edit | Copy as Link | Document Link (or View Link or Database Link) to copy a link into the Clipboard.
3. Return to the document where you want to place the link.
4. Highlight the text or graphic that you want as a hotspot.
5. Select Create | Hotspot | Link Hotspot from the menu bar.
6. Display the Hotspot Properties InfoBox. Right-click on the hotspot or click on it once and select Hotspot | Properties.
7. In the Hotspot Properties InfoBox, click to check or uncheck showing a border around the hotspot, and use other pages in the InfoBox to define the appearance of the hotspot text.

NOTE A bitmap graphic is treated as a text character when you define it as a hotspot. You can drag the mouse pointer across the graphic to highlight it, and you can position it as if it were text.

The link hotspot will work only when the document is in the Read mode.

Creating a URL Link Hotspot

A URL is a Uniform Resource Locator, which is the way sites are addressed on the Internet. If your workstation has access to the Internet through the local area network or via a direct

connection or a dial-up connection, you can access the Internet from within a Notes document. All you need is the address—the URL—of the site you want to view. The link to a URL can be made automatic by creating a URL link hotspot.

To create a URL link hotspot:

1. Highlight the text or graphic that you want to make into a hotspot.
2. Select Create | Hotspot | URL Link from the menu bar.
3. Type in the URL address, or copy the address from the Internet and paste it into the Hotspot Properties InfoBox.

You can define the appearance of the link on the other pages of the InfoBox.

Figure 6.17 shows a text document link and a URL link as it is defined in the Hotspot Properties InfoBox.

Figure 6.17.
A link to the World Wide Web is defined as a hotspot link.

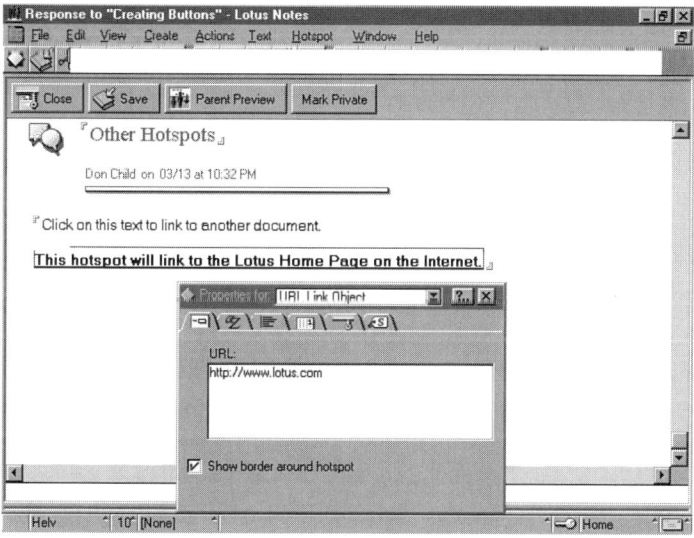

When you click on a URL link, Notes will use whichever Web browser you have defined in your current Location document. You will learn about this document on Day 12, and you will learn about using the Web on Day 14.

Creating an Action Hotspot

When working with buttons, you learned how to make a hotspot perform an action. The same process is used to create an action hotspot.

1. Highlight the text you want to make into a hotspot.
2. Select Create | Hotspot | Action Hotspot from the menu bar.

3. Define a simple action, as described under the topic of Buttons.
4. Define the appearance of the text or graphic button in the Hotspot Properties InfoBox.

Creating Pop-up Hotspots

Text or graphics that appear in a Rich Text field can be made into a text pop-up to help the reader understand the document. The pop-up is similar to a footnote. When you click on the hotspot, hidden text is displayed as long as you hold down the mouse button.

The text pop-up is similar to other hotspots in that you define a portion of a Rich Text field that becomes a hotspot. But the text hot-spot differs in that it does not perform an action or link to something outside the current document.

To create a text pop-up:

1. In the edit mode, highlight the text or graphic that you want to make into a hotspot.
2. Select Create | Hotspot | Text Pop-up from the menu bar.
3. Enter the text that you want to appear in the pop-up in the Hotspot Properties InfoBox. Click on the checkmark to update your text, or click anywhere outside of the InfoBox.
4. Define the appearance of the hotspot text on the other pages in the InfoBox.
5. When you are done defining the pop-up, the hotspot will be displayed with an outline around it, if you selected that option. Figure 6.18 shows a pop-up being defined, and the result of the pop-up is shown in the background text.

Figure 6.18.
A text pop-up hotspot, shown as outlined text, is defined in the Hotspot Properties InfoBox.

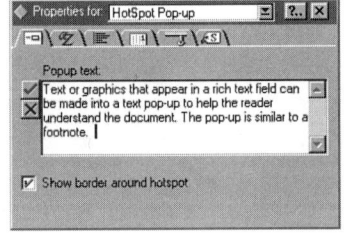

You can also create pop-ups that use a formula to determine all or part of the text that appears in the pop-up. An example of a formula pop-up is shown in Figure 6.19. When you click on it, the pop-up will display the name of whoever's Notes ID is being used to access the document. This pop-up was created using the following simple Notes formula:

"You are using the Notes ID of " + @Name([CN];@UserName) +"!"

Figure 6.19.
A hotspot can use a formula to display information such as the name of the userID being used.

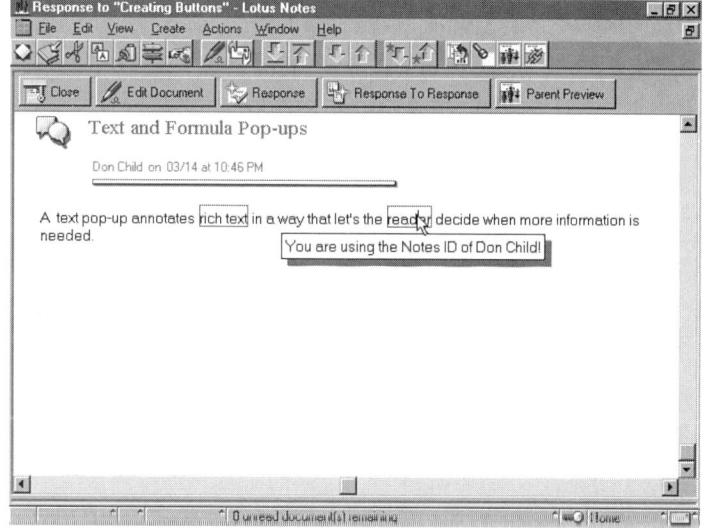

As an end user, you do not need to learn how to write Notes formulas, but you should be aware that they can be used to make Notes documents more interactive and relevant to others.

 **TIP** You can have fun with the @UserName function shown above. See if you can figure out how to personalize your own message to any person reading the document.

Editing Hotspots

For all types of hotspots, the editing process is the same. Place the document in the Edit mode, and then do one of the following:

- Right-click on the hotspot and select Edit Hotspot from the floating menu.
- Select Hotspot (or Button) | Edit Hotspot from the menu bar.

The Hotspot Properties InfoBox will be displayed. Make changes to the hotspot in the InfoBox, and then save the document.

Removing a Hotspot

There are two ways to remove a hotspot, depending on the type of hotspot.

For all hotspots, you can highlight the hotspot and press the Delete key, or delete the text, graphic, or button using the backspace or Delete keys.

For any hotspot other than a button, you can remove the hotspot but leave the text or graphic in place. To do this, select Remove Hotspot from the floating menu or from the Hotspot menu on the menu bar. Removing the hotspot leaves the text or graphic intact, but removes any hotspot characteristics.

NOTE You must be in the Edit mode before you can remove or delete a link.

Summary

In this lesson, you extended your knowledge of Rich Text fields, and got a glimpse of how extensible Notes is. Notes documents are containers for all sorts of data, and not all of the data is Notes data. You can embed spreadsheets, link cells from a database, and launch a word processor or a graphics application—all from within a Notes document.

You can also use the document as a multimedia container. You can attach multimedia files, including sound and video files, presentations, ScreenCam shows, MathCad or AutoCad files.... The Notes document can contain anything from an organization chart to a complete proposal.

You also learned how to create a variety of interactive elements known as hotspots. These include buttons, links to external applications, internal links, and pop-up annotation of a document. The only thing you did not learn was how to use Notes formulas to create truly programmable hotspots. But you can accomplish a lot using the simple predefined actions that are included in the Design pane when you are creating action hotspots and buttons.

When you combine the Rich Text features from yesterday's lesson and the graphic and interactive features from today's lesson, there is no reason you cannot create very rich documents. Your imagination is practically the only barrier you will encounter.

Workshop

The Workshop section presents quiz questions to help you cement your new knowledge and exercises to give you experience using what you have learned. Try to understand the questions and exercises before moving on to the next lesson. Answers are in Appendix A.

Q&A

Q I have a document that has embedded data in it, but I cannot edit the data. Why not?

A If you are going to edit data in a Notes document, you have to be in the Edit mode. This includes editing data in an embedded document. If you cannot get the embedded object to launch at all, it may be that you do not have an application capable of editing the material. Finally, it may be that object is not embedded at all. It is also possible that the object was pasted into the document rather than being embedded. A pasted object is nothing more than a bitmap graphic.

Q I tried to create a linked object, but when I go to paste it into the Rich Text field, the Paste as Link is grayed out. Why?

A When you copy something to the Clipboard in another OLE2-compliant application, you must keep the application open while pasting a link. If you close the source application, you can only embed the object; you cannot link it.

Q Sometimes, I launch an embedded object and I can still see the Notes document. Other times, I launch the object and then I see the source application. Why?

A That is the difference between OLE (Object Linking and Embedding) and OLE2. Notes can display the editing interface for OLE2 applications within Notes.

Q Can I use OLE or OLE2 on a workstation that runs the OS/2 operating system?

A You can accomplish the same thing on an OS/2 workstation. Notes uses DDE rather than OLE to share data between applications in the OS/2 environment. The future (and the present) of Notes includes additional ways to share data, including ActiveX and Java applets.

Q I created a button, and copied a formula that was supposed to open another database, but the database doesn't open. Why?

A Any formulas or actions that you create have the same access privileges that you have in the ACL. Perhaps you are not authorized to open the database. If that is not the case, then there is something wrong with formula. You might want to consider furthering your Notes education with a course in application development, or read a book on Notes application development. You will learn more about simple formulas in Notes as you continue to study this book, but the book is not intended to give you a grounding in the design and development of Notes databases.

Quiz

1. Can you import data into a Notes field that is not a Rich Text field?
2. You have a library of documents that were written using Microsoft Word, and now your company wants you to share those documents with Notes users in another location. How would you use Notes to share those documents?
3. What sort of link could you create to display the Inbox in your Notes Mail file?
4. Can a DocLink display a document that is not visible in any view?
5. If you have a document that contains an embedded Lotus 1-2-3 worksheet, can you update the source by editing the embedded object?
6. Do you have to write a formula in order to create a hotspot that modifies data in a document?

Exercises

1. Paste objects into a Notes document from various applications. What format is used to paste the data? Can you determine from this whether the data is OLE or OLE2 compliant?
2. Create a second discussion database. Then create a button that will copy a document to the second discussion database and delete it from the first database.
3. Create a spreadsheet on the file server. Link part of that spreadsheet to a Notes Rich Text field. Edit the document from within Notes. Close Notes and see if the changes got saved on the file server. Do the same thing with a word processing document and a graphic.
4. Create documents illustrating each type of hotspot and pasted, embedded or linked objects in your discussion database. Write one or two sentences describing in which circumstances you would use each one.

Week 1

Day 7

Exploring a Notes Database

Today's lesson sweeps up a lot of details that were not covered earlier because you had to have enough time to start building a database full of documents. Hopefully, you've been following along and doing the exercises at the end of each lesson. If you have, you should now have a discussion database with quite a few documents in it—Main documents, Response documents, and Response to Response documents, along with several different views.

If you haven't been following along and reinforcing what you learned by doing the exercises, then you may need to find another database to use for today's lesson. You could use the Help database, or your personal mail database, for example, or one of the databases you use in your organization. What is important is that you have a database that you can follow along in, if you want to work with a live screen. Otherwise, you can follow along with the book, learning from the illustrations. That should be sufficient to explain what you're missing.

What we are going to do today is tour the database, taking a closer look at some key elements.

Using Your Notes Password

Before going too far, let's look at the Notes password. If you are trying to access a database on a Domino server, you won't even be able to open the database until you provide a password. The first time a UserID is required during a Notes session—normally when you first try to open a database that resides on the Domino server—Notes will prompt you for a password.

> **NOTE** The password is stored as part of your Notes UserID.

The password prompt is illustrated in Figure 7.1.

Figure 7.1.
Enter your password so Notes can verify who you are.

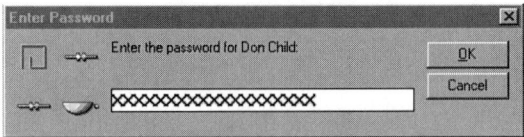

Type in your password and press Enter or click on OK. Here are some important characteristics about passwords:

- Passwords are case sensitive. If you create a password using the word "password," then each of these passwords would be distinct: "Password"; "PASSWORD"; "PassWord"; "password".
- Passwords cannot contain spaces. Therefore, you could use "Pass_Word" but you could not use "Pass Word" as two separate words.
- For each character you type in the prompt box, Notes will display a random number of Xs. That means that somebody watching your screen as you type will not see your password, nor will they be able to tell how many characters there are in your password.
- After the first four characters of your password are typed, each subsequent letter is represented by a set of four hieroglyphic-like characters (glyphs). The pattern of these characters is different for each person's password.

Tip

Get to know the pattern of glyphs for your password, so you will know if they come up wrong. This is a security feature known as anti-spoofing, and it only works if you pay enough attention to the pattern of the glyphs to know when they change unexpectedly.

Here is how the glyphs work. Somebody intent on stealing your password could create a dialog box that looks just like the password dialog box. When you click on OK, the password you entered would be surreptitiously mailed to the password thief without you ever knowing it. Without the glyphs, a single dialog box could be displayed for all users, and every password in the organization could be captured. But with the glyphs, the thief would have to create a separate "spoof" dialog box for each user, and would have to know the pattern of glyphs that are displayed for each person's password.

This is an unlikely occurrence, especially because it requires access to your Domino server and the ability to override the design of the password dialog box. But if it's possible, some hacker will try it.

Changing Your Password

There is no automatic expiration on passwords. If you want to ensure security, you will have to periodically change the password on your Notes UserID.

Note

When you first receive your UserID from the Notes administrator, it will have a default password. This assumes that the administrator did not change the Notes default that requires user IDs to have a minimum eight-character password. The default is assigned by the administrator, and may be a common password (such as "password") that is used for all new user IDs, or it may be a password that is intentionally very obscure and difficult to remember. This will encourage you to change the password to something of your own choosing as soon as possible. In either case, you should change the password to something that only you know, and that meets any password policies your company may have.

To change the password on your UserID:

1. Select File | Tools | UserID... from the menu bar.
2. Enter your current password to verify that you are authorized to use the ID. The UserID dialog box will be displayed (see Figure 7.2).

Figure 7.2.
The UserID dialog box is used to make changes to your Notes UserID.

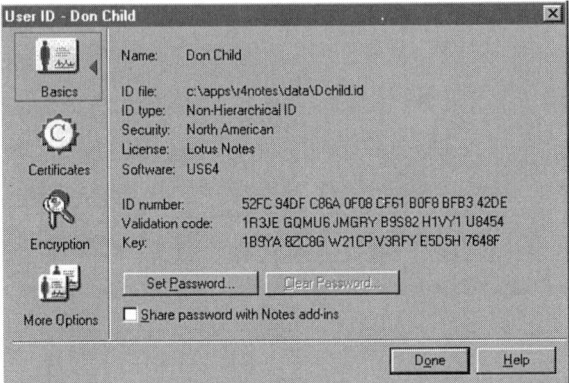

WARNING

Do not make changes to settings on pages other than the "Basics" page of this dialog box unless you are instructed to do so by your Notes administrator. Making the wrong change could make your ID unusable.

3. Click on the Set Password... button.
4. Notes will again ask you for your current password to verify that you really are authorized to change the password on this ID. After you enter your current password, click on OK.
5. Notes will display the Set Password dialog box shown in Figure 7.3. This dialog box tells you whether you have a required minimum length, and reminds you that passwords are case sensitive.
6. Type your new password. Only Xs will be displayed as you type. Press OK when you're done.
7. Type your new password again to confirm the password.
8. Click on OK to accept the new password, or click on Cancel if you change your mind and do not want to make the change.

Figure 7.3.
The Set Password dialog box describes parameters for new passwords.

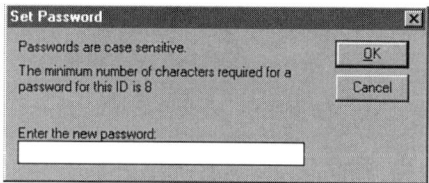

WARNING

Do not forget your password. The Notes administrator cannot recover a forgotten password for you. If you forget a password, your only recourse is to have the Notes administrator create a new ID for you, but you will still lose access to any data that you have encrypted or protected with a digital signature. Some administrators keep a secure backup of all ID files with their original default passwords as a hedge against users forgetting their passwords.

Touring the Database

Now that you have gotten beyond the Password dialog box, it is time to open up the database. After opening the database and looking at the default information, you will learn how to manage the documents in the database, including:

- How to use views to their fullest potential through the use of unread marks and sorted columns.
- How to work with folders.
- How to create your own private view.

After you have learned about views, you will have a chance to take a closer look at documents, and finally, you will explore database properties.

Looking at Default Opening Pages in the Database

The first time you open a database, you may see the About This Database document. This document usually contains information about the purpose of the database, and who to contact if you have any problems. You saw this document on Day 2, "Exploring the Notes Workspace," when you clicked on the About button while opening a database.

Figure 7.4 shows the About document for the discussion database you created.

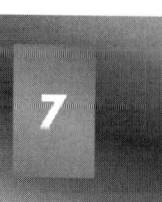

Figure 7.4.
The About This Database document is shown when the database is first opened.

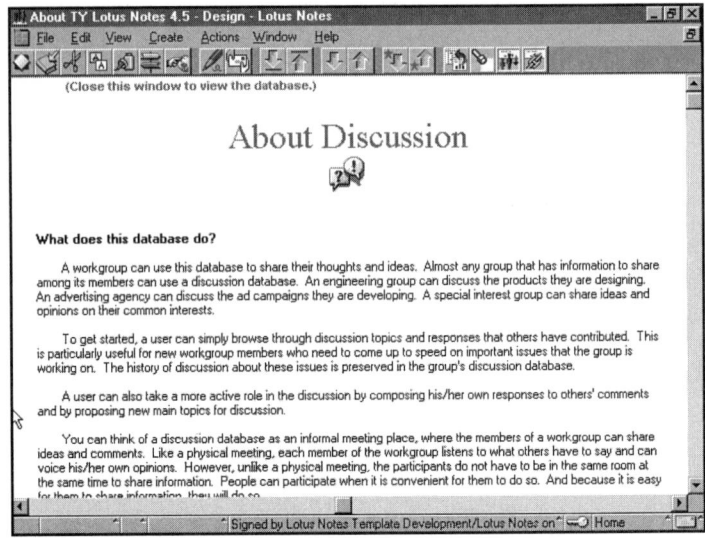

The About document can be customized by the application developer, but the document shown in Figure 7.4 is the example that comes with the Discussion database template. After you read it, press Esc (or select File | Close) to close the About document.

NOTE The application developer can control when the About document actually displays. You may see it only the first time the database is opened, see it if it has changed, never see it, or you may see it every time you open the database.

The About document can also be used as a "splash screen" for an application, giving you a nice lead-in to the work you do in the database.

How to Use Views

As soon as you close the About document, you see the default view of the database. Again, the default view is determined by the database developer.

The default view can be a graphic navigator or it can be a "folders" view that lists the various views and folders. Because the discussion database has a simple graphic navigator, we will stick with that for now, and concentrate instead on the documents in the view.

NOTE The default view is the first view you see when you open the database. Depending on how the application was designed, the database may open up to the default view every time, or it may open to the last view you were in when you closed the database.

If you have been following along and doing the exercises, you should by now have quite a few documents in your discussion database. Use that database or another database that has at least a dozen or more documents in it and several different views.

NOTE Some views may be too wide to fit in the view pane. The first time you look at a view, you may need to display the horizontal scroll bar by selecting View | Show | Horizontal Scroll Bar. After setting it once, it should "stick" so that it is available the next time you open the view.

Working with Unread Marks

Set up your discussion database by selecting Edit | Unread Marks | Mark All Unread.

You will see how unread marks are used in a moment.

NOTE You can work with unread marks for any database from the Edit | Unread Marks menu. The unread marks are stored on your Notes desktop along with your database icon, so other people using the database are not affected when you mark documents as having been read, or when you change documents from read to unread.

TIP You can determine how many documents there are in a database by marking all documents unread.

Now that all documents have been marked as unread in the discussion database, open the default view. Figure 7.5 shows the default view of the TY Lotus Notes 4.5 database, with all documents marked as unread.

Figure 7.5.
The default view of a discussion database with all documents marked as unread.

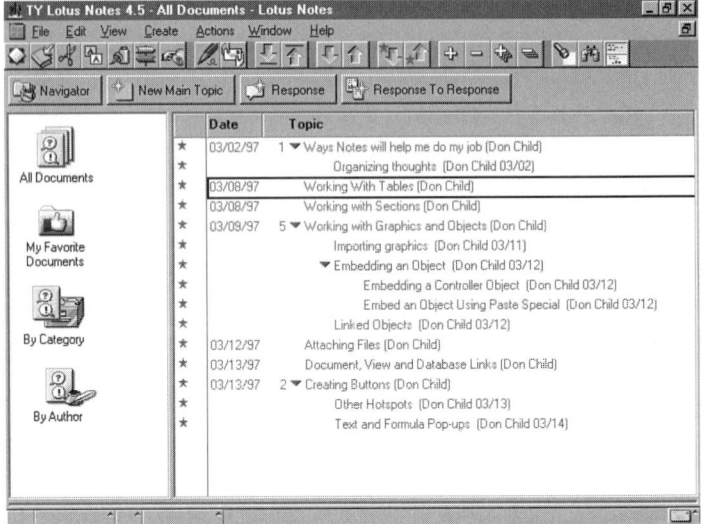

Look at the narrow column just to the right of the navigation pane. The stars beside each document in the column indicate that the documents are unread. You probably cannot tell in this black-and-white picture, but the unread documents are also displayed in a red typeface, while documents that have been read are displayed in a black typeface.

NOTE "Unread" in this case just means that the document has an unread marker beside it. Reading a document means opening the document up from a view and closing it again. The unread marks are simply an indicator that helps you manage the documents in a database.

To see how the unread marks work, double-click on the first document to open it for reading. Now close the document and look at the document in the view. The asterisk has been removed, and the document is displayed in black.

NOTE Unread marks are commonly used in databases, but they are an optional feature. You may find that some databases do not distinguish unread documents from those that you have already read.

Navigating Unread Documents Using SmartIcons

When you are reading through a Notes database, you can move from one document to another using the SmartIcons. The six SmartIcons you want to use are illustrated in Figure 7.6.

Figure 7.6.

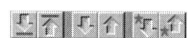

SmartIcons can be used to navigate to the next main topic, the next document, or the next unread document.

To see how these SmartIcons are used, open the first document in your discussion database again and try the SmartIcons to see how they behave. They will have the following effects:

- *Navigate Next (or Previous) Main Document.* The SmartIcons with arrows and underscores or overscores are used to navigate to main documents. In the hierarchical main view of the discussion database, main documents are shown left justified, and may be collapsible if there are responses to the document. When you click on the SmartIcon while reading a document, you will be taken to the next or previous main document in the currently selected view.
- *Navigate Next (or Previous) Document.* If you click on the plain up- or down-arrow SmartIcons, you will be taken to the next or previous document in the currently selected view, regardless of which type of document it might be.
- *Navigate Next (or Previous) Unread Document.* The SmartIcons that have arrows with asterisks are used to navigate to unread documents in the database, skipping any intervening documents that have already been read.

The unread marks may not make much of a difference in a small database. But some databases can grow until they have tens of thousands of documents in them. A single Notes database can be up to 4GB in size. If you use a database of that size frequently, you will want to use every tool available to manage the documents. The unread marks are one tool.

Marking Selected Documents Unread

In a view, you can highlight selected documents and perform a variety of batch functions on those documents—copying, deleting, or printing the selected documents, for example. You can also highlight documents and mark the selected documents as read or unread.

To mark or unmark individual documents:

- Click once in the narrow column (the View Marker column) to the left of the document you want to mark. A checkmark will be displayed beside the document when it has been selected.
- Click once on a checkmark to uncheck it. Unchecking a document means the document is no longer selected.

To mark several documents at once:

- Click and hold down the left mouse button beside the first document you want to select, and then drag the mouse up or down the marker column. Documents will be marked as you drag the pointer past them.
- Click on a checkmark and hold down the mouse pointer, and then drag it up or down to uncheck multiple documents.

Figure 7.7 shows selected documents marked as read.

Figure 7.7.
In a view, selected documents can be marked as having been read.

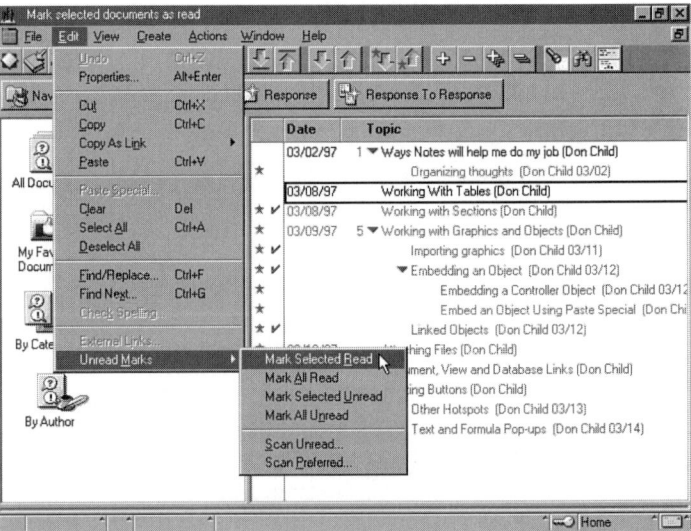

Managing Documents by Switching Views

You can also manage documents by switching to another view that may provide easier access to the documents by sorting them and selecting them in a different manner. For example, Figure 7.8 shows the same database that was shown above, only now it has been sorted by category.

Figure 7.8.
The categorized view groups similar documents for easier access.

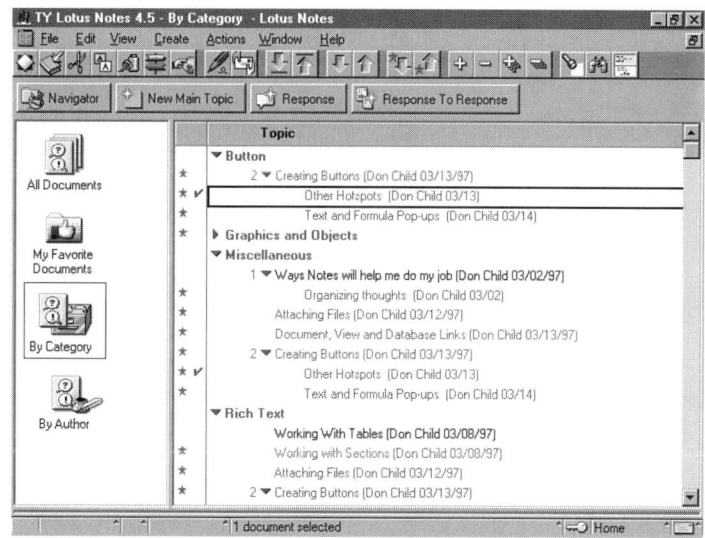

The categorized view shown in Figure 7.8 has a couple of features that you should take note of:

- The "twisties," the small triangles beside categories or categorized documents, indicate whether a category is expanded or collapsed. A right-pointing triangle indicates that the category is collapsed. A downward-pointing triangle indicates that the category is expanded. You can expand or collapse a category by clicking on the twisty or by double-clicking on the category. Alternatively, you can press + on the numeric keypad to expand a category; press - to collapse the category; Shift and + or - to expand/collapse all categories; or * to expand selected categories including all children in nested categories. These options are also available from the View menu on the menu bar.

- If a document is categorized under multiple categories, the document will show up in the categorized view in multiple places. For example, in Figure 7.8, the document titled "Other Hotspots" shows up under multiple categories. The document was selected once (with a checkmark), but the checkmark is displayed beside every instance of the document. There is only one document, even if it is in the view in multiple places. This means, for example, that you cannot delete the document from one category and not from another, or mark it as having been read in one category but not in another category.

- Categorized main documents have a column that indicates how many responses there are to that document. If there are no responses, the document is not categorized.

NOTE There are no hard and fast rules about how views display documents. It is really up to the discretion of the application developer whether the view has elements such as an unread document indicator, twisties beside categories and categorized documents, and response documents indented under main documents. Sometimes practicality dictates a particular solution. For example, if you have documents that are also categories, then double-clicking on the document would open the document. There should be some indicator that helps you, the Notes user, determine how to use the database.

Re-categorizing Views Using Sorted Columns

The discussion database is a fairly simple database, with only three views and one folder (to be discussed shortly). However, other databases are more complex. These complex databases allow you to dynamically re-sort views by clicking on the view column header.

To demonstrate this, I made a small design change to the discussion database. The version of the All Documents view shown in Figure 7.9 enables you to sort the dates in ascending or descending order by clicking on the Date column header.

Figure 7.9.
Dynamic columns let you re-sort data in a view by clicking on the column header.

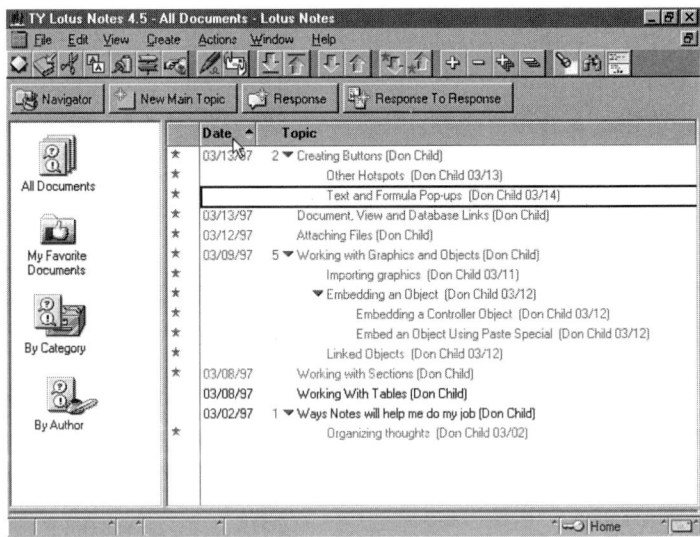

Notice the small up and down arrows next to the Date column header in Figure 7.9. If you see these small arrows, you can click on the column header to cycle through differently sorted views. In the example shown here, the view has been re-sorted so that the newest main document shows up first in the view, rather than being appended at the end of the view. Click on the header again to return to the ascending date sort.

TIP

You can sometimes resize columns, as well. If the designer made this feature available, you can click on and drag a column border in the header to resize the column. If the column is resizeable, the mouse pointer will change shape when you point at the column boundary.

Working with Folders

You will notice, in the discussion database, that there are actually only three available views: All Documents, Categorized, and By Author. The fourth view, called My Favorites, is actually a folder. You can put documents that you refer to frequently into the folder for quick reference.

NOTE

A view uses a formula to select documents, while a folder only contains the documents that you place into it.

Adding Documents to Folders

To put a document into the folder, click on the document and drag it over to the Navigation pane. Drop it on the My Favorites icon.

Click on the My Favorites icon and you will see that the folder contains the document you dragged to it.

WARNING

Before you try removing the document from the folder, read on. Do not delete documents to remove them from the folder. Deleting documents in a folder deletes them from the entire database. See the section "Removing Documents from Folders" later in this chapter.

If you want to move multiple documents to the folder, select the documents by placing a checkmark next to them, and then drag all the selected documents to the folder.

NOTE If you are not accustomed to dragging and dropping, you can move documents to a folder by selecting Actions | Move to Folder from the menu bar.

Removing Documents from Folders

The only way to remove a document from a folder without deleting the document is to highlight the document and select Actions | Remove from Folder. It will no longer be shown in the folder, but it will still be visible in any views that select the document.

Creating Your Own Folder

You can create your own folder in any database even though you are not the designer of the database; all you need is Reader access. The folder is based on the design of any one of the views in the database, but the documents you put into it are only available to you.

To create a folder, first select the view on which you want to base your folder.

WARNING The type of view makes a difference, even in a simple database like the discussion database. For example, if you select a categorized view, then you cannot move response documents into the folder unless you also include the main document.

After you decide which view you are going to use, follow these steps to create a folder:

1. Select Create | Folder from the menu bar to display the Create Folder dialog box shown in Figure 7.10.

Figure 7.10.
Enter a folder name and location, and then use the Options button to select a view to base your folder on.

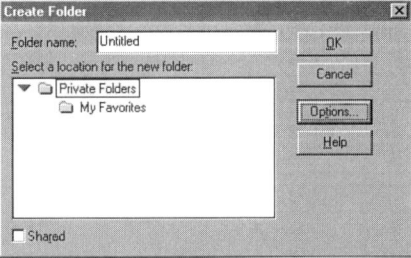

2. Enter a name for your folder.
3. Click on the folder within which you want your private folder listed.

NOTE Although there is a check box for creating shared folders, you cannot create shared folders unless you have at least Editor access to the database. If you have Author or Reader access, which is the norm, then you can only create your own private folders.

4. Click on the Options button to select the view on which you want to base your folder. Click on the view you want to use. The folder will use the view's design for layout purposes, even though the folder holds only the documents you place there.
5. Click OK twice, once to save your view option and once to save the folder.

NOTE If you do not define a view, Notes uses the database's default view as a template for the folder.

To view the folder you created, select View | Goto... from the menu bar, and then select your folder. The Go To dialog box displays all the views and folders from the Navigation pane.

To move documents to your folder, highlight the document and select Actions | Move to Folder.... When the Move to Folder dialog box is displayed, click on the folder you want to move the document(s) to, and click on Add. If you do not see a folder you want to use, you have the option of creating a new folder from within the Move to Folder dialog box.

Changing or Removing a Folder

If you create a folder and then decide that you want to change the name or location of the folder, or if you want to delete the folder, the steps are essentially the same.

1. Open the folder you want to edit or delete.
2. Select Actions | Folder Options... from the menu bar.
3. Select Rename... to give the folder a new name.
4. Select Move... to move the folder to a new location in the view and folder structure for the database.
5. Select Delete to delete the folder. Documents are not affected when you delete a folder.

NOTE  There is also a Design option on the Folder Options menu. As a novice user, it is easier to delete the current folder and re-create it using another view as a template. If you want to learn to design views, refer to the online Application Developer's Guide, or refer to one of the excellent books on Notes application development from Macmillan Computer Publishing.

Creating a Private View

You can create a private view using a process that is similar to the process of creating a private folder. What is the difference between a view and a folder?

In a view, the system uses a formula to determine which documents should be included. The only control you have over what gets included in a view is what you put into documents. For example, if a view only shows documents in a particular category, you can remove a document by changing the category field so the document is no longer included.

In a folder, the only documents that get stored there are the documents that you decide to put there.

To create a new private view, you do the following:

1. Select Create | View from the menu bar. The Create View dialog box will appear, as shown in Figure 7.11. The dialog box has already been filled in.

Figure 7.11.

Create a private view based on a view template, and create a simple selection formula.

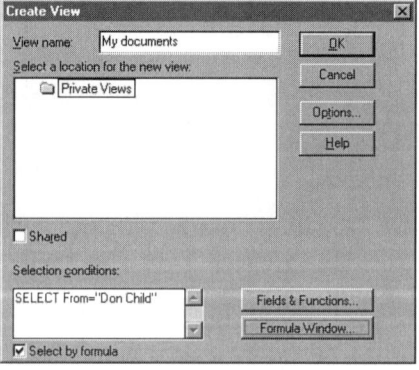

Exploring a Notes Database

2. Enter the view name.
3. Select the view location. Because you are creating a private view, the location has to be under Private Views. Only the database manager, designer, or editor can create shared views—that is, views that can be seen by other Notes users.
4. Click on the Options button and select the view that the private view should be patterned after. Click OK to return to the New View dialog box when you are done selecting a template view.
5. Enter a formula to select documents. If you do not select by a formula, all documents in the database will be selected by default.

NOTE The selection formula in Figure 7.11 includes any document where my name appears in the From field. The documents will be displayed in the By Author view. If the database were available to other Notes users, documents they created would not be displayed in this private view.

If you uncheck Select by Formula, a Conditions button will be displayed. You can then enter the conditions that will be used to select documents using a Search Builder dialog box. The Search Builder dialog box is similar to the one you will be learning about in tomorrow's lesson.

Printing Notes Documents

You can print an individual Notes document when the document is open for reading or editing, or when the document is highlighted in a view. You can also print multiple documents by selecting them in a view and then sending them to a printer.

In this section, you learn first how to print from within a document. You will then learn how to print documents from a view, and how to print an entire view without printing the documents in the view. Finally, you will learn how to tailor your printing by using headers and footers.

Printing an Individual Document

You can print an individual Notes document whenever the document is open for reading or editing. The process should be fairly intuitive to anyone who has used any Windows applications. You can do any of the following to display the File Print dialog box, shown in Figure 7.12:

- ☐ Click on the Printer SmartIcon, if you have a Printer SmartIcon showing.
- ☐ Select File | Print from the menu bar.
- ☐ Press Ctrl+P.
- ☐ Click on the Print button on the action bar, if one is available.

Figure 7.12.
The File Print dialog box is used to set print parameters and to start printing a document.

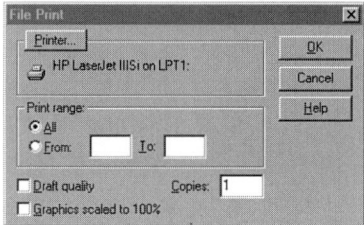

In the File Print dialog box, you have the following options:

- ☐ *Printer.* See the next section, "Setting Up a Default Printer."
- ☐ *Print Range.* The default is to print the entire document. However, if you inserted page breaks in your document, you can select a range of pages.

NOTE Because Notes is formatted for the online environment, it may be difficult to ascertain which pages you want to print. You may have to use trial and error to print the correct portion of a document.

- ☐ *Draft Quality.* This prints the document without graphics.
- ☐ *Graphics Scaled to 100%.* This will cause any graphics to be printed at full size, even if the aspect ratio has been rescaled for the online version of the document.
- ☐ *Copies.* Enter the number of copies you want to print.

Click on OK and the document will be printed on your default printer.

Setting Up a Default Printer

You set up your default printer first within Windows or whichever other operating system you are using. Lotus Notes uses the same printer drivers, and even the same dialog boxes, as your operating system for setting up printers. Once a printer is set up at the operating system level, you can access the printer and select options from within the Notes File Print dialog box.

To set up your printer within Notes:

1. Select File | Print from the menu bar to display the File Print dialog box.
2. Click on the Printer button to display a Print Setup dialog box. This dialog box displays a list of all the printers that you have available to your system.
3. Highlight the printer you want to set up, and click on the Setup... button.
4. A printer-specific setup dialog box will be displayed so you can change printer options. When you close this dialog box, the print options you selected will be in effect for all subsequent print jobs.

Setting Page Specifications for a Notes Database

You can specify the size of margins and how Notes documents fit onto the page. Select File | Page Setup from the menu bar to display the Page Setup dialog box shown in Figure 7.13.

Figure 7.13.
The Page Setup dialog box is used to define how the printer handles Notes documents.

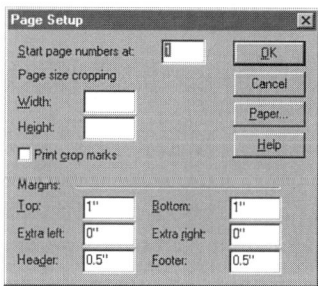

In this dialog box, you can define the following:

- *Start Page Numbers At.* This sets the beginning page number in headers or footers.
- *Page Size Cropping.* You can force Notes to print on only part of the page by setting the paper width and height. The width and height are measured from the top-left corner of the paper.
- *Print Crop Marks.* If you set the width and height, you can have Notes print crop marks on the paper to assist in trimming.
- *Paper.* Click on the Paper button to set paper feed characteristics. For example, you can set the paper so the first page feeds manually, allowing you to put in letterhead for a cover page.

- *Margins.* You can create top and bottom margins for printing. In addition, you can define how far the left and right margins should be indented (i.e., if you enter ".5" for extra left and the left margin defaults to 1 inch, then you will have a 1.5 inch left margin) and how much space there should be between the body of the document and the header and footer.

Click on OK to accept your Page Setup options.

Headers and Footers for Printed Documents

You can define headers and footers for Notes print jobs. The headers and footers can be set at any of three different levels:

- Database headers and footers print for all documents in the database (except for any documents that have a document or form header or footer specified), and for printing lists of documents from views.
- Form headers and footers print for all documents that use a particular form in the Notes database. Form headers and footers override database headers and footers. You have to be the manager or designer of a database in order to define form headers and footers.
- Document headers and footers can be defined for a specific document. If a header and footer are defined for the document, this will override any database or form headers or footers.

NOTE Database headers and footers are stored locally as part of the database icon, rather than being stored with the database itself. Therefore, you do not have to be a designer to create the headers and footers, but by the same token, your headers and footers cannot be accessed by other Notes users. If you remove a database icon from your desktop and then restore it at a later date, the headers and footers are lost, and will have to be re-created.

Creating the Header and Footer

The following steps define how to create a header and footer for a document. The same steps are followed if you want to create a header and footer for a Notes database or for a form, except that you use the Database or Form Properties InfoBox.

1. Open a document or highlight the document in a view.
2. Open the Document Properties InfoBox by using the Properties SmartIcon, by right-clicking on the document, or by selecting Edit | Properties from the menu bar.
3. Click on the Printer tab to display the Header Footer page in the Document Properties InfoBox (see Figure 7.14).

Figure 7.14.
The Printer tab of the Document Properties InfoBox is used to create headers and footers.

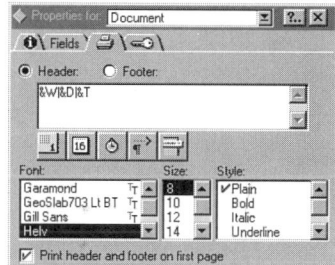

4. Enter a header. (The process is described below.)
5. Set the font, typesize, and style for the header.
6. Click on the Footer radio button and create a footer.
7. Set the font, typesize, and style for the footer.
8. If you want the header and footer printed on the first page of the document, make sure the print option at the bottom of the screen is checked. If you do not want the header and footer to print on the first page, click on the check box to uncheck it.

When you print the document, it will be printed with the header and footer you defined.

The header and footer are created in the large scroll box in the middle of the InfoBox page shown in Figure 7.14. In this box, you can type characters, or you can insert codes by clicking on the five buttons that are directly beneath the scroll box. The five buttons, from left to right, insert the following codes:

☐ *Page number.* When you click on this button, the code "&P" is displayed, and the current page number is printed at that location on the header or footer.

☐ *Date.* When you click on this button, the code "&D" is displayed, and the header or footer displays the date the document is printed.

☐ *Time.* When you click on this button, the code "&T" is displayed, and the header or footer displays the time the document is printed.

☐ *Tabs.* More about tabs in a minute.

☐ *Title.* When you click on this button, the code "&W" is displayed, and the content of the document's Title field (the field that is normally displayed in a view, whether it is labelled "Title" or something else like "Subject") is printed.

The codes do not have space inserted between them, so you have to insert your own spaces. For example, if you want to display the date and time together, you would enter "&D &T" with a space in between the two codes.

Using Tabs to Determine Position

The header and footer are each divided into three parts: a left side, a middle, and a right side. The three parts are delineated by vertical bars that you can insert by clicking on the Tab button.

Characters and codes to the left of the first tab are left-justified. Characters and codes between two tabs are centered. Characters and codes to the right of two tabs are right-justified. Two codes separated by a single tab are displayed on the left and right sides of the header or footer.

The following are examples of headers or footers:

```
Document Title: &W
```

Left-justified, for example, "Document Title: Using Graphics"

```
&D | &T | Page &P
```

Left, center, and right tabs, for example, "03/17/97 (left) 10:37:54 (centered) Page 2 (right)"

```
||Page &P
```

Right-justified page number, for example, "Page 2"

```
Capitol Creek Ranch | &W
```

Text string left-justified, document title right-justified

> **Tip**
>
> You can also enter a hard return and then enter another line, thereby creating a multi-line header or footer.

After you create a header, define the font, typesize, and style for the header, and then click on the footer button and do the same for the footer.

> **Note**
>
> Remember, you can set the header and footer for an entire Notes database. If you do so, and then later you create a different header and footer for an individual article, the article header/footer takes precedence.

Looking at the Database Characteristics

You have already done a lot in this database. But there are a few loose ends that have been skipped—things that you can examine in a database before you even open it. On Day 2, you learned how to display information about a database on its icon from the view menu. But today, besides working with views and reading documents, we examine a few other database details.

The first thing you should be aware of with any Notes database is its availability to other Notes users. If you can open a database and work with it, it is being made available to you either from your local Notes client workstation, or it is being accessed through a Domino server (a Notes server, in earlier versions of Notes).

If a database is local, the ACL for the database might not be enforced. That depends on whether the database is a replica of a database on the Domino server, and if it is, whether the ACL is uniformly enforced on all replica copies of the database. And if the database is local, it cannot be read or updated by other Notes users, unless a replica of the database exists on a Domino server. You will learn more about replica databases on Day 12, which is all about using Notes when you're out of the office.

If the database is on a server, then the ACL is enforced automatically, and the documents in the database are probably available to Notes users other than yourself.

You can determine the location of a database from the database icon on the desktop, as described on Day 2. But you can also learn about the database location and a whole lot more from the Database Properties InfoBox.

Examining the Database Properties InfoBox

From the Notes desktop, click once on the database icon you want to examine—for example, the TY Lotus Notes 4.5 icon. Then display the Database Properties InfoBox in any of the following ways:

- ☐ Click on the Properties SmartIcon.
- ☐ Right-click on the database icon and select Database Properties from the floating menu.
- ☐ Select File | Database | Properties from the menu bar.

The first page of the Database Properties InfoBox is shown in Figure 7.15.

Figure 7.15.
The Database Properties InfoBox provides information and resources for managing databases.

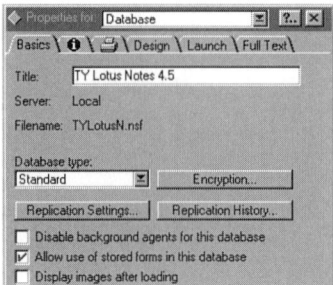

In the next sections we walk through the first two pages of this InfoBox. The other pages are covered at various times throughout the course of this book.

Page One of the Database Properties InfoBox

On the first page of the InfoBox, you will find the following:

- *The database title.* If you want to change the title on the database icon, this is where you enter the new title. Changing the title does not affect the ability to replicate the database.
- *The Server.* This is the system through which you are accessing Notes. Refer back to the earlier discussion of the difference between a local and server-based Notes database.
- *The Filename.* This is the name under which the Notes database is stored.
- *The Database type.* Most databases are Standard databases. Personal Journals are only for a personal journal database, which does not get shared with other users. Libraries are used to catalog Notes databases, and Address Books are the other types. There should be no reason to change the database type.
- *Encryption.* This button is used to encrypt your local database. When you click on the Encryption button, an encryption dialog box, shown in Figure 7.16, is displayed.

Figure 7.16.
The Encryption dialog box is used to define local database security.

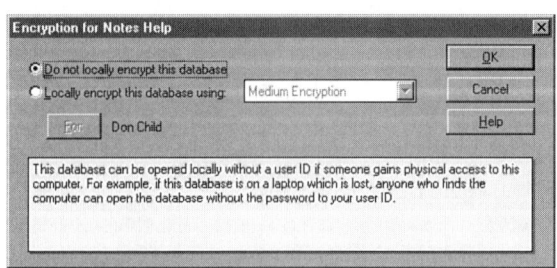

By default, local databases are not encrypted. If you set encryption to simple, medium, or strong, then you can define the user whose ID must be used in order to access the database. This is used if you are storing secure information, or if you are carrying a portable computer and want to ensure the security of your data. Encrypted databases cannot be opened unless you have the ID for which the database was encrypted.

- *Replication settings.* These are discussed on Day 12 when you learn about Mobile Notes.
- *Disable background agents.* Checking this option will keep agents (macros) from running on your database. You will learn about agents on Day 13 when you learn about automating Notes.
- *Allow use of stored forms.* When a complex document is mailed or pasted into a database, it can only be displayed if the database has a form that maps to the same fields as the data. The prime exception to this is stored forms, which ensure that a document is seen in its original format. Stored forms take up space and impact database performance, so you may want to disable this for large databases.
- *Display images after loading.* This speeds up the display of text in graphics-intensive databases.

Page Two of the Database Properties InfoBox

The second page of the Database Properties InfoBox is also of interest to us at this time. It is the information page, and is shown in Figure 7.17.

Figure 7.17.
The information page of the Database Properties InfoBox.

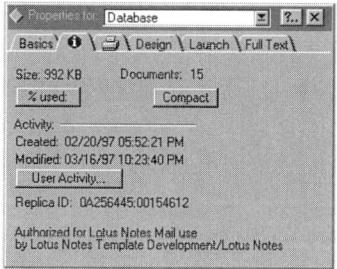

This page, as its name implies, displays information about the database.

The first bit of information is the current size of the database, and the number of documents in the database. The database grows as documents are added and edited, but over time, as documents are deleted or edited, the database develops *white space*, unused space that is still being taken up by placeholders where documents have been deleted.

Click on the % used button to see how much of the total database file size is actually being used.

When the amount of space being used dips below 80–85 percent of the database, you can compact the database by clicking on the Compact button.

> **TIP**
>
> In a large database, you may find that you can reclaim quite a bit of space, but you will lose some system performance while the database is being compacted in the background.

The bottom part of the Information page shows database activity. The date and time of creation are shown, as well as the last time that the database was modified.

Click on the User Activity... button to see statistics such as who has been using the database, how many times the database has been opened for reading, or how many times it has been written to in the past day, in the past week, and in the past month.

These statistics are gathered if you check the Record Activity check box, as shown in Figure 7.18. This is checked by default for databases on the Domino server, but it can be turned off for all databases by the Notes administrator. The option can then be turned on for individual databases. Recording user activity increases the size of the database by 64KB.

Other options in the User Activity dialog box include Activity is Confidential, which makes the User Activity dialog box available only to those with Designer or Manager access to the database, and Copy to Clipboard, which can be used to create a hard-copy version of the User Activity log.

Figure 7.18.
Track database usage in the User Activity log.

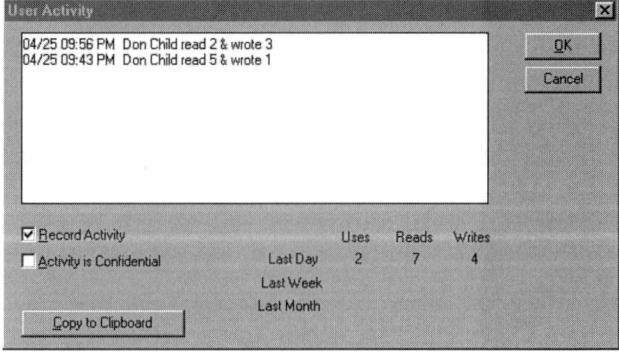

NOTE If you do not see a User Activity button on the Information page of the Database Properties InfoBox, it means that Activity is Confidential has been checked, and you are not a designer or a manager in the database.

Near the bottom of the Information page in the Database Properties InfoBox, you will see the *Replica ID*. The Replica ID is a code that the Domino server uses to identify the database. The Replica ID is unique for all new databases and copies of databases, but a Replica Copy of the database will have the same Replica ID no matter where it resides.

NOTE The importance of the Replica ID will become increasingly apparent when you learn about database replication on Day 12.

The final bit of information shown on the Information page is the message shown at the bottom, which states that the database has been authorized for Lotus Mail use. Notes users with Lotus Mail licenses can only use certain types of databases. If a certified database has its design changed, Notes Mail users may no longer be able to use the database.

Summary

You spent the last couple of days creating various types of documents in the discussion database you created on Day 4. Today, you got to take a tour of that database now that it has been populated with enough data that it begins to make sense. You can see how the different views and folders in the database are used to provide quick access to a variety of documents.

Views can be fairly complex, and they can contain a large number of documents. Knowing how to keep track of the documents you have already read in a database can make the information more useful to you in the future. Learn how to navigate and control the use of unread marks in views, and you will find that Notes databases quickly become more accessible to you.

In addition to reading documents in views and folders created by the database designer, you created your own folder and your own view. This is something that you can do as an end user of the database, even if you do not have designer access. This is a more advanced function, one that you may want to revisit as you become more competent with Notes. It is a good way to tailor a database for your own use.

You then learned about printing Notes documents. As mentioned earlier, Notes is not a page-layout application, but you can control the appearance of printed documents by using margins, by setting up a printer, and by creating headers and footers for some or all documents in the database.

You have now learned how to create a database, how to fill the database with documents, and how to manage the documents in the database. You have peeked under the hood of the database. You should now be fairly comfortable with a simple Notes database.

Workshop

The Workshop section presents questions and answers, quiz questions to help you cement your new knowledge, and exercises to give you experience using what you have learned. Try to understand the questions and exercises before moving on to the next lesson. Answers are in Appendix A.

Q&A

Q While playing with views, I lost the graphic navigator. How do I get it back?

A In some Notes databases, you can toggle back and forth between a graphical navigator and a folder view of the database by clicking on a Navigator button on the action bar at the top of the screen. If there is no button, try selecting View | Show from the menu bar and selecting the name of the navigator you want. You can also toggle from the navigator to the folder view by selecting View | Show | Folders.

Q My database icon says there are several unread documents in one of my databases, but I open up the database and all the documents are marked as having been read. Why?

A First, check other views to see if the unread documents are selected by another view. If unread documents are not selected by any view, try using the Navigate Next Unread SmartIcon. If an unread document is not selected in any view, Notes will offer you the option of viewing the document using the database's default form.

Another possibility is that unread documents are ones that you are not allowed to access because of a reader names field or because the document has been encrypted and you do not have a key needed to decrypt the document. You can turn off the unread marks by selecting Edit | Unread Marks | Mark All Read.

Q Does Notes have a "master document" feature for printing documents that are drawn from several databases?

A No. Each database has its own headers and footers. You can define the starting number on a print job, and you can copy the header or footer field from the Database Properties InfoBox in one database to another database, but you cannot create a universal master document like you can with powerful word processors.

Q I have two databases that are supposed to be replicas of each other, but they have different names. How can they be replicas, if they have different names?

A All Notes cares about is the replica ID on the Information page of the Database Properties InfoBox. If two databases have the same replica ID, they are replicas. If two databases have different replica IDs, then they are not replicas, even though they might have identical documents in them.

Quiz

1. What is the difference between a view and a folder?
2. You delete a folder that is full of documents. What happens to the documents?
3. Can a view have categories nested inside categories?
4. Can a document also be a category?
5. How do you select 10 documents from a view at the same time?
6. How do you unselect a document that has been selected in a view?
7. How many ways can you create a header or footer for printing if you have Reader access in the database ACL? If you have Manager access?
8. How do you change the name of a database?

Exercises

1. Set all documents as unread in your discussion database. Figure out two different ways to mark some of the documents as read without opening the documents.
2. In any Notes database, create a private view that displays all documents that have been edited in the last five days.
3. Create a header and footer for printing documents in your discussion database. Do the headers and footers print out when you set the printer to print in draft mode? Can you suppress the printing of the database header and footer on a single Notes document? (Hint: Create a blank header or footer.)

In Review

Now that you have finished your first week, you should already be fairly proficient using the basic functionality of Lotus Notes 4.5 : creating and reading documents.

The Notes environment is complex, but as an end user, these complexities are more or less transparent. However, it does help you to have a basic understanding of the complexities. What does matter is understanding where the data is stored, and how that can effect what you can do with the data.

You learned that you need a Notes UserID to access data on a Domino server, and that the same UserID determines what you can do on any Notes database because of the Access Control List, commonly referred to as the ACL.

You learned all about the parts of the Notes workspace that are used for navigation, and then you learned how to put a database onto your desktop. This is fundamental to everything you do. You have to put a database on your desktop in order to open it and work with the documents that are in it.

You also learned how to work with workspace pages, the tabbed pages on your desktop that you can use to organize your database, and how to change the user preferences to tailor the way your workspace functions. The user preferences can be left with their default settings in most instances, but as you become more accustomed to Notes, you may want to return to Day 2's lesson. You can also work with the user preferences pages by referring to the online Help.

After you were familiar with the Notes environment, you got to start creating your own Notes documents in a database that you created from a Notes template. In a Discussion database, you learned to create a Main Topic, and then a response. All Notes documents, no matter how complex or how simple, are either main documents, responses, or responses to responses.

These documents were populated with several different data types—text, rich text, numbers, time, keywords, authors, readers, and names field types. Although you entered data into some fields, Notes handled other fields by computing what went in and displaying the data by default.

After creating simple documents, you learned the complexities of Notes documents, aside from the communications that take place within Notes. Those complexities started simple, with the word processing functions within Notes. You learned how to format text, and how to use styles to make that process more automatic and efficient. You also learned how to work with data in tables to make it more presentable, and how to use the 80/20 rule to hide information unless the user needs it by using collapsible sections.

The Notes document is a container that can hold virtually any type of information you can put onto a computer. The Rich Text field is the primary container within the Notes document. In a Rich Text field, you can embed anything from multimedia files to spreadsheets. You can link individual cells with a database application or a spreadsheet application. You can launch a word processor or a graphics application within the Notes workspace, you can cut and paste from another application, or you can attach files. The choice depends on your environment and how the information is to be used.

Besides being a container for external data, the Rich Text field can be used to link other Notes documents, views, or databases, and to launch other programs from links. Among the elements you learned to create are hotspots, DocLinks, and pop-ups. In learning to work with these, you were introduced for the first time to the Notes programming environment in a very small way—creating hotspots that performed simple actions.

As you followed along in the exercises, the Notes discussion database you put onto your desktop was filled with a variety of documents. You got to explore the database with all of the documents in it, learning to use views and folders to gain quick access to the information you need.

You learned how to keep track of which documents you had worked with by setting and removing unread marks, and how to navigate from document to document within a view using the SmartIcon shortcuts.

You then learned a more advanced function available to you as an end user: how to create your own custom views and folders. What you did was basically no more than copying and modifying an existing view, but that is a valid method of designing a Notes database.

Finally, this week, you learned how to print Notes documents. Printing and page layout control is probably one of the weakest points about Notes. There are valid reasons for some of the difficulties, but one can't help but wish that you could format and print documents as easily as you can with more sophisticated page layout and desktop publishing applications. But then again, when is the last time you tried to collaborate with a workgroup that was geographically dispersed while working with PageMaker? Notes is good at what it's good at...collaboration, communication, and coordination.

After this first week, assuming you have attempted to answer all of the quiz questions and done all of the exercises, you should be feeling fairly comfortable with Notes. You should be ready to appreciate some of the richness of the Notes environment beyond your desktop, beyond a simple database. You will get a good dose of the complexities in Week 2.

At a Glance

After a week of working with Notes, you should have the basics down pretty well. You should be able to locate a database on your workstation or on a server on your Notes network. And, once you have a database on your desktop, you should be able to navigate within the database and create documents, or understand why you may not be able to create documents.

What's Ahead?

During the second week, you will be looking at several more complex issues having to do with Notes. One objective of this second week is to move beyond how to use Notes so that you can begin to understand why and when Notes may be appropriate. Notes is not just documents and not just a glorified bulletin board, as you will quickly learn.

On Day 8, you will learn how to do complex searches on a Notes database or on multiple databases using a full text index. This index allows you to use Boolean searches to locate data based on its context. You will learn how to create and manage an index, as well as how to search through an index that has already been created.

On Day 9, you will begin to learn about Notes Mail. Some critics claim that Notes is nothing more than glorified e-mail. By the end of this week, you will be laughing every time you hear someone say that. But meanwhile, you should learn the strengths of the communications side of Notes, and that begins with Mail. You will learn the basics of using Notes Mail, and then on Day 10, you will learn some of the more advanced mail features that let you tailor your mail environment. For example, you can create your own mail templates, and you can modify the type of stationery you use when you send mail.

On Day 11, you will still be working within the Notes Mail database, but you will be working with the Calendaring and Scheduling functions, which let you create and manage a variety of items on your personal calendar. You will also learn how to use the calendar in a collaborative environment, learning, for example, how to send invitations to others in your workgroup after checking to see if they have free time on their personal calendars.

On Day 12, you will take Notes on the road. You will learn how to set up communications ports, and how to set up Location documents so that you can change your entire Notes environment with a couple of clicks of the mouse. You will also learn how to share data between your mobile location and the replica database on the Domino server in your office. When you work on the road, you can modify a Notes database that is on your desktop, and then go online to share your modifications with your coworkers. The first time that happened in my office, one of our key people was on the road for two days before anyone even realized he was out of the office, because he was still contributing to discussions on the server-based databases. Learn this well enough, and maybe you can sneak out for a awhile.

On Day 13, you will learn how to automate Notes using Agents and programmed Actions. That is the strength of using a computer—being able to make the computer do the repetitious work, rather than having to do it yourself.

And finally, on Day 14, you will slip the surly bonds of Notes and escape onto the Internet by learning how to set up Notes to automatically launch a browser whenever you click on a Web link, or whenever you enter a URL on the Search Bar or from a SmartIcon. The browser could be the Notes Personal Web Navigator, which you will learn about, or another Web browser. And you will learn how to use the Weblicator, another Lotus product that delivers a portion of Notes functionality to anyone with a Web browser. And as a finale, you will get a look at the Kona Java applets that hint at the future direction of Notes.

Week 2

Day 8

Searching for Information in Notes Databases

On Day 3, "Using Notes Help," you explored the Notes 4.5 Help database and learned various ways to locate data in that database. Today, you are going to get a review of some of the techniques you learned on Day 3, but you are also going to learn more techniques.

Starting with the discussion database that you created on Day 2, "Exploring a Notes Workspace," you will learn to search for documents using standard Windows search functions. You will then learn to extend that simple search by creating and managing a full-text index. If you remember, the Help database already had its own search view. But with the discussion database, there is no index. Because you created the database, you are the Manager of the database, and therefore, you have the ability to create and update an index.

Getting Started with a Simple Search

Presumably, you have created enough documents in your discussion database to make a search worthwhile. If not, perhaps you can make a copy of a discussion database from your organization's Notes installation, or use one of the Notes help databases.

To make a copy of a database, click once on the icon of the database you want to copy to select it, and then select File | Database | New Copy from the menu bar. Give the database a title and a file name, and place it on your local hard drive.

Open the database by double-clicking the database icon and make sure that you are in a view with plenty of documents; for example, the All Documents view. Try a simple Quick Search. Remember, in the Help database, how you could type the first couple of letters, and then press Enter and find your way quickly to a specific location?

Try a Quick Search in the All Documents view. It doesn't work. Why? Because the view is set up incorrectly. The first column is a date field, and it is only the first column that is searched in a Quick Search.

TIP A Quick Search will only work if the first column in the view is sorted alphabetically.

Because a Quick Search will not work, you will have to try another type of search, called a simple search. It is a type of search you are probably familiar with if you use a graphical word processor. To search for a word or a text string that appears anywhere in a view, do the following:

1. Select Edit | Find Next from the menu bar, or press Ctrl+G. Notes displays the search box shown in Figure 8.1.

Figure 8.1.
Use the Find dialog box to locate the first occurrence of a text string in a view or document.

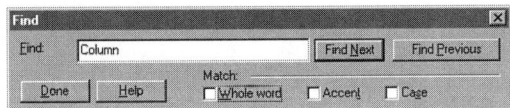

2. Enter the word you want to search for.
3. Optionally, click on the check box to indicate that you want to search for the text string only if it is a whole word.
4. Optionally, click on the check box to indicate that you want to match any accents you entered in the text string.
5. Optionally, click on the check box to indicate that you want the search to match the case of the characters you entered as a search string.
6. Press Enter or click on OK to search for the string.

Notes will then look for the first instance of the search string in the view.

TIP You can do the same search in a document, and Notes will find the first occurrence of the search string in the document.

NOTE When in a view, you also have the option of selecting Edit | Find/Replace from the menu bar to search for a text string. Because you cannot edit documents unless you are in a document and in the Edit mode, Notes displays the Find dialog box.

Find and Replace Text in a Document

While we're looking at the Edit | Find/Replace option on the menu bar, let's use it in a document. To replace a text string in a document:

1. Open the document in the Edit mode. Tip: You can put a document into the Edit mode by pressing Ctrl+E. If you highlight a document in a view and press Ctrl+E, the document will open in the Edit mode.
2. Select File | Find/Replace from the menu bar. Notes will display the Find/Replace dialog box shown in Figure 8.2.

Figure 8.2.
Use the Find and Replace dialog box to replace one text string with another in a document.

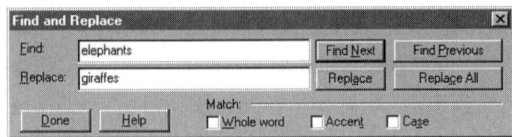

3. In the Find field, type the text string that you want to replace.
4. In the Replace field, type the new text string that you want to substitute for the first string.
5. Click in the check boxes to indicate if you want to search for full words only, paying attention to accented characters and to case.
6. Click on Find Next to search for the next occurrence of the search string.
7. Click on Replace to replace the highlighted string.
8. Click on Replace All to replace all occurrences of the word from the cursor to the end of the document.
9. Click on Find Previous to search from the current location to the top of the document.

Those are simple searches, and in many cases, they might be sufficient for your purposes. But to really put the power of Notes into practice, you can use a full text search.

What Is a Full Text Search?

A *full text search* is a way to locate words and phrases, alone or in relation to other words and phrases, anywhere that they appear within a Notes database. You can even extend that definition to include words that are contained in attached files, in embedded graphics, and in other databases.

You can define the search criteria using Boolean logic. But don't worry if the word "Boolean" doesn't really mean anything to you. The full text search function has its own search builder to help you build a search that adheres to all the ins and outs of Boolean logic.

Displaying the Search Bar

You can actually do a limited full text search of a database that has not been indexed. To search a database, you have to display the Search Bar, shown in Figure 8.3.

Figure 8.3.
The Search Bar is used to perform full text searches.

1. Display the Search Bar by selecting View | Search Bar from the menu bar.
2. In the large, white entry field, type the word you are looking for.
3. Click on the Search button.
4. A new temporary view will be created that displays only documents containing the text string you searched for.

> **NOTE** Doing a full text search without indexing the database limits your options for working with search results, and is far more inefficient, because Notes has to search through every document in the database.

Examining the Search Bar

While you have the Search Bar in mind, take a closer look at the elements on it, shown in Figure 8.3. You will be using these later on.

- ☐ *Full Text Indicator.* The finger pointing to a book indicates that the search bar is focused on performing full text searches. Click once on the icon and it turns into a finger pointing at a globe, indicating that the search bar is focused on searching the World Wide Web for a Web page (if you have an Internet connection). For full text searches, make sure the icon shows a finger pointing at a book.
- ☐ *Text field.* Type your search commands in this field.
- ☐ *Search.* Click on this to perform a search based on the search commands you entered.
- ☐ *Reset.* This clears the results of a search, allowing you to enter another search without exiting from the database.
- ☐ *Options button.* This button displays a menu of options used to tailor the way a search is performed on your workstation.

These Search Bar options are described in detail later in today's lesson.

Creating a Full Text Index

If you think back to the first database you created, there was a button that allowed you to create a full text index at the same time the database was created. While that is one option, it is probably more common to create an index on an existing database. in this section, you will create an index for the discussion database you already created.

NOTE A full text index can only be created by a Manager or Designer. Therefore, you are most likely to index databases that reside on your own Notes client workstation, whether the database is one that you created, or a replica copy of one that is on the server.

To create a full text index, select a database that is on your local hard drive; for example, the discussion database that you created, a help database, or any other database for which you have Designer or Manager access. Select or open the database, and follow these steps:

1. Display the Database Properties InfoBox by selecting File | Database | Properties; by clicking on the database with the right mouse button and selecting Properties from the floating menu; or by clicking on the Properties SmartIcon.
2. Select the last page of the InfoBox, the Full Text page shown in Figure 8.4.

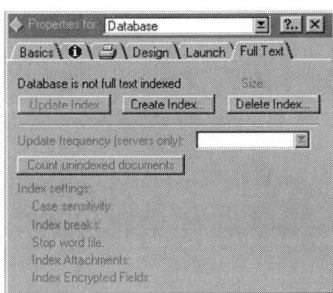

Figure 8.4.
Create a full text index from the Full Text page of the Database Properties InfoBox.

3. Click on the Create Index... button to display the Full Text Create Index dialog box, shown in Figure 8.5.

Figure 8.5.
Select full text index options in the Full Text Create Index dialog box.

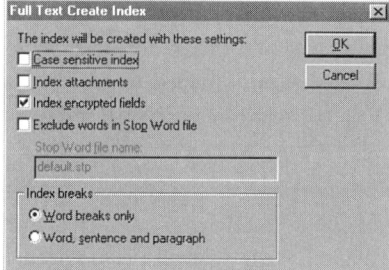

 **TIP** Whenever you see a menu item followed by an ellipsis (...), the ellipsis means that the menu item leads to a dialog box. This is a standard function on all applications that run in Windows.

1. Select your index options in the Full Text Create Index dialog box, and then click on OK to start the background indexing process.

On the status bar, Notes will display the following message: `Your request to index this database has been queued locally. You may search the database as soon as indexing is completed`. While the indexing process is taking place in the background, you can continue working.

 **NOTE** This assumes that you set the workspace property to allow background indexing. You learned how to do this on Day 2 with a check box on the first page of the User Preferences dialog box. If background indexing is not selected, you will have to wait until the database is indexed before you can continue working.

Index Options

You have a lot of options for tailoring your full text index. You select these options in the Full Text Create Index dialog box shown above in Figure 8.5. The options include the following:

☐ *Case Sensitive Index.* By default, every word in a database is indexed once. If you elect to create a case-sensitive index, then a word such as "Notes" could be indexed twice—once with an uppercase *N*, and again with a lowercase *n* if the word "notes" appears in the document. Every uppercase word that starts a sentence would be indexed separately from its lowercase counterpart. You could then search for "Notes" without locating documents with the word "notes." The case-sensitive option increases the size of an index by 5–10 percent, depending on the percentage of text versus graphics in the database.

- ☐ *Index Attachments.* If you select this option, Notes indexes the text in attached files and embedded objects within the database. You can then search for text even when it is included in attached files, although the text string will not be highlighted in the attached file the way it is in a Notes document. Indexing attachments increases the size of the index based on the number of text-based attachments in the database. With embedded objects, only the ASCII text in the object gets indexed, and only if the object is not compressed.

- ☐ *Index Encrypted Fields.* If you select this option, then encrypted fields in documents will be indexed. You still cannot see the encrypted data, but you can determine which documents contain a search screen. The option is turned on by default.

WARNING

> If you have highly sensitive data in encrypted fields, you may want to see that this option is turned off to prevent people deducing the content of your secure documents. Besides being able to locate documents that contain an encrypted string, they could also access the full text index, where the encrypted words are not encrypted, even though they are out of context. Also note that in order to create the index, the Domino server must have the encryption key in memory during indexing. Any other databases using that same encryption key could be compromised.

- ☐ *Exclude Words in Stop Word File.* This option tells Notes to *not* index certain words that appear in a text file known as a Stop Word file. If you select this option, then words in the Stop Word file are excluded from the index, and you cannot include them in search strings. The Stop Word file is a text file called DEFAULT.STP, and it is located in your Notes program directory. This file contains words such as *a*, *the*, and *an*, along with the numbers 0–9. You can add other words, if you want, or remove words. For example, if you want to be able to search for numbers, do not use the Stop Word file or remove numbers from the file. Using the Stop Word file can reduce the size of your index by up to 15–20 percent.

NOTE You can create customized Stop Word files that contain words that are used so frequently in a particular database that they are not useful in searches. The Stop Word file must have a file name of eight characters or less, with an extension of .STP, and it must be located in the Notes program directory. You can select the Stop Word file you want to use when indexing a particular database. Custom Stop Word files do not get replicated to other servers when the associated database is replicated.

- *Index Breaks.* By default, only word breaks are indexed. However, you have the option of indexing word, sentence, and paragraph breaks. If you do this, you can search for words in proximity to each other. For example, you could enter the search string "embed sentence graphic" to locate documents in which *embed* and *graphic* appear in the same sentence. This greatly increases the size of the index. A word break index is 50 percent of the size of text in the database, while a word, sentence, and paragraph index is 75 percent of the size of the text in the database.

Information about the completed index is available from the Full Text page in the Database Properties InfoBox, shown in Figure 8.6.

Figure 8.6.
Selected full text options are shown on the Full Text page of the Database Properties InfoBox.

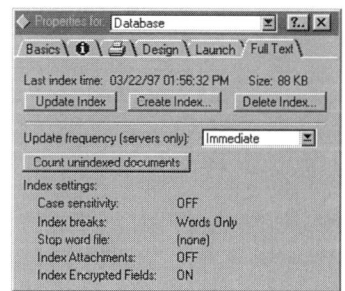

When you generate the full text index, it is placed into its own subdirectory beneath the data directory in which the indexed database is located. For example, if your discussion database is named C:\NOTES\DATA\DISCUSS.NSF, then your full text index files can be found in a directory named C:\NOTES\DATA\DISCUSS.FT\. Each full text index has its own directory (and several subdirectories).

Removing an Index

A quick word about removing a full text index before we get into searching for data. There are two ways to remove a full text index—a right way and a wrong way.

The right way to remove an index is by using the Database Properties InfoBox. On the Full Text page shown in Figure 8.6, click on the Delete Index... button. After you confirm that you want to delete the index, the .FT directory and all its files and subdirectories will be removed from your computer.

The wrong way to remove an index is to delete the .FT directory and all its associated files and subdirectories from Windows or DOS. If you do this, the index will no longer work, but Notes will still think the index exists.

You should delete the index from within Notes.

Using a Full Text Search

Now that you have indexed your database and displayed the Search Bar, it is time to do a search. For starters, we will do a simple search by entering a single word.

Figure 8.7 shows the results of a search on the discussion database that has been used to illustrate various types of data entry in this book.

Figure 8.7.
A simple full text search finds documents that contain the search string "object".

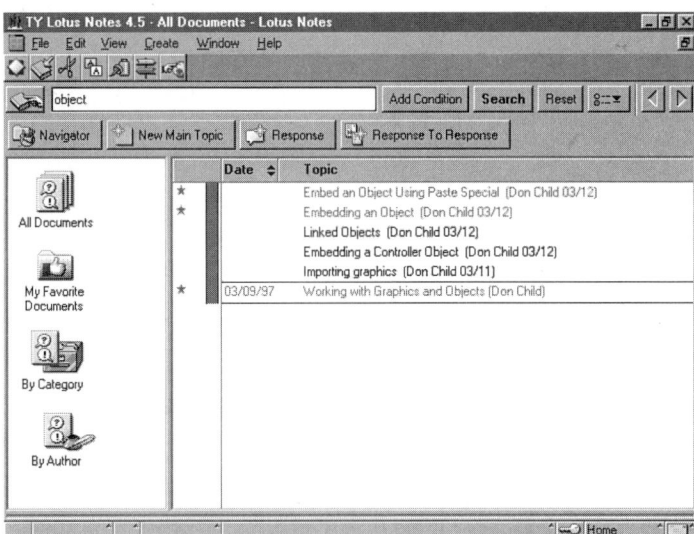

In this search, there are six documents found that contain a mention of the word "object."

If I edit a document by adding more occurrences of the search string, what happens? Nothing at all. Notes is searching the full text index, not the database itself. If I want the full text search to show the latest changes in the database, I have to refresh the index.

To refresh the index, open the Database Properties InfoBox to the Full Text page and click on the Update Index button.

> **NOTE** You can schedule regular updates for server-based databases. However, local full text indexes have to be manually updated so they contain pointers to your latest changes.

In Figure 8.8, a few edits have been made to documents, and the index was refreshed. Doing the same search now results in a view that is sorted by relevance.

Figure 8.8.
The search results ranked by relevance.

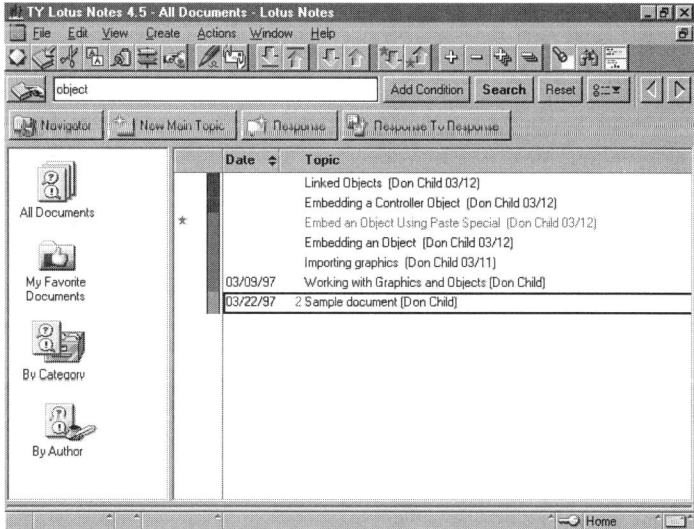

Notice the bar with graduated shades of gray. The documents at the top of the view have a greater number of hits by the search criteria. Those at the bottom of the view are less likely to be relevant because there are fewer matches on the search string.

Controlling How Documents Are Displayed

The Options button, on the right side of the Search Bar, lets you control, to some degree, which documents are selected and how they are displayed in the search results view. Clicking on the Options button displays the menu of choices, which are shown in Figure 8.9.

Figure 8.9.
The full text Options menu is used to set local parameters for your search.

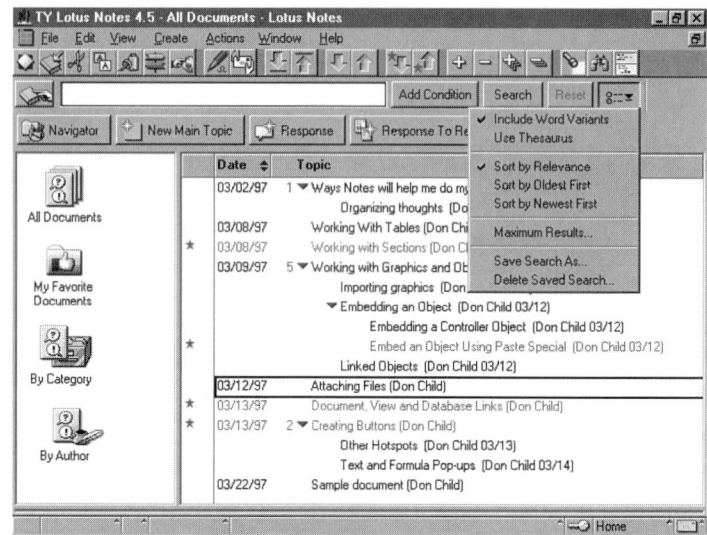

The options that you can select include:

- *Include Word Variants.* Word variants are words that have the same semantic base. For example, if you search for "computer" and its variants, you would also find any instances of "compute," "computing," and "computational." Notes automatically searches for variants, but you can exclude them by clicking on this option to remove the checkmark.
- *Use Thesaurus.* If you select this option, Notes uses an internal thesaurus to locate synonyms for search words. The thesaurus cannot be viewed or edited.
- *Sort by Relevance.* This is the default sort for search results when a database is full text indexed. Relevance sorting is what you have already seen, where the document with the most matches ("hits") on search words is moved to the top of the search results view.
- *Sort by Oldest First.* This moves the oldest documents to the top of the search results, and turns off relevance ranking.
- *Sort by Newest First.* This moves the newest documents to the top of the search results, and turns off relevance ranking.
- *Maximum Search Results.* This displays a dialog box in which you can define the maximum number of documents you want displayed in a search. The default is 250 documents.

The other two options involve saved searches, which you will learn about shortly.

Looking at the Search Results

When you open documents located by a full text search, the search string is highlighted wherever it is visible within the document. For example, Figure 8.10 shows the results of a search in the Help database for the word "thesaurus."

Figure 8.10.
Text strings located by a full text search are highlighted in the document.

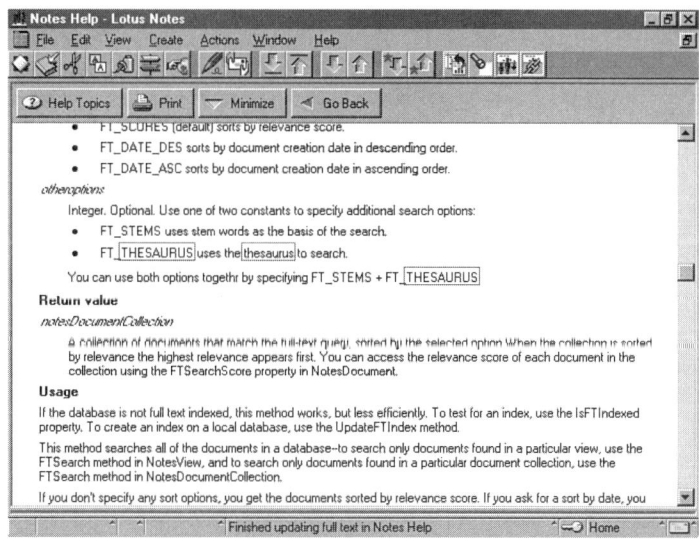

 **TIP** If you open a large document and want to locate the search string, press Ctrl and + on the numeric keypad. Every time you press Ctrl +, you will move to the next occurrence of the search string. You can move backward to locate the search string by pressing Ctrl – on the numeric keypad.

You might not be able to see the search string in a document, even if the document was located by a full text search. If you cannot see the search string, then why was the document selected?

Notes documents can have hidden fields. The contents of these hidden fields, as well as the contents of encrypted fields, the text content of embedded objects, and the contents of attachments, may have the search string. You will not be able to see the string in these documents.

When you print a document located by the search, the highlights around words will also be printed. If you copy or forward the document, the highlight is removed.

>  **TIP** To print documents with the highlight hidden, create a folder and put the documents into the folder. Then click on the Reset button on the Search Bar to remove the search results. You can then print the documents without the highlights, and delete the folder when you are done.

Performing Boolean Searches Using the Search Builder

You can refine your searches using Boolean logic. Don't panic just yet. You do not have to learn Boolean logic, and you do not even have to know what it is. But if you happen to be familiar with it, you can type your search query on the Search Bar to locate specific combinations of information.

For example, suppose you are working with a Sales Tracking database. You want to see all purchase orders for widgets in the western region in the past six months. How do you go about it?

The hard way goes like this. Search for all documents containing the word "widgets." That might be 200 or more documents. Now, using the Search Results view, do a new search for "west" and hopefully, that will locate mostly invoices from the western region, because you have a "region" field that is required. If you still have too many documents, you can search for 1996 or 1997, assuming that is the way Notes is storing the year. Now you might be getting close. Gradually, you might narrow your search to the point that you can locate the documents you need, but it can be a laborious process.

If you know Boolean logic, you can construct a detailed search that looks for widgets and west, but no documents that were created earlier than 1996.

The easier way is to use the Search Builder, and let the Search Builder create your complex search for you.

To use the Search Builder, click on the Add Condition button on the Search Bar. The Search Builder will be displayed as shown in Figure 8.11.

Figure 8.11.
The Search Builder helps you build a complex search.

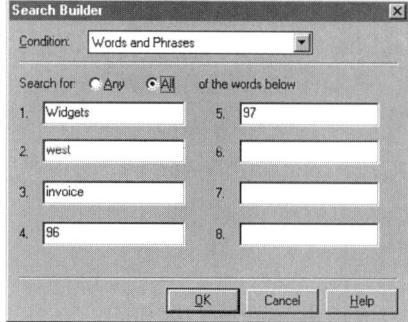

In this illustration, the Search Builder has been used to create a complex search. There are several types of search condition available in the Search Builder. Each one is described below.

Searching for Words or Phrases

In the Conditions field, select Words or Phrases. This is the default condition for the Search Builder. You have the option of searching for any or all of the words or phrases you type in the eight available fields. This is what you can expect:

- ☐ If you search for any of the search words or phrases, you will get a larger selection of matches. For example, if you are searching for documents that contain any of the choices "apple," "orange," or "banana," then a document that has just "apple" would match the search conditions. This is an OR search in Boolean logic.

- ☐ If you search for all the words or phrases, then documents do not get selected unless they match every one of the search fields. If you search for "United Airlines," "Honolulu," and "Los Angeles," then a document that mentions Los Angeles and Honolulu will not be selected unless it also mentions United Airlines. This is an AND search in Boolean logic.

TIP Do not be too restrictive in your search. It is easier to narrow your search than it is to start over. You can always enter one condition, and if it returns too many documents, you can add additional criteria until you narrow the search to a workable number of documents.

Searching by Author

You can search for documents based on whose name is in the Author field. You have the option of searching for all documents where the Author field contains a specific name, or you can search for documents where the Author field does not contain specific names.

To ensure that you spell names correctly, enter the names from a Names dialog box that lets you pick names from a Notes Address Book. Figure 8.12 shows the Names dialog box.

Figure 8.12.
The Names dialog box is used to select user names from a Notes Address Book.

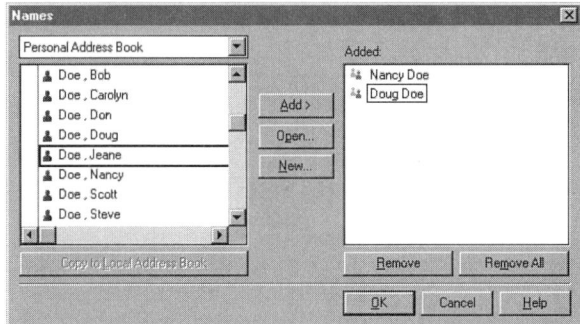

In this Names dialog box, do the following to select one or more names:

1. Select the address book you want to search by clicking on the first drop-down arrow in the top-left corner of the dialog box to display a list of available address books.
2. Highlight a single name or click beside several names to add more than one person at a time.
3. Click on Add. The names are added to the column on the right.
4. Alternatively, you can remove names from the list on the right by highlighting them and clicking on Remove or Remove All to remove all names and start over.
5. You have the option of adding names from a Public Address Book to you Personal Address Book by clicking on the Copy to Local Address Book button when the name is highlighted.
6. You have the option of opening the address book to look at the Person document for an individual.
7. You have the option of adding a person to the address book by clicking on New and entering details about the individual. In most organizations, you can only add people to your Personal Address Book, because you are not likely to have sufficient rights in the Public Address Book to create new people.

8. When all the names you want are added to the right column, click on OK to copy them back to the field in the Search Builder dialog box.
9. Click on OK in the Search Builder dialog box, and the names will be added to the Search field on the Search Bar.

When a search is performed, Notes will find any documents that have the names of the people you entered as authors.

Searching by Date

You can search for documents based on the date the documents were created, or the date they were last modified. You can select from among a number of criteria, including:

- ☐ Created on, before, after, or between specific dates.
- ☐ Not created on or between specific dates.
- ☐ Older than a certain number of days.
- ☐ In the past certain number of days.

Using these criteria, you can use a variety of strategies for defining which documents you want by date.

Searching by Field

You can search for documents based on the content of any field in the database. There are a lot of hidden fields, but the Search Builder dialog box provides a list of field names, so you don't have to guess, and you don't have to know the design of the database.

Looking back at the scenario described at the beginning of this section, you can now be much more specific. Instead of looking for the word "west" anywhere in a document, you can say that you want only documents where the Region field contains the word "west."

When using the By Field search condition, you do the following:

1. Select the name of the field you want to search on.
2. You elect whether you want the field to contain, or not contain, the search data.
3. You then enter the search data.

In the example used above, you would select Region as the field, you would select Contains as the option, and the data would be west.

Searching by Form

This is an interesting one. You can display the fields on any form in the database, and fill in the fields with the data that retrieved documents must have. Again, remember the caution to be conservative. If you are too explicit, you may eliminate the very documents you want to retrieve.

The Search Builder dialog box displays a list of available forms.

NOTE: Forms must be set up in advance by the database designer. If a form is given the design characteristic of being searchable, then it will be listed in the Search Builder. Only forms with that characteristic set by the designer will be available.

Go through the form field by field, filling in any fields in which you want specific data retrieved. Leave other fields blank.

This is just an elegant way to define search criteria for more than one field in the database.

Searching by Form Used

This is a simple search. You can limit the search results to documents that use a particular form, for example a Purchase Order form.

A list of available forms will be displayed. Again, the only forms that appear on the list are those that have been defined by the application developer as searchable. Select the form or forms that you want, and click OK to copy the information to the Search Bar.

Launching a Search after Using the Search Builder

As you select data for different search conditions, the data is copied to the Search Bar. You can return to the Search Builder and add new conditions. A Boolean search is created on the search bar using the data that you provide. Once you have defined all criteria, you conduct the search as usual:

1. Click on the Search button.
2. Locate the document you want, or further refine your search.
3. When done, click on Reset to return to the view you were in before beginning your search.

Saving a Search

Searches can be complex to build. If you create a complex search that you want to use again, you can save it, and use it again rather than having to rebuild your search from scratch.

To save a search:

1. Build the search on the Search Bar so it will select the documents you want.
2. Click on the Options icon on the right side of the search bar.
3. Select Save Search to display the Save Search dialog box shown in Figure 8.13.

Figure 8.13.
Save a search so you can reuse it at any time.

4. Enter the name under which you want to save the search.
5. If the search is in a database on the Domino server, and you have at least Designer access to the database, you can elect to save the search as a shared search. This allows others to use the same search.
6. Click on OK to save the search.

You can then run the search at any time by selecting it from the menu displayed when you click on the Options icon.

Deleting a Saved Search

To delete a previously saved search, select Delete Saved Search... from the Options icon on the Search Bar.

Click on the search you want to delete so it is highlighted, and then click on OK. The saved search will be deleted.

Searching for Documents in More than One Database

Using the search techniques described above, you can locate virtually any textual information within a Notes database. If that information spans multiple databases, you can extend the full text searching capabilities to gather documents from all databases on a site.

To search multiple databases, you create a special database based on the SRCHSITE.NTF database template. When you create this database, you are automatically the Manager, and can define the site-wide search criteria you want.

NOTE The Site Search database is enabled for the Web. This is one of your first glimpses into the Internet connectivity of Notes. When a Web user accesses a Search Site database from a Domino server, they are able to perform the equivalent of a database full text search over the World Wide Web. You can also use the Site Search for your own searches.

You create a Site Search database the same way you create any database. To review:

1. From the Notes workspace, select File | Database | New.
2. Accept Local as the location for your database.
3. Give the database a title.
4. Give the database a file name that is no more than eight characters long without spaces. Give it an NSF file extension, such as MYSEARCH.NSF.
5. Click on the check box to show Advanced Templates. If necessary, select another template server until you locate the Search Site template.
6. Click on OK to create the database.

After the database is created, you can set up your site search. Take a deep breath, because the setup can be a complex process. It starts with setting up individual databases so they can be included in the search, and then moves to the Search Site database, which needs to be set up for full text searching. You should have enough experience by now to successfully complete the setup.

Setting Up Databases for Inclusion in a Site Search

For each database that you want to include in a site search, do the following:

1. Open the Database Properties InfoBox.
2. Select the Design page.
3. Click on the check box beside Include in Multi Database Indexing.

The database can now be included in site searches.

Setting Up the Search Site Database

After you set up databases so they can be included in a site search, it is time to configure your site search.

1. Click on the Site Search database icon to select it.
2. Select Create | Search Scope Configuration. Notes displays the document shown in Figure 8.14.

Figure 8.14.
Define the scope of your Site Search and define the level of index you want to create.

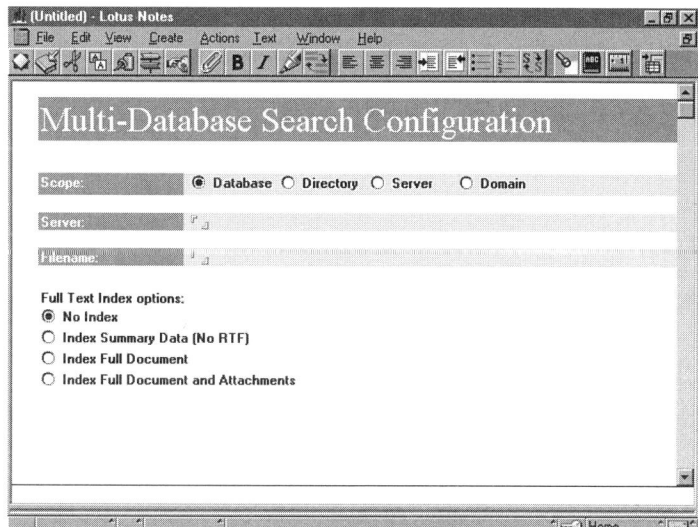

3. Select the scope of your search. Because you are working on a local workstation, the only options that will work for you are Database or Directory. Database lets you specify the databases that get included in the site search. Directory lets you name a Notes data directory in which all databases (all that have been set up as described above) are included in the search.
4. Define the full path and file name of the database you want to add to your site search, or the full path of the directory in which you have multiple databases that you want to include in your site search.
5. Select the full text option you want to set for your search site. Options include Index Summary Data, which indexes everything except for rich text fields; Index Full Document; or Index Full Document and Attachments, which will also index ASCII text in any embedded objects (as long as the objects are not compressed).

6. If you want to include all databases in a directory except for one, you can set the index option for that one database to No Index.
7. When done, press Esc to close and save the document, or select File | Close.
8. Open the Full Text page in the Database Properties InfoBox for the Site Search database.
9. Create a full text index for the Search Site database, or Update the index if one already exists.

Doing a Search on Your Site

To do a search on your site, open the Site Search database, and then do one of the following:

- [ ] Select Create | Search Form from the menu bar.
- [ ] Click on the Create Site Search if the database is already open.

Notes will display the Site Search Form, shown in Figure 8.15.

Figure 8.15.
The Site Search Form is used to perform a simple site search.

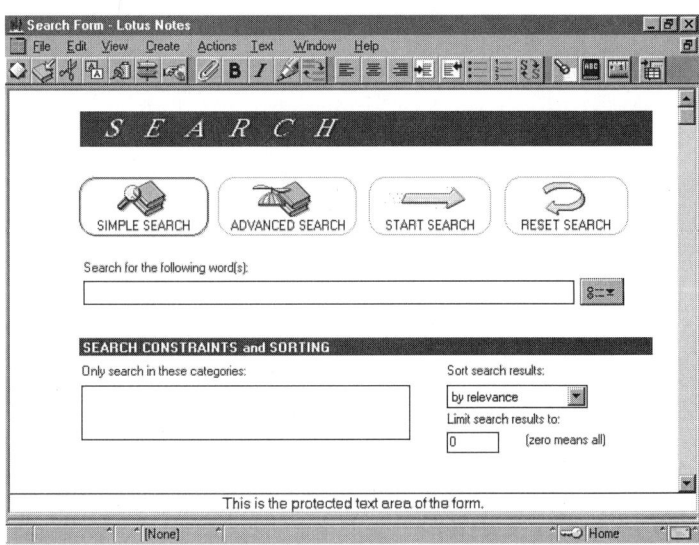

There are two types of Site Search available. The Simple Search is like using the Search Bar. Enter a word or phrase to search for, and click on Start Search to perform the search. You can also expand the search options by clicking on the Options button and defining constraints and sorting, just as you did with a regular full text search.

The Advanced Search is similar to the Search Builder, letting you create more complex searches by including multiple words with an Any or All option, and searching for documents by date. Other search options are not available because form-based searches require all searched databases to have the same forms.

Figure 8.16 shows part of the Advanced Search page.

Figure 8.16.
Advanced Search options are similar to the Search Builder options on a database full text search.

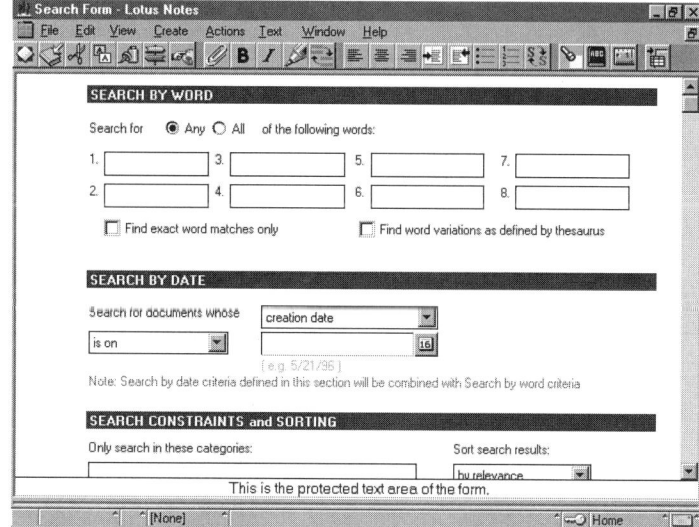

Not shown in Figure 8.16 are the Save Search and Open Search buttons at the bottom of the form. You can save a search for later use. If you want to run a saved search, click on the Open Search button, and run the saved search from there.

WARNING

The Site Search functions are similar to the full text searches you have already performed in databases. Play around with the new interface to see how it performs, but remember this: The full text indexes can take up a lot of disk space, so use them judiciously. Unless you really need them, save site searches for your Notes administrator to set up on the Domino server.

Summary

Notes is valuable for its workflow applications, and for facilitating communication. But right up there, in terms of corporate value, is the repository of knowledge that builds up in Notes databases over time. To realize that value, you have to be able to get at the data. The full text searching techniques you learned in today's lesson are the primary tools you as an end user can use to mine that data.

You were able to search without creating a full text index, but the searches were limited. You could locate a text string in a view or in a document. If you were an editor, you could find and replace data within a document. But you did not have the flexibility to build complex searches, and the searches that you could do were much slower than a full text search.

You learned to create an index for a database, and then used the Search Bar to perform a simple full text search. After that, you learned how to build complex searches using the Search Builder dialog box.

You then built on that same skill to create a Site Search database. That involved first setting up your Notes application databases so they could be included in a site search. Then you created your Site Search database and configured it so you could perform site searches. That makes it possible to integrate data from multiple databases in a single search.

Workshop

The Workshop section presents questions and answers, quiz questions to help you cement your new knowledge, and exercises to give you experience using what you have learned. Try to understand the questions and exercises before moving on to the next lesson. Answers are in Appendix A.

Q&A

Q I was going to set up full text indexes, but I don't want people to have access to any encrypted data. Is there any way I can ensure that the encrypted data is safe?

A Encrypted data is indexed by default. But you can turn off indexing of encrypted data when you define your full text index. If the data is not indexed, it cannot be found using a full text search.

Q I think my full text index is corrupted. Is there any way to repair it?

A Delete the old index, and create a new one.

Q I did a full text search on some information that I know is in the database, but the search is not finding it. What is wrong?

A The likely problem is that you need to update the index. Indexes on local systems are only updated when you go to the Full Text page in the Database Properties InfoBox and update them. Server-based indexes can be updated on a scheduled basis, or updated immediately whenever a new document is added. An index cannot find documents that have been added to the database since the index was last updated.

You may also be locating the document, but don't see any matches on search data because the data is in hidden fields.

Q I set up indexing for attachments, but the attachments and OLE objects don't seem to be indexed.

A Indexing only works for objects and attachments if they are not compressed. When you create an object, you have the option of compressing it to save space. This may be your situation.

Also, if you do find that a document with an attachment is selected, the search string will not be highlighted in the attachment.

Quiz

1. Can you do a full text search on a database that has not been indexed?
2. How can you tell if full text search results are ranked by relevance?
3. Where is a full text index stored?
4. If you save a search, can it be used by other users?
5. Can you build a full text index for a database that is stored on the Domino server?
6. True or False. If you set a Site Search to search all databases in a directory, you do not have to do anything to the databases to make them searchable.

Exercises

1. Create a full text index for your discussion database. Try different settings to see how much space the index takes up if you accept the default, if you make the index case sensitive, and if you index sentence and paragraph breaks.

2. Create a site search for all active databases on your desktop. After searching for documents, which form is used to display documents? Is it the same form, no matter which database the document is in?
3. Select one document. Try to locate the same document using a quick search, using Edit | Find, and using a full text search.
4. Create a complex search using the Search Builder. Save the search and close the database. Open the database again and run the saved search from the Options icon on the Search Bar.

Week 2

Day 9

Notes Mail Basics

Today, you will begin learning about Notes Mail, which is undoubtedly the most widely used Notes application. I say this at risk of making anyone think that Notes is nothing more than glorified e-mail, as some of the press pundits and Notes competitors have claimed in the past. Notes Mail enables a lot of the communication, collaboration, and coordination, but it is only a workgroup enabling technology. You have already seen how rich the Notes document environment can be. That richness is enhanced by the workflow capabilities when you harness Notes Mail.

Notes Mail goes far beyond the simple ability to send and receive mail. While today's lesson focuses on the fundamentals, you will also learn a little about the concepts that make Notes Mail so handy for workgroup computing.

Notes Mail Overview

Lotus Notes uses a store-forward mail paradigm. That means that e-mail is stored in a central repository until it is collected by the recipient's mailbox.

If you follow the basic path of an e-mail memo in Notes, it is very similar to (but much faster than) the U.S. Post Office.

1. You create a memo on your desktop and drop it in the mail by saving it.
2. If you are on a LAN or WAN, the mail goes immediately into a mailbox on the Domino server. If you are working on a workstation that is only occasionally connected, for example via a dial-up modem, then the memo is stored in a mailbox on your local workstation, and is transferred to the mailbox on the server as soon as you establish a connection.
3. The mail process on the server uses the Notes Public Address Book to determine where the addressee's mail is stored. If the addressee is in the same mail domain, the mail is forwarded to the addressee's home server and placed in the addressee's mail inbox. If the addressee is in another domain, the address book tells the server how to connect to the other domain. Whenever there is a scheduled connection to the other domain, the mail is forwarded to that domain for processing. High priority mail can be scheduled for immediate delivery.
4. Once mail is deposited in the addressee's mailbox, it sits in the inbox until he or she decides to open it.

If that process rings a bell, it should. Let me help you translate it. You write a letter, put it in an envelope, and drop it in the mailbox. If the mailbox is at the post office, it goes straight to the sorting room. If it is your local mailbox, the mail carrier picks it up during the daily mail route, and takes it to the post office for sorting. In the sorting room, improperly addressed mail is returned to the sender. If the mail is properly addressed to someone local, it goes directly into their mailbox, where they can pick it up at their convenience. If the mail is going to another ZIP code, it gets forwarded to another sorting room when the mail truck makes a scheduled run. There, it is put in the addressee's mailbox. If the mail is going overseas, it gets forwarded to another postal system. There is no way of knowing if the address is correct, so it is up to the other postal system to sort out the addressing.

Of course, it gets much fancier than that—certified mail, return receipt requested, fancy stationery, mass mailing, parcels—but the parallel with Notes Mail carries right through. Once mail is in the system, it gets delivered to the addressee as soon as possible, based on various parameters such as priority, scheduled delivery times, and so forth. When an addressee's mail file is available, mail delivery is virtually instantaneous.

A Tour of the Notes Mail Database

To help you get oriented, let's take a quick tour of the Notes Mail database. Your mail database should be on your Notes desktop. If you cannot find it, you can always open it by selecting Open Mail from the mail icon on the right side of the status bar at the bottom of

the screen. The database will usually have a file name that is the same as your username, for example, my mail file is DCHILD.NSF.

The default view of the Mail database is shown in Figure 9.1.

Figure 9.1.
The Notes Mail database has several unique views for managing mail.

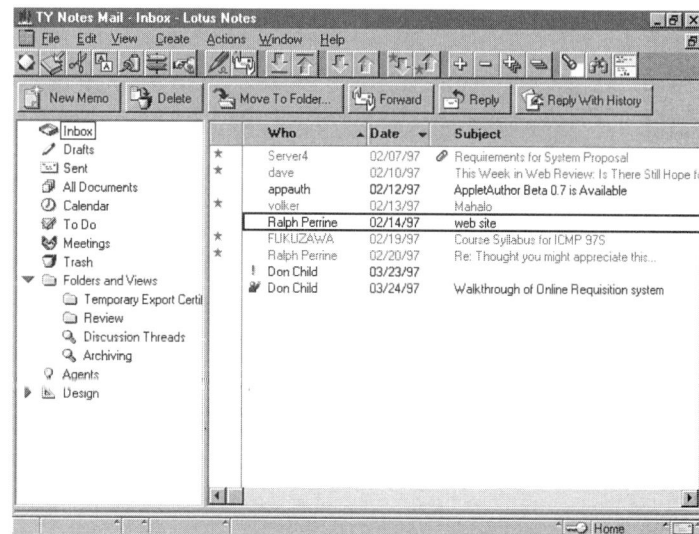

As with any Notes database, the default view has three panes: a navigation pane, a view pane, and a preview pane, which remains hidden until you show it by dragging the border or clicking on the Show Preview SmartIcon.

The database opens up to your Inbox, which is a folder that holds incoming mail until you decide what you want to do with it. There are several other views and folders, most of them unique to the Notes Mail database. They are the following:

- *Inbox.* This folder holds incoming mail until you decide what to do with it.
- *Drafts.* This view holds various types of mail documents that you created and saved, but have not yet sent.
- *Sent.* This view holds various types of mail documents that you send to others. Saving sent documents is optional.
- *All Documents.* This view is a collection of all documents in the various views and folders.
- *Calendar.* The calendar is a special view used for the mail database's built-in Calendaring and Scheduling (C&S) functions, which are described on Day 11.
- *To Do.* This view is a part of the C&S function. It keeps track of tasks that you have to perform or that you can assign to others.

- *Meetings.* This view is part of the C&S function, and is used for interactively scheduling meetings with others in your organization.
- *Trash.* This folder holds documents that have been marked for deletion, and provides a single location for checking on documents before they are irretrievably deleted.
- *Discussion Threads.* This view organizes documents so that Reply documents are grouped with the memo documents to which they are responding. This makes it easier to follow threads when you have a complex exchange of documents discussing a topic.
- *Archiving.* This view is used to group documents that will be archived out of the mail database based on archive parameters you have defined. You can review documents before they are archived to another database and deleted from your mail file.

The available folders will vary depending on whether you have created folders, and what you have created. For example, if you create a temporary export certificate, a Temporary Export Certificate folder is automatically created on your desktop.

You will see how to use these views to your advantage as you move through the next three lessons.

Sending an E-Mail Message

Although Notes Mail is at the heart of most workflow activities, sending a basic e-mail message is what most people think of when you talk about e-mail. In Notes, the basic e-mail message uses the memo form.

If your mail file is set up correctly—as a local file when you are working remotely, or on the server when you are working on a LAN—you can create a memo from anywhere within Notes. You can create a memo from anywhere within Notes in any of the following ways:

- Select Create Memo from the mail icon on the status bar.
- Select Create | Mail | Memo from the menu bar. If you have the Mail database highlighted or open, the menu option is just Create | Memo.
- Press Ctrl+M (hold down the Ctrl key while pressing M).
- If the mail database is already open and you are in any view besides a Calendaring and Scheduling view, click on the New Memo button on the Action bar.

Notes displays the Memo form shown in Figure 9.2.

Figure 9.2.
The Memo form is used to create a basic e-mail message.

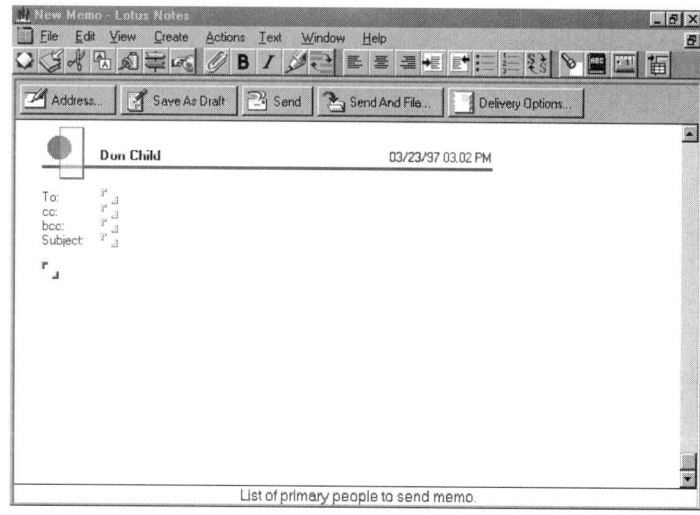

This basic form has only five fields. The first three fields are used to address the memo to one or more individuals. One field provides the subject of the memo. This subject appears in views so the receiver will know what to expect when they open the memo. The final field is a Rich Text field in which you create the body of your message, including attachments and graphics...everything you've already learned about Rich Text fields.

Addressing an E-Mail Memo

There are three fields used for addressing a memo.

- ☐ The To: field identifies the primary recipient of the memo, and is a required field.
- ☐ The cc: field is an optional field for sending a "carbon copy" of the memo to individuals other than the primary addressee.
- ☐ The bcc: field is used to address the memo as a "blind carbon copy." People addressed in this field will receive the memo, but other recipients will not see their name on the memo.

In each of these fields, names have to be entered in a way that Notes recognizes them, but this is made easy for you. Names are looked up in the Public Address Book or in your Personal Address Book, and converted to addresses that Notes recognizes. Therefore, all you usually have to do is type enough of a person's name that Notes can recognize it as a unique name, and Notes will type ahead, finishing the name for you. Lotus calls this *recipient name type-ahead*.

If you want to address a memo to person whose name is not in one of the address books, you have to spell out their full e-mail address. The Notes address books are examined later in today's lesson.

An alternative way to address a memo is to look up names from a Notes address book and have them added to any of the address fields automatically. If you have been following along through all of the lessons in this book, then you are already familiar with looking up names from an address book. Addressing a memo is similar. You do the following:

1. Click on the Address button. Notes displays the Mail Address dialog box shown in Figure 9.3.

Figure 9.3.
Enter addresses for a memo using the Mail Address dialog box.

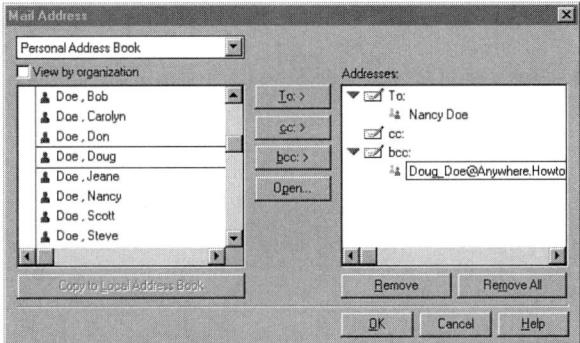

2. Select the address book you want to look in.
3. Highlight the name you want to add to one of the address fields.
4. Click on the To:>, cc:>, or bcc:> button to add the selected name(s) to one of the address fields on the right side of the dialog box.
5. If you want to remove a name from an address field, highlight the name and click on the Remove button.
6. When you have selected all the people to which you want to address the memo, click on the OK button to copy the names to the memo.

NOTE  You can also address memos to predefined groups, such as a project team. A copy of the memo will be addressed to each member of the group.

Completing Your Memo

After addressing your memo, enter a subject for the memo. The subject is a short description of what the memo contains. The contents of the Subject field are displayed in views.

Next, you create the body of your memo. Because this is a Rich Text field, you can import text, paste in graphics, link objects, create buttons, create sections, and so forth.

Figure 9.4 shows a completed memo ready to send. There is a primary addressee in the To: field (required) and another person addressed in the optional bcc: field. When Nancy and Doug Doe receive this memo, they will see "Can you help me with my memory upgrade?" in the view.

Figure 9.4.
A completed mail memo ready to be sent.

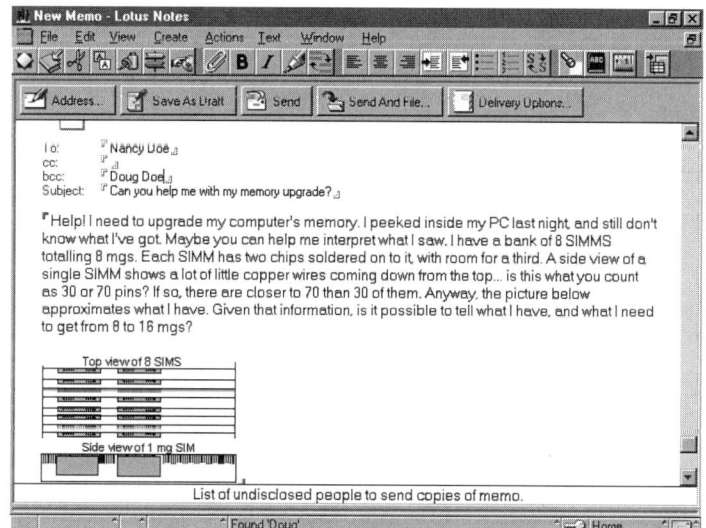

Sending the Memo

You have three options for sending the memo that are available from buttons on the Action Bar:

- *Save As Draft.* When you select this option, the memo is saved in the Drafts folder in your mail database, but the memo is not sent. You can open the memo at a later time and edit it before sending it.

- *Send.* When you click on Send, the memo is sent immediately. Whether the mail gets saved depends on the Mail options you set up in the User Preferences dialog box, described later in this chapter.
- *Send And File.* If you select this option, the memo will be sent immediately and saved based on your Mail options, but you will also be presented with a list of available folders in your mail database, as shown in Figure 9.5. Click on a folder to select it, or create a new folder by clicking on the Create New Folder button. Creating a folder is identical to the process you learned on Day 7.

Figure 9.5.
Save outgoing mail in folders within your Mail database.

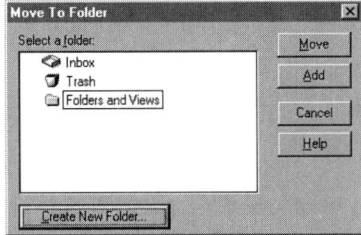

Selecting Delivery Options

Another button on the Action Bar lets you select delivery options for your memo. Delivery options determine how your memo is handled when it is delivered to the addressee.

NOTE When you send mail to users with mail systems that are outside of Notes, the memo loses many of its formatting features. What does get through the SMTP gateway from Notes is primarily text and file attachments. Therefore, most of the enhancements to Notes Mail such as the Delivery Options are lost, or at best unpredictable. One of the enhancements you can expect in future releases of Notes is a universal mail client based on emerging e-mail standards.

If you want to set delivery options, they must be set before you send the memo. To set delivery options, click on the Delivery Options button. The Delivery Options dialog box, shown in Figure 9.6, looks like an envelope. You fill out the fields on the envelope to define delivery options.

Figure 9.6.
The Delivery Options dialog box lets you determine how your memo gets delivered.

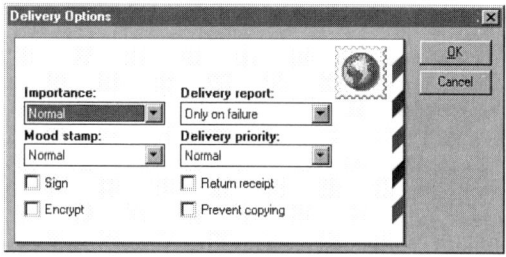

This is what the fields on the Delivery Options envelope mean:

- *Importance.* You can set an importance marker of high, normal, or low. Notes Mail uses icons to indicate when mail is of high or low importance. Normal mail does not have an icon associated with it.

> **NOTE** These Importance icons are part of the Notes view. They are not available with Internet mail or foreign mail systems.

- *Delivery Report.* By default, you only hear about e-mail that fails to get through to the addressee. You can also opt to receive a delivery report as soon as the memo is put in the addressee's mailbox, or you can opt to receive a report from every point on the delivery path between your Domino server and the user's mail server. You can also opt to have no notification, success or failure. Delivery Reports do not work beyond the SMTP server that connects to outside mail systems.

- *Mood Stamp.* You can personalize your memo by putting a mood stamp on it. After the memo is saved and opened for reading, the mood stamp will be displayed at the top of the Body field. Mood stamps can add personality and indicate the purpose of the memo for other users of Notes Mail. Mood Stamps include Personal, Confidential, Thank You, Flame, and Question stamps.

- *Delivery Priority.* You can send your memo to other Notes Mail users as normal, high, or low priority mail. Normal mail is delivered immediately to people who are connected to your network, but is sent during the next scheduled delivery to people outside of your network. High priority mail is sent immediately, regardless of scheduled connections. Low priority mail is only sent when there is a delivery scheduled during inexpensive connection times in the middle of the night.

You can also select a variety of options by clicking on check boxes:

- ☐ *Sign.* If you select this option, Notes attaches your digital signature to the message. This digital signature provides proof that you, or at least somebody using your Notes user ID, created the memo.
- ☐ *Return Receipt.* If you select this option, Notes generates a memo to you at the moment the addressee opens your memo. That way, you know that the user not only received but actually opened your memo to read it. Again, this works only for Notes Mail users.

TIP Some users do not appreciate you generating out-going e-mail on their mail system, so use your discretion when using return receipts. Be sensitive to the possible reactions of those you send mail to. They do not want to feel mistrusted by you.

- ☐ *Encrypt.* If you elect to encrypt this memo, then the only person who will be able to read it is the person to whom it is addressed.
- ☐ *Prevent Copying.* If you select this option, the recipient cannot copy the data in the memo electronically. This prevents them from forwarding the memo to others if they are using Notes Mail. Once you send the memo to someone outside of the Notes environment, you lose the protection of this feature.

NOTE Each of these options increases the size of the file and the amount of processing needed by the system to handle the memo.

Making Delivery Options Applicable to All Outgoing Mail

The delivery options that you select for an individual can also be applied to all outgoing mail. You can set universal mail delivery options in the User Preferences dialog box. To set these options, select File | Tools | User Preferences, and click on the Mail icon. This displays the page shown in Figure 9.7.

Figure 9.7.
Set delivery options for all outgoing mail in the User Preferences dialog box.

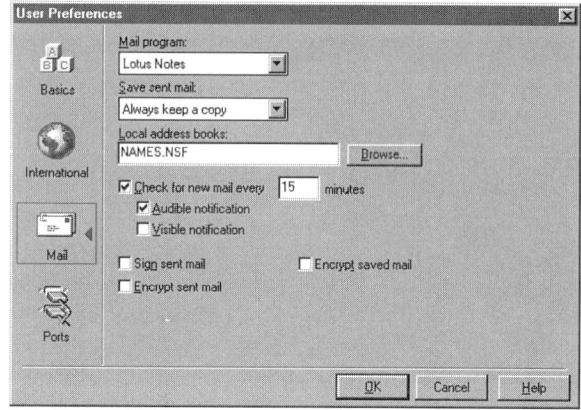

In this dialog box, you can tell Notes to automatically save all sent mail, or to prompt you to decide whether to save it. You can also set the delivery options to sign all sent mail and to encrypt all sent mail. In addition to these options, which were just explained, you also have these options:

- *Mail Program.* If you have cc:Mail or another VIM-based mail program installed, you can select another mail system besides Notes Mail.
- *Local Address Books.* You can set up multiple local address books, and tell Notes which ones to search when looking for e-mail addresses.
- *Check For New Mail...* You can tell Notes how often to poll your mailbox on the Domino server to see if you have any new mail. If you have new mail, you can have Notes sound a chime to inform you, or you can select a visible notification. The visible notification is a message box that pops up on the screen when you have new mail. When Notes polls the mailbox, a message is displayed on the status bar by default.
- *Encrypt Saved Mail.* This option causes all mail that you send and save, including drafts that are stored in your mail database, to be stored in encrypted format. Even if someone were able to obtain a copy of your saved mail, they could not read it without your user ID and password.

You can now create a simple mail memo, and control how the memo is sent. Now let's look at how to handle your incoming mail.

Opening and Reading Your Mail

When you open your mailbox, you will see your incoming mail in your Inbox folder. That is your default view, if you have mail waiting. Otherwise, you see whatever view you were in when you last closed your mail database. For now, let's look at the Inbox, as shown in Figure 9.8.

Figure 9.8.
The Inbox holds all your incoming mail until you place it in other folders.

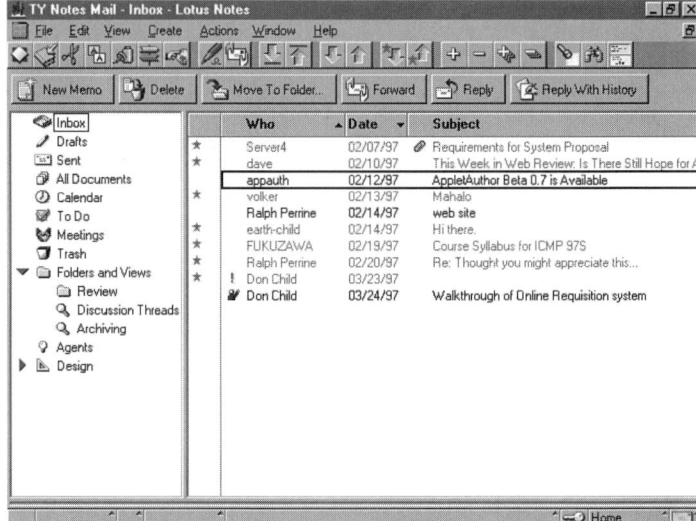

In this folder, you can see several icons that indicate what type of mail you are receiving. For example, the mail from Server4 contains an attached file. You can tell because there is a paper clip indicating an attachment. The document sent from Ralph Perrine (a fellow author who contributed to *Lotus Notes and Domino Server 4.5 Unleashed*) on February 20 is a response to another document, because the document title starts with a "Re:". The document from me was sent high priority, because it has an exclamation point in front of it. And, of course, you can see that a couple of the documents have been read, but they remain in the Inbox folder.

You can read these documents just like any Notes document. But what is important is how you can respond to a document, and how you can file it away for future reference.

For example, I want to refer to the document about the AppletAuthor later, so I'm going to move it to the private "Review" folder that I created. There, it will be easier to locate. I could drag it and drop it on the folder, or I could click on the Move To Folder... button to display the dialog box shown in Figure 9.9.

Figure 9.9.
Moving a memo from the Inbox to a folder is one way to manage documents in the mail database.

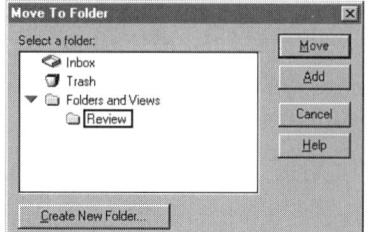

After the document is moved to another folder, it disappears from the Inbox.

You can mark a document for deletion from the mail database by clicking on the Delete button. Alternatively, you can move the document to the Trash folder, or you can press the Delete key to mark it for deletion.

The other buttons provide shortcuts for creating new memos.

Forwarding a Document

You can forward a document by highlighting the document and clicking on the Forward button. This is something you can actually do from anywhere within Notes with any Notes document by selecting Actions | Forward from the menu bar. But for now, we will forward a mail memo.

NOTE

> You cannot forward mail if the delivery option Prevent Copying is set.

When you forward a document, the original document is embedded in the body of a new memo, and it is given the same subject as the original memo. You can address the new document as you would address any memo. You can change the subject to one of your own choosing, and you can add your own comments in the body field before forwarding the document. An example of a forwarded document is shown in Figure 9.10.

Figure 9.10.
A forwarded document is embedded in the body of an e-mail memo.

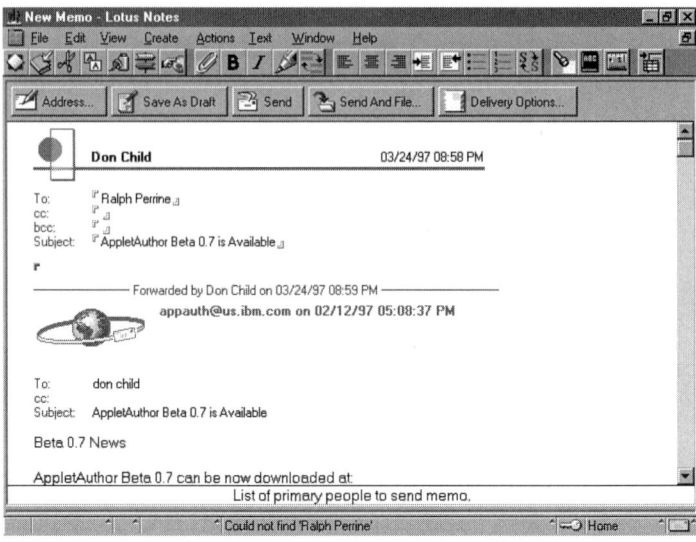

Replying to a Memo and Replying with History

You can reply to any memo by highlighting the document and clicking on the Reply button. The result is a memo addressed to the person who sent the memo, with the document subject defaulted to "Re:", plus the subject of the original document.

If you have ever participated in Internet mailing lists, you may have noticed that replies can contain an entire history of documents and responses. In Notes, you can do the same thing by creating a Reply with History.

A Reply with History is created by highlighting the document and clicking on the Reply with History button. The document is just like an e-mail memo, with one exception: You can click on the Reply to All button so that your response gets sent to anyone whose name appeared in the To: or cc: fields, in addition to being addressed to the sender of the original document.

> **TIP**
>
> This same Reply to All is also available when you create a Reply document.

Figure 9.11 shows a Reply with History document. The Reply to All button was selected in this example to illustrate how the addressing fields are filled out. Note that the original memo had a name in the bcc: field, but this person's name was not put into any of the address fields on the reply. Therefore, the Reply to All will not go to the bcc: person or persons, because their name is not in any of the addressing fields.

Figure 9.11.
A Reply with History can be sent to everyone addressed in the original memo.

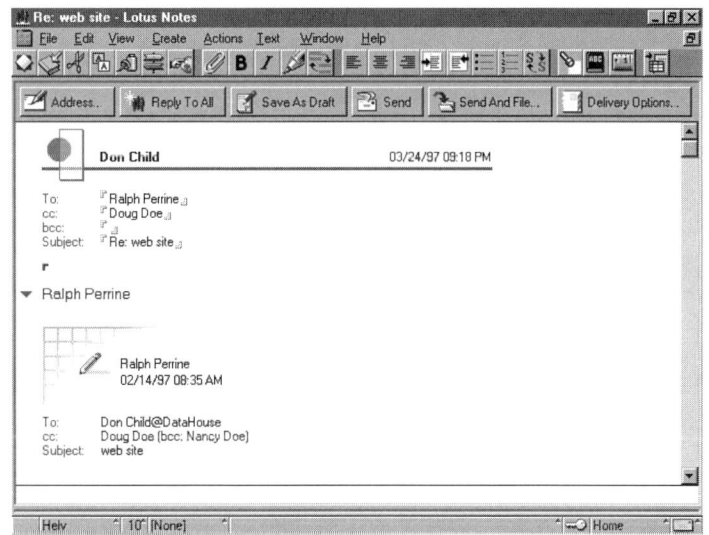

Creating Special Mail Documents

There are other mail documents that you can create aside from a regular mail memo and replies. Two of these—Task and Calendar Entry—are covered on Day 11. The other special document types are used for various types of workflow and communication, and are found under the Create | Special menu in the Mail database. Each document type is described below.

Creating Mail Bookmarks

When you learned to work with Rich Text fields, one of the objects that you could embed was a DocLink. If you want to make sure that your colleagues see a document that is in a shared database, you can send them a DocLink to the document. The question is, how do you do that efficiently?

You can already copy the document as a link, and then open your mail database, create a memo, and paste the DocLink into the rich Text field. But there is a quicker way to do it.

Mail is an option on the Create menu no matter where you are within Notes. When you find a document that you want to share with others, select Create | Mail | Special | Bookmark from the menu bar. All you have to do is address the Bookmark to your colleagues, and send it. Notes puts in the title of the document, creates a link to the document, and includes a message to the recipient. A Bookmark document is illustrated in Figure 9.12.

Figure 9.12.
Create a Bookmark document as a shortcut to send DocLinks to your fellow workers.

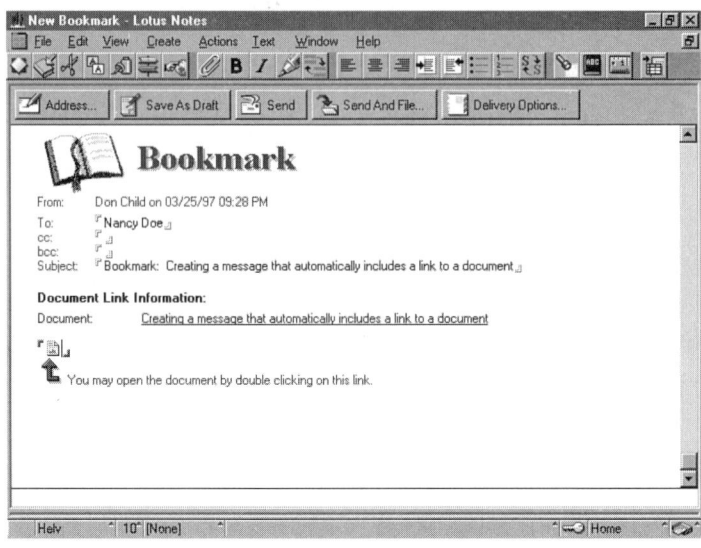

NOTE You should only send Bookmarks that link to documents if the recipient has access to the database that holds the linked document. If he or she does not have access, the link will not work.

Creating Phone Messages

Phone messages are simple memos with a specific purpose: to send a message regarding a contact with someone outside the workgroup. The phone message, like any Notes memo, must have a To: field so Notes knows who to send the message to. There are a couple of text fields to identify the person who called or otherwise left a message. And further down the screen, scrolled out of sight in Figure 9.13, there is a Rich Text field in which you can enter a more detailed message.

Creating Serial Route Memos

If you want a memo to go to several individuals in a particular order, you can send a Serial Route memo. Simply enter the name of individual addressees, with each name separated by a comma.

When you are done creating the memo, click on Send to Next Person to route the memo to the first person on the list of names in the Route to: field. An example of a Serial Route Memo is shown in Figure 9.14.

Figure 9.13.
The Phone Message lets you use Notes to take a message and forward it to a colleague's mailbox.

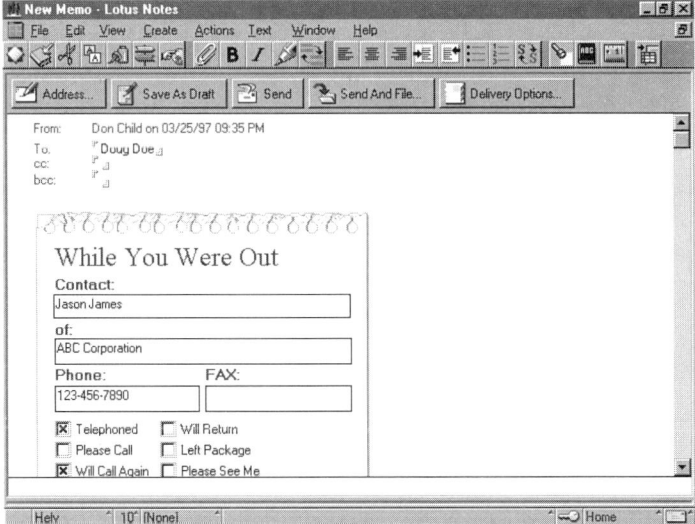

Figure 9.14.
A Serial Route Memo is sent to a list of individuals one person at a time.

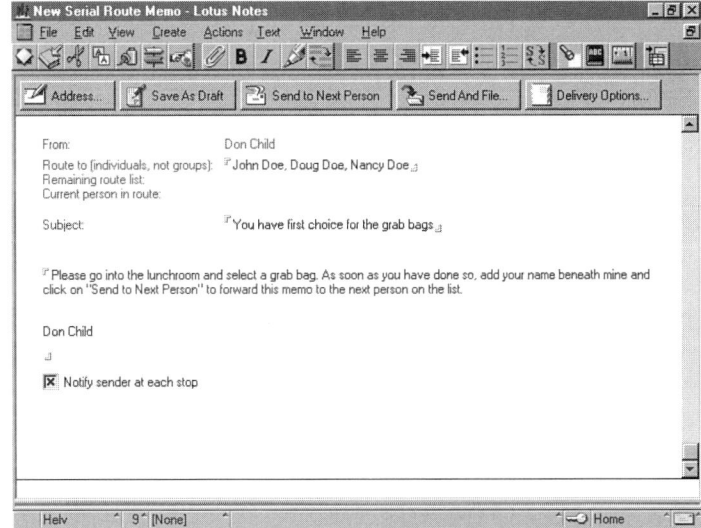

When an individual receives the memo, there are a couple of things he can do. He can add a message if he wants to, and then he can click on Send to Next Person to forward the memo to the next person. Saving the memo does not automatically send it, as it does with a regular memo. The memo does list who has it at the current moment, and the names of the people remaining on the Route to: list.

NOTE If a recipient does not click on Send to Next Person, then this "chain e-mail" is broken. For that reason, you might want to check the Notify Sender at Each Stop check box. When you check this option, Notes automatically generates an e-mail to you whenever anyone on the list sends the memo to the next person on the list. If the memo does not get forwarded within a reasonable amount of time (for example, someone on the list might be out of the office), you can send another copy of the memo to the individuals who have not yet received it.

Create a Temporary Export Certificate

This topic, creating a temporary export certificate, could just as well be listed under Notes Security or under Mobile Notes, but it is found on the Mail | Special menu. If you have Notes on your computer and you are travelling overseas, this section is a must-read.

The RSA encryption security used by Notes is considered a restricted "weapon" by the United States government. If you have a North American Notes license, you need a temporary export certificate to take Notes overseas.

There are various levels of encryption security, with the levels based on the number of bits used in mathematical computations during encryption and decryption. Within North America, Notes uses up to 512-bit encryption, depending on the version of Notes you are using, and it changes all the time. If you are interested in the topic, there is a Web page (**http://www.crypto.com**) that tracks changes in government policy regarding encryption technology. Until very recently, the strongest encryption allowed on software exported from the U.S. was 40 bits, with stronger security available if additional bits are available to the U.S. government. Notes was providing 64-bit encryption at last report. This has been increased in some instances, and restrictions may eventually be dropped altogether, but in the meantime, the law's the law.

NOTE Even 64-bit (40 + 24) encryption is virtually unbreakable unless you have a supercomputer. For all but extremely sensitive data, the question of how many bits your encryption uses is pretty much irrelevant. If it's encrypted, the data is not going to be stolen as it is communicated between your computer and your coworker's computer, even if your coworker is on the other side of the world.

How do you get an export certificate? You do not have to go to a Federal building and stand in line. Instead, you can create the certificate within Notes, and print it out. Carry the printed certificate with you until you return to the United States.

To create the temporary export certificate:

1. Select Create | Special | Temporary Export Certificate from within Notes Mail, or Create | Mail | Special | Temporary Export Certificate from elsewhere within Notes.
2. If your Notes username is not your legal name, enter your full legal name as it appears on your passport.
3. Enter the name of the company you work for.
4. Enter the names of the countries to which you will be travelling.
5. If you have any additional Notes versions or other encryption products, enter their names and versions.
6. Enter the departure and return dates of your travels.
7. Read the document and click on the check box indicating that you accept the terms described on the certificate.
8. Print and save the certificate, and carry it with you while travelling.

The certificate is shown in Figure 9.15.

Figure 9.15.
Fill out and print the temporary export certificate when travelling overseas with a North American licensed version of Notes.

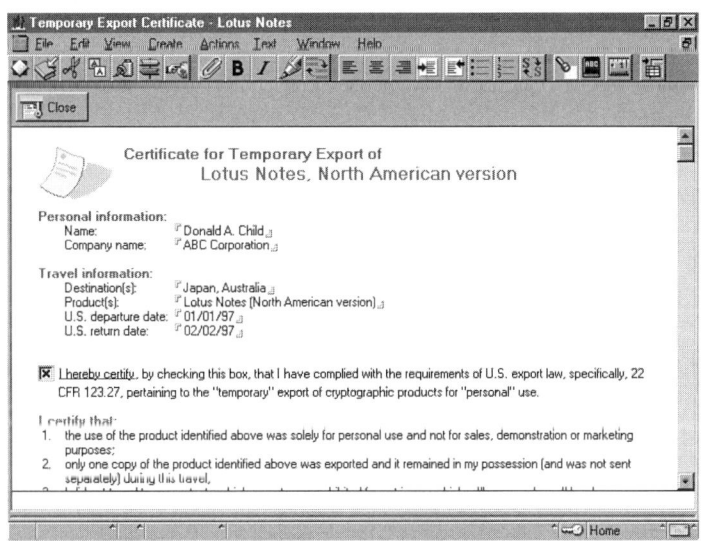

WARNING

> Encryption policies may also vary within different countries. For example, France does not allow 64-bit encryption. Therefore Lotus was required to develop a special French version of Notes with less robust encryption security. If you are travelling overseas, it is always advisable to check to see if there are any restrictions in your destination country.

Creating a Memo for the Database Manager

If you are working with a Notes database and need to communicate with the database manager, for example you need to have your security role modified, you can address a memo to the manager by selecting Create | Mail | Special | Memo to Database Manager. You can type your message in the memo form and send it to the database manager without worrying about how to address the memo.

The alternative is to create a regular memo after you look at the Database ACL to determine who the manager is, and then look up the manager's e-mail address in the Public Address Book.

Working with Mail Views

You have now seen most of the document types you can create in Notes Mail. While demonstrating these various types of memos, I have been building up a lot of documents in my All Documents view. This view shows all documents in the mail database, regardless of whether the documents are ones I created and saved as drafts, ones that are in my Trash folder, or new documents in my Inbox that have not yet been moved to other folders.

Figure 9.16 shows the All Documents view with a number of different document types, indicated by icons.

In Figure 9.16, you can see the following types of documents as they show up in views:

- Memos sent by other Notes users.
- Replies sent by others Notes users.
- Normal, High, and Low Priority documents that have been sent to other users.
- A high priority memo that was received in the Inbox.
- A reminder and an appointment. (Calendaring functions are discussed on Day 11.)
- Draft documents that have not been sent.
- A temporary export certificate.

Figure 9.16.
The All Documents view shows several document types.

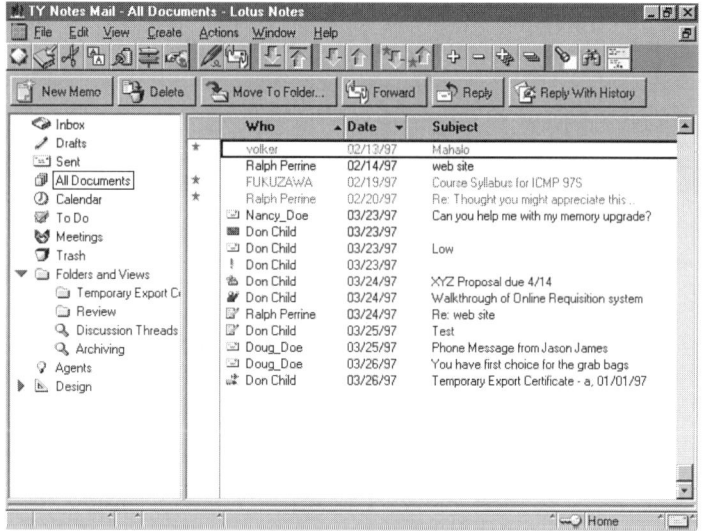

Using the Views and Folders

The first several views in the navigation pane are available to all Notes Mail users. The views and folders at the bottom of the pane may vary depending on how you set up and use your mail system.

Using the Discussion Threads View

The Discussion Threads view is a special view that keeps track of main documents and responses related to the main document. Using this view, you can follow an entire discussion regardless of who responded or when they responded to a document. Without this view, you would have to depend on "Re:" document titles to give you a clue about which document was being referred to. This is the Notes Mail database equivalent of a Discussion database.

NOTE

If you follow any Internet discussion groups, you may understand better what a discussion thread is. In a non-threaded discussion, new documents are always displayed at the top of the list. If you see a new response document at the top of the list, you might have to scroll down through several other documents to find the subject addressed by the response. A threaded discussion, on the other hand, links all responses to the subject document that is being addressed. In that way, you can follow a discussion regardless of the order in which documents were created.

The Discussion Threads view contains all documents in the database. If there is no discussion associated with a document, it still appears in the view as a Main document. Responses (replies) and Response to Responses appear indented beneath the document to which they replied.

An example of the Discussion Threads view is shown in Figure 9.17.

Figure 9.17.
The Discussion Threads view associates main response documents with the documents to which they reply.

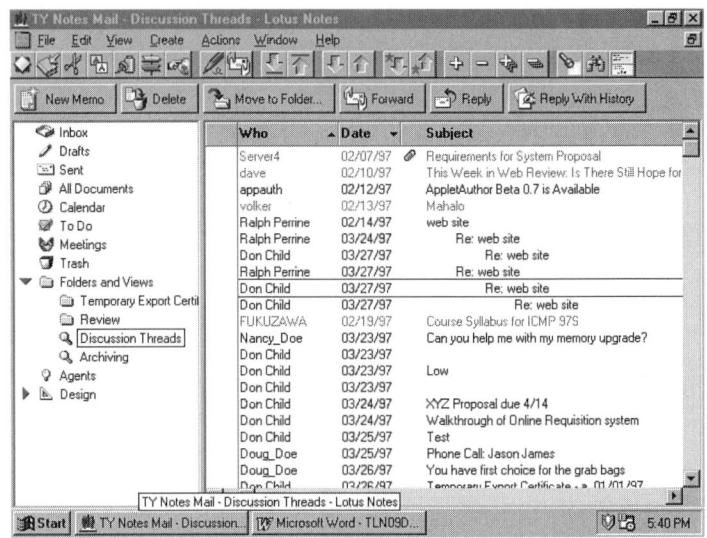

Archiving Documents

If you use your mail file to keep track of old documents, events, or discussions, then the file will eventually get very large. And unless you have a very generous file storage system on your Notes server, you are likely to have the Notes administrator sending you messages asking you to please reduce the size of your mail file.

NOTE The Notes administrator can set up your mail so it has a maximum file size, in which case you will be notified automatically whenever the database gets too large.

When you archive a document, it is copied to another database on your local hard drive or on a file server, and is removed from your mail file. You can set Notes up to archive documents automatically when they meet certain criteria, or you can archive documents manually. In either case, you must first set up the archive database.

Creating an Archive Database

To create an archive database, navigate to the Archive view in the Mail database. Tip: An application developer can also set up an archive database for other Notes databases by copying the Archive view and its associated actions to the database in which you want to set up archiving.

Click on the Setup Archive button on the Action Bar at the top of the view. Notes displays the Archive Profile, shown in Figure 9.18. In this Archive Profile, you can select the options for your archive database.

Figure 9.18.
Define how documents are archived by creating an Archive Profile.

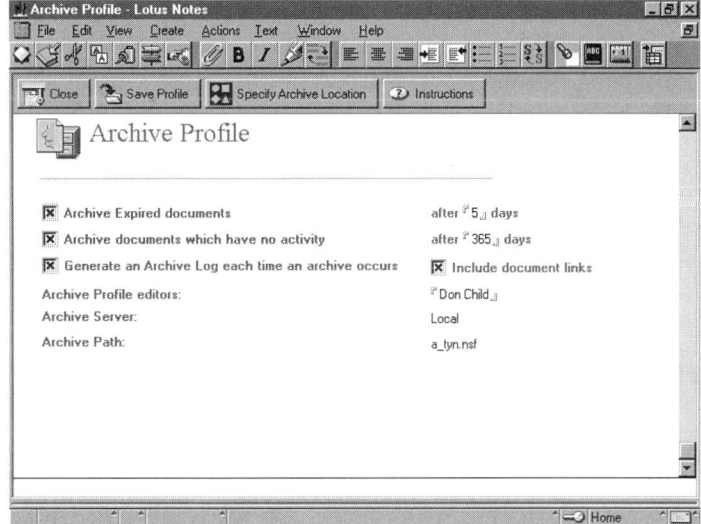

The options in this document include:

- *Archive Expired Documents.* You can choose this option if you want Notes to wait for a designated number of days before archiving documents that have expired. Later, you will learn how to set an expiration date on a memo, after which time the document is no longer needed in the database.
- *Archive Documents Which Have no Activity.* You can specify the number of days of inactivity, after which mail is archived automatically if you have schedule archiving enabled.
- *Generate an Archive Log Each Time an Archive Occurs.* If you select this option, Notes will generate a log every time documents are archived. The log is in the form of a memo in your database, with DocLinks to the archived documents in your archive database.

- *Archive Profile Editors.* After you save the profile, your name is inserted as the editor. You can allow others to edit your archive profile by entering their names in this field.
- *Specify the Archive Location.* You can specify the server and the path to the archive database to which documents will be archived. The archive database will be created automatically when you save your Archive Profile. To specify the location and server, click on Specify Archive Location at the top of the Archive Profile.

NOTE The archive database should normally be on a server. However, if your database is local (as it would be for mobile users), then the archive database must also be local.

When creating an archive database, you normally only have to specify the server and the file name for the database. Notes assumes the default Notes data directory for the database unless you enter an explicit path for the database.

You can also create a new archive to replace an old archive. Figure 9.19 shows the dialog box for creating a new archive database.

Figure 9.19.
Define the directory and file name for a new archive database.

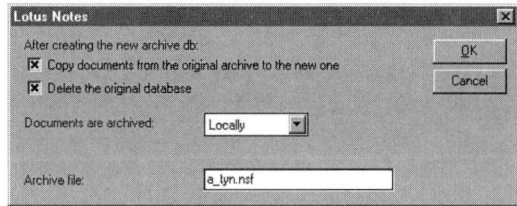

How to Archive Documents

You can archive documents manually or on a scheduled basis.

If you want to archive documents on a scheduled basis, you must first click on the Enable Scheduled Archiving button. Documents will then be archived as soon as they pass the expiration date, for example five days after they have been inactive for 364 days.

To give you a better idea, here is what happens to a document. After 365 days (or whatever period you designate), the document is moved into the Archive view. You then have a waiting period during which you can reactivate a document, if you want it to remain in your database. After the waiting period, the document is copied to the archive database, and then deleted from your regular mail database.

If you want to archive documents manually, select the documents in any view in your mail database. After you highlight the documents you want to archive, select Actions | Mail Tools | Archive Selected Documents from the menu bar. The documents will be archived immediately.

With either technique, an archive log document, as shown in Figure 9.20, is added to your Archive view if you selected the Archive Log option in your Archive Profile.

Figure 9.20.
Archived documents are listed with DocLinks in an Archive Log document.

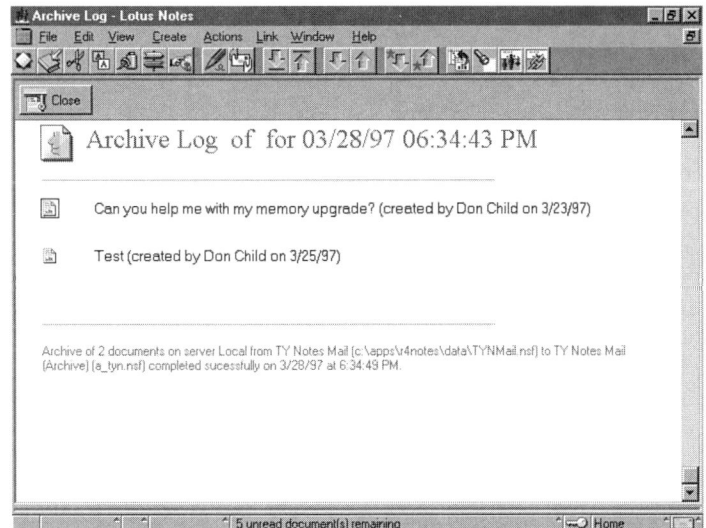

Reading Archived Documents

You can read documents that have been archived by clicking on a DocLink in an Archive Log document. You can also open the archive database (which uses the same mail template as your Notes Mail database) and read the documents as you would read any Notes document.

If you want to return a document to your regular Mail database from the archive database, follow these steps:

1. Highlight the document in the archive database.
2. Select Edit | Cut from the menu bar.
3. Open the Mail database.
4. Select Edit | Paste from the menu bar.

The document will now be back in your Mail database.

Setting Expiration Dates on Documents

Setting the expiration date on a document was not covered earlier when you were learning to create memos. If you are using an archive for your mail, the expiration date can be a handy tool. The expiration date tells a user that this mail memo is not important after the expiration date, so it can be archived immediately.

NOTE As with mail options described earlier, this functionality is liable to be lost if you are sending mail to someone who does not use Notes Mail.

When creating a document, you can set an expiration date by selecting Actions | Special Options... from the menu bar. Notes displays the Special Options dialog box shown in Figure 9.21.

Figure 9.21.
Set the expiration date for a document in the Special Options dialog box.

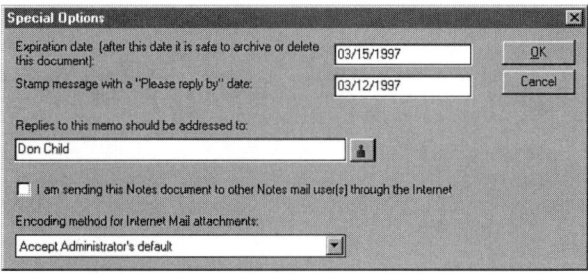

In this dialog box, you can do the following:

- To set an expiration date, type the date after which the memo is no longer needed in the Expiration date field.
- To display a "Please reply by" date on the memo when a person opens it, enter the date in the Please Reply By field.
- To route replies to another individual, enter the name of the individual in the Replies ... Should be Addressed to field.
- To send the memo to other Notes users via the Internet, click on "I am sending this Notes document...." Ordinarily, Notes documents lose much of their formatting if they are sent over the Internet. Checking this ensures that the document retains its formatting.
- Select an encoding method for attachments if you are mailing them to people who use non-Notes mail. You can accept your system's default, but if people have special requirements, you can specify MIME (base 64), UUEncoding, or Quoted Printable attachments.

Summary

Today you learned the basics of Notes Mail. You learned how to create and send a memo, and how to work with mail that was sent to you. Specifically, you learned how to respond to a document, and how to forward a copy of the document to which you are responding.

The Mail database has several other types of documents that are used for different purposes, such as a phone message, a message to a database manager, and a message that forwards any document in any Notes database.

You learned how to use views to see related documents, and how to use folders to make it easier to manage the documents in your Inbox.

You can work with Notes Mail from anywhere within Notes, accessing your Inbox or your mail database views from the mail icon on the status bar. You can create e-mail memos from the Create | Mail menu, or by pressing Ctrl+M at any time.

In tomorrow's lesson, you will learn several advanced mail techniques, including how to customize your mail forms, and you will learn more about addressing memos using the Public and Private Address Books. You will also learn how Notes can be used with non-Notes e-mail packages.

Workshop

The Workshop section presents questions and answers, quiz questions to help you cement your new knowledge, and exercises to give you experience using what you have learned. Try to understand the questions and exercises before moving on to the next lesson. Answers are in Appendix A.

Q&A

Q I send mail to people exactly the way described, but they say they never get it. Where does it go, if they don't get it?

A If you are working on a mobile Notes workstation, the mail goes into an Outgoing Mailbox. This mail gets forwarded to a Domino server for delivery when you dial in to the server. If you do not communicate with the server, the mail will simply accumulate in the Outgoing Mailbox. If the mail goes to the server but cannot be delivered from there, you can set your mail options (using File | Tools | User Preference) to notify you of errors. Otherwise, work with your Notes administrator to trace your mail.

Q I look at the mail in my Inbox folder, but it just keeps piling up. It never empties after I read it.

A If you want to hold only new incoming mail, you must dispose of mail in the Inbox by moving it to another folder. If you do not move it to a folder or delete it, it remains in your Inbox.

Q Our Notes administrator said that we use a shared object store. What is that, and how does it affect my mail?

A The shared object store holds the contents of the Body field whenever mail is addressed to more than one individual on a Domino server. A single copy of the body is held in the shared object store, and individuals receive a memo that actually only contains a pointer to this shared store. When you open your mail, you see the shared object, but it is exactly as if all of the data were in your own mail file.

This will not affect the way you use mail unless you are a mobile Notes user, or you move your mail to a new home on another Domino server. Then you have to copy all the shared objects into your mail database so you can still access them. Talk to your Notes administrator if you are having any problems with a mail database that uses a shared object store.

Quiz

1. Can you create a memo and save it to be mailed at a later time?
2. How do you send a reply to several people?
3. Can you carry a laptop computer overseas if it has the North American version of Notes on it?
4. If you archive documents and they get deleted from your Notes Mail, can you get the documents back?
5. Can you archive documents in other databases besides Notes Mail?
6. If you open up a document that is serially routed, does the document get sent to the next person when you are through reading the document?

Exercises

1. Address a memo to three of your colleagues using the "To:", "cc:", and "bcc:" fields. Ask them to respond to your memo, then compare their responses. Locate them in the Discussion Threads view.
2. Create an archive database for your Notes Mail so that documents are automatically archived after two months of inactivity.

Week 2

Day 10

Notes Mail Advanced Features

Yesterday, you learned the basics of Notes Mail: how to create memos and how to read mail and use views. In this day, you extend that knowledge by learning how to customize your Notes Mail using stationery and letterhead templates, how to delegate the answering of your mail to others, and how you can respond to your e-mail when you are out of the office.

After you have been through all the capabilities of the Notes Mail template (aside from Calendaring and Scheduling, which you will learn tomorrow), you will get a glimpse of how you can use Notes even if you want to continue to use another e-mail package.

Addressing Users Using the Name and Address Books

The simple addressing of mail memos in yesterday's lesson assumed that all users were registered on your Notes system by the Notes administrator. The names were already in the Public Address Book and the users were connected via the same LAN. But, in reality, you will probably be sharing e-mail with a variety of users, and they will not all be part of your local Notes organization.

Using the Public Address Book

The Notes Public Address Book is automatically put on your desktop the first time you connect to the Domino server when your Notes client workstation is first set up. Unless you have worked with your Location documents, then your Notes client will automatically use the Public Address Book when addressing mail. When you put somebody's name in the To: field, how does Notes find them? To gain a better understanding, look at the Person document in a Notes Public Address Book, shown in Figure 10.1.

Figure 10.1.
The Person document in the Public Address Book is used by Notes to deliver mail.

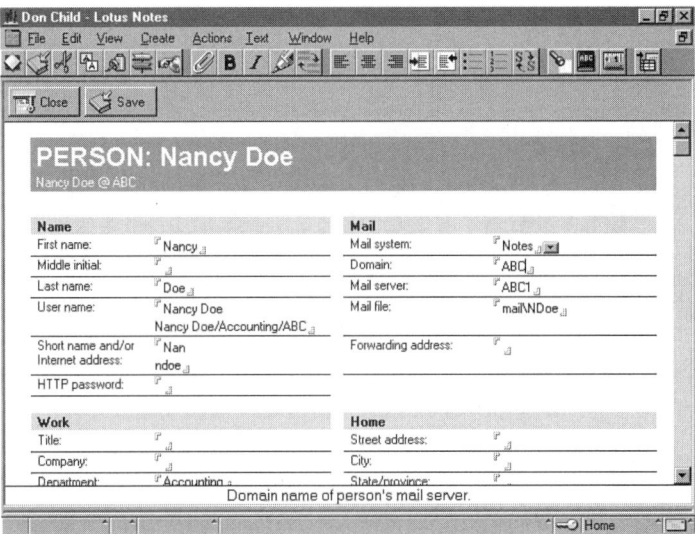

This document is used to resolve the address of the person listed in one of the address fields.

It works like this. You enter a name or part of a name, and Notes tries to guess who you mean.

- If you enter "Doe," Notes will list every member of the Doe clan so you can select the one you want to send mail to.
- If you enter "Nancy," Notes lists every Nancy in the address book so you can select which Nancy you want to send mail to.
- If you enter "Nancy Doe," or "ndoe," or "Nan," or "Nancy Doe/Accounting/ABC," then Notes will find a unique match, and will send the mail to that individual without asking you for confirmation.

 **NOTE** Notes uses type-ahead. As you start typing in a name, Notes will try to guess based on a lookup in the Public or Private Address Book, so you might not have to fill in the entire name.

Once a unique mail address is located in the Public Address Book, the Domino server takes that memo, looks at the name of the mail server, and places the memo in the mail file on that server.

If the person's mail is in another domain, on another Domino server, or uses another mail system, Notes is still able to resolve the routing of the memo through the address book. If the Person document refers to another domain, then Notes looks elsewhere in the Public Address Book to determine which route and which connections to use in order to send the mail. Of course, all of this depends on the Notes administrator getting everything set up properly in advance.

Using a Personal Address Book

Although the process above describes the Public Address Book, most organizations will not give author access to the Public Address Book, except possibly for your own Person document.

If you want to send e-mail regularly to someone who is not in the Public Address Book, you cannot add a Person document for them. The Person document normally gets created when the Notes administrator registers them as a Notes user, although a document could be added manually. You could type in their full address every time, including the complete path to their mail domain, but that gets tiresome. The solution lies in the Personal Address Book.

You can create a Personal Address Book on your desktop, and use it to enter the names and mail addresses of people you want to correspond with.

To add a Personal Address Book to your desktop:

1. Select File | Database | New from the menu bar.
2. Enter a title, such as "My Address Book."
3. The default file name for the database is NAMES.NSF. Accept this name or give it another name of your choosing.
4. Select the Personal Address Book template (pernames.ntf)
5. Click on OK when you are done.

The Personal Address Book has four views that you will be concerned with:

- Companies, used to store information about companies
- Groups, used to create a mailing list
- Locations (covered on Day 12)
- People, used to store Person documents for people who are not in the Notes Public Address Book

Creating a New Person Document

To create a new Person document as a shortcut for sending mail:

1. Switch to the People view.

    Click on the Add Person button on the Action bar at the top of the screen to display a blank Person document, or you can select Create | Person from the menu bar. The Person document in Figure 10.2 has already been filled in with essential information.

Figure 10.2.
The Person document in the Personal Address Book.

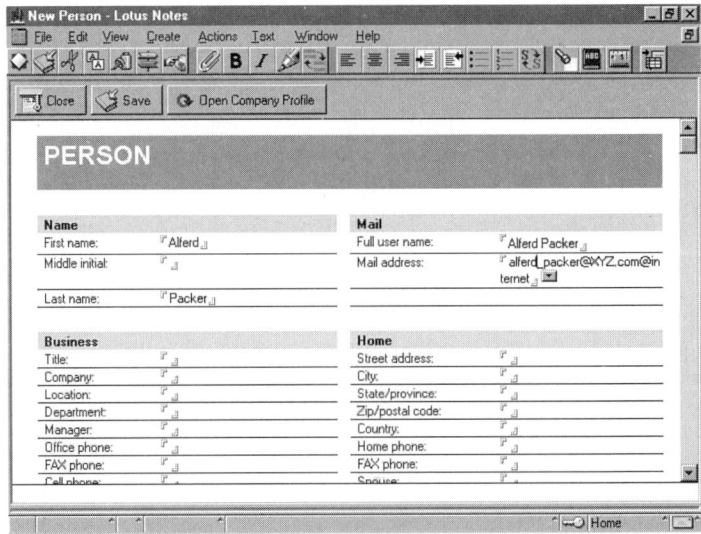

2. Fill in at least the First name, Last name, Full user name, and Mail address. The other information is optional.

NOTE: If you fill in the first and last names, Notes will fill in the User Name field automatically.

There is an even easier way to add a name to your Personal Address Book, if you receive mail from the person you want to add.

1. Open or highlight a memo from the person you want to add.
2. Select Actions | Mail Tools | Add Sender to Address Book from the menu bar.

That's it. Notes uses the From address in the mail document to create a Person record. You can open the record and edit it if you want to add more detail. You don't need to add the person to the Public Address Book, because your Personal Address Book is primarily for people who cannot be reached through other address books.

Creating Addressing Shortcuts with Group Documents

Another shortcut for addressing mail is to create a Group document, and then address mail to the group, rather than addressing each person individually. It is a quick and easy shortcut if you find yourself sending mail to the same group of individuals. The Notes administrator can create groups in the Public Address Book, but you do not have to wait for the administrator in order to take advantage of groups. You can create your own personal groups in your Personal Address Book.

To create a Group document:

1. Open your Personal Address Book to the Groups view.
2. Select Create | Group from the menu bar or click on the Add Group button on the Action Bar. The Group document is shown in Figure 10.3.
3. Enter a Group name. This is the name to which you will send mail. The name can contain spaces, for example, "Notes Developers."
4. Select a Group type. The default is Multi-purpose, but you can also create a group that can be used only for Access Control Lists, only for mail addressing, or only for a Deny Access list.

TIP: The ACL and Deny Access options are vestiges of the Public Address Book, without much application to you as an individual Notes user. Select the multi-purpose option, then you can enter the group name into reader or author access fields in addition to using it for mail addressing.

Figure 10.3.
Create a mailing list by adding names to a Group document.

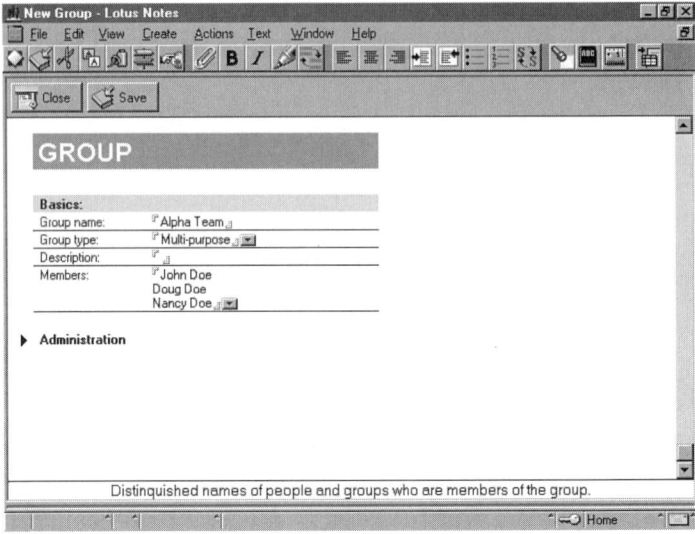

5. Enter an optional description of the group.
6. Enter the names of group members. You can add names from an address book, or type the names of the members of the group, separated by commas, or press Enter and place each name on a new line. If you add names from the address book, you have the assurance that there are no typos that would result in a person's being accidentally excluded from the group.
7. Close and save the document when done.

Using Groups is an easy way to send mail to a list of individuals.

Defining Which Address Books Notes Uses

You can have multiple Notes Address Books on your desktop. You just learned how to work with a Personal Address Book, and you have a Public Address Book. You can have any number of address books. When you address a memo or enter a name in any field where you can look up the names from an address book, you have the option of selecting which address book you want to look in. However, you have to define which address books are available to you for lookups. Notes refers to this as Cascading address books.

To make an address book available for lookup, you use the User Preferences dialog box.

Select File | Tools | User Preferences. Click on the Mail icon to display the Mail page. Enter the names of address books in the Local Address Books field, separating address books with commas. You can click on the Browse button to locate and select address book databases one at a time.

NOTE To define how databases are used for type-aheads, you have to edit the Location document, which you will be using on Day 12. We will not be looking at the Location document yet, but when we do, you will find two fields in the Mail section that let you set the Mail database precedence that is used for type-ahead lookups.

Customizing Notes Mail Documents

You can customize Notes memos in a couple of ways: You can create a stationery template for repetitious documents, and you can select a letterhead or create your own personal letterhead.

Working with Stationery

Stationery is essentially a document that is reused as a template. It is a good way to save time when you have to create the same type of document over and over, especially if it is a fairly complex document.

When you create stationery, it is stored in your Drafts folder. Every time you open the stationery template in the Drafts folder, a new document is created. You can modify the text, and when you close the new document and select the option to send the memo, it is sent just like any mail memo. The stationery template document does not get modified. The only modifications are to the new document created from the template.

There are two ways to create stationery: using a regular memo form and using a special personal stationery form.

Creating Stationery Using a Memo Form

You can create stationery from scratch using a Memo form, or you can convert any existing memo, Reply, or Reply with History into stationery. If you put a lot of effort into formatting a document, and you have to re-use that same document later with slight revisions, you can reopen the original document and convert it into stationery.

To create stationery from scratch, do the following:

1. Select Actions | Mail Tools | Create Stationery while you are in the Mail database.
2. You will be given the option of using a Memo or using Personal Stationery. Select Memo.

3. A standard Memo form will be displayed. Fill in the form as if you were creating a memo. Address the memo, enter a subject, and fill in the body with file attachments, embedded objects, tables, pages, collapsed sections—anything that you can do in a Rich Text field.
4. Click on Close when you are done. You will be asked if you want to save the memo as stationery. Answer Yes, as shown in Figure 10.4.
5. You will be asked to provide a title for the memo. Enter a title and click on OK.
6. The stationery will be saved in the Drafts folder under a Stationery category.

Figure 10.4.
Save a Memo form as stationery, and then use the stationery as a template.

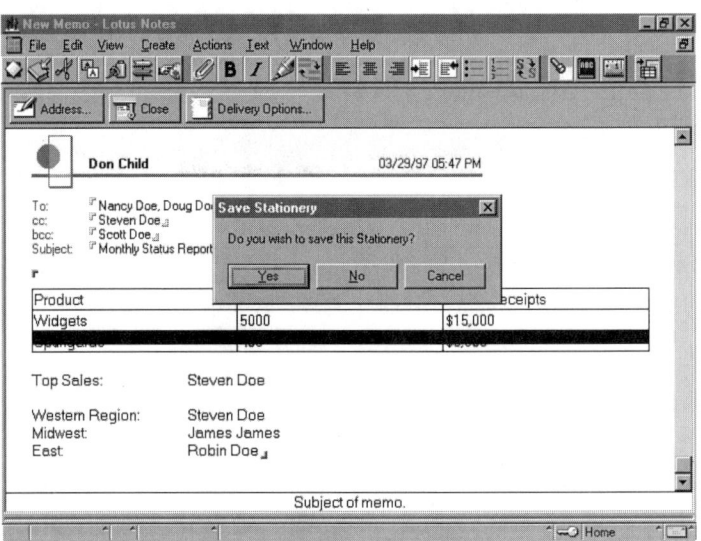

After it has been saved, you can use the stationery. To use it, go to the Drafts folder and open the stationery. It will be opened as a memo, but will contain all the information you entered when you created the stationery. You can edit it and then close it, and if you choose to send it, it will be mailed to anyone listed in the address fields.

You can also create stationery from an existing memo, or from a Reply or Reply with History. To create stationery from an existing memo, open the document in the Edit mode, and then select Actions | Save as Stationery... from the menu bar. All you have to do is enter the name under which you want to save the stationery.

Creating Stationery Using Personal Stationery

Personal stationery is a special memo form that lets you put in your own header and footer in Rich Text fields, in addition to the usual addressing fields and a body field.

Notes Mail Advanced Features

You create stationery using this form just as you would with a Memo form.

1. Select Actions | Mail Tools | Create Stationery....
2. Select Personal Stationery.
3. Fill in the form.
4. Close the form and save it as stationery.

An example of the Personal Stationery form is shown in Figure 10.5.

Figure 10.5.
With personal stationery, you can create your own headers and footers.

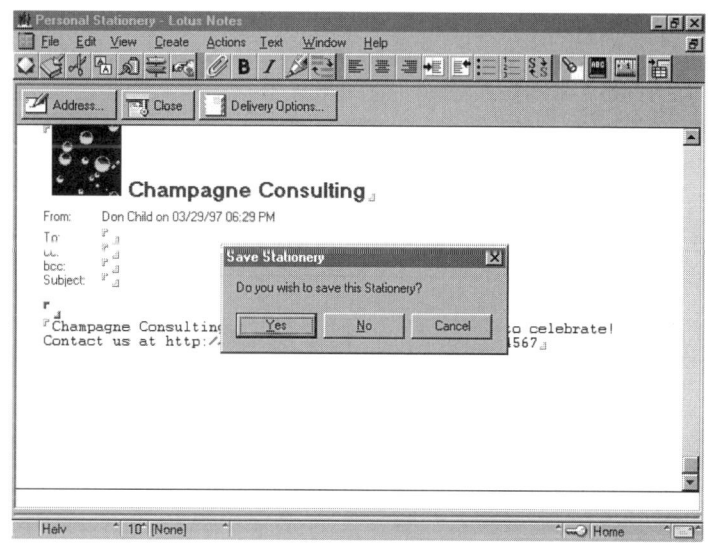

Notice in Figure 10.5 that a graphic and rich text were put into a header field at the top of the Memo form, and a rich text footer was also created. When a memo is sent using the Personal Stationery memo form, it will have the header and footer attached as part of the document.

 **TIP** This is one way you can create a memo that has a tag line, similar to using a "sig" file that displays a standard message at the bottom of all outgoing correspondence. The *sig* file is commonly used on the Internet as a way of spicing up an e-mail or a bulletin listing.

Customizing Your Memos with Letterheads

When you create a Notes memo, the memo always uses a default letterhead—the graphic that appears at the top of the memo. There are over 30 letterheads that come with Notes, and you can select any one of these letterheads as your personal letterhead.

To select a new letterhead:

1. In the mail database, select Actions | Mail Tools | Choose Letterhead from the menu bar. Notes will display a list box of letterheads, as shown in Figure 10.6.

Figure 10.6.
Select the letterhead you want to appear at the top of mail memos.

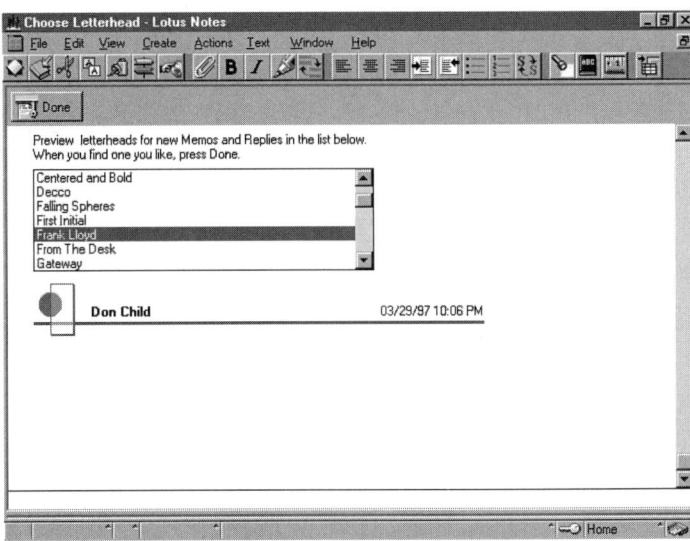

2. As you select different letterhead names, a sample of the letterhead is shown. Locate the letterhead you want, and then click on Done.

The next time you create a memo, the new letterhead will be used.

If you want to create a custom letterhead, you have to do a little bit of database design. You can add your own logo to a letterhead using the steps described below.

NOTE Note that the Memo form properties also have to be changed so that the form is stored inside all documents created with the form, if you want others to be able to see the new letterhead. Storing the form in

> documents will increase the size of all your memos. Within your own organization, you can have the Notes administrator make the described changes to the Notes Mail template and have everyone refresh the design of his or her mail database. In this way, everyone within your company can see the new letterhead without storing the form in documents.

To create your own letterhead (assuming you know some basic Notes application development techniques):

1. Open up the design menu for your mail database and select the subform for any of the existing letterheads.
2. Give the new subform a new name.
3. Delete the graphic in the subform, and then save the new subform.
4. In a graphics program, copy the new artwork for your letterhead into the clipboard.
5. In your new subform, select the layout region, and from the menu bar, select Create | Layout Region | Graphic. The graphic in the clipboard will be pasted into the layout region for the subform. Save and close the subform.
6. Edit the hidden form "(LetterHead Chooser)" to change the keywords for the LetterHeadChoices list box so it includes the name of your new subform.

Save your changes, and then select your new letterhead from the Choose Letterhead dialog box.

Letting Other Notes Users Work with Your Mail Database

You are the manager of your own Notes Mail database. Normally, without your Notes user ID and your password, nobody—not even the Notes administrator—can look at your mail database. However, there are exceptions where you can allow others to have limited access.

One exception involves the use of Calendaring and Scheduling functions, which you will be learning about tomorrow. You can also allow limited access for e-mail–specific functions.

Consider this scenario. You are going on a sabbatical, but are involved in several ongoing projects where individuals work with your workgroup through your e-mail. You could inform everyone of your impending absence, but then it would disrupt the flow of the project. It is better if you remain "on the job" as far as others are concerned. Therefore, you decide to delegate the authority to use your mail database to an assistant while you are gone.

To do this, set up a Delegation Profile, which allows limited access to your mail database. Do this as follows:

In your mail database, select Actions | Mail Tools | Delegation Profile.... Notes displays the Delegation Profile document, most of which is shown in Figure 10.7.

Figure 10.7.
Delegate access to your mail database using the Delegation Profile document.

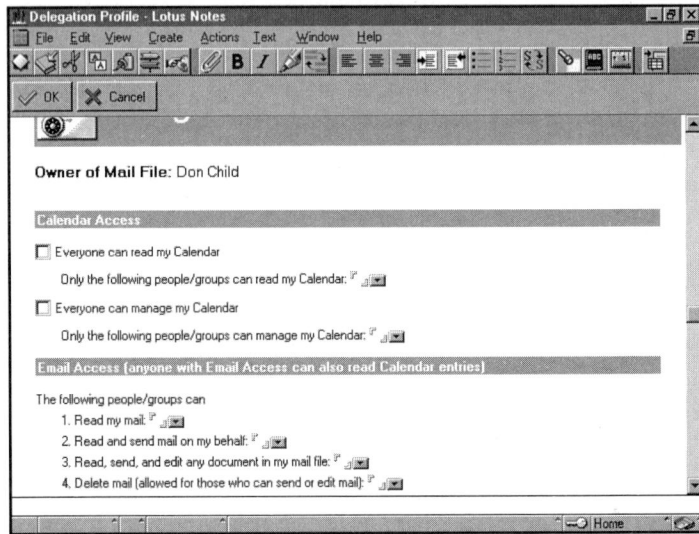

In the E Mail Access section of the document, enter names of people to whom you want to delegate responsibilities in your mail database. You can delegate people to perform the following functions:

- ☐ *Read My Mail.* People listed in this field will be able to read your mail, but they cannot create or modify any documents in the database.

- ☐ *Read and Send Mail on My Behalf.* People listed in this field will be able to read mail and will be able to create new mail memos using your mail file. However, they cannot edit documents that they did not create, and they cannot delete documents that they created unless they are also listed in the Delete Mail field.

- ☐ *Read, Send, and Edit Any Document in My Mail File.* People listed in this field will have the same rights as those listed in the previous field, but they also can edit any document in the mail file.

- ☐ *Delete Mail.* Users can delete mail only if they are listed in this field, which extends the privileges of the previous two fields. If they have read and send privileges, then they can delete documents they created. If they have read, send, and edit privileges, they can delete any document in the mail database.

When done, save the Delegation Profile. The individuals will then be able to perform the functions that were delegated to them. To remove privileges from a person, you have to go back into the Delegation Profile and remove his or her name from the related fields.

Sending Messages to Others Automatically When You Are Out of the Office

You can create an Out of Office Profile document that automatically generates replies to mail messages while you are gone from the office. You can tailor your replies to specific individuals or groups.

This is similar to delegating the right to handle your mail, but in this case, you are depending on an automated agent to handle your mail until you get back from your trip. Which alternative you choose depends on your circumstances.

NOTE Before you can enable an Out of Office agent, you must have the authority to create agents on the Domino server on which your mail database resides. Check with your Notes administrator if you are not sure you have this ability.

To create an Out of Office Profile:

1. In the mail database, select Actions | Mail Tools | Out of Office....
2. The Out of Office Profile will be displayed. Enter the date you are leaving and the date you are returning. Dates are entered in MM/DD/YY format, e.g. "04/15/97." The profile will be in effect during the time you specify.
3. Create a default message that will be sent as a reply to most people's messages. (An example of this default message is shown in Figure 10.8.) You can modify the Subject and the tag line. Both of these are plain text fields. Once the profile is activated, this simple message will be sent to anyone not included in the next two categories of people who should receive a special message, or people who should receive no message.

Figure 10.8.
Create a default message that is automatically sent to people while you are out of the office.

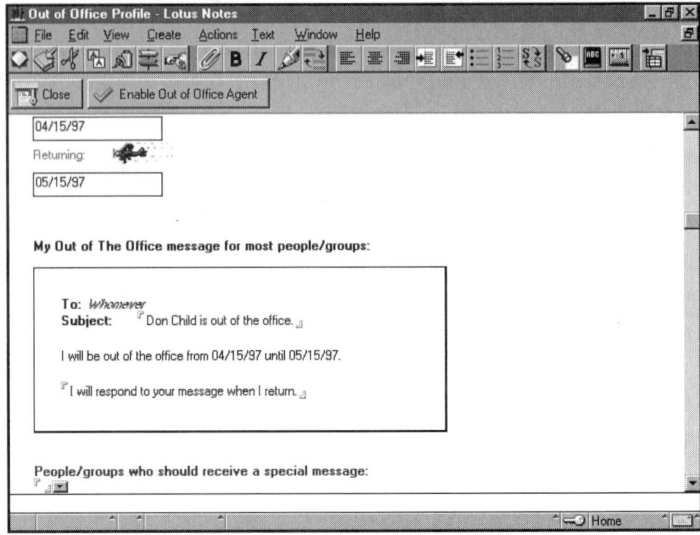

4. Scroll down the Out of Office Profile document to the next field, which contains a special message for select individuals or groups. Enter the names of the individuals or groups, selecting them from a Notes address book so that Notes will recognize them when they send e-mail.
5. Enter a special message for the select individuals or groups. Again, you can modify the Subject and the tag line, as illustrated in Figure 10.9.

Figure 10.9.
Enter a special message for selected individuals, and send no message to others.

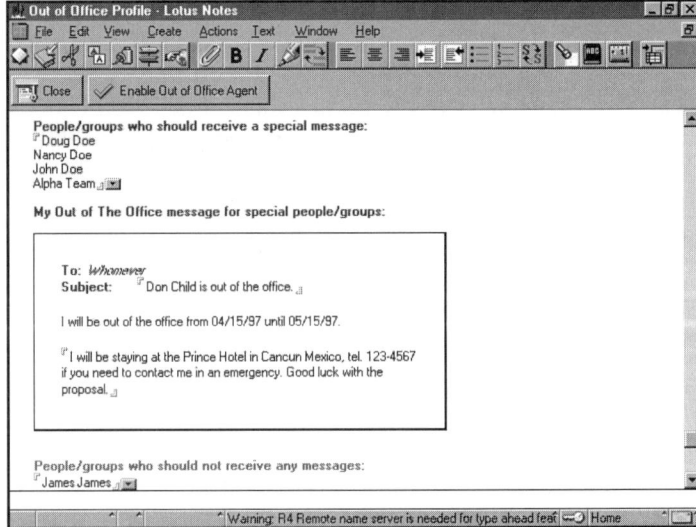

6. Enter the names of any individuals or groups who should not receive any Out of Office message.
7. Click on the Enable Out of Office Agent button to activate the Out of Office Profile. A dialog box will be displayed asking which server you want the "Out of Office" agent to be run on. Enter the name of the server on which your Notes Mail database resides.
8. Notes will display a message, shown in Figure 10.10, informing you that your Out of Office message will be sent during the specified period.

Figure 10.10.
Notes confirms that a message will be sent during your absence.

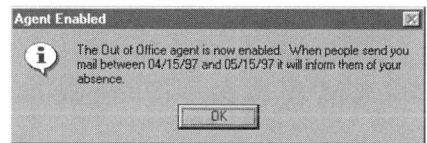

What happens then? Does your Notes Mail "spam" everyone, sending countless messages every time they send mail to you? No. Quite the opposite. Notes sends only one message to each individual, even if they send numerous messages to you.

A log is maintained of everyone who received the Out of Office message. On the date you are scheduled to return, Notes sends you a "Welcome back" message, along with a list of everyone who received your Out of Office message. You can then respond to the people to tell them that you are back in the office.

You will continue getting "Welcome back" messages until you disable the Out of Office agent. To disable the agent:

1. In the mail database, select Actions | Mail Tools | Out of Office....
2. Click the I Have Returned to the Office button.

If you return to the office early, you can disable the Out of Office message in the same way. If you do not disable the message, it will continue to be sent to people the first time they send you a memo.

Using Other Mail Systems with Notes

Notes underwent a big transformation in the appearance of its user interface when it moved from Notes 3.x to Notes 4.x in December 1995. At that time, the interface took on the three pane look that cc:Mail already had. Today, Notes Mail and cc:Mail look very similar, and share quite a bit of functionality. They are still distinct mail systems under the surface, although they are both moving toward a common standard. Given the speed of the evolution of computer technology, the two mail systems will merge at some point in the near future.

Lotus is committed to common standards. They have promised that Domino 5.0, when it is released, will be a fully standards-based server platform, making it possible to interoperate with virtually any standards-based mail package. Meanwhile, Notes 4.5 has already gone a long way in that direction. You can use cc:Mail or other Vendor Independent Mail (VIM) systems with Notes. You can also use Microsoft mail-enabled programs and Microsoft Exchange with Notes.

Using cc:Mail and VIM Programs with Notes

You can use cc:Mail and VIM programs only if you are using a 16-bit Windows version of Notes.

> **TIP**
> To find out if you have the correct version of Notes installed, select File | Tools | User Preferences. Click on the Mail icon to display the Mail page. Click on the Mail Program drop-down list to see if other mail programs are available. If other programs are available, you have the option of using them instead of Notes Mail.

If you have the right version of Notes on your desktop, and you have cc:Mail (or another VIM program) installed and running, you can enable it by setting the Mail Progam in the User Preferences dialog box to your mail program. Enter the full path and file name for the EXE file that runs your program, and exit the User Preferences dialog box. Your mail system is now cc:Mail, even though your are using Notes.

There are several common mail functions that are slightly different when using another mail system from within Notes. These are described below. Note that the descriptions depend on your familiarity with the mail system you are using.

Creating a Mail Memo Using cc:Mail in Notes

To create a memo if you have cc:Mail set as your mail system:

1. Select Create | Mail | Open from the menu bar.
2. If necessary, enter the location of your mail system's post office, your mail username, and your password. Notes will start your mail system.
3. Create a memo the way you normally would in your mail system.

Forwarding a Document Using cc:Mail in Notes

To forward a Notes document to other users:

1. Open or select the document you want to forward.
2. Select Actions | Forward from the menu bar.
3. Click on the Address button and address the memo.
4. Modify the document if necessary, and send it.

NOTE You can forward a document as an attachment if the person to whom you are sending the attachment is also a Notes user. The attachment is saved as a Notes database that the user launches in Notes by double-clicking on it to view the attachment. To forward a document as an attachment, select Create | Mail | Forward as Attachment.

When you create a document in Notes using another mail system such as cc:Mail, the document may contain a field that lets you define how the document should be formatted. The choices that you have include the following:

- *Text.* If you select this, the message will be sent as plain text, and can be read just like any other document in the recipient's mail program.
- *Encapsulated.* This sends the document as an attachment in Notes database form so you can launch Notes by double-clicking on the attachment. In cc:Mail in the User Setup dialog box, you have to select Message in the Preference part of the dialog box, and Run Double-Click as a view/run option.
- *Both.* This lets you send the document as both text and as an attachment so the user can select the version he or she wants.
- *Memo.* This sends a text document without any header information. The user will see a document, rather than an e-mail memo with all the summary addressing fields.

How Notes Documents Are Displayed in cc:Mail

cc:Mail does not support rich text in the same sense that Notes does, so the information in a Notes Rich Text field gets broken down into different elements within cc:Mail.

Text is converted into 8-point Courier text, which is the only supported font in cc:Mail. However, cc:Mail approximates the same paragraph grouping and justification, including tabs and line spacing.

Bitmaps become PCX files attached as file items. Also attached as file items are Notes file attachments, TIFF and CGM graphics, and graphic DDE link symbols.

OLE links are carried over to cc:Mail, with the OLE object file attached as a file item. The link is displayed as text or pasted as a separate file item if it is a graphic.

Some of the text formatting is carried over from Notes to cc:Mail, but the formatting is rendered in different background colors (italic = green, bold = blue, and underline = red, e.g.) to represent the rich text formatting of Notes. Superscript, subscript, and strikeout are indicated in parentheses.

All the elements are translated in one way or another, except for fonts and font size, and DocLinks, which are lost in the translation. Also, large Rich Text fields are broken down into multiple cc:Mail text items.

This is something you can expect to see for now if you are a cc:Mail user, but eventually, cc:Mail and Notes Mail are sure to become more interchangeable.

Using Microsoft Mail-Enabled Programs and Microsoft Exchange with Notes

With Windows 95 and Windows NT, you can set up Microsoft Exchange to access a Notes Mail database, and you can set up Microsoft-enabled mail programs so you can use them to send mail to Notes users.

Most of the setup for this interchange takes place at an administrative level. The Notes administrator has to create a profile that lets you use Notes Service Providers for the Messaging Application Programming Interface (MAPI). This is done during installation.

After it is set up, here is what you can do to send mail from your Microsoft-enabled mail application:

1. In the Microsoft-enabled mail application, select File | Send.
2. Select the profile for the Notes Service Provider.
3. Complete the message and send it as you normally would in your mail application.

Addressing is done using the address book you specified in your Notes Server Provider profile.

When you use the Lotus Notes Service Provider for a MAPI application such as Microsoft Exchange, you can use the Exchange interface to access the Notes Mail database. You will actually use the Exchange commands to create, send, and read mail, and you can address mail using an Exchange address book, but it must be resolved using a Notes Public Address Book, and you will be using the Notes Mail database to store mail.

The level of integration is amazingly complete. You can use the Inbox, the Outbox, Drafts, All Documents, and Trash folders, along with personal folders that closely match the Exchange default information view. You can create and send rich text messages, attach files, and even read messages that were encrypted in Notes. You cannot verify the signature on encrypted data, however.

> You must use the Notes mail template when accessing Notes from a MAPI application. You cannot change the design of this template.

The Hidden Role of Notes Mail

Notes Mail plays a hidden role within Notes— one that you don't have to do anything about, but one that you should be aware of. Any form in a Notes database can be mail enabled with the addition of a couple of fields: an address field that tells where the document should be mailed, and a mail options field. The document can be set up so that a status change or some other event triggers the mail option. The document can be mailed to another database or to a user.

For example, imagine a requisition application. A requisition is created, and then goes through an approval process. As soon as the final approval is given, the requisition is automatically mailed to another database, where it becomes a purchase order. There are no forms from the Mail database involved, but Notes Mail is central to this workflow operation. Mail is one of the keys to creating a successful application for a workgroup.

An interesting application of Notes Mail can be seen in the Discussion database that you created and worked with. You can create an Interest Profile (on the Actions menu in the Discussion database) that automatically mails a notice to you whenever documents meeting a certain profile are created. An example of this Interest Profile is shown in Figure 10.11.

This simple form triggers e-mail whenever Nancy Doe creates a document in the Discussion database, whenever there is a document categorized under "Education," and whenever a document includes the words "Lotus Notes," "e-mail," or "embedded object."

In this instance, Notes Mail is being used in the background to inform me of targeted changes in the discussion database. Aside from setting up my Interest Profile, I don't have to do anything. Notes Mail handles everything.

Figure 10.11.
The Discussion database Interest Profile triggers e-mail from a non-mail database.

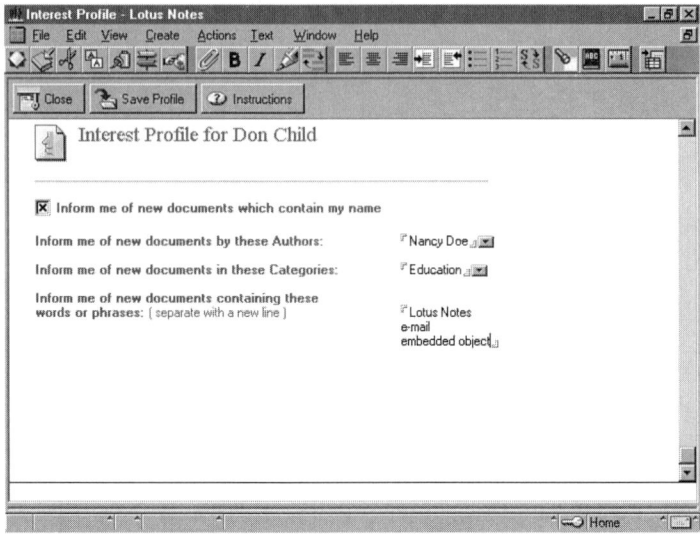

Summary

Today's lesson added to your knowledge of Notes Mail, building on what you learned in yesterday's lesson. You learned first about the Notes Public and Personal Address Books, which let you customize more than mail addressing. Just about every time a name is used in Notes, the name is validated in an address book to be sure that Notes recognizes it.

The Notes administrator creates most entries in the Public Address Book by registering Notes users. You can enter names in your Personal Address Book automatically by using an Action to create an entry for anyone who sends you mail. You can also create groups in your Personal Address Book, and use them in Reader Name fields, for example, or in memo addresses.

You then learned how to customize your mail using letterheads, and how to create shortcuts when you have memos that you want to resend periodically by creating Stationery—a reusable document template.

You then learned how to let others use Notes Mail for you. You can create Delegation Profiles that define what others can do in your Notes Mail database, and you learned how to delegate some of the responsibility for your Notes Mail database to Notes itself. When you create an Out of Office document, Notes responds to mail that lands in your Inbox.

You then learned how to use cc:Mail or another Vendor Independent Mail application as your mail application. In addition, you saw how to use Microsoft-enabled mail systems, including how to use the Microsoft Exchange client to work with your Notes Mail database.

Finally, you saw how Notes uses mail not just for sending e-mail messages to others, but how it uses the mail function in the background for various workflow applications—the backbone of Notes as a groupware application.

Workshop

The Workshop section presents questions and answers, quiz questions to help you cement your new knowledge, and exercises to give you experience using what you have learned. Try to understand the questions and exercises before moving on to the next lesson. Answers are in Appendix A.

Q&A

Q I use Microsoft Exchange with Notes the way it was described in today's lesson. Do I have to use the Notes Public Address Book, or can I just use the Exchange address book?

A You can use the Exchange address book, but you must also have the Notes Public Address Book in your profile so that Notes can resolve any addresses it gets from Exchange.

Q Can I send mail to people if they are not in a Notes address book?

A You can, if you include a full path that allows Notes to deliver the memo to the other person's mail system—for example, `john_doe@abc.com@internet`.

Q I created a letterhead, and I see the letterhead whenever I create a memo. But when somebody sends a Reply with History, I see another letterhead, not mine. Does that mean others are not receiving my letterhead?

A You have to set the Form Properties to Store Form in Document if you want people to see your private letterhead, unless the Notes administrator is willing to change the mail template. Another alternative might be to create Personal Stationery, which has your graphic embedded as rich text.

Quiz

1. Where do you go to create a document from a Stationery template?
2. Do you have to enter a user's full name in order for him or her to receive e-mail?
3. How many address books can you use to look up usernames on your Notes desktop?
4. How do you register a new address book so Notes can use it?

5. Can a delegated mail user read your encrypted mail?
6. How often does an Out of Office memo get sent to somebody if he or she sends you e-mail every day?

Exercises

1. Create a Personal Address Book. Make it so that when you create a memo, Notes looks up names in the Personal Address Book before looking up names in the Public Address Book.
2. Create a weekly status report. Save it as stationery, then create a revised status report using the stationery.
3. If you have access to cc:Mail, mail a Notes document to a cc:Mail user. Include a variety of text formatting in the body of the memo, and compare the memo in Notes and in cc:Mail.
4. Create an Out of Office profile. Set today as the beginning date for you to be out of the office, and have a fellow Notes Mail user send you a message. Disable the profile, then compare Notes with your workmate. What sort of message did he or she receive? What sort of message did you receive?

Week 2

Day 11

Calendaring and Scheduling

When Notes was released in December 1996, Calendaring and Scheduling was introduced. Calendaring and Scheduling lets you keep a personal calendar for tracking your own meetings and appointments, and maintaining to do lists. But that is only the tip of the iceberg.

You can also do group calendaring and scheduling. You can use the power of Notes, the power of groupware, and the power of your computer to help you schedule meetings and activities efficiently, taking into consideration the times that other members of your workgroup are free. You can share your calendar, allowing a coworker to manage your schedule for you.

When you schedule tentative meetings, you can send out invitations, reserve a room, and reserve the items you need for your meeting. You can then track the RSVPs of those you invited.

You will learn how to handle all of these functions in today's lesson.

Taking a Tour of the Calendar View

There are three views in the Notes Mail database that were skipped over during the past two days' lessons. One of those views is the Calendar view, which we will be working with in this lesson. The Calendar view is shown in Figure 11.1.

Figure 11.1.
The Calendar view lets you view scheduling using a calendar interface.

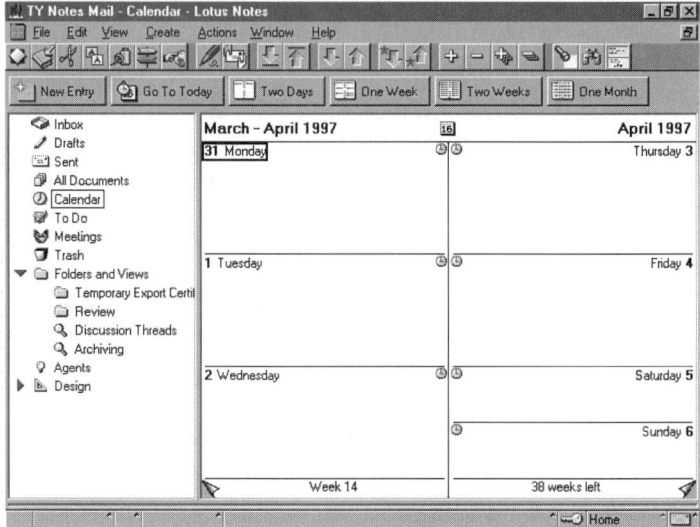

This view shows one week in April 1997. Right now, the calendar is empty, but we will be filling it with information such as appointments, meetings, and reminders as we progress through today's lesson.

Look at the Action Bar at the top of the calendar. You can click on buttons to change the calendar so it shows two days in hourly increments, a two-week view, or a one-month view. These other views of the calendar will be shown as the lesson progresses.

Moving to Another Page on the Calendar

No matter how many days you have showing on the calendar, you can page forward to the next page, or back to the previous page.

Notice the curled up corners in the lower-right and lower-left corners of the calendar shown in Figure 11.1. Click on the right corner to move forward to the next page, and click on the left corner to move back to the previous page.

Moving to a Specific Day

You can move to a specific day by clicking on the small 16 icon to display a small monthly calendar, as shown in Figure 11.2.

Figure 11.2.
Move to a specific day by displaying the small navigator calendar.

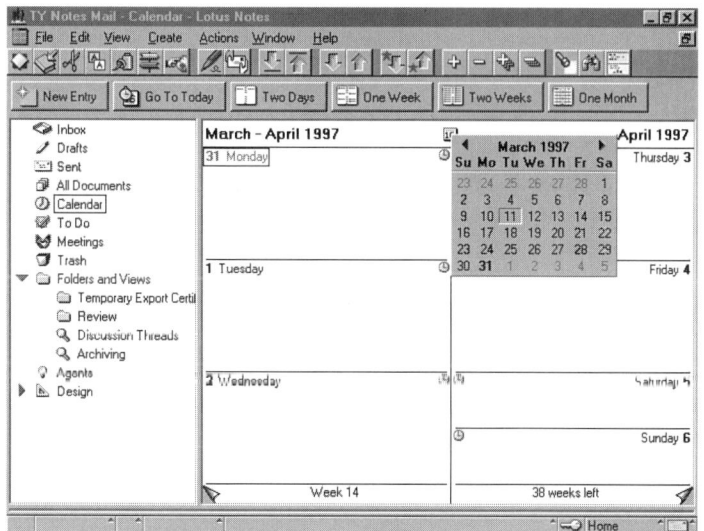

On the navigator calendar, click on the right arrow to move forward a month at a time, or click on the left arrow to move back a month at a time.

When the month you want is displayed, click on the day you want. The calendar will be reset so that the selected day is included in the visible time frame.

For example, suppose you want to take your vacation during the second week of August. Display the navigator calendar, move to August, and select any day during the second week. The calendar will move ahead to that date, and you can see whether there are any conflicting events scheduled for that week.

To return to today's date from anywhere on the calendar, click on the Go to Today button near the left side of the Action Bar.

Displaying a Day in Hourly Increments

In the Two Days, One Week, or Two Week view of the calendar, you can toggle between a full day and a day divided into hourly increments. To toggle between a daily and hourly display, click on the small clock icon in the top right corner of the cell. If all hours do not fit in the cell, you can scroll by clicking on arrows on the right side of the cell. This is illustrated in Figure 11.3, which shows Monday, March 31, segmented into one-hour increments.

Figure 11.3.
Divide a day into one-hour increments by clicking on the clock icon in the corner of the cell.

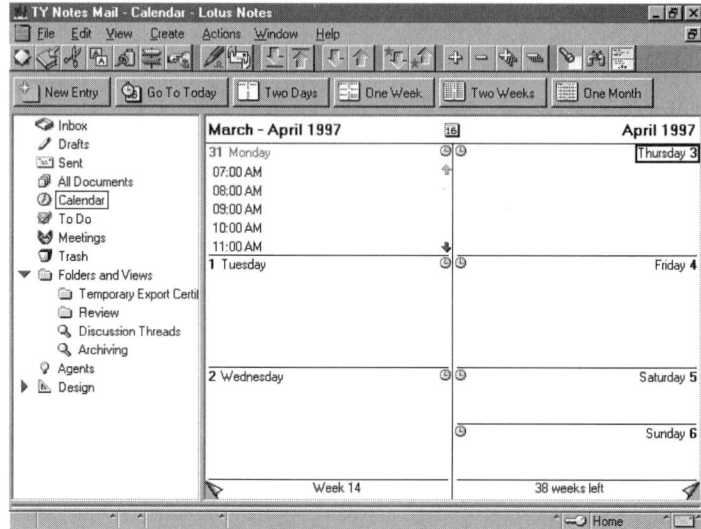

Now that you know how to navigate in the calendar, you can start looking at how the calendar is set up.

Setting Up Your Calendar Profile

You can define how your calendar handles various types of calendar entries. You do this by editing a Calendar Profile document. The Calendar Profile controls several elements in your calendar, and the options will make more sense to you if they are discussed in context.

For now, though, you will see the first part the Calendar Profile. It gives you access to Delegation Profile, which you learned about in yesterday's lesson.

The Calendar Profile is displayed automatically the first time you open the Calendar view in your mail database. You can also display the Calendar Profile by selecting Actions | Calendar Tools | Calendar Profile... from the menu bar. The Calendar Profile document is shown in Figure 11.4.

Calendaring and Scheduling

Figure 11.4.
The Calendar Profile gives you access to the Delegation Profile.

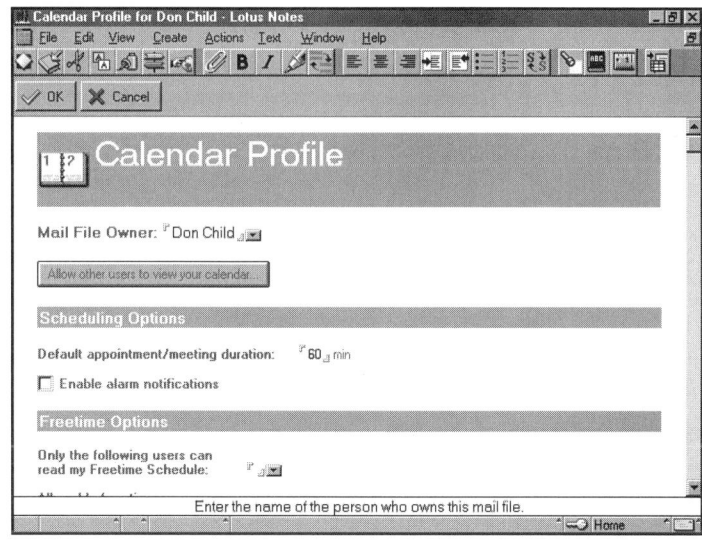

From the Calendar Profile, you can access the Delegation Profile to define which individuals, if any, should have access to your calendar.

To access the Delegation Profile, click on the Allow Other Users to View Your Calendar button. The Calendar Access portion of the Delegation Profile is shown in Figure 11.5.

Figure 11.5.
Use the Delegation Profile to define who else besides you can access your calendar.

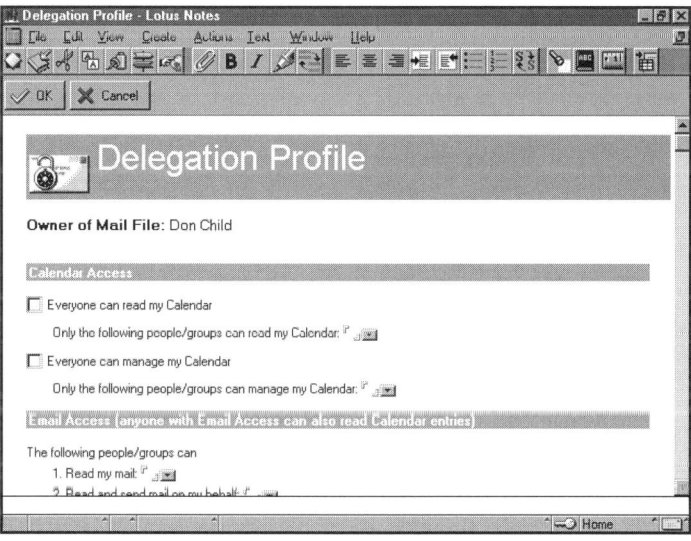

In the Delegation Profile, you can define who can read public events on your calendar, and who can create or modify public events on your calendar. A public event is any event that you have not marked as private.

If Everyone can read my Calendar is checked, then everyone will be able to read your calendar entries. If it is not checked, then you can select the names of specific individuals or groups who should be allowed to read your calendar.

If Everyone can manage my Calendar is checked, then everyone will be able to create, modify, or delete public calendar items. They cannot work with calendar items you have marked as private, and they cannot view or work with the rest of your mail. If Everyone is not checked, you can enter the names of specific people who will be able to open and work with your calendar.

When you give another Notes user access to your calendar, they can open it from within their Notes mail database. Likewise, if you are given access, you can open another user's calendar by selecting Actions | Calendar Tools | Open Another Calendar. In the dialog box that is displayed, shown in Figure 11.6, select the address book that contains the user's name. Highlight his name, and click on OK to open his calendar, if it is available to you.

Figure 11.6.
Select the person whose calendar you want to view, assuming he has given you access.

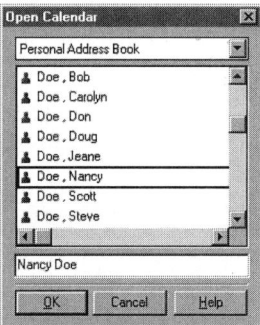

Why would you want access to someone else's calendar? Picture yourself supervising a Help Desk. Your staff has training sessions they have to go to. They also support the consulting staff. Who are you going to schedule on the Help Desk, if they are all pretty much independent? A tough job, unless you have access to their calendars. When you look at their calendars, you can see only calendar-related views if you have Read Public Documents access. You can switch from the Calendar to the Meetings view to see their invitations and appointments. Viewing others' calendars can be very convenient in the right circumstances.

Defining Scheduling Options

Before you learn how to create calendar items, we will set some scheduling options. This is also done on the Calendar Profile document. Figure 11.7 shows the Scheduling Options section of the Calendar Profile document.

Figure 11.7.
Select scheduling options from the Calendar Profile document.

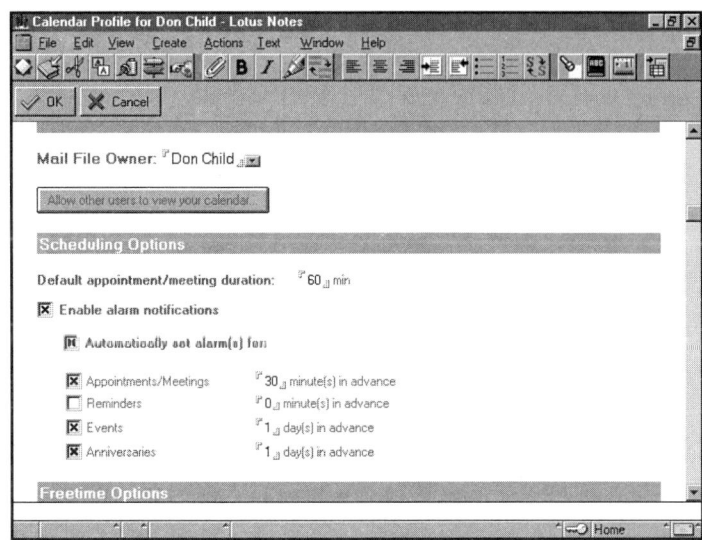

The Scheduling Options section is collapsed when you first open the Calendar Profile document, except for two fields:

- *Default Appointment/Meeting Duration* lets you customize your calendar so that when you create appointments, it matches your work style. If your average appointment is two hours long, then set the default time for appointments to 120 minutes. If your average appointment is only 10 minutes, set the default duration to 10 minutes. It will save you keystrokes when you create appointments or meetings on your calendar.
- *Enable Alarm Notifications* is turned off by default. If you want to have your Notes workstation display alarms to alert you when an appointment is approaching, click Enable Alarm Notifications to expand the Scheduling Options so you can define which alarms you want set and how far in advance you want them. When you receive an alarm notification, a pop-up window is displayed on your screen. You can acknowledge the alarm, or click on a "snooze" button so the alarm will persist.

With the alarm notifications expanded, you can click on Automatically set alarm(s) for: to expand a list of available alarms. The alarms represent some of the document types you can create for your calendar:

- ☐ Appointments/Meetings have a default reminder 30 minutes before the start time.
- ☐ Reminders do not have beginning time, therefore there is no alarm by default. However, you can set a time, if desired.
- ☐ Events have a one-day alarm, by default.
- ☐ Anniversaries also have a one-day alarm by default.

Entering Data in Your Calendar

There are basically two forms used for creating entries in your calendar: a Calendar Entry form and a Task form. That statement is deceptive, though. At the top of the Calendar Entry form, you can select from five types of entries in your calendar: Appointments, Invitations, Events, Reminders, and Anniversaries.

The information required for some of these calendar entries is fairly basic, but you have several options that you can set, and with the Invitation entry in particular, the processing is fairly complex. Each Calendar Entry type is described in detail in the following sections.

Creating a Calendar Entry

To create a new Calendar entry, you can do any of the following:

- ☐ Select Create | Calendar Entry from the menu bar if you are in the Mail database.
- ☐ Select Create | Mail | Calendar Entry if you are anywhere else in Notes.
- ☐ Double-click on any date cell in the Calendar view.
- ☐ Click the New Entry button in the Calendar view.

The default Calendar Entry will be displayed. Unless you changed it on your Calendar Profile, the default Calendar Entry is an Invitation.

Creating an Appointment

When you first create a Calendar Entry document, you have a choice of any of the five types of document. Click the Appointment radio button to hide any fields not related to appointments, and to display the fields that are required.

You will see an Appointment screen like the one shown in Figure 11.8.

Figure 11.8.
Create a new Appointment using the Calendar Entry document.

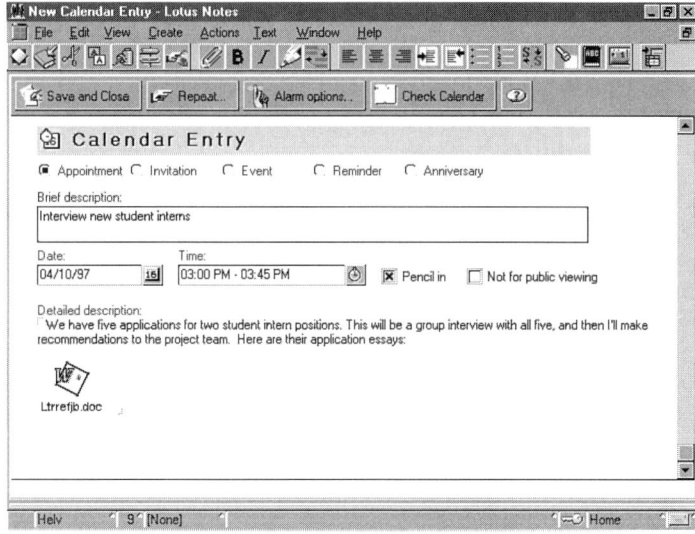

Enter the following details:

- A brief description that will appear on the calendar.
- The date of the appointment. You can click on the small Date icon to display a navigator calendar for selecting the date of the appointment. The navigator calendar is just like the one you already saw in the Calendar view.
- The time of the appointment. You can type in a range of times, but you also have the option of displaying a slide bar, shown in Figure 11.9. You display the slide bar by clicking on the small clock icon, and set the duration of the appointment by dragging the beginning and end of the slide bar up and down until they rest on the beginning and ending times for the appointment.

Figure 11.9.
Use the slide bar to define the beginning and end times of your appointment.

☐ Pencil in. If you select Pencil in, the appointment will not show up on your Free Time schedule, because the appointment is only tentative. You will be learning about free time later in today's lesson.

☐ Not for public viewing. Earlier, you set up your calendar so that others could view it and work with it. Even if you give others access to your calendar, you can still hide personal appointments by clicking on the check box to indicate that this appointment should not appear on your public calendar. The appointment will block free time, even if it cannot be seen by others.

☐ Detailed description. This is a Rich Text field that you can use to include various items such as a more detailed description, attach related files, and so forth.

In addition to the fields in the document, you have a couple of options on the Action Bar at the top of the document. For example, if you want to view the calendar to see if there are any conflicting appointments, you can click on the Check Calendar button to display the calendar. When you are done looking at the calendar, press the Escape key to return to the Calendar Entry document.

Creating a Repeating Appointment

You can turn a single appointment into a repeating appointment, with repetition based on a number of parameters. To create a repeating appointment, click on the Repeat button. The Repeat Rules dialog box will be displayed (see Figure 11.10).

Figure 11.10.
Set up repeating appointments in the Repeat Rules dialog box.

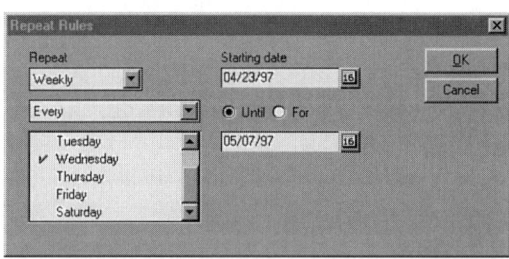

In this dialog box, you enter the type of repetition in the Repeat field. You can have appointments that are repeated weekly, monthly by date (the 15th of each month), monthly by day (the second day of the month), yearly, or on a custom basis.

Depending on the option you choose, the remaining options in the dialog box may change, but they do follow a pattern. After you choose the length of period on which you want to base the repetition, you choose the frequency. For example, you can choose a weekly interval, and make the interval every three weeks on a Friday. You can choose a monthly interval and make it every six months.

After establishing the frequency and the interval, you set the start and end dates or the duration of the repetitions.

After you save the Repeat information, multiple appointments are created automatically based on your definition.

If you attempt to delete or modify an automatically generated repeat appointment, a dialog box will be displayed to warn you that it is a repeat appointment. You will have the option of canceling your action, modifying just the current appointment, all previous appointments, all future appointments, or all appointments previous and future related to this one. The dialog box is shown in Figure 11.11.

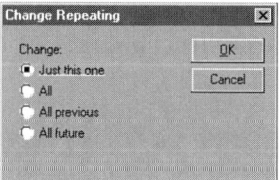

Figure 11.11.
When you modify or delete one repeating appointment, you can decide how to handle related appointments.

NOTE You can only set up repeat appointments when an appointment is first created. You cannot go back in the Edit mode and change a single appointment to a repeat appointment.

Setting Alarm Options

You learned how to set default alarm options in the Calendar Profile document. However, the options you set may not be appropriate for all instances. You can override the default options for an individual appointment by clicking on the Alarms button.

If no alarm is set up, you will be asked if you want to set one up at this time. Answer Yes, and you will see the Set Alarm dialog box shown in Figure 11.12.

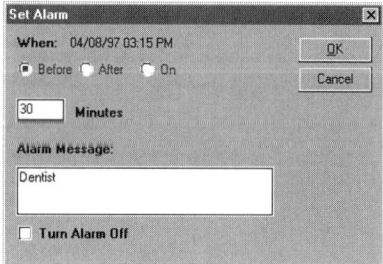

Figure 11.12.
You can set one-time alarm settings for an individual appointment

In this dialog box, define when you want an alarm to sound in relationship to the beginning of the appointment. You can also create a message to appear with the alarm. When it is time for the alarm, the system will beep and display your alarm message. When the alarm goes off, you can acknowledge it or click on a "snooze" button so the alarm will repeat in a set amount of time, such as 10 minutes.

NOTE An alarm can be set at any time; it does not have to be created when the appointment is first created. To set an alarm after the document has been created, open the document and click on the Edit button, and then you can set or reset an alarm.

Creating Invitations

The Invitation document is used to organize meetings using all the workflow features of Notes. You will find that this one application within the calendar interface is a simple but elegant argument for using Notes. The Invitation is used to set up a meeting. You can invite individuals and define what happens when they receive the invitation. You can also verify that those you are inviting to the meeting do not have conflicting appointments.

To create an Invitation, you start by creating a Calendar Entry by double-clicking on the day you want to create the meeting, by clicking on the New Entry button, or by selecting Create | Calendar Entry from the menu bar. After the form is displayed, click the Invitation button to display the screen shown in Figure 11.13.

Figure 11.13.
Set up a meeting using the Invitation Calendar Entry.

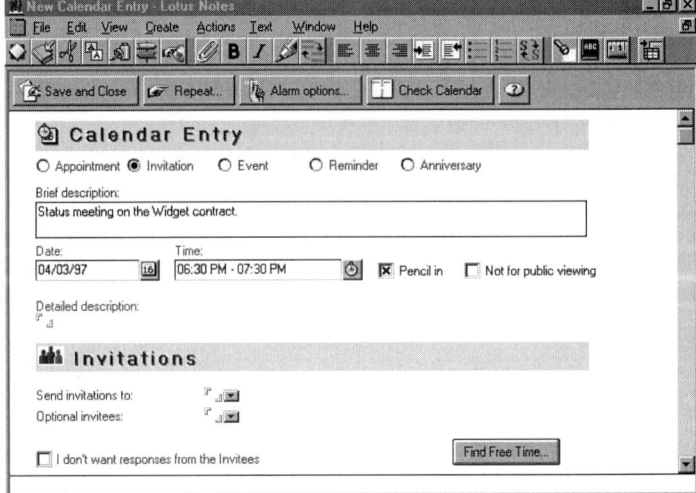

You will notice that the top part of the document is the same as the Appointment document. You can enter a description, a date, and beginning and ending times. You can choose to pencil in the meeting, and you can choose to hide it from public view. You can enter a detailed description in a Rich Text field, which means, for example, that you can attach files for invitees to review before the meeting.

What distinguishes the Invitation, though, is the Invitations section of the document. It is here that you enter information inviting other individuals to the meeting.

Build a list of invitees and optional invitees by looking them up in your Notes address books. If necessary, refresh your memory on how to add names from an address book. You learned this skill on Day 9, "Notes Mail Basics," when you learned about Notes Mail basics.

After you have a list of invitees, you can use the Free Time function to determine the best time for the meeting.

Working with Free Time

The people that you want to invite to your meeting are, with any luck, maintaining their own appointments on their Notes calendars. On the Domino server, there is a Free Time database that keeps track of the times when users have obligations marked in their calendars, such as appointments and meetings, and times when they are normally out of the office. Any other time is considered free time—a time when the person is presumed to be available for meetings and appointments.

When you click on the Find Free Time button, Notes goes out and searches the Free Time database for free time listings, using the list of individuals you provided. If you have access to the free time listings for individuals, their free time will be shown in the Free Time dialog box, as shown in Figure 11.14.

Figure 11.14.
Select a meeting time when all or most individuals have free time and will be able to attend.

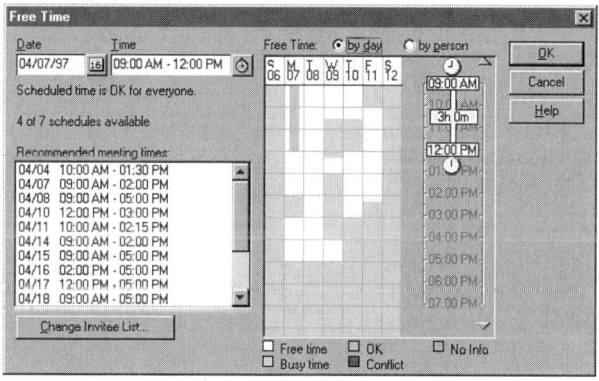

In this dialog box, you can see free time and busy time illustrated by day or by individual, and you can see a list of suggested meeting times. If you want to accept one of the recommended meeting times rather than the time you initially set, click on the recommended time to highlight it, and then click on OK to set the meeting date and time.

If any individual has a conflict with the meeting time you selected, a red "conflict" will show up on the Free Time schedule. Times that are okay are shown in green. If it is important that everyone attend, you can always select one of the times that Notes suggests.

Setting Up Your Free Time

You set up your own free time options in your Calendar Profile document (Actions | Calendar Tools | Calendar Profile). Scroll down until you can see the Free Time Options section, shown in Figure 11.15.

Figure 11.15.
Define how other users see your free time in the Calendar Profile document.

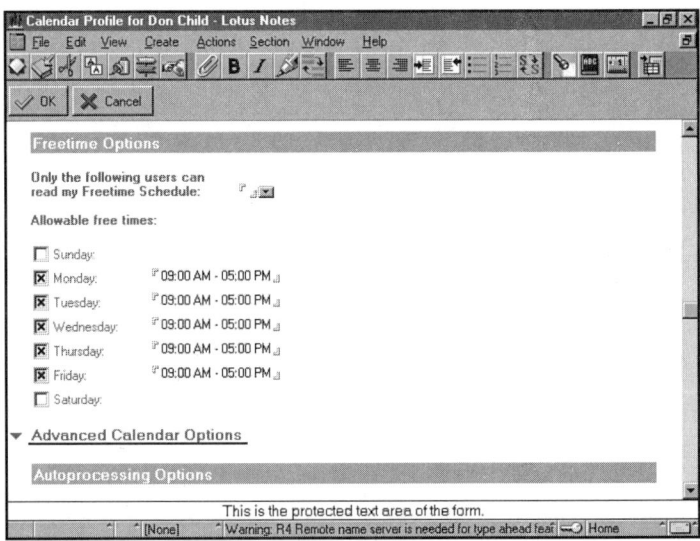

By default, all users can see your free time. If you want to restrict who can see your free time, enter only the names of those who should have access.

NOTE People who can see your free time can only see what time is blocked out. They cannot read your calendar to see what your appointments are unless you gave them access to your calendar in your Delegation Profile.

In the Calendar Profile, you can also define which days and hours you are available for appointments. If you spend your mornings being productive, then you can set your free time schedule so that you cannot be booked for meetings until after 11:00 AM. And if you work an odd schedule, you may want to set the calendar so you are available on Saturday and Sunday, but not on Tuesday and Wednesday, for example.

Looking Up Free Time on Your Local Workstation

You can set up your local Free Time database so it selectively replicates free time from your organization's Free Time database on the Domino server.

You will be learning the details of replicating and setting up the Replication Page in tomorrow's lesson. For now, I will give a high-level description of what you have to do to set up Free Time replication.

On the Replication Page, there is a Free Time icon. If you double-click on the directional arrow next to the Free Time icon, the dialog box shown in Figure 11.16 will be displayed.

Figure 11.16.
Define how much free time is replicated from the server to your local Free Time database.

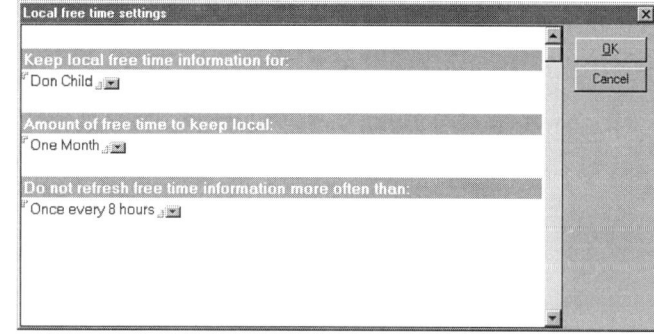

In this dialog box, you can define the following:

- ☐ The names of people whose free time you want to replicate.
- ☐ The amount of free time you want to maintain, ranging from one week to one year.
- ☐ How long the minimum refresh cycle should be, ranging from one hour to eight hours.

After setting up and saving the parameters for your replication, you can click the check box next to the Free Time icon on the Replication Page to activate Free Time replication. After Free Time replication is set up, you can tentatively set up meetings, even if you are disconnected from the local area network.

Setting Up a Broadcast Meeting

When users get an invitation to a meeting in their Notes mail, they can click on a button to RSVP to the invitation. But not all meetings require an RSVP. For example, I belong to a local chapter of the Society for Technical Communication (STC). If we are having a monthly meeting, I can send an invitation to everyone, but it is not important for me to know who is attending (unless they happen to be the speaker for that month's meeting).

I can broadcast an invitation by creating an invitation as described above (minus the Free Time search), and clicking on the check box to indicate that I do not want responses from invitees.

NOTE When an invitation is created using your calendar, you are considered the chairperson. The only way you can assign the meeting chair to another individual is to create the invitation using his calendar. Before you can use someone else's calendar to create an invitation, he must give you access in his Delegation Profile.

Reserving Rooms and Resources

You can also reserve a room for a meeting, and reserve resources, such as a video projector and a microphone, for a meeting at the same time that you create the invitation. As you would expect, the Reservations section of the Invitation form follows the Free Time scheduler, because you normally cannot reserve the room until you know when the meeting will take place.

Rooms and resources are set up in a Resource database on the Domino server. The records are similar to your free time schedule—your resource manager can define blocks of time during which the rooms and resources are available. When you select a room and/or a resource for your meeting, you select the site—the West regional office, for example—and then select the room/resource for your meeting.

NOTE Resources cannot be set up if your organization uses flat names, which were common in earlier versions of Notes. Only hierarchically named organizations can use the Resource database. In most organizations, one individual will be responsible for setting up and maintaining resources.

Responding to an Invitation

When you receive an invitation to a meeting from another Notes user, you will see three buttons on the top of the invitation.

You can click on a button to accept the invitation or to decline the invitation. In either case, a message is sent directly to the person who invited you. You do not have to do anything else when you respond.

You may, however, want to send a note to the person who invited you. For example, you may want to accept with stipulations. You can select Accept as the action to be taken, and then include a note to the person who invited you saying that you would like to see the question of "allowable expenses" included on the agenda. To do so, click on the Other button. A dialog box will be shown that lets you send a brief message, along with one of the following actions:

- *Accept.* This is the same as clicking Accept on the Action Bar, except that you can now add a note to the chairperson.
- *Decline.* This is the same as clicking Decline on the Action Bar, except that you can now add a note to the chairperson.
- *Delegate.* You can delegate the acceptance to another user. When you delegate your acceptance, you also enter the name of the person to whom you are delegating attendance at the meeting, and include a note to the chair. When you save your response, an invitation is automatically sent to the person you delegated the meeting to. After you delegate the invitation, you are no longer considered an invitee, and will not receive any further correspondence regarding the meeting invitation unless you are invited again.
- *Propose Alternative Time/Location.* If you select this as an action to take, you can enter a proposed time and/or a proposed location. When done, you can click a button to send a counterproposal. You will then get a response from the chairperson accepting or declining your counterproposal.
- *Pencil In.* If you pencil in an appointment, it is just like accepting the invitation, but doing so tentatively. The meeting will show up in your calendar, but free time will not be blocked by the meeting.

Any action that you take to accept a meeting sends a message to the chairperson, and creates a meeting document in your mail database.

If you later have to change your mind and decline the invitation, you can open the meeting document and click on Other, and then select Decline or Delegate. Changing your response will generate another e-mail to the chairperson.

Automating Your Response to Invitations

Let's take one last look at the Calendar Profile document, accessed by selecting Actions | Calendar Tools | Calendar Profile. Scroll down to the bottom and open the Advanced Calendar Options section. This section is shown in Figure 11.17.

Figure 11.17.
In the Advanced Calendar Options, you can automate responses to invitations.

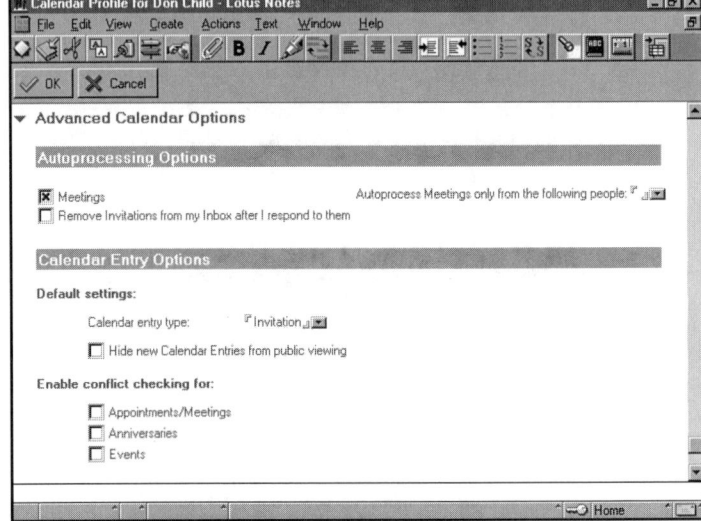

Notice that there are two autoprocessing options.

The first option lets you elect to autoprocess meeting invitations. If you click on this, you can fill in a field to identify individuals from whom you will automatically accept invitations. If you leave this field blank, then all invitations will be autoprocessed. If any individual (an individual from whom you accept autoprocessing) sends you an invitation, the invitation is automatically accepted if you have free time at the time of the meeting. The invitation shows up as a meeting on your calendar.

If the individual sends you an invitation that conflicts with another appointment or meeting, a meeting conflict is created. When you have a conflict, the invitation is not automatically processed. Instead, you can work with the conflicting appointments by opening them individually to accept or decline them, as previously described.

If you click the second box in the Autoprocessing Options, then documents are automatically removed from your Inbox as soon as they are autoprocessed. Otherwise, they would remain in your inbox until you handled them.

Notice that you can select other advanced options that affect your autoprocessing. If you enable conflict checking, then you will see conflicts for any appointments, meetings, anniversaries, and events.

> **NOTE** You can also define which type of Calendar entry is displayed by default, and you can elect to have Calendar entries hidden from public view as a default.

After you save your autoprocessing options, you will be asked on which server the agent should be run on. You should select your home (that is, Mail) server.

Handling Responses from Invitees

When you get responses from invitees, their responses show up in your Inbox with a thumbs up icon if they accepted your invitation, or a thumbs down icon if they had to decline the invitation. You can look at each response individually if you want to, but there is an easier way to get an overview of everyone's status regarding attendance at the meeting.

Open the original invitation. Near the bottom, you will find a button labeled Display Invitee Responses.... Click on this button to display a summary of responses.

A summary will be shown that lists invitees under the categories Accepted, Counter Proposed, Delegated, Declined, No Response, and Removed. If you want, you can send confirmations to individuals from the summary screen by clicking on the Send Confirmation button.

Making Changes to a Meeting

You can change a meeting after it has been set up. If you open the original invitation and change the date or the location, a Reschedule document is sent to all original invitees. When they open the Reschedule document and accept the new time, their calendars are automatically changed.

If you need to cancel a meeting, highlight the invitation and select Actions | Cancel Meeting. A cancellation notice will be sent to all invitees, and when they open the cancellation, the original meeting notice will be automatically removed from their calendars.

If you need to uninvite someone who has already accepted an invitation, open the invitation and select Actions | Remove | Invitees and select the names of the invitees who no longer need to attend the meeting. When they open the memo informing them that they do not need to attend, the original invitation is automatically removed from their calendars.

Creating an Event

The Event type of Calendar entry is a simple document that is virtually identical to an Appointment type document. The only difference is the time increment. Appointments were in increments based on an hourly schedule. An event is something that you can put on your calendar that spans one or more days.

For example, if you want to put your annual vacation on your calendar so that others will not mistakenly think that you have free time available, you can create an Event. Figure 11.18 shows the Event type of Calendar entry.

Figure 11.18.
Use an Event to record an event on your calendar when the event will last for one or more days.

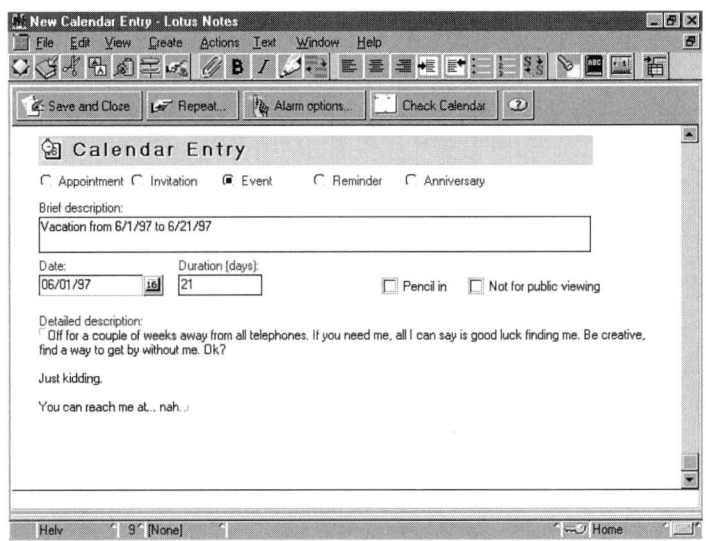

Creating a Reminder

Use Reminders when you need to have Notes provide an alarm to remind you of anything that does not fit into the other Calendar categories. The document is a simple Calendar Entry document with a date and a single time, rather than a start and end time as there is with an Appointment.

Creating an Anniversary

An Anniversary type Calendar entry is another simple document type, an annual reminder rather than a reminder that takes place at a specific day and time. No more excuses for forgetting the boss's birthday.

 **TIP** Remember, you can set up your Calendar Profile so that Anniversaries display conflicts on your calendar.

When you set repeat options for an anniversary, you have the option of moving the anniversary to a Monday or Friday if it falls on a weekend.

Using the Meetings View

The Meetings view gives you an alternative to using your calendar. If you have a lot of To Do tasks, which we will be looking at next, they can clutter your calendar and make it difficult to use.

When you switch to the Meetings view, you can view all Calendar entry documents in one place. The documents are sorted by date.

 **NOTE** You can change the sort order by clicking on the column header. This changes the order so the latest start date appears at the top of the view, rather than appearing at the bottom of the view.

Figure 11.19 shows an example of the Meetings view.

Figure 11.19.
The Meetings view shows all Calendar entries and responses in a single view.

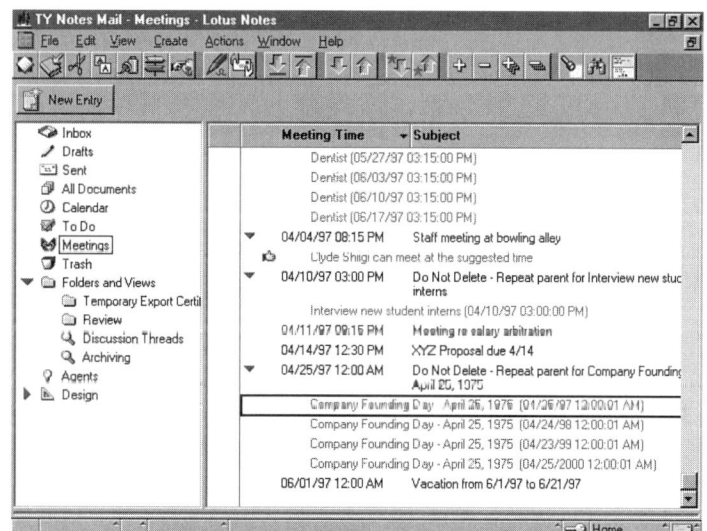

The view displays all Calendar entries and responses to invitations. It also consolidates repeat events under a single parent document.

WARNING

If you delete the parent document, the individual repeated events are also deleted. However, you can delete individual repeated events without effecting the parent event.

Creating a To Do List

I know several people who wouldn't be caught dead without their To Do lists—long lists that get crossed off one item at a time, or get carried forward to the next day. Another list has deadline items, those that cannot slip onto the next day's calendar. The Notes Calendaring and Scheduling function has its own To Do list.

Switch to the To Do view and click on the New Task button. The Task form will be displayed as shown in Figure 11.20.

Figure 11.20.
You can create a To Do document and give it a priority.

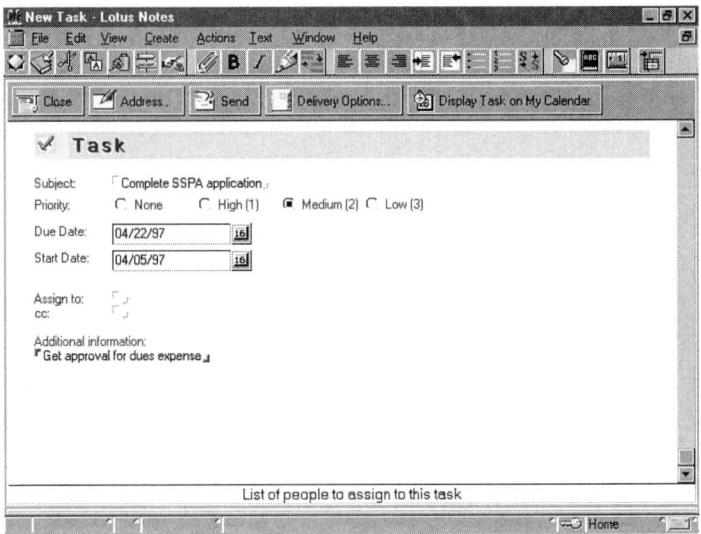

In Figure 11.20, I have already created a task. The fields on the form include:

- *Subject.* This is what you will see in the To Do view and optionally on your calendar.
- *Priority.* You can leave the priority unset, or you can indicate a high, medium, or low priority task. This affects how the document gets sorted in the To Do view.
- *Due Date.* This is the date when the task should be completed. It is not required, but when you do use it, it determines how the item is sorted in your To Do list.
- *Start Date.* The start date indicates when you should start working on the task. It is used by the system to calculate whether the task is a current task or a future task. If you do not enter a start date, then Notes assumes the task is current, and gives it today's date as the start date.
- *Additional Information.* This is a Rich Text field that you can use to provide additional information.

Creating a Task While Reading Mail

You can create a task while reading your e-mail. There is an Action on the Action menu that lets you convert any document into a task.

For example, I received a document in my mail from Nancy Doe asking me to go on and begin filling out a nomination for the Beacon Award. While reading the document, I decide to convert this into a task for myself. I select Actions | Convert to Task from the menu bar, and Notes creates a new task document, with the original document copied into the Rich Text field. I can then enter any scheduling details at the top of the form, and voila! A new task!

Assigning a Task to Others

I don't really have time to do some tasks myself—too many other deadlines. Therefore, I can assign the task to someone else by clicking on the Assign to Others button, and entering the name of the person to whom this task is being assigned. This is shown in Figure 11.21.

Figure 11.21.
A task can be created from e-mail, and then forwarded to others to complete.

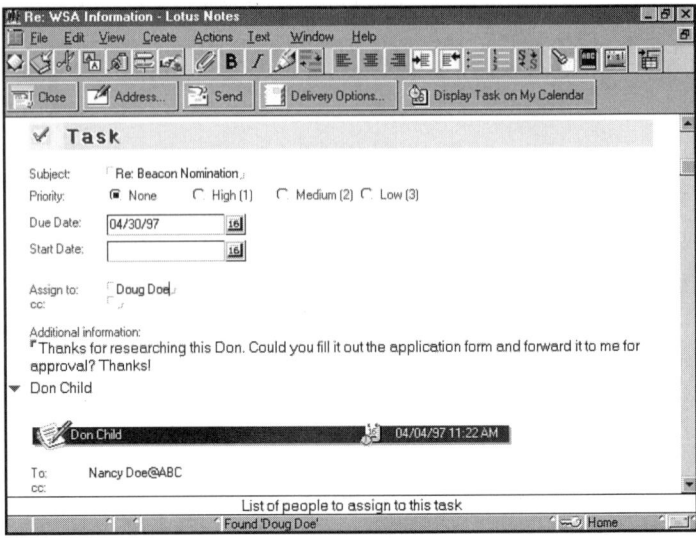

When you save the task, it will automatically be mailed to the person to whom you assigned the task.

Notice that you also have the option of displaying this or any other task in your calendar by clicking on the Display Task on My Calendar button. The task can also be removed from your calendar, if it is already there, by clicking on the Remove from Calendar button.

Looking at the To Do View

The To Do view holds all of your tasks. As you can see from Figure 11.22, the tasks are categorized by status. Overdue tasks show up at the top of the view, followed by Current tasks, Future tasks, and Complete tasks.

If tasks have been assigned to others, they are listed in the view, and their completion is updated by clicking on the Update Tasks button.

When you complete a task, highlight it and click on the Mark Completed button. The task will be marked as completed, and will be moved to the Complete category. Once a task has been marked as complete, it cannot be reactivated.

TIP If you want to remove the completed tasks from the view, highlight them and click on the Remove from To Do View button.

Calendaring and Scheduling

Figure 11.22.
The To Do view displays your tasks sorted by status and priority.

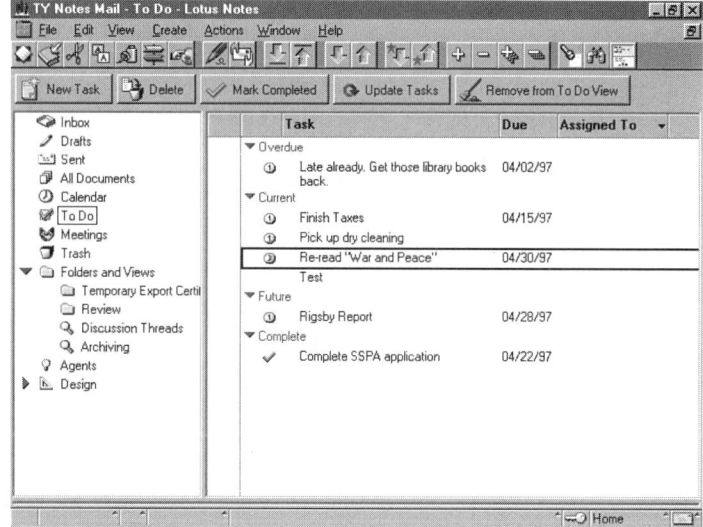

Working with Documents in the Calendar View

Now that you have created a lot of appointments, meetings, and To Do tasks in your calendar, let's take another look. Figure 11.23 shows the One Month view fully populated with various activities.

Figure 11.23.
The One Month view of the calendar shows all times that you have tasks or appointments.

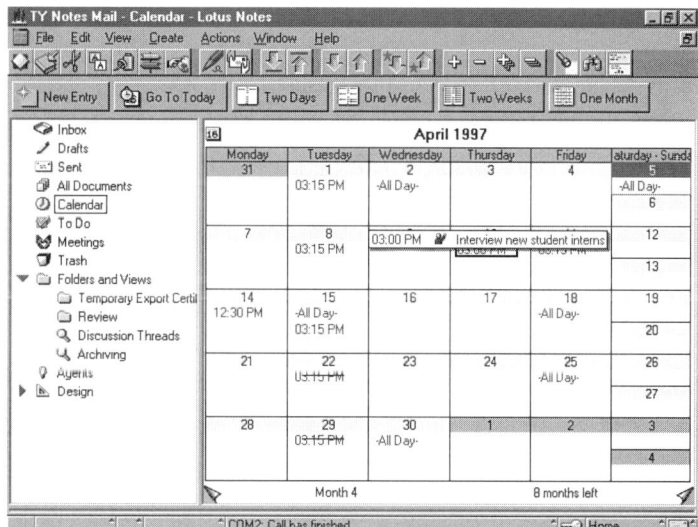

There are a few things to note in this view.

- There is not enough space to tell what is happening for any period of time marked on the calendar. Hold the mouse pointer over a marked time, and a pop-up will tell you what the event or task is. In the example, the appointment on April 10 is shown in a pop-up.
- You can delete an event or task by highlighting it and pressing the Delete key. Deleted documents are indicated by a line drawn through them. When you close or refresh your mail, you will have the option of permanently deleting the documents.

NOTE This assumes you have retained the default settings on the Mail page of the User Preferences dialog box.

- You can copy a document and paste it on a new day, creating a new instance of the same Calendar entry or Task. The new copy is identical to the original, except the date is changed. Note: If you copy and paste a repeating entry, the new pasted version of the document is saved as a non-repeating entry.
- You can move a document from one day to another by pointing to it and holding down the left mouse button. Drag the document to a new day, and then release the mouse button to drop it on the new day.

NOTE If you move a repeating entry, a dialog box will be displayed giving you the option of moving just the current entry, moving all future entries, all previous entries, or all entries.

You can also move appointments from one hour to another hour by dragging and dropping on a Two Day view of the Calendar. Figure 11.24 shows the Two Day view. I am in the process of moving my dentist appointment from 9:00 in the morning to a new time during the day. Trivia question: Which is the most painful task or appointment on the day shown?

Figure 11.24.
You can move appointments from hour to hour by dragging and dropping.

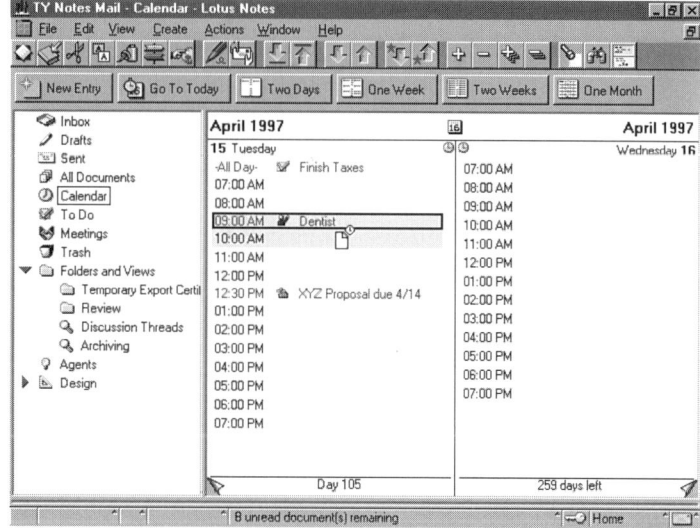

Summary

Look at your Notes Calendar. You have now completed 11 days of learning how to use Notes. If you had known about these calendar functions before you started, you could have created a To Do list, and checked off each day's lesson as you completed it. Hopefully, you would have given each day's lesson a high priority.

Of course, you had other things to do during the past 11 days, as well. You probably have had a couple of deadlines to meet, a meeting or two with your coworkers, maybe your spouse's or child's birthday to remember. And did someone send you an e-mail asking you to go back and look up how to set up his computer so that he can see that nifty marbled desktop like you have? Maybe you changed that e-mail into a task, and assigned it to him, telling him to find out for himself using the online help.

Did you have to set up a meeting? You could have. You would set a tentative meeting time, entered a list of the people you wanted to invite, and then done a free time lookup to see if everyone could come at the time you wanted. If someone had a conflicting appointment, Notes would tell you when everyone was likely to be available. Using Notes Calendaring and Scheduling, you can save yourself a lot of time playing phone tag, and become an efficient manager of your own and everyone else's time.

Workshop

The Workshop section presents questions and answers, quiz questions to help you cement your new knowledge, and exercises to give you experience using what you have learned. Try to understand the questions and exercises before moving on to the next lesson. Answers are in Appendix A.

Q&A

Q I have been using Lotus Organizer for Calendaring and Scheduling. Can the Notes Calendar use information in my Organizer calendar?

A While Notes provides a C&S function, it does so in a Notes database format. The Organizer's ORG files are not Notes database files, so cannot be used directly in your Notes Calendar.

Q I assigned a task to several people. Some completed the task and some didn't. Can I mark the task as completed?

A When another person completes a task you assigned to him, it shows up in your mailbox as completed. However, if the task was assigned to multiple people, the task is not completed until everyone indicates that they are finished.

Q Can I automate the scheduling of appointments with users who do not have Notes Mail?

A The Calendar Entry document gets sent to other individuals as e-mail. If you have set up your address book so Notes can find a route to the individual, you can send him an invitation to a meeting. Some functionality such as the ability to automatically respond to an invitation will be lost, however.

Quiz

1. Can other Notes users see your e-mail if you give them access to your calendar?
2. If you hide a Calendar entry from public view, can others see the entry when looking at available free time?
3. If you change a repeating appointment, can you change all future occurrences of the same appointment?
4. Do Tasks show up in your Meetings view? Do they show up on your calendar?
5. What happens to someone who has already accepted an invitation if you change the time of the meeting?

6. How do you create a general meeting announcement where others are not obliged to attend or RSVP?
7. What is the difference between an appointment and an event?
8. Does Notes save an appointment if you already have another appointment at the same time?

Exercises

1. Working with two of your fellow Notes coworkers, create a meeting invitation and have them respond to the invitation. Have one accept and one decline the invitation. View their responses from within the original invitation, and then cancel the invitation. Check with your coworkers to see what sort of mail they received regarding the meeting.
2. Create a To Do list for yourself. Include everything that you have on your agenda for the next two weeks. If you want, display your tasks on your calendar.
3. Using the Calendar Profile document, define which types of Calendar entries you want reminders for, and set how long before the start time you want to be notified.

Week 2

Day 12

Mobile Notes: Using Notes When You're Out of the Office

Today, you are going to learn how to work with Notes when you are not in your office. So far, everything you've learned has been based on the assumption that you were working on a Notes workstation attached to a Domino server via a local area network (LAN) or a wide area network (WAN). But, in reality, many people in today's workforce are mobile, or they take work home and use their own PC to carry on with what they were doing in the office.

You will be learning about replication, and about three key parts of the Notes interface: the Location document, the Server Connection document, and the Replicator Page on the Notes desktop. By the end of today's lesson, you should be able to set up your home Notes workstation to communicate with the Domino server in your office.

Sharing Data Between Different Locations

When Netscape bought Collabra, it was hoping to target one of Lotus Notes' strong points, its ability to share data across different platforms and different locations. When Bill Gates talked about information at your fingertips, he may have had a very real vision of where computing was going, but people's experience with Microsoft Exchange has once again demonstrated just how sophisticated the Notes model for data sharing really is. What Netscape and Microsoft call "replication" is a limited attempt to implement a small part of the technology that Notes was built on, and has been building on since the beginning of the 1990s.

Notes advertises itself as using the three C's: communication, collaboration, and coordination. These concepts are the backbone of Notes, and their implementation lets you truly have information at your fingertips, no matter where you are, as long as you have a telephone line available to you.

The primary way that Notes shares information between locations is through replication. *Replication* is the synchronizing of the data in two databases over a period of time. Two databases that replicate with each other do not necessarily contain identical data, because it is possible to replicate only certain parts of a database, but the data that is replicated gets synchronized every time replication takes place.

NOTE Replication can only take place between a Notes client workstation and a Domino server, or between two Domino servers. There is no workstation-to-workstation replication.

You learned earlier that you could work with documents on your local workstation, or you could work with a shared database on a Domino server. But it is also possible for the database on your local workstation to be a replica of a database on the server.

If your local workstation is connected to the office LAN, there is normally no need to have replica databases. But as soon as you put Notes onto a laptop computer, or start using Notes at home or in an outlying office, the capability to replicate data is vital.

The classic scenario is the Notes user on the road. You make replicas of the databases you need to work with while you are gone. You get on an airplane, open up a Notes database, and start creating documents or editing existing documents. You delete documents. You change the design of a database. You read your mail and your respond to people via e-mail. You can send out invitations to meetings, including looking up the free time of those you are inviting. You can even browse the Internet, as you will see on Day 14. And you can do all of this while you are disconnected from any network.

You get to your hotel room at the end of the day, plug your modem into the phone jack, and replicate with the Domino server in your home office. All the work you did on the airplane is replicated to the server so others using the database in the office can see your changes. You can see the changes others made since you last replicated with the databases on the server. You can participate in a threaded discussion in a discussion database. You can read new e-mail, and the memos you wrote to others are forwarded to the Domino server. From there, the memos find their way to the addressees.

There is a lot of setup that goes into making all this happen, but most of the setup is automated, and takes place only once, when you first install Notes on your workstation. At that time, you define communication ports and modems, and you define Location documents. After that, you can replicate databases with one or two clicks.

Setting Up Communications

You have to have a modem before you can communicate with the Domino server over the phone line. Part of the setup process for your workstation is to set up communications ports. You will also have to do this if you are setting up a workstation so you can dial in to a Domino server.

You set up communications on the User Preferences page. Select File | Tools | User Preferences. Click on the Ports icon to display the port setup page shown in Figure 12.1.

Figure 12.1.
Set up communication ports in the User Preferences dialog box.

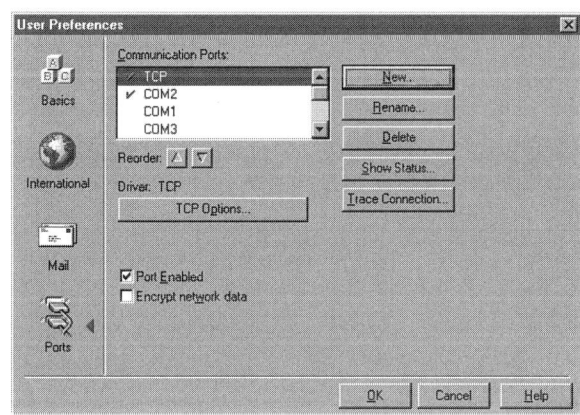

The top part of this dialog box lists the ports that can be made available to you if you have a way of connecting. In addition to the TCP and COM ports shown, you can define a port as a LAN, as SPX, or VINES. For all practical purposes, though, you will be using either a TCP or COM2 port.

TCP is the protocol that you use to communicate with the Domino server if you have a connection to the Internet for your PC, as well as a connection to the Internet for the Domino server on the other end.

COM ports are the standard ports through which you computer communicates with outside devices such as printers and modems. Most modem connections use the COM2 port. The COM2 port is predefined to use XPC protocol, the "language" that the Domino server uses to communicate with another computer via a modem. You cannot change the protocol.

Setting Up a Modem Connection

Highlight COM2 and click on the COM2 Options... button to display the Additional Setup dialog box shown in Figure 12.2.

Figure 12.2.
The Additional Server dialog box is used to set up the modem for your Notes workstation.

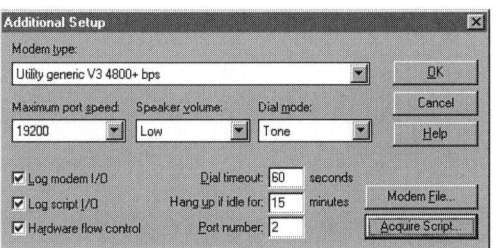

In the Additional Setup dialog box, select the type of modem you have. If you cannot find your modem, you can select one of the Utility Generic modems, or use the autoconfigure option located at the bottom of the modem list.

Select the nearest port speed setting at or above the maximum speed of your modem. If you have problems communicating, you can always pick a slower speed.

Select the speaker volume for your modem, and indicate whether you have tone or pulse dialing.

The log settings are useful if you are having troubles getting your modem to work properly. Your system administrator may be able to help you if you have the I/O and Script logs from your modem.

Leave Hardware Flow Control selected unless your modem does not support flow control. Check your modem documentation if you are not sure.

You can customize modem files (text files that enable your computer to talk to a modem) and acquire scripts (a text file that is used to communicate with an ISDN modem before the modem script is run) if necessary. If you need help with these, contact your system administrator.

The basic thing that you need to worry about in this dialog box is to find the correct modem type. The rest of the dialog box is fine tuning, and every situation will be different. When you are done setting up your modem, save your selections and return to the User Preferences Ports page.

If you want to test your connection to see if it works, click on the Trace Connection... button. Enter the name of the Domino server you want to call, and in the Call Server dialog box, enter the number to dial to reach the server. Notes will attempt to dial the server, and will log the entire search path to the server. You can use this to determine where you are having problems, if you cannot connect. An example of the Trace Connections log is shown in Figure 12.3.

Figure 12.3.
Trace a connection if you want to see whether you can communicate with a server.

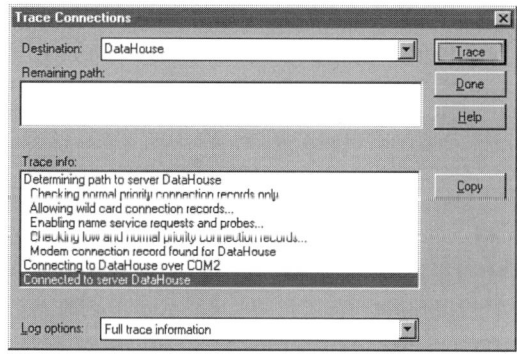

 **NOTE** It may seem obvious, but in order to connect to a Domino server via a modem, you have to know the telephone number to dial. Ask your Notes administrator which number you should use to contact the server.

Setting Up an Internet Connection

An Internet connection also requires a modem, and it requires TCP as the driver. There is not much setup for the modem with a TCP port. All you can do is define the duration of connection time-outs (the amount of time your computer should wait before trying to reconnect, if a connection is broken).

In addition to your TCP connection, you need to establish a PPP or SLIP connection to an Internet service provider (ISP). You establish a connection using software such as Trumpet Winsock, which should be available from your ISP or from shareware resources, or Dial Up Networking, which is included in Windows 95.

Setting Up a Location

After you set up a communication port, you need to set up a location from which you will be communicating with the server. To set up a location, you create or modify a Location document in your Personal Address Book. You can set up multiple locations for different purposes. For example, you might have the following locations, which Notes creates by default:

- Home, for working from home.
- Network, where you are connected via a network connection.
- Internet, for connecting over the Internet using TCP and a dial-up connection.
- Travel, where you have to dial 1 plus your area code before dialing the server's number.
- Island, where you are disconnected from the server. This lets you work while you are disconnected from all communications devices without Notes trying to connect to servers when there is no way you can connect to them.

You can create new Location documents, or you can modify the standard locations that Notes provides for workstation installations. All the locations listed above are standard Notes locations, except for the Internet location.

To create or modify a Location document:

1. Select File | Mobile | Locations from the menu bar to display the Locations view of your Personal Address Book.
2. Click on the Add Location button to add a new location, or highlight a location and click on Edit Location to edit an existing location. The Location document will be displayed.

Mobile Notes: Using Notes When You're Out of the Office

3. Fill out the fields on the Location document. The document is complex, so it is described section by section in the paragraphs that follow.

Figure 12.4 shows the top part of the Location document.

Figure 12.4.
The Location document is used to set up communication parameters so you can quickly switch settings in different locations.

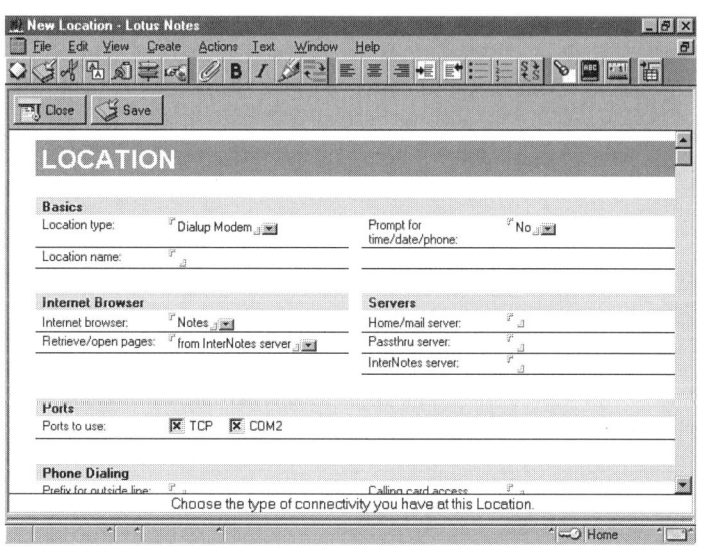

Defining Location Basics

The Basics section of the Location document is used to define the following information:

- ☐ *Location Type.* You have a choice of setting up a Local Area Network connection if you have a permanent connection to the server, a modem connection if you have to dial to reach the server, a combination of a LAN and modem connection where you have a choice of connections, or no connection at all for a Location Type where you have no connection to communications devices. Depending on the Location Type you select, some of the fields described below may be hidden—for example, phone numbers are not relevant if you have a LAN-only connection.

> **NOTE** An Internet connection is a type of Local Area Network connection, because the Domino server treats you as if you were communicating over the LAN, as opposed to communicating over a dial up phone line.

- *Location Name.* This is the name you give the location. The name will appear in the list of locations when you want to select a new location setup.
- *Prompt for Time/date/phone.* If you select Yes, you will be prompted for the phone time, date, and phone number every time you want to connect to the Notes server. For example, if you travel around the country and have a choice of servers to which you can dial in, you can set up several different locations, but you might want to select the phone number and time zone every time you call the server. This allows Notes to accurately determine which documents have already been replicated based on the time the documents were last modified.
- *Web Proxy.* If you select a LAN location, the Web proxy field will be visible. Depending on how your system is configured, you can have a direct Internet connection or a connection through a proxy server. The proxy server acts as a buffer between your LAN and the Internet. If you connect through the LAN and have an HTTP Proxy server, then you enter the IP address of the proxy server in this field. You can click on the HTTP Proxy icon to display a dialog box that will assist you with entering proxy information. If you need help, please contact your Notes System Administrator.

Defining an Internet Browser

You will be learning more about how Notes connects to the Internet on Day 14, but for now, you will set up a Web browser for the location you are defining.

You can select the Notes Web Navigator, Netscape Navigator, Microsoft Internet Explorer, or another browser as your option. When you launch an URL from within Notes, the browser you have selected for the location will be used.

If you select the Notes Web Navigator, you have a choice of where to retrieve stored Web pages from. You can retrieve them from the Web Navigator database on the Domino server, or from your local Web Navigator database. You can also elect to retrieve Web pages directly from the Internet, bypassing any Web pages stored in the Web Navigator database.

Defining Servers

You can define a home/mail server and a passthru server for each location, in addition to an optional InterNotes server. The home/mail server is the server on which your mail database is located when you are working on your organization's LAN. This information is needed so Notes can route your mail.

The passthru server is usually the same as your mail server. A passthru server acts as a conduit to other Domino servers, if you have multiple servers set up in your organization. With a passthru server, you can connect to a single server, and then work with databases on other servers by passing through the first server (the passthru server). Again, if you have questions, please contact your Notes system administrator.

The InterNotes server is only available if you selected the Notes Web Navigator as your preferred browser, and elected to retrieve Web pages from the server-based Web Navigator database. The InterNotes server is the Domino server where the server-based Web Navigator database is located.

Setting Up Phone Dialing

If the location you are creating uses a modem to dial up the server, then the Location document will have a Phone Dialing section. In this section, you can set up your workstation so you can call the server during scheduled replication using a variety of prefixes for your call, such as an international dialing code and a calling card number. You can also specify a different telephone number to use for your server when you are at this location.

The Phone Dialing section is shown in Figure 12.5.

Figure 12.5.
Set phone dialing rules for a location, and set up mail and replication.

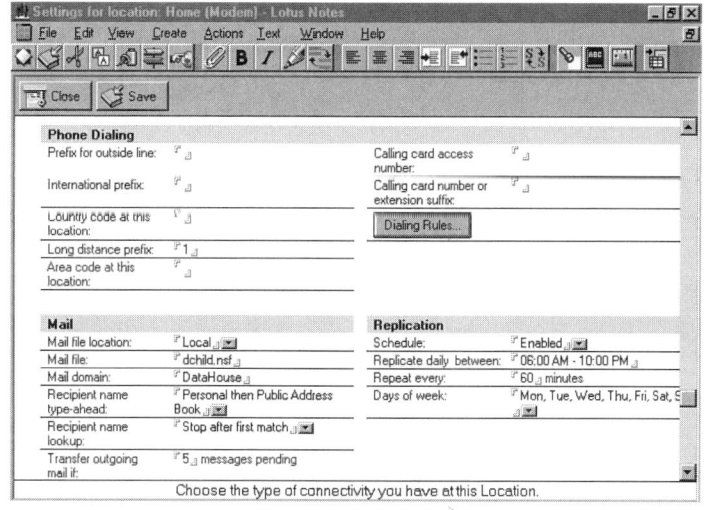

You can set up specific phone dialing instructions in the Phone Dialing section. You will be setting up a Server Connection document before you are done getting set up, but you can also specify the rules that Notes should use for a specific location, such as an overseas travel location. You can specify the following:

- *Prefix for outside line.* If you have to dial a number to get an outside line, enter it in this field.

- *International prefix.* Enter the number you need to dial to make international calls.
- *Country code.* Enter the country code for the location.
- *Long distance prefix.* Enter the prefix you need to dial to make long distance calls.
- *Area code* at this location.
- *Calling card access number.* This is the access number you want to use when you want to charge calls from this location to a calling card.
- *Calling card number or extension suffix.* Enter the number of the calling card you want to use.
- *Dialing rules.* You can specify a different number to use when calling the server from this location. For example, you might have an 800 number you can call to connect to your server when you are in another area code.

You can always override these dialing instructions by dialing manually using the telephone dialing SmartIcon.

Setting Up Mail

For each Location document you create, you should define your mail setup. Notes handles most of the setup for you, but you can modify the settings if necessary.

The fields in the Mail section of the Location document include:

- *Mail file location.* If you are using a modem connection, the default location is Local. If you are using a LAN connection (TCP, for example), the default location is On Server. If you want to store mail in a local outgoing mailbox and then send it when you connect to the server, set your mail to Local.
- *Mail file.* This is the database name for your mail file.
- *Mail Domain.* This is the domain where your home server (the location of your server-based mail file) is located. Notes fills this in by default, but if you need to know your mail domain's name, ask your Notes System Administrator.
- *Recipient name type ahead.* When you address a memo, Notes looks in various Notes address books and inserts the addressee's full name as soon as you type enough information to distinguish the name from others. You can disable type-ahead, or you can set up the location so that it uses your Personal Address Book only, or the Personal Address Book then the Public Address Book. Using a Personal Address Book for type-ahead reduces the need to communicate with the server, which makes lookups quicker, and also ensures accuracy of addressee names no matter what Location you are using.

- *Recipient name lookup*. You have the option of stopping lookups after the first match, or continuing to check all available address books. Consider the scenario where you have five people in your address book named "Andrew," for example. You address a memo to "Andrew," and the first Andrew's name always gets inserted by the type-ahead feature. If you set "Recipient name lookup" to check all address books, then when you attempt to send a memo to "Andrew," Notes will tell you that there are multiple possible addressees...which one do you want?
- *Messages pending*. This determines when Notes will call the mail server to empty the outgoing mail box. Normally, this will take place anytime there is a connection to the server for replication, including scheduled replications. If you have at least five messages in your outgoing mailbox, for example, Notes will try to call the server to deliver the mail, even if there is no replication scheduled.

Setting Up a Replication Schedule

If you want to replicate databases with the server, you can do it manually on an ad hoc basis. However, you also have the option of setting up scheduled replication from a specific location. For example, I frequently work from home, where it is a local call to the server in my office. I turn the computer on in the morning, and once an hour Notes dials the server and replicates databases that I have set up for replication.

If scheduled replication is disabled, the Replication section of the Location document is empty. Change the schedule to Enabled and the section expands to let you fill in the following information:

- *Schedule*. Enabled or disabled.
- *Replicate daily between*. This defines the range of time during which replication takes place. If your computer is turned on during the defined hours, then replication will take place based on the schedule you set up.
- *Repeat every 60 minutes*. The repeat interval lets you establish the number of minutes between replications. How often you replicate depends on the type of information you are working with, and how important it is to have the information current. If you work in virtual real time, for example working with the latest stock market quotes, you may want to replicate every five minutes. If you work with static data, you can probably get by with once a day at the most. The repeat interval starts from the completion of the last successful replication. For example, if you have a replication interval of 120 minutes and you finish replicating at 9:37 a.m., then Notes will call the server again at 11:37 a.m. to start replicating again.
- *Days of the week*. You can set scheduled replication so it only takes place on certain days of the week, for example, during working hours from Monday to Friday.

After you set up scheduled replication, you still need to set up your Replicator Page for the location. This is described later in today's lesson.

Working with Advanced Settings

The Advanced Settings section of the Location document is used primarily for Web Retriever and Java settings. However, you can set a few standard settings, including:

- ☐ *Local time zone.* Set the local time zone so that Notes can resolve time differences between different locations.
- ☐ *Daylight savings time.* If you observe daylight savings, set this so that Notes can adjust its internal clock.
- ☐ *Only for user.* You can define the location so that you are the only one allowed to use it, if others share your Notes workspace. This works in combination with the next setting.
- ☐ *User ID to switch to.* You can have Notes automatically switch to another User ID when you switch to this new location. This could be used if you work with more than one Notes organization, and have separate Notes IDs for each organization, or if multiple users share the same workstation.
- ☐ *Load images.* You can have your Notes Web Navigator download and display text from Web pages before graphics are loaded and displayed. This speeds up the navigation of Web pages.
- ☐ *Remote LAN idle timeout.* If you set up a remote LAN server, Notes makes a connection to the server whenever it needs to access a database on the server. Notes will hang up the remote LAN connection after *n* seconds if there is no activity. This is where you set the number of seconds of inactivity before Notes hangs up the connection.

If you are working over a LAN connection (a TCP location, for example), you can also set up a secondary TCP/IP Notes name server, a secondary TCP/IP host, a secondary NDS Notes name server, and a secondary NDS name server. See your Notes System Administrator for details.

The other two subsections in the Advanced section, Web Retriever configuration and Java applet security, are discussed on Day 14.

Setting Up a Server Connection

You have now set up a communications port and a Location document, but you still need to tell Notes which phone number to call. You do this by creating a Server Connection document. This document defines how Notes should connect to the server. You have to create a Server Connection record for every server you want to communicate with.

To create a Server Connection:

1. Select File | Mobile | Server Phone Numbers from the menu bar. This will display the Server Connections view in your Personal Address Book.
2. Click on the Add Connection button to display the Server Connection document shown in Figure 12.6.

Figure 12.6.
Use the Server Connection document to define how to connect to a server.

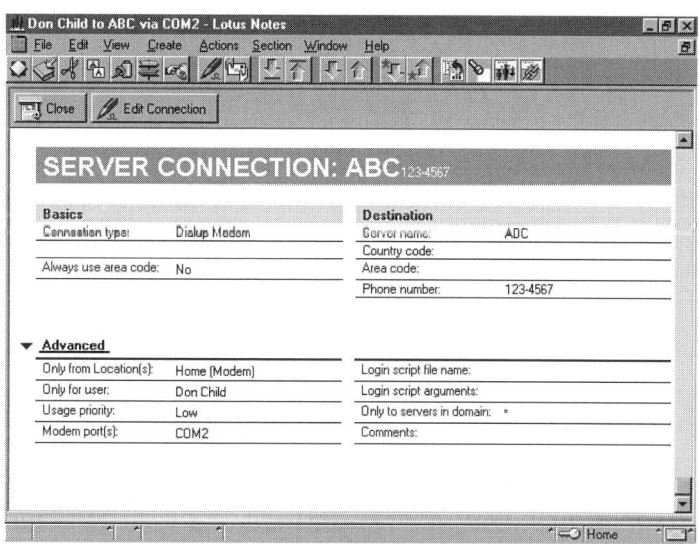

The Server Connection document is actually fairly simple, but in Figure 12.6, the Advanced section has been expanded to show all the possibilities.

The information you need to fill in includes:

- *Connection type.* You can define any one of five different connection types: Local Area Network, Dialup Modem, Passthru Server, Remote LAN Service, or Hunt Group. Check with your Notes System Administrator to determine which type of connection you should be using. The connection type you select will determine which other fields are displayed.

NOTE You have already encountered most of these, but Hunt Group is a new term. A *Hunt Group* is a way to set up multiple passthru servers for your organization.

- *Server name.* Enter the name of the server you want to access.
- *Always use area code.* Select Yes if you need the area code in order to contact the server. This and the other phone number fields are only displayed for Dialup Modem or Hunt Group connections.
- *Country code.* Enter the country code if it is needed in order to call the server.
- *Area code.* If you enter an area code, it will only be used if you also select Always Use Area Code.
- *Phone number.* The telephone number that you call to connect to the server.
- *Use LAN port.* This is only shown for a LAN connection, and lets you select which enabled port should be used when connecting to this server.
- *Passthru server name or hunt group.* This is only shown for a Passthru server connection, and defines which server or hunt group to go through to get to the destination server. A *hunt group* is a group of passthru servers that can be accessed with a single connection, sometimes used in larger organizations to balance the load between several passthru servers.

When setting up a Remote Access Service, an expanded section is displayed. In this section, you enter the name of the RAS (either Microsoft Remote Access Service or Appletalk Remote Access), and then enter the name of the remote connection, your login and password, the telephone number, and any additional information.

In the Advanced section of the Server Connection document, you can define the following:

- Which locations this connection can be used from.
- Which Notes users can use the connection.
- Which priority this connection should have. If Notes cannot connect with a higher priority connection, it can retry using a lower priority.
- Which of the active modem communication ports should be used.

You can also define a login script file to be used, the login script arguments to be used, and you can restrict the login to servers in a specific domain. Most users will not require these settings. If you are an advanced user with special requirements, work with your Notes System Administrator to set up these fields correctly.

When you're done, save the Server Connection document.

In the Server Connection view, you will see all connections listed, with icons to indicate whether they are Dialup, LAN, Passthru, RAS, or a Hunt Group.

Verifying Your Connection

After you create a connection, you need to verify that the connection is set up correctly. The easiest way to do that is to call the server and see if you can connect to it.

A good way to verify your connection is to try to open a database that is on the Notes server. To do that from your workstation with a Dialup connection, follow these steps:

1. Select File | Database | Open from the menu bar, or press Ctrl+O.
2. In the Open Database dialog box, type the name of the server in the Server field.
3. Click on Open to view databases on the server.

Notes will display a dialog box asking `Make call to server ABC on port COM2?`, substituting the name of your server and whichever communications port you are using.

If you click on Yes, Notes will display a dialog box like the one shown in Figure 12.7, with the name of the server and the highest priority telephone number for contacting the server. If you have other routes to the server, these will also be shown so you can determine which connection to use.

Figure 12.7.
If you have the right server and the right phone number, click on Auto Dial to call the server.

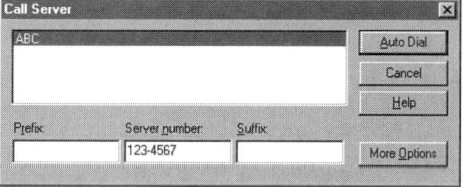

When you have verified that the correct server and the correct connection are selected, click on Auto Dial. Notes will call the server so you can select a database to open. If you can see a list of databases on the server, your connection is okay. If the connection fails, review your setup.

TIP You can enter a telephone number in the Call Server dialog box, overriding any connections you have set up. If no connection is set up, you can enter a phone number and call the server directly by entering a number and clicking on Auto Dial.

NOTE  If you have an acoustical modem, click on More Options in the Call Server dialog box, and then click on Manual Dial. Notes will display a series of help dialog boxes that walk you through the process of dialing and connecting to the server.

Understanding Replicas

You are now set up to replicate databases. The only thing you need are databases that can be replicated. I will assume that you are setting up replicas on a computer that is using a dial-up connection to a Domino server. You can also create a replica database over other types of connection, but most mobile users are likely to use a dial-up connection.

A replica database is not just a complete copy of another Notes database. When you copy a database (using File | Database | New Copy), you get a copy of the database design, the documents within the database, and even a copy of the ACL, but you do not get a replica of the database because one vital element is missing—the Replica ID.

Every database has a Replica ID number that is unique to the database and its replicas. If you make a replica copy of the database, the two databases have an identical Replica ID number. It is this Replica ID number that identifies two databases as replicas of each other, not the design of the database or the documents within the database. In fact, two replica databases can contain different sets or subsets of documents through a process referred to as *selective replication*.

To help you understand why you want to selectively replicate documents between replica databases, look at the ABC corporation with all of its widget sales people. They have a database at headquarters that lists all the latest price changes and sales incentives...information that everyone needs. They also list quotas, keep all purchase orders and invoices, and keep a running tally of everyone's sales by region. Now, if I'm the western regional sales person and I have limited disk space on my laptop, I don't want all the invoices and correspondence and so forth for the southern, eastern, and northern sales districts, thank you. Maybe a summary of sales would be nice, because I feel competitive, but I don't need all of the nitty gritty details. But I do need to replicate my own information with the server at headquarters, so I set up selective replication, and my local database ends up with only a subset of the documents on the main corporate Domino server.

The Replica ID for each database is seen on the Information page of the Database Properties InfoBox. To refresh your memory, you can open the Database Properties InfoBox by clicking on a database icon on the Notes desktop, and then selecting File | Database | Properties. Click on the second tab to display the Information page. Near the bottom of the page is the Replica ID, as you can see in Figure 12.8.

Figure 12.8.
Every Notes database has a 16-digit Replica ID number that uniquely identifies it and its replicas.

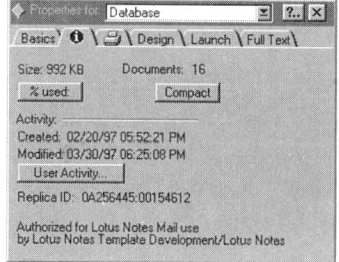

In the example shown above, the Replica ID is 0A256445:00154612. You do not have to remember this number. That is the computer's job.

Creating a Replica Database

To make a replica of a database, follow these steps:

1. Connect to the server and open a database you want to replicate, or place the database icon on your desktop without opening the database.
2. Highlight the database icon or open the database.
3. Select File | Replication | New Replica... from the menu bar. Notes will display the dialog box shown in Figure 12.9.

Figure 12.9.
Define the properties for your replica database in the New Replica dialog box.

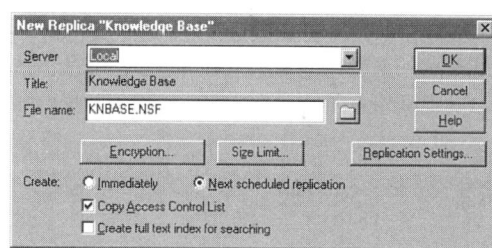

4. Leave the "server" on which the replica stored as Local, and give the replica a new file name if you want to. Include a full data path if you want the replica stored anywhere besides the default data directory. Leave the other settings as they are for now. You can set up database encryption and size limit here just as you did when creating a new database.

Click on the Replication Settings button to define what which parts of the database you want to replicate, if you want to create replication settings in advance. You can also access the Replication Settings dialog box after creating a database replica.

A *replica stub* (a space holder for the new replica) will be put on your Notes desktop, and the dialog box shown in Figure 12.10 will be displayed.

Figure 12.10.
Limit the size of a replica by defining replication settings.

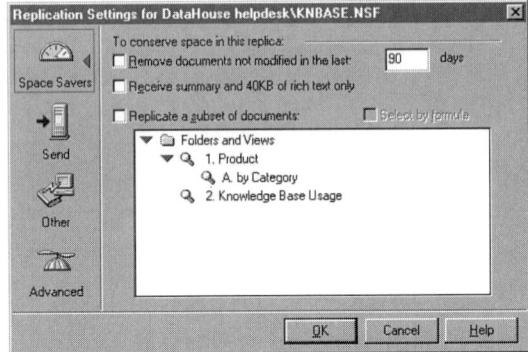

Controlling What Gets Replicated

You can use the Replication Settings dialog box to control the size and content of your local replica of a database. You can do this when creating a new replica copy of a database, or you can do it after the replica has been created by highlighting the replica database and selecting File | Replication | Settings from the menu bar.

In the Replication Settings dialog box, you can control the size of your replica by using the following fields:

- *Remove Documents not Modified in Last 90 Days.* If you have Manager access to your local database, then older documents will be deleted from the database unless they have been updated recently.

- *Receive Summary and 40KB of Rich Text Only.* This limits how much of larger documents gets replicated.

NOTE
If you replicate just part of a document and subsequently discover that you need to replicate the entire document, you can request that the entire document get downloaded from the Actions menu by selecting Retrieve Entire Document.

- *Replicate a Subset of Documents.* You can highlight the folders of views that you want to replicate, or you can replicate only documents that meet specific criteria by entering a simple formula.

TIP Look at the formulas used to select documents for views. They identify a field name, and then specify what must be in that field if a document is to be replicated.

On the Send page of the Replication Settings dialog box, you can define what gets sent from your database to the one on the server. You can define the following:

- *Do not Send Deletions Made in This Replica to Other Replicas.* If you set this, you could replicate an entire database, and then delete the documents you do not need, without deleting the documents on the server copy of the database.
- *Do not Send Changes in Database Title and Catalog Info to Other Replicas.* You can change settings locally, giving your database a unique name and telling Notes not to publish the database name in a database catalog that lists all databases available in the local data directories and makes databases available in the Open Database dialog box. If you select this option, these changes will not effect the server-based copy of the database, even if you are the manager of the database.
- *Do not Send Changes in Local Security Property to Other Replicas.* This is selected by default. If you do not replicate the ACL and locally enforce it, then you are the manager of your local database. If you make changes, for example, to give another user Manager access, you can prevent these changes from replicating to other replicas of the database.

NOTE Remember that you cannot change the ACL on other copies anyway, unless you are manager of the database.

On the Other page of the Replication Settings dialog box, you can do the following:

- *Temporarily Disable Replication.* This lets you make local design changes and test your changes without accidentally replicating the changes to the server copy of the database, if you have Designer or Manager access on the server.
- *Scheduled Replication Priority.* You can set a database as a high, medium, or low priority database, and then you can limit what gets replicated by replicating only high priority databases when you are in a hurry.
- *Only Replicate Incoming Documents Saved on or Modified After....* You can set replication so it is date sensitive to make sure that you are only replicating recent changes.

- *CD-ROM Publishing Date.* You can publish a database to a CD and distribute it. Then users can copy the database from their CD, and then set up replication from the server for documents added or revised after the CD-ROM publishing date.

The Advanced page of the Replication Settings dialog box is shown in Figure 12.11.

Figure 12.11.
For finer control of replication, you can use the Advanced page of the Replication Settings dialog box.

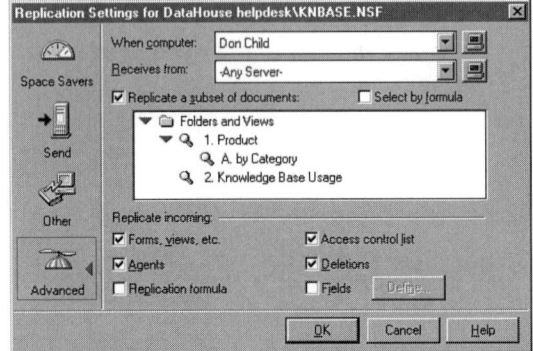

On the Advanced page of the Replication Settings dialog box, you can do the following:

- Centrally control replication by defining which computers and which servers the replication is between.
- Define a subset of documents for replication between the servers and computers you define.
- Define which elements, aside from documents, you want to replicate. These elements include forms and views and other design elements; agents; replication formulas such as those you set up on the top of the same dialog box page; access control lists; deletions; and fields.

NOTE These advanced functions assume that you are an advanced user with Manager access to the database helping other users set up replication formulas.

Replicating a Single Database

When you first create a replica copy of a database, a replica stub is placed on your desktop, unless you specified that Notes should replicate the database immediately.

The replica stub is basically a placeholder. It is an NSF file with a name and a replica ID, but not a whole lot else. It cannot be opened, and cannot be used until you replicate at least once. Figure 12.12 shows a Knowledge Base database that resides on a Domino server, and a replica stub of the same database.

Figure 12.12.
A replica stub is created on your desktop.

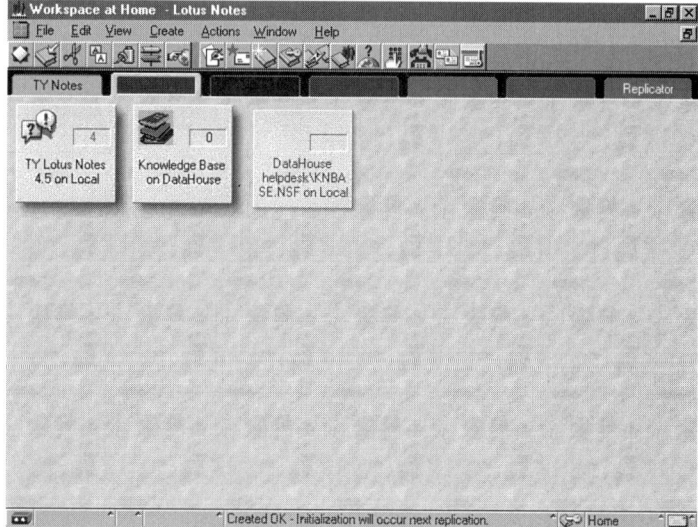

To replicate the stub with the database on the Domino server, do one of the following:

- Highlight the replica stub and Select File | Replication | Replicate from the menu bar.
- Highlight the replica stub and click on the File Replication Replicate SmartIcon.
- Right-click on the replica stub and select Replicate....

After you initiate replication, Notes will display a dialog box asking you to select one of two replication modes. You can replicate via background replication, which allows you to continue working while replication takes place; or you can replicate using one-time-only replication options that override anything you set up in the Replication Settings dialog box. The selection dialog box is shown in Figure 12.13.

Figure 12.13.
Select background replication or you can override replication settings for a one-time replication.

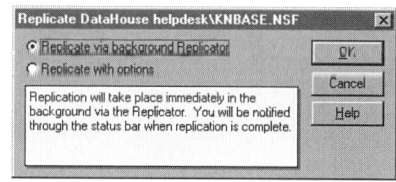

After you make your selection, replication will take place. You may hear your modem dialing in the background. Also, you may be required to enter your password, if you haven't yet entered a password during the current Notes session.

Notes then communicates with the server, using the communication parameters you set up earlier in today's lesson. The Replica ID for your database is compared to the Replica ID on databases on the Domino server until a match is found. Then documents, design changes, a database icon—any part of the database replica you did not exclude—gets sent to your local replica. And if you had any changes that you had made locally, they would be sent to the server-based copy, assuming your ACL privileges let you make the changes on the server-based copy.

When replication is done, you have two copies of the database on your desktop: the original server-based copy, and your local replica copy.

NOTE This assumes you did not delete the icon for the server-based copy before replicating.

You can save space on your desktop, and save yourself a lot of confusion, by stacking replica icons. Select View | Stack Replica Icons to create a single stacked icon for all replicas of the database. Figure 12.14 shows the stacked icon for the Knowledge Base database that was just replicated for the first time.

Figure 12.14.
You can stack the database icons for all replicas of a database.

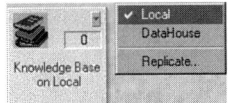

Notice the small expander arrow in the upper-right corner of the icon. This indicates that there are multiple replica icons stacked on top of each other. In Figure 12.14, I clicked on the expander button so you can see the list of locations for the stacked icons. The checked location is the one that is on the top of the stack; it is the one that will be opened when you double-click on the database icon.

TIP The icon on top of the stack is Location-specific. When you switch to another Location, the icon on top of the stack will be the icon for the replica you used the last time you used this Location.

You can replicate the database at any time by clicking on the expander arrow and selecting Replicate... in the expander box.

Using the Replicator Page

Although you can replicate single databases at any time, the real power of working in an extended workgroup environment comes from being able to schedule replication in the background. You started that process by setting up a Location document. Now you will learn to work with the Replicator Page, which makes it easy to manage complex replications.

The Replicator Page is a permanent part of the Notes workspace, whether you work with replicas or not. It cannot be deleted or removed from the workspace. In that way, it is unlike the other workspace pages. There is another difference, too. One look at the Replicator page, shown in Figure 12.15, will show that there is a big difference in how you work with databases on this page.

Figure 12.15.
The Replicator page is used to manage all replication tasks from a single location within Notes.

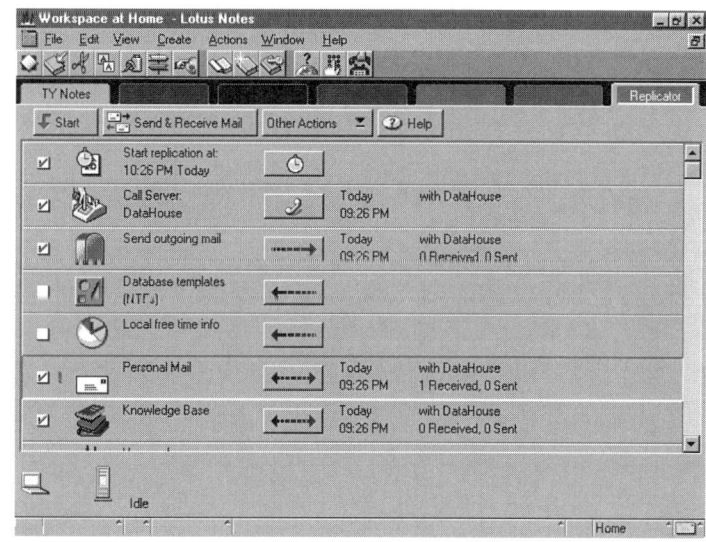

As I have been working with Notes, Notes has been quietly populating the Replicator page with databases. For example, when I created the replica of the Knowledge Base database, the Knowledge Base icon was put onto the Replicator page. When I set up my Calendar Profile, a freetime database was added to the Replicator page so my free time could be shared with others in the organization.

Elements of the Replicator Page

The Replicator page has three basic sections:

- The Action Bar with its buttons at the top of the Replicator page.
- The various replication action icons and icons for replicable elements, each on a separate line in the center of the screen.
- A status section at the bottom of the screen that keeps track of replication as it occurs.

Database Line Items on the Replication Page

Each line in the center of the screen contains common elements. As an example, we will examine the Knowledge Base line in detail.

- On the left side of the line is a check box. If an item is checked, then it is active and will be replicated. If you want to temporarily turn off replication for a database, you can just click on the check box until there is no checkmark.
- If a database is high priority, it will have a red explanation mark (!) next to it. The Personal Mail database is a high priority database.
- The database icon is the same icon you see on the Notes desktop. Replication actions such as Call Server and Start Replication are also marked by icons.
- The name of the database or a brief description of the action performed by the line follows the icon.
- The arrow icon indicates the direction of replication. Arrowheads that point to the right mean that data is being sent from your workstation to the Domino server. An arrowhead pointing to the left means that the Domino server is sending information to your workstation. A two-headed arrow means that documents are sent in both directions during replication. Double-click on the arrow to change your replication settings. The dialog box shown in Figure 12.16 is displayed so you can modify how replication works for that database.

Figure 12.16.

Modify your replication settings from the Replica page by double-clicking on the arrow.

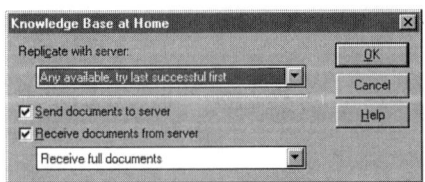

- In this dialog box, you can specify which server should be used if there are multiple replicas available, which direction(s) documents should be sent during replication, and whether the replication should include full documents, summary data, or summary data plus 40K of rich text. The default setting is to send and receive full documents.
- Next on the line is the last time that you replicated, followed by a message indicating the results of the replication.

When you start replication (you can start it manually by clicking on the Start button), Notes moves from the top row to the bottom, stopping at each line that has a checkmark beside it. In Everyone's Replicator page will be unique, because the page is somewhat dependent on which replica databases you have on your computer. In the example shown above in Figure 12.15, replication will perform the following actions:

- Start Replication... is checked, which means that scheduled replication is enabled. At 6:00 a.m., if my computer is turned on, it will try to call the server to replicate. Double-click on the clock icon to open the current Location document if you want to change the schedule.
- Call Server... is checked, which means that the server will be called as soon a replication begins.
- Send Outgoing Mail is checked, which means that the first thing Notes will do after it establishes a connection with the server is forward any outgoing mail memos to the mail router on the Domino server. Documents will be sent to the server, but no documents will be received from the server in this database.
- Replication of templates is turned off, so the Database Templates line will be skipped.
- Local Free Time Info is not checked, which means that free time on my home calendar does not replicate to the free time database on the Domino server.
- Personal Mail will be the first database replicated, and it will send and receive documents.
- Knowledge Base will be replicated, and it will send and receive documents.
- The last item, not visible in Figure 12.15, is a Hang Up line that automatically hangs up the phone as soon as replication is completed.

If you want to change the order in which databases get replicated, you can point to a line on the Replicator page, hold down the left mouse button, and drag the line to a new location on the page.

Selecting Options with the Buttons on the Action Bar

You've seen how you can initiate replication by clicking on the Start button. The other two buttons (excluding the Help button) give you finer control over replication.

If you click on Send and Receive Mail, Notes calls your home server (where your Mail file is stored). Mail in the outgoing mailbox is sent to the server, and from there, it gets delivered to the addressees. New mail in the server-based mail database is then retrieved, and Notes hangs up again. It is a quick way to work with your mail without taking the time to replicate.

If you click on Other Actions, you have several options, including:

- *Replicate High Priority Databases.* If you select this option, Notes will call the server, replicate only databases marked as High Priority (databases that have an exclamation point (!) next to them on the Replicator page). When done, Notes will hang up.
- *Replicate with Server....* You can replicate with a specific server by selecting this option. First, make sure that only the databases you want to replicate are checked, and then select the server that you want to replicate with.
- *Replicate Selected Database.* You can place a checkmark next to the databases you want to replicate, and then click Replicate Selected Database to initiate replication.
- *Send Outgoing Mail.* This type of connection sends the mail in your outgoing mailbox and then hangs up immediately.

The same options are also available from the Actions menu on the Replicator page menu bar.

Strategies for Speeding Up Replication

A quick true/false quiz: When you replicate a document, the entire document gets replicated.

The answer is true and false, depending on the circumstances. When you replicate a new document, the whole document gets replicated unless you opt to replicate only summary data, or to replicate summary data and 40KB of rich text.

When you replicate documents that have been modified, the only part of the document that gets replicated is the field in which changes have been made.

NOTE  If two or more users modify the same field on a document, then the entire document gets replicated as a Replication or Save Conflict, and gets saved as a response to the original document so you can decide which changes you want to keep. If two or more users modify different fields on the same document, the changes can be merged into a single document if a form has been designed to allow the merging of replication conflicts.

Because replication takes place at the field level, replication is considerably faster than copying or sending complete documents back and forth between your workstation and a Domino server, or between two servers.

You have seen several ways to limit the size and number of documents that replicate in databases, primarily using the Replication Settings dialog box. You have seen how to limit which databases get replicated from the Replicator page. But sometimes, you have to get off the phone...maybe you have a memo that contains a huge attachment, and the replication is taking forever.

You can skip to the next database on the Replicator page by clicking on the Next button. You can also stop replication by clicking on the Stop button.

TIP If a document contains a large attachment, you have the option of opening the server-based copy of the database and viewing the document there, dealing with the large attachment and deleting the document from the database before replicating.

Figure 12.17 shows the Replicator status bar during replication. You can see an estimate of how much time remains for the current database. Notes changes its estimates as it goes along based on the size of the documents replicated so far.

Figure 12.17.
The Replicator Page status bar provides a constantly updated status during replication.

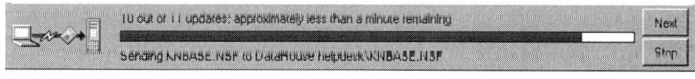

Because replication usually takes place in the background, you can continue working within Notes while replication is taking place.

Adding and Deleting Databases from the Replicator Page

Database icons on the Replicator page are just pointers to databases on the Notes desktop. You can remove an icon from the Replicator page by clicking on it to select it, and then pressing the Delete key. The database will be removed from the Replicator page, but the database itself is not effected, other than the fact that it will no longer replicate from the Replicator page.

To put an icon onto the Replicator page, drag the icon and drop it on the Replicator tab. When you create new replica databases, they are automatically put onto the Replicator page, so you only need to add icons if they have previously been removed.

You can also remove the Call Server and Hang Up icons from the Replicator page. If you remove them and then need to add them back to the page, select Create | Call Entry or Create | Hangup Entry from the menu bar on the Replicator Page.

Switching Locations

Now that you have set up various locations, and have them so they work on a schedule, you will find that life has suddenly become much easier. Are you doing temporary duty from your hotel room near a branch office that has its own LAN?

To set up your Notes workstation, click on the Location button near the right side on the status bar at the bottom of your Notes workspace, as shown in Figure 12.18. Select Travel (Modem) or whatever location you have set up for the occasion.

Figure 12.18.
Select a new location from the status bar, and Notes remembers all of your setup for that location.

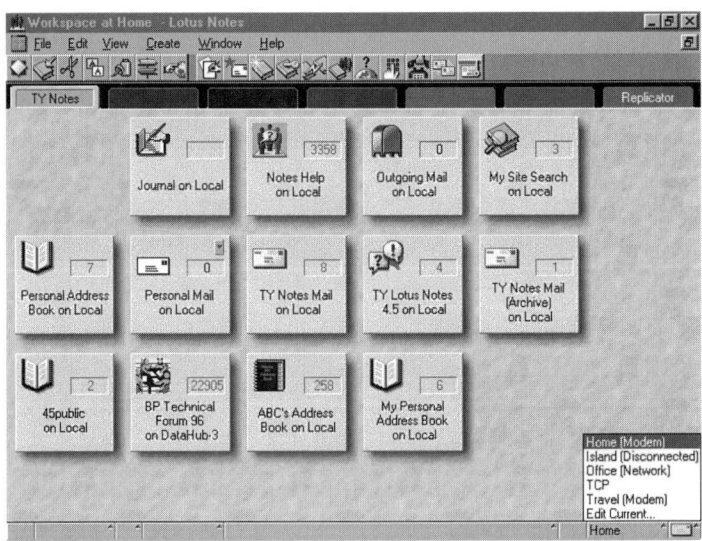

That's it. You're all set up. Notes remembers all your settings. If you have scheduled replication set up, all you have to do is plug in your computer to the phone line, start Notes, and provide your password. You can start working, and Notes will replicate in the background.

Doing a presentation for a client? Switch your Location to Presentation or whatever you have defined. Now your workstation will automatically use the "demo" User ID and the settings you defined for "demo."

Back in the office? Select Office as your Location, and you are working with databases on the LAN, and do not need to replicate.

TIP You can also select your current location by selecting File | Mobile | Choose Current Location.... And if you need to edit the location, select File | Mobile | Edit Current Location... from the menu bar or select Edit Current... from the status bar.

After you set up your computer so it works at a particular location, you do not have to do anything else besides select that location. Notes will refer to the Location document for that location to use your preferred communication port, call the server you defined using the number you defined, and the replica you last used will be the one that opens when you double-click on a stack of replica icons.

Summary

You have just set up your computer for mobile computing. Now, with a single click, you can repeat all the setup you did. Here is what you learned today.

1. You set up the communications ports on your workstation.
2. You set up Server Connection documents and defined which phone numbers Notes should call to connect to your Domino server.
3. You created replica copies of the databases you want to work with on the road.
4. You used the Replicator page to set up one-step replication from your current location.
5. You selected a Location from the status bar, or from the File | Mobile menu on the menu bar.

Five steps is all it takes to set yourself up so you can have the latest information on your desktop from anywhere in the world. All you need is a computer, a Notes license, and a way to connect so you can communicate with your Domino server.

Workshop

The Workshop section presents questions and answers, quiz questions to help you cement your new knowledge, and exercises to give you experience using what you have learned. Try to understand the questions and exercises before moving on to the next lesson. Answers are in Appendix A.

Q&A

Q If I set up TCP as a port, does that mean I can use the Internet?

A It means that you can communicate with your Domino server (assuming it also uses TCP/IP) using a SLIP or PPP connection. In other words, you can use the same protocols the Internet uses. To actually get onto the Internet, you still have to have an Internet connection through an Internet service provider, or through your organization's LAN.

Q Can I have a different set of icons on my desktop for different locations?

A No. The desktop is defined in a file called DESKTOP.DSK. You would have to create a new desktop file, and switch desktops using your computer's operating system. What you can do, though, is to set up your workspace pages so that the databases you use on the road are all on a single page.

Q How does a Passthru Server connection work?

A Your System Administrator has to set up a server as a Passthru Server, and define which other servers you can reach using passthru. Then you dial a single number, and can access databases on any of those servers defined by the System Administrator.

Quiz

1. Do you have any Location documents when you first set up your Notes workstation?
2. How would you replicate data between your workstation and another user's workstation?
3. True/False. Two databases can replicate as long as they have an identical design and they contain identical documents.
4. When you try to call the server, there is no answer. How can you verify that the problem is on the server's end, and not on your end?
5. Can you replicate a database using Internet protocols?
6. Can you schedule replication to take place only once a day except on weekends?

Exercises

1. Create a Location document that automatically dials long distance and uses a calling card to connect to your home server.
2. Create a new replica of the Discussion database. Set the replication up so your local replica discards documents older than 45 days, and only selects documents created by members of your workgroup.
3. Create new documents, modify existing documents, and delete documents in your local replica of the discussion database. Replicate your changes to the server-based copy, and then open the server-based copy and look for your changes. Are they there? Now make changes on the server-based replica, and replicate them to your local replica copy of the database.

Week 2

Day 13

Automating Notes with Agents and Actions

Today, you will learn about a more advanced topic: how to create agents and actions to automate Notes. *Agents* run on a scheduled or manual basis, performing repetitive tasks on selected documents. *Actions*, on the other hand, are launched from buttons or hotspots in Notes documents and views. First, you will learn about agents.

Creating and Using Agents

Think about all the things you can do with Notes, the things that are repetitious.

- ☐ You can mine a knowledge base for new documents that mention topics you are interested in. When you find a document that interests you, you copy it to another database so you can refer to it later.
- ☐ You can make a "newsletter" that contains DocLinks to the new documents in a database, and mail the newsletter to others so they can locate the documents that interest them with a single click.

- ☐ You can categorize incoming orders for products, and assign fulfillment to members of your workgroup based on criteria such as locale, product, or volume.
- ☐ You can change all occurrences of a word or phrase within a Notes database. For example, suppose the person who authorizes purchase orders retires from the company. Because you have your P.O. process automated in Notes, you now have to go through and change the Authorization field in all of your P.O.s. With an agent, you can let Notes do all the repetitive work.
- ☐ You can look at logs and export them to word processing or spreadsheet files.

The list is endless. Use your imagination. Look at what you do everyday in Notes, or once a week, and you can probably create an agent to handle most of the tasks for you by launching the agents either automatically or manually.

You can create an agent for any action if you can define when you want the action to take place, which documents you want to perform the action on, and what action it is that you want to perform.

What Is an Agent?

Think about the world at large, and some of the things that you hire agents to do for you.

If you have to move to a new town, you might hire a moving and storage company to act as your agent. It will pack your household items, load them in the truck, ship them to your new city, hold the items in storage until you are ready for them, and then deliver them to your new house.

If you want to produce a calendar using an overseas printer, you would hire an agent to deal with the printer, the shippers, and customs.

If you want to go on a vacation, you would hire a travel agent to book your airline tickets, your rental car, hotel, and tours.

These are all things that you could do on your own, but it is far more efficient to have a professional agent do them for you. In the same way, an agent within Lotus Notes performs the same functions that you could do yourself, but Notes uses the power of the computer to do things for you, leaving you free to concentrate on other activities.

Think back to the lessons on Notes Mail. When you were out of the office, you could run an Out of Office agent. The agent looked at all documents that were added to the InBox. The first time a person sent you e-mail, the agent would respond, telling him or her that you were out of town, and when to expect you back at your desk.

TIP Think of Notes agents as macros, because that is what they are. They perform repetitive functions for you.

Personal Agents and Shared Agents

Your ability to create agents is somewhat like your ability to create views. You can create personal agents that are only visible to you, and the agents can only perform tasks within the database that you yourself would be able to perform. Personal agents act on your behalf.

A personal agent is stored in the database, but the database could be stored on your local hard drive, or it could be in a database on the Domino server. It doesn't matter where the database is stored, you can still run a personal agent that you have created. And you can run it on documents within a shared view, or within a private view or folder that you created and that is only accessible to you.

NOTE The database ACL can be tailored to restrict people from creating and running personal agents. If they are not restricted in the ACL, anyone with Reader access or above can create personal agents.

A shared agent has many of the same characteristics as a personal agent, but it is more limited in its scope as far as you are concerned as an individual user. First, a shared agent can only be created by someone who is a Designer or a Manager in the database ACL. The agent is stored in the database just like a private agent, but it can only run on the server. If the database is local, shared agents will not run. And if the database is on another Domino server, the agent will not run. It runs only on the server where the database resides. In addition to those restrictions, a shared agent can only run against documents in shared views and folders.

Given those restrictions, what is the purpose of a shared agent? Access. Chances are, your personal agent has only Author access or Reader access in most databases. A shared agent has at least Designer access, which means that it can make global changes within the database. If you need an agent that is going to touch every document in the database, then that agent is going to need, at a minimum, Editor access to the database on the server. Keep that in mind as you learn to create agents.

Taking a Cautious Approach to Creating Agents

Before you create an agent, consider for a moment what could happen if you make a mistake. The agent can modify documents in the database, and after you run the agent, there is no way to undo the edits that have been made. Therefore, you want to make sure that the agent is selecting the correct documents, and is performing the correct actions on the documents once they are selected.

There are two possible approaches to ensure the integrity of your documents when creating an agent:

- You can create a copy of the database and create your agent in the copy. That way, if there is a problem, the damage is limited to your test data. When the agent works the way you want it to, you can copy it and paste it into your production database.
- You can create and test your agent one step at a time. First, define which documents should be selected, but do not define an action for the agent. Run the agent and make sure the correct documents are selected. Then select a single document (or a copy of a single document) and define the action you want to be run on the document. If the action is successful, you can combine the selection and the action into a single agent.

Of course, the two techniques can be combined.

To copy the agent from your test database into your production database:

1. Navigate to the Agents view in your test database.
2. Click on the agent you want to copy.
3. Select Edit | Copy from the menu bar, or press Ctrl+C.
4. Switch to your production database.
5. Navigate to the Agents view.
6. Select Edit | Paste from the menu bar, or press Ctrl+V.

The agent will be shown in the list of agents in your production database, and you will be able to run it.

Creating an Agent

We will now walk through the process of creating an agent. At a high level, the steps for creating an agent are the following:

1. Highlight the database in which you want to create an agent and select Create | Agent from the menu bar. An Agent Builder window will be displayed, as shown in Figure 13.1.

Figure 13.1.
Notes guides you through the process of creating agents in this Agent Builder window.

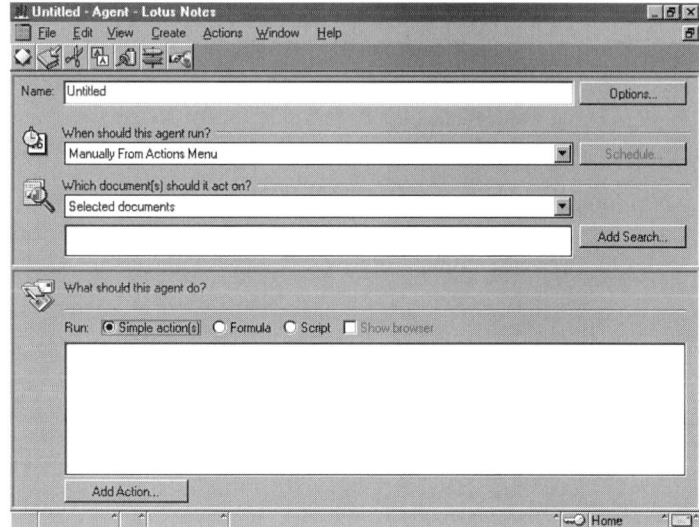

2. Name your agent.
3. Define when the agent should run.
4. Define which documents the agent should run on.
5. Define what the agent should do.

Each of these is covered in detail below.

Naming Your Agent

Give the agent a name. That may sound like a simple task, but there are several caveats. It is simple if you only have one or two agents, but what if you have 20 or 30 agents? How do you find the one you want?

The answer depends in part on which platform you are using. If you use Windows, OS/2, or UNIX, you can select menu options by typing the first character of the option. This assumes that each option starts with a different letter of the alphabet, or with a number. You will notice, when you look at a menu, that the first character of a menu option is underlined, for example Copy.

If two agents begin with the same letter of the alphabet, you can define which letter is used as the shortcut key. For example, if you had the Copy option and a Clear option, only one of the two can work when you press "C" as a shortcut key. In that instance, if you cannot rename either of your agents, you can instead define another letter as the shortcut letter.

To define a letter other than the first letter of the name as a shortcut letter, type an underscore (_) before the letter that you want to use as a shortcut. For example, to make the "l" into a shortcut in Clear, enter the name as "C_lear." It will show up in the menu as "Clear."

TIP If you want to display your agents in a particular order, consider numbering them, as they are displayed on the menu in alphabetical order.

Creating a Cascading Menu of Agent Names

You can also create cascading names to help you organize numerous agents. To create a cascading menu for your agents, use a backslash to separate the agent name from the top level menu entry.

NOTE The maximum number of bytes for the entire name is 127 bytes including the cascading menu and the backslash, which is a two-byte character.

As an example of cascading names, you might have a menu option labeled "Move to Folder" and under that menu, you could have agents named "Publisher," "Projects," "Archive," and so on.

To create the first of these agent names, you would enter "Move to Folder Agents\Publisher," and then for subsequent folders, "Move to Folder Agents\Projects," and so on.

Setting Options for Displaying the Agent Name

You can set options for the agent by clicking on the Options button beside the Name field. This will display the Options dialog box shown in Figure 13.2.

Figure 13.2.
Select options for your agent.

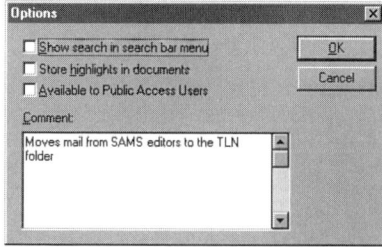

In this dialog box, you can choose from the following options:

- *Show Search in Search Bar Menu.* If you check this, you will be able to view the search selection for the agent from the Special Options button on the search bar. When you define which documents get selected, you can use the Search Builder to build a full text search, and then have the agent run against the selected documents.

- *Store Highlights in Documents.* If you select this, the red lines that highlight words in a full text search will be saved in the document after the agent is done selecting documents.

- *Available to Public Access Users.* Users who have no access to the database in the ACL may be given the right to read or create certain public documents in a Notes database. If you check this option, then this agent will be available for use by these public access users.

- *Comment.* You can create a comment that describes the agent. The first 30 characters of the comment appear beneath the agent name in the Agents view.

Defining When the Agent Should Run

There are several options for determining when an agent should run. The option you select will determine which documents can be selected for the macro to run on, and whether you have the option of scheduling the agent to run automatically.

Let's look at the options.

- *Manually From Actions Menu.* This is the default. There are no restrictions on which documents you can choose. The only way you will be able to run the agent is from the Actions menu, or from the Search Bar Options menu if you selected the option to show the agent there.

- *Manually From Agent List.* If you select this option, the only way you will be able to launch the agent is from the Agent view. Click on the agent to highlight it, and then select Actions | Run from the menu bar to run the agent.

- *If New Mail Has Arrived.* This agent works only when documents are first deposited into your InBox.
- *If Documents Have Been Created or Modified.* When you select this, you can schedule the agent to perform an action on any document that has been created or modified within the database since the agent last ran.
- *If Documents Have Been Pasted.* Every time a document is pasted into the database, the agent will run against that document. The agent cannot be scheduled, and runs only against documents that are added to the database by being pasted from the clipboard.
- *On Schedule Hourly (Daily, Weekly, Monthly).* You can determine the schedule that will be used for running the agent. The Schedule button is described below.
- *On Schedule Never.* This option is used only for working with macros that were created under Notes R3. In that version, you could temporarily prevent a macro from running by telling it to run never. If you want to disable an agent running in Notes 4.5, use one of the other options described below.

To define a schedule for agent, select one of the On Schedule options, and then click on the Schedule button.

The dialog box that is displayed will vary slightly depending on the scheduled interval you select. Figure 13.3 shows the Schedule dialog box for an hourly interval.

Figure 13.3.
Tailor the schedule for an agent in the Schedule dialog box.

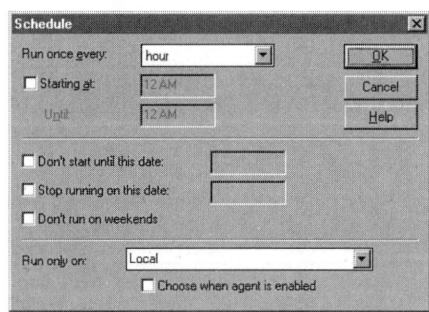

The top part of this dialog box enables you to tailor the interval. In the hourly dialog box, you can elect to run the agent once an hour, or every two, four, or eight hours. You would use this type of agent for high priority databases where it is vital that the information is up-to-date, and there are frequent changes in the database. By default, the hourly agent runs from midnight to midnight, 24 hours a day. You can change the start and end times if you do not want the agent running the entire day.

With a daily schedule, the agent runs once a day, and you can specify the time of day. By default, the agent runs at 1:00 a.m.

With a weekly schedule, you can set the day of the week and the hour at which the agent runs.

With a monthly schedule, you can set the day of the month on which the agent runs, and the time of day.

The second part of the dialog box is essentially the same for all intervals. You can set the date on which the agent starts running, and the date on which the agent stops running if you want to. For hourly and daily schedules, you can also select an option to prevent the agent from running on a weekend.

The bottom part of the dialog box lets you define where the macro will run. Because you are creating a personal agent, you can accept the default selection, which is to run the agent on your local database, or you can choose the server on which your database resides.

Note The ability to create personal agents can be denied in the ACL. With server-based databases, make sure that you are authorized to create personal agents.

Define Which Documents the Agent Should Run Against

After you define when an agent will be run, you can define which documents the agent should be run against.

The selections you made as to when the agent is run will determine which documents can be selected to run the agent against.

If you selected an option to run the agent manually, then you can select any of the following to run the agent against:

- ☐ *All Documents in the Database.*
- ☐ *All New and Modified Documents Since the Agent Was Last Run.*
- ☐ *All Unread Documents in View.* The view you are in at the time the agent is run will determine which documents the agent runs against. You can create a full text search, which will select documents in an ad hoc view, and then the agent will run against documents in that view.
- ☐ *All Documents in View.* Again, the view you are in at the time the agent is run will determine which documents the agent runs against. You can create a full text search to create an ad hoc view and run the agent against documents selected in that view, similar to the way you can run an agent against selected documents.

NOTE A database must be full-text indexed before you can run an agent against all documents in the database or against all or selected documents in a view.

- *Selected Documents.* You can manually select a single document or multiple documents in a view. You can also create a full text search to select documents, and then run the agent against documents that are selected by the search.
- *Run Once.* If you select this, you can use Notes @functions that are used in Notes application development to perform complex selections.

TIP Refer to Day 8, when you learned about full text searching. Those selections that utilize a full text search let you click on the Add Search button, and then you can build a search using the Search Builder dialog box. You can build a search query to limit the documents selected by any method. For example, you can limit the selection of new mail for processing to documents that come from selected individuals.

When you run an agent against all new mail, against documents that have been pasted, and against documents that have been created or modified, the selection criteria is implicit in the type of agent. You cannot modify the selection.

When you run an agent using a scheduled time interval, you have two options. You can run the agent against all documents in the database, or you can run the agent against all documents created or modified since the last time the agent was run.

NOTE Remember the caveat at the beginning of this section about running agents. Test the selection criteria, and make sure that your agent is accurately selecting the documents against which you want to run the agent. Define what the agent does only when you are sure that the correct documents are being selected.

Define What the Agent Should Do

The bottom half of the Agent Builder window is used to define what the agent does. It is similar to the design pane that is used to create formulas for forms and views. In today's lesson, you will be defining simple actions that require no programming ability.

You will notice in Figure 13.1 that you have the ability to run a simple action, a formula, or script. Make sure the Simple action(s) radio button is selected.

Click on the Add Action button to define which actions you want to run in this agent. The Add Action dialog box will be displayed as shown in Figure 13.4.

Figure 13.4.
Use the Add Action dialog box to define what your agent should do. For example, change the Account Manager in all selected documents by entering the new Account Manager's name.

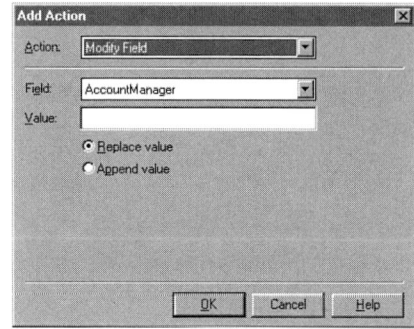

Using Simple Actions

In the Add Action dialog box, there are several actions from which you can select. Depending on the action you select, different options will be presented in the dialog box.

The actions are described in Table 13.1.

Table 13.1. Simple actions.

Simple Action Name	What It Does	What You Input
Copy to Database	Makes a copy of documents and pastes them into another database. Useful for archiving documents.	Identify the database to which documents should be copied.
Copy to Folder	Makes a copy of documents and pastes them into a selected folder. The original would remain in an uncategorized folder such as your mail InBox.	Identify the folder using a view-like navigator.

continues

Table 13.1. continued

Simple Action Name	What It Does	What You Input
Delete from Database	Removes the selected documents from the database. They cannot be recovered if there is no backup.	No information required.
Mark Document Read	Removes the unread mark from the selected document.	No information required.
Mark Document Unread	Changes documents with "Read" marks to "Unread," useful for counting the number of documents in a database.	No information required.
Modify Field	Replace the information in a field, or add new information to the end of the field.	Identify the field and the value to be added or substituted. The dialog box displays a list of all fields in the database.
Modify Field by Form	Replace one or more fields' values by entering the data you want in a form.	Select the form, then enter data in any field you want to modify.
Move to Folder	Moves the selected document to a folder. As a result, the document would be removed from uncategorized folders such as your mail InBox.	Select the folder from a view-like navigator.
Remove from Folder	Removes the document from the folder and back into an uncategorized view.	Select the folder from a view-like navigator.
Reply to Sender	Creates a "Reply" document as in the mail database. This document could be used to automatically respond to people who send Internet	Select who to reply to, whether to include a copy of the original document, and whether to send this reply to an individual one time only.

Simple Action Name	What It Does	What You Input
	mail to a database, for example, to create an "out of office" memo.	You can also create a text body of the document.
Run Agent	Runs another agent.	Select the agent to run from a list of available agents.
Send Document	Mails a document that is mail-enabled.	No information required.
Send Mail Message	Creates a mail memo. For example, you could create an agent that looks at a project database and automatically assigns and mails action items to individuals.	Address, subject, body, add DocLink and include copy of document are options. The "More" button gives you access to additional fields that can be filled by entering text or formulas.
Send Newsletter Summary	Creates a mail memo with links to selected documents.	To, Subject, and Body fields can be filled. Optionally include a summary of each document using a selected view. Specify how many documents to gather before sending. "More" button lets you use text or formulas for filling various fields.
@Function Formula	Lets you create your own agents using Notes programming functions.	Option to update existing document when run, create new document when run, or select document when run. The Notes @Function formulas give you greater flexibility, but you do need to know how to use Notes programming functions.

Using Multiple Simple Actions

You are not limited to a single simple action. For example, in Figure 13.5, I have created an agent to archive documents from one mail database to another. The agent first creates a newsletter summary for the documents it selects. It then copies the selected documents to the new database, and deletes the document from the original database.

Multiple actions in an agent run one at a time on each selected document. Therefore, if you have a Delete Document action, you want to make sure that it is always placed last.

To insert a simple action, click in between two actions, or use the arrow keys to move the cursor.

To delete an action, highlight it and click on the Delete key.

To move an action, highlight it, select Edit | Cut, move the cursor to the new location, and select Edit | Paste.

You can also use standard Windows keyboard shortcuts such as Ctrl+X to cut and Ctrl+V to paste data.

Figure 13.5.
An archiving agent that uses multiple simple actions.

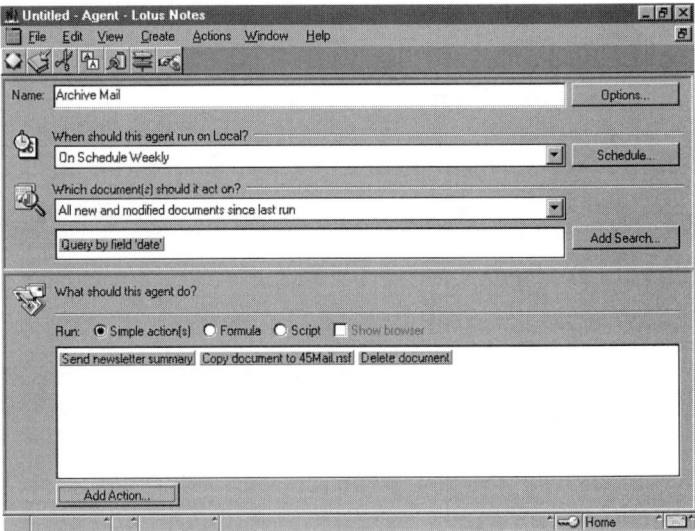

Working with Actions

What is the difference between an agent and an action? You already got a taste of working with simple actions when you created an agent. The same actions can be used in other places, including action hotspots within an individual document, an Action button on the button bar within a Notes form, or an Action button on the button bar within a Notes view.

The first one, the Action button, synthesizes two things you have already learned: creating a hotspot, and selecting a simple action. The other two involve the design environment, so you will be getting your feet wet in Notes development.

Creating an Action Hotspot

You can create an action hotspot in any Rich Text field. But first, you need some text or a graphic object to make into a hotspot. You then highlight the text or graphic and select Create | Hotspot | Action Hotspot. Select a simple action and fill in the appropriate fields, just as you did when creating an agent.

Figure 13.6 provides an example of how you might create an action hotspot in a document. In the background of the figure, an invitation is being created to everyone in the corporation, inviting them to attend a planning meeting (okay, so it's a small corporation). There are two action hotspots: one to send a positive response, and one to send regrets. The simple action being created will send an e-mail telling me that you can attend. When the simple action is completed, all you have to do to RSVP is click on "Yes, I will be able to make it." Perhaps the action could be expanded to create an action item in your calendar, too.

Figure 13.6.
Create an action hotspot to send an RSVP to an e-mail invitation.

Creating an Action Button on a Form

Pop quiz time. What must your role be in the database ACL before you can modify the design of a database?

If you answered Designer or Manager, you get a passing grade. And by default, what sort of access do you have in local databases? Again, you should have answered Manager. Unless the database is a replica of a database on the Domino server, and the database ACL is locally enforced, you will have Manager access in local databases. That means that you can modify the design, assuming you are using a full Notes license, also known as the Notes Design license. You must have the full Notes client if you want to modify a form.

Pick out a local database to modify—preferably a copy of a database, not a production database. Try the TY Notes 4.5 discussion database, for example.

NOTE If you modify the design of certain databases, Notes will display a message informing you that the database is certified for Notes Mail, and modifying the form may break the database, or that the database is created from a template and your design changes may be lost. Ignore the messages, because you are just practicing.

To add an Action button to a form, follow these steps:

1. Open the database you want to modify. At the bottom of the Navigation pane, there should be a Design view marked by a designer's triangle icon. If you see a graphical Navigator, select View | Design. If the design view is not showing, select View | Show | Design to display the view. Once you see the Design view, click on the Design triangle to expand the view.

2. Click on Forms to display a list of all forms in the database in the View pane, as shown in Figure 13.7.

Figure 13.7.
With the Design view expanded, select Forms to see a list of all forms in the database.

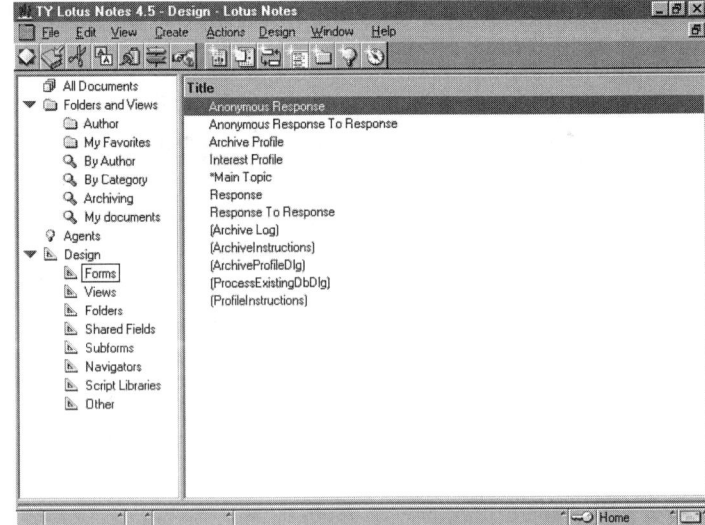

3. Double-click on the form named *Main Topic. The asterisk indicates that this is the default form in the database.
4. A dialog box will be displayed telling you that your design changes may be lost. Click on OK to acknowledge the message. Your changes will only be lost if you refresh the design of your database from the Discussion template. You may want to disable refreshing the design for your database (hint: search through the Database Properties InfoBox).

The design window will be displayed (see Figure 13.8).

5. In this window, the top half of the screen is a rich text area called the Design pane, where you lay out the form, adding elements such as static text, fields, and graphics. As you can see from the complexity of the form, there are many parts of the document that get hidden from the user when they are creating documents in the database. You will not need to concern yourself with this part of the design window, because you will be putting your Action button on the button bar.

The bottom half of the form is the Programming pane, where you enter formulas and scripts to define the characteristics of different design elements.

The top right corner is the Action pane, where you define a new action for the form. If the Action pane is not showing, you can display it by clicking on the View Show/Hide Action Pane SmartIcon, by selecting View | Action Pane from the menu bar, or by dragging the right edge of the Design pane.

Figure 13.8.
The Notes design window lets you make changes to the design of Notes forms.

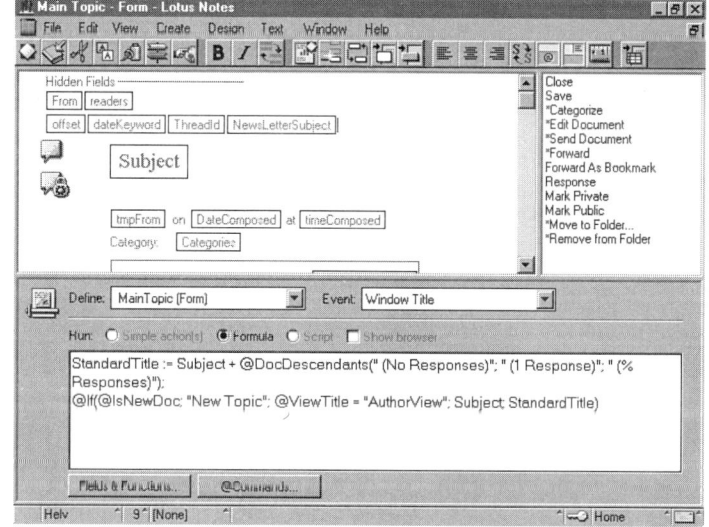

Select Create | Action from the menu bar to display the Action Properties InfoBox shown in Figure 13.9.

Figure 13.9.
Define how your action is displayed in the Action Properties InfoBox.

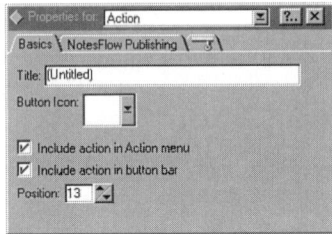

6. Enter a title for your action, for example, **Forward for Review**.
7. Click on the Button Icon down arrow button to display a gallery of icons that can be displayed on your Action button. This gallery is shown in Figure 13.10.

Figure 13.10.
Select from a gallery of icons to display on your Action button.

8. If you want the action to be available on the Actions menu, leave the check box marked beside Include action in Action menu. Otherwise, click on the check box so it is unchecked to remove the action from the Action menu.
9. Leave the check box marked beside Include action in button bar so your action appears on the button bar at the top of the Main Topic form whenever it is displayed on the screen.
10. The Position box determines where your action shows up on the button bar in relation to other buttons. Many of the buttons are situational, so they will only show up if certain conditions are met; for example, a button may only be available

when the document is in Edit mode. Look at the list of actions in the Action pane. The actions marked by an asterisk (*) are predefined actions that are available for all forms, if you choose to use them. By clicking on the up and down arrows beside the Position box, you can position the button where you want it.

11. You will not be using the other two pages on the Action Properties InfoBox. NotesFlow Publishing is used for applications that use OLE to integrate other applications into the workflow. The final page is used to determine when the Action button is displayed or hidden from view. Click on the X in the corner of the InfoBox to close it so you can concentrate on adding an action.
12. In the Programming pane, select Simple Action(s) as your run option. You should now be in familiar territory.
13. Click on the Add Action... button.
14. Select and define your action.
15. Save your changes to the form. You can press the Escape key or select File | Close from the menu bar.
16. Test your button. Open an existing document in the database and click on the Action button you just created to test whether it accomplishes what you expected.

The primary difference between this button and the action hotspot that you created earlier is that you can use this button from all documents created with this form, and the button will remain at the top of the screen, even when you have to scroll down through the document.

The action hotspot is only available from a single document, unless you build it into the body of the form. And it will scroll off the screen, so you have to place it where the user will see it when they need it.

Creating an Action in a View

Creating an action in a view is similar to creating an action in a form. Rather than walk through the entire process step by step, only the high points will be described. You need a full Notes client to make design changes to a view, just like you did when making design changes to a form.

1. Navigate to the Design view and click on Views.
2. Select the view where you want to create an action button. Figure 13.11 shows Design window for the (Default) view in the Discussion database.
3. Display the Action pane using SmartIcon or the View menu.

Figure 13.11.
Create an Action button associated with a view by using the View design window.

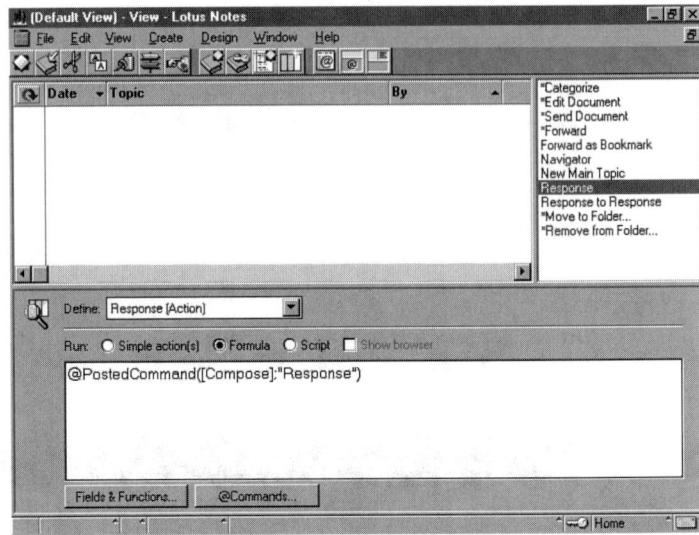

4. Select Create | Action.
5. Define the action in the Action Properties InfoBox.
6. Click on Add Action in the Programming pane.
7. Select and define a simple action.
8. Save the view and test your action.

The action you define can be launched from the Action menu or from the button bar at the top of the view. Actions in a view have the obvious advantage of being able to work on multiple documents at one time.

Editing an Action

To edit an action, open the form or view that contains the action.

Double-click on an action in the Action pane to display the Action Properties InfoBox. If you want to edit the what the action does, you can add, delete, or modify one or more simple actions in the Programming pane.

When you are done making your changes, save and test your changes.

Copying an Action to Another View or Form

You can copy an action from one form or view and paste it into another. To do so, open the form or view where the action exists, highlight the action in the Action pane, and select Edit | Copy from the menu bar. Navigate to the form or view where you want to paste the action, open the Action pane, and select Edit | Paste from the menu bar.

WARNING

The functioning of an action depends on the context in which it is used. Be sure to test your action in its new location to make sure there are no unexpected results.

NOTE

Action buttons can only be copied one at a time. There is no convenient way to copy multiple actions from one form or view to another.

Deleting an Action

To delete an action, highlight the action in the Action pane, and press the Delete key, or select Edit | Cut.

Summary

Today, you looked at two techniques for automating Notes. You learned how to create personal agents, which you can build in any Notes database to automated functions that involve multiple documents and/or repetitious activities.

You already had some experience with agents in the Mail database. Other agents are built into the Discussion database, and other databases built with Notes templates. The personal agents you learned to build use a set of predefined simple actions that can be combined to perform complex functions.

With agents, you defined when and how the agent would be initiated, and then you defined which documents would be effected by the agent. After testing the agent one step at a time, you were able to run it on your database.

You then used the same simple actions to create an action that could be embedded within an individual document as an action hotspot, or within a form or view, where it would be displayed as an Action button or accessed from the Action menu on the menu bar.

These methods of automating Notes are things that you can do as an end user. But they hint at another level of integration that Notes uses: workflow applications that integrate multiple Notes databases into a single application.

Workflow applications use the Notes messaging structure to automate work, delivering data when and where it is needed. Many workflow applications use more advanced programming functions to determine when and how to trigger the movement of information, but the principles are the same as what you learned today. The application developer determines when an action should be triggered, which documents the action should process, and what actions should be performed.

When you use such applications, you do not need to know where the information came from, as long as you know it is accurate and timely.

Workshop

The Workshop section presents questions and answers, quiz questions to help you cement your new knowledge, and exercises to give you experience using what you have learned. Try to understand the questions and exercises before moving on to the next lesson. Answers are in Appendix A.

Q&A

Q I sometimes access Notes databases through a Web browser. Can I still run Notes agents?

A All agent triggers work over the Web except for manual triggers. Scheduled agents, mail agents, add or change agents, and paste agents all still work when you are working with Notes databases served to the Web via the Domino server.

Q If I create a scheduled agent in a local replica copy of a database that resides on the server, will the agent get replicated to the server?

A The agent will only be replicated to the server if you are a Designer or a Manager in the database ACL. Likewise, your personal agents cannot do anything that exceeds your privileges in the database. In other words, you cannot modify documents unless you are an authorized editor, and you cannot view documents or forward documents unless you are an authorized reader.

Q How do the other ways of creating actions—functions and scripts—differ from simple actions?

A They work pretty much the same way as simple actions, but give you extended flexibility and added functionality. For personal agents, a simple action is likely to be all that you need.

Quiz

1. True or False? You cannot create an agent in a database unless you have at least Designer access.
2. Where does a database have to reside if you want to run a shared agent against it? What about a personal agent?
3. You create an agent doing everything correctly, but it will not select any documents when you run it. What is likely to be the problem?
4. What sort of agent would mail out a list of DocLinks and a summary of all new documents in a database?
5. In what order do actions get run when you have an agent that runs multiple actions?
6. Can you create an agent that runs another agent?

Exercises

1. Create an agent that mails you a summary and DocLink of all new or modified documents in a discussion database. Automatically transfer the incoming summary document to a special folder in your mail database.
2. Create a database from the Notes mail template. Then create your own archiving agent to select older documents and move them to the archive database. When you are sure everything is working correctly, add to the agent so that the original document is deleted from your mail after it has been archived.

Week 2

Day 14

Notes and the Internet

Today, we will be looking at the future of Notes: the Web. Notes is not restricted to the Notes environment that you have been learning about for the past two weeks. A big part of the Notes environment, and what promises to be even a bigger part of Notes in version 5.0, is the capability to launch Web pages directly from within Notes, and the capability to interact with Notes databases using Web browsers.

The Domino server translates Notes documents into HTML on-the-fly, making them available to Web users. For Notes applications that have been designed with the Web in mind, a user can use either a Web browser or a Notes client. Documents can be read, and you can enter data into forms and submit it back to Notes through the Domino server. Once back on the server, the data can be managed using replication, agents.

In this lesson, we will be exploring applications that use the power of the Web to enable users in a distributed environment to manage content. We will look at different ways to set up your Notes workstation so you can easily access the Web using your favorite Web browser, or using the Notes Web Navigator. We will then look at the Weblicator, which provides functionality similar to Notes replication over the World Wide Web. You will learn how to keep track of changes on your favorite Web pages, and how to do a full text search on information found on Web pages. Finally, you will get a glimpse of a feature that Lotus calls "Kona," which is downloadable Java applets for Notes over the Web.

Looking at Web-Enabled Notes Applications

With a Web-enabled Notes application, you absolutely need to use the Notes client if you are doing application development or doing certain administrative tasks on the Domino server. Even at that, many Notes developers have built into their applications functions that allow them to do things like adding new users to the Public Address Book via a Web browser.

As you learn more about Notes on the Internet, you will see that there are certain limitations to using the Web, but those limitations have been minimized through the use of Agents, LotusScript, and now Java.

The limitations on the Web are the result of a difference in how information is processed over the Internet and how it is processed over a local area network.

The Web does not require a constant state of connection, even though it may appear to you that you are constantly connected when you are working with Web pages. You enter a Uniform Resource Locator (URL), the standard way of defining a Web page's address on the Internet, and this URL is sent as a request to the Internet server where the Web page is stored. The server sends HTML code (*HyperText Markup Language*, the universal formatting language of the Web) and files to your computer, where your Web browser interprets the code and displays a Web page. If there is animation on the Web page, the animation is being created by downloaded code, for example in the form of a Java program or an ActiveX program. You are not connected to the Web server as long as you are on that page. Another connection is made only when you request another URL, either by typing it in or by clicking on a hypertext link.

This disconnected state means that you do not work directly with data on the server. Instead, you work with a local representation of the data. If you interact with the data, all the interaction takes place on your local computer. Therefore, when you fill out a form on the Web, you are filling it out while disconnected from the source of the data. If a field on the form does a lookup, the lookup has to come from data that has been downloaded as part of the form, or you have to reconnect to the Web server to download the data. With most Web technologies, you have to maintain a connection to the Internet so that your requests can be sent to the Web server when necessary, but you are not connected to the Web server itself.

When you save a form that has been filled out over the Web, the data is not saved directly to a database. The form is sent back to the Web server, which has its own program that takes the data and writes it back to a database. In the case of Notes, the server is a Domino server, and the database is a standard Notes database.

In contrast, when you work on a local Notes database or work directly in Notes with a database that is stored on a Domino server, you are making changes directly to the database itself, and you are constantly connected with the database. That is why, when you are using a mobile Notes client, you replicate the data back to the Domino server. Replication only requires a brief connection, even though you may have been working on your local database for hours or even days before replicating with the server. When you work directly with the database, lookups occur using the live data in the database, and more complex interaction is permitted.

The difference between a live connection to your data, as you have with Notes, and a virtual connection, as you have with the Web, accounts for most of the differences you will encounter when working with a Web browser client as opposed to a Notes client.

An Intranet Example

An *intranet* uses Internet technology to make information available over a secure internal network. Internet technology means using TCP/IP as your communication protocol, and using a Web browser to access data that is delivered as an HTML document.

In a Notes-based intranet, the HTML documents are being served by the Domino server, which is also the server for your Notes network. Therefore, you have a choice of how you access data. If you have a Notes client, you can open the database directly on the Domino server. If you have a Web browser, you can download the data as an HTML document, work with the data, and then submit it back to the Domino server. In either instance, you have the latest available data from anyone using the database.

Because the intranet is internal, you do not need to connect directly to the Internet if everyone is in a single location. However, if you want people to have access from different locations, such as from a remote office or from their home computers, you can still create an intranet, but it has to be accessible from the Internet and should require a login procedure so users can verify their identity.

A similar authentication process takes place when you use the Web as the one that takes place with Notes. However, with Notes, you must have your ID file with you. Over the Web, the only ID available to the Domino server is your name in the Public Address Book, so your user name and your password are vital elements of intranet security. The Notes administrator controls whose name can be listed in the Public Address Book.

The Notes databases on the intranet must be designed and maintained using a full Notes client. They can be designed into a workflow application, with agents handling the workflow whenever there is a trigger, for example, a new document being saved to the database. Agents can create DocLinks, which work when using a Web browser. Users can create and launch file attachments using a Web browser. They can do almost anything that a regular Notes client can do, except that they cannot work with rich text in the same sense that they can in a Notes client. Data can only be entered as text or as a file attachment. Any formatting has to be triggered on the back end after the document is submitted.

So you have an intranet. Any registered user with a Web browser can look up data, such as access an information library. They can see graphics, read text, and follow links. If they have Author or Editor access, they can click on an Action button to put the document into Edit mode, make changes, and then submit those changes back to the Domino server. They can create documents using forms that were designed for Web or Notes use. After they submit their changes, they can refresh the page and see the changes immediately. They can search the database using special search forms. They can browse through a categorized view, expanding and collapsing categories as they go.

Any user with a Notes client can do the same things. In addition, they can create and run personal agents, create their own personal views, and they can run agents from the button bar or from the Actions menu. They can also format rich text and paste graphics into their documents, and they can create buttons and hotspots. They can replicate databases.

If these additional functions are important to you, then you need a Notes client. If not, a Web browser may suffice. With every new release of Notes, the distinction between the two clients will become less significant.

An Internet Example

The intranet is used for internal data. But the same principles apply for a Notes database that is exposed to the Internet via the World Wide Web. Typically, some of the information in an application is made available to the public via a Web site, while some information is used internally. The workflow functionality you have already learned makes Notes ideal for this sort of an arrangement.

In the exercises in yesterday's lesson, you created an agent to archive documents by copying them from one database to another, and then deleting them from the first database. For an Internet application, you might want to remove the deletion part of the formula. Have the first database, the one in which the agent runs, be the database that is being published to the Web. Make the second database into a secure Notes database that is behind your Internet firewall—a logical barrier that protects your network from external prying—in other words, it is not accessible from the Internet. Now, what can you do with that arrangement? A lot!

If you let Web users submit new product solutions, submit questions to your help desk, or order products, you do not necessarily want those documents sitting on the Internet where anyone can see them. So as soon as they are submitted, move them to your internal database, where they can enter into a workflow process:

- ☐ A standard "Thank you, your idea is under consideration" can be sent out automatically to anyone submitting a new product suggestion. Product development can review ideas submitted by the public and discuss them internally before responding directly to the user.
- ☐ Questions to the help desk can be answered from a knowledge base or escalated to in-house experts. Only when a response has been approved does it get copied back to the public database.
- ☐ Product orders can be routed to the credit, accounting, and fulfillment departments, all within Notes, and all done automatically.

That is information on your desktop when and where it is needed. That is information automatically published on the Web as soon as it has been approved for public release. That is why you hear the Domino advertising tagline, "Work the Web."

You will be learning more about how people without Notes clients can work with Notes databases, but first, we will look at how you can use a Web browser from within Notes.

Using a Web Browser from within Notes

There are at least five places within Notes from which you can launch a Web browser:

- ☐ You can launch a Web browser by clicking on a URL link within a Notes document (see Figure 14.1).

Figure 14.1.
You can go directly to a Web page by clicking on an underlined URL in a document.

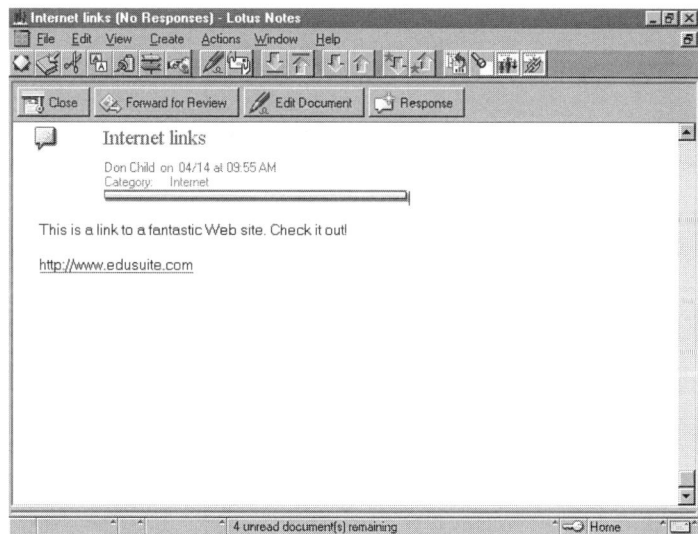

> **TIP** On the User Preferences page, you can set your workspace to underline URL links.

- [ ] You can launch a Web browser by selecting File | Open URL from the menu bar (or use the keyboard shortcut Ctrl+L) and entering the URL you want to launch.
- [ ] You can launch a Web browser by clicking on the Open URL SmartIcon and entering the URL you want to launch.
- [ ] You can launch a Web browser by changing the Search Bar into a URL address bar (see Figure 14.2).

Figure 14.2.
The Search Bar becomes a URL Bar by clicking on the icon on the left side of the bar.

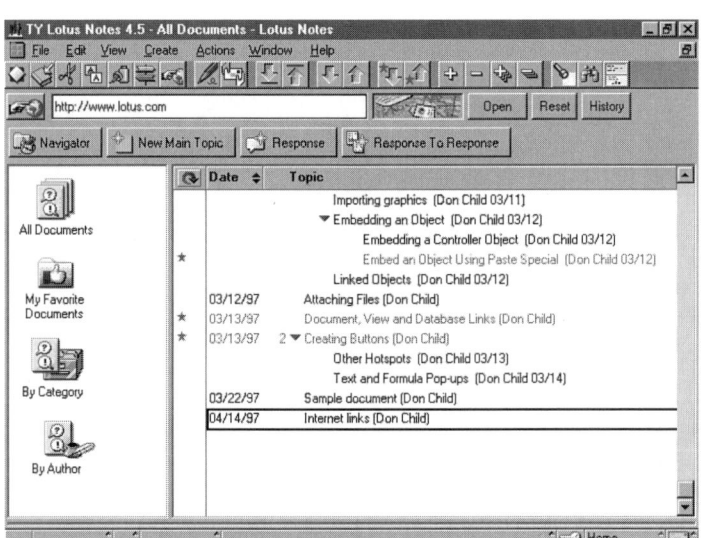

- [ ] You can open the Notes Web Navigator as a database and browse the Web within that database.

When you launch a Web page using any of the first four options, Notes will use whichever browser you have set up as your default browser.

Setting Up Your Default Browser

Lotus Notes ships with three browsers: its own Web Navigator, the Netscape Navigator, and Microsoft Internet Explorer.

You can install either the Netscape or Microsoft browser when you install Notes, or you can download them from the Internet.

To use any browser from within Notes, you must have some sort of connection to the Internet: a direct connection, a connection through a proxy server that acts as a buffer between your computer and the Internet, or a dial-up connection. And you must have a TCP/IP communications port enabled, or use the Notes Server Web Navigator, which has its own Internet connection.

Your Web browser is set up in your Location document. You open the Location document for your current location by clicking on the location on the status bar and selecting Edit Current... or by selecting File | Mobile | Edit Current Location....

Enter the name of your preferred browser in the Internet Browser field, as shown in Figure 14.3.

Figure 14.3.
Select your default Internet browser in the Location document.

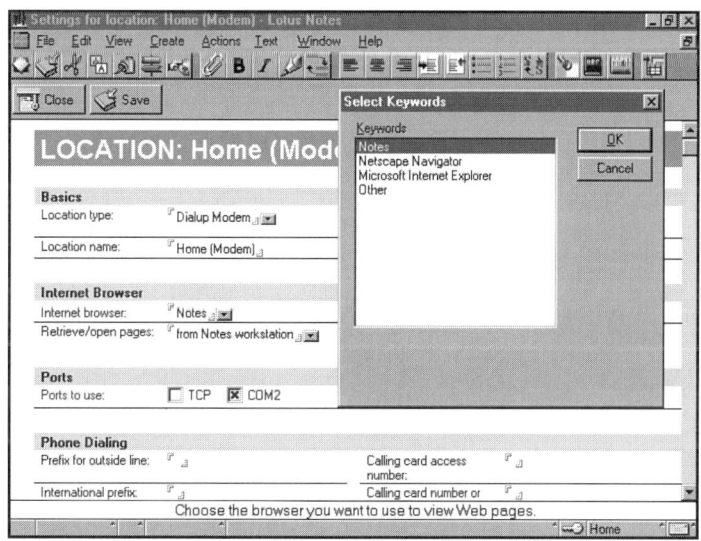

If you select the Notes browser, you have to indicate whether you want to retrieve and open pages from your local workstation (Personal Web Navigator database) or from the Domino server (Server Web Navigator database). If you select the option to not retrieve documents, you can still use Web Navigator to look at documents that have been copied from elsewhere.

When you are done, save your Location document. The browser you chose will be launched the next time you open a Web page from within Notes.

NOTE If you have a browser other than Notes, Microsoft, or Netscape, select Other. You can then define the search path to your preferred browser.

If you selected any browser besides Notes, presumably you know how to use that browser. The next section of today's lesson will take you through the Notes Web Navigator.

Setting Up the Web Navigator

After selecting the Notes Web Navigator as your browser of choice, you can set up additional options that determine how the Navigator functions.

In the lower-right corner of your workspace, click on the location and select Edit Current... from the menu.

In the Location document, scroll down until you see the Advanced section. Expand that section and scroll down to Web Retriever Configuration. You can work with the following fields:

- *Web Navigator Database.* This is the name of the database in which your Web pages will be stored when you surf the Web. If you changed the name of your Web Navigator database, or set up a new one, you can point to it by entering the new name here.

- *Concurrent Retrievers.* This is how many browser windows you can have open at one time. Depending on the speed of your computer, the practical limit is around six. You can move between open retrievers from the Window menu on the menu bar. If you open more retrievers than the number you specified for the location, the URLs will be queued and opened as soon as there is a spare retriever.

- *Retriever Log Level.* You can send status messages to a log database on your workstation (LOG.NSF). The log database is created automatically, and you can place it on your desktop if you want to. Messages can be set at one of three different levels: None, Terse (a short message), and Verbose (a detailed description of any messages).

- *Update Cache.* The cache for the Notes Web Navigator is the stored Web page in the Web Navigator database. You can have Notes refresh the pages in this database once only during an online session, every time you open a Web page in the database, or never (you have to manually refresh pages by clicking on a refresh icon).

- *Accept SSL Site Certificates.* SSL certificates enable you to access sites secured using RSA security. If you enable SSL site certificates in this field, certificates will be downloaded to your computer, allowing you to access the site. The safest way to access these sites is to NOT accept certificates by default. You will then only be able to access SSL sites when you already have a certificate from a common certifier. If you need to perform secure Web transactions, you should study the Notes online help to understand the HTTPS protocol in greater detail.

If you enabled Java on your User Preferences document, you may also want to set the following Java Applet Security fields in the Advanced section of the Locations document to determine on a server-by-server basis what level of access Java applets have. Regardless of the level of access, Java applets cannot access your system resources.

- *Trusted Hosts.* You can limit the servers from which you will accept Java applets, for example, the servers on your corporate intranet. Enter the IP address or domain name of trusted hosts, for example "*.lotus.com". Note that you can use wildcards.
- *Network Access for Trusted Hosts.* This determines what level of network access trusted hosts have when you run Java applets. The options, quoted from the Notes online help, include: *Disable Java* means the trusted host cannot run applets on your system. *No Access Allowed* means the trusted host can run an applet on your system, but cannot make network HTTP connections on any host. *Allow Access to Any Originating Host* means that the applet can make network HTTP connections on the host where the applet was retrieved. *Allow Access to Any Trusted Host* means that the applet can make network HTTP connections only on trusted hosts. *Allow Access to Any Host* means the applet can make network HTTP connections on any host. The default is Allow Access to Any Trusted Host.
- *Network Access for Untrusted Hosts.* This determines what level of network access Java applets from untrusted hosts have on your network. The same options are available as described above, except that with untrusted hosts, you do not have the option of allowing access for trusted hosts.
- *Trust HTTP Proxy.* If you use an HTTP proxy server, you cannot run the Java applet directly, but rather you must rely on the HTTP proxy server to run the applet. Set this field to Yes if you want the HTTP server to be able to run Java applets for you.

Using the Notes Web Navigator

The Notes Web Navigator can function either as a local application, known as the Personal Web Navigator, or as a shared application known as the Server Web Navigator. The Notes Web browsers differ from other popular browsers such as Netscape and Microsoft in terms of what Notes is able to do with Web pages after they have been downloaded.

The Notes Web Navigators give you the option of saving Web pages as Notes documents. And you already know what you can do with Notes documents. You can full text search them. You can forward them to other Notes users. You can manipulate them with agents. You can even replicate them, and you can take them along with you on your laptop computer.

You will see in a moment how to use the Web Navigator. But first, what is the difference between the Personal Web Navigator and the Server Web Navigator?

The obvious difference between the two navigators is the location of the database. The Personal Web Navigator is a local database, and as such, is available only to you. The Server Web Navigator is on the Domino server, and can be accessed by anyone with access to the server who is not excluded in the ACL.

The Server Web Navigator follows in the footsteps of the earlier Notes application known as InterNotes, which marked the first Notes foray into cyberspace. InterNotes gave rise to the term *team surfing*, whereby a workgroup could share the Web surfing of any member of the team. Web pages were saved to a common database, and could be opened from that database instead of going out to the Internet to retrieve the pages. The InterNotes server did all the Web retrieval, and was the only machine that had to have TCP/IP and an Internet connection. Notes users could use any communication protocol supported by Notes, because all they had to do was to access the InterNotes database on the Notes server and tell InterNotes which Web page to retrieve from the Internet.

The Server Web Navigator is essentially InterNotes. If you have the database on your desktop, you can open it up using any protocol—for example, SPX or AppleTalk—and have the server retrieve documents from the Web. Then others can see the same pages without going to the Internet, saving on connection costs. In some environments, this can be a very effective way to make the Internet available in a limited fashion. This also increases the security of your internal network.

The Personal Web Navigator lets you retrieve Web pages directly from the Internet. That means you have to have an Internet connection either directly or via a proxy server, and you have to enable a TCP/IP communications port.

Setting Up the Notes Web Navigator

Whichever version you elect to use, the setup process is the same (aside from the necessity of setting up the ACL on a Server Notes Navigator). You have to put the database on your desktop, and then you need to tailor it to your needs.

To put a new Personal Notes Navigator database on your desktop, follow these steps:

1. Select File | Database | New from the menu bar.
2. Set the Server to Local.
3. Give the database a name, such as Personal Web Navigator.
4. Give the database the file name PERWEB.NSF.

Warning

If you assign another file name, Notes will not recognize the database. Instead, another database with the name PERWEB.NSF will be created the first time you open a page on the Web. This can lead to confusion, with Web pages not being stored where you expect them.

5. Scroll through the list of templates and select Personal Web Navigator 4.5.

Notes will create the database on your desktop, and will display the dialog box and About document shown in Figure 14.4.

Figure 14.4.
You can tailor the setup of your Personal Web Navigator database.

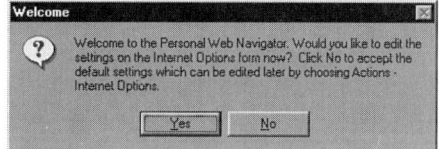

Click on OK to display the Internet Options document. This document is used to define a number of options, including your default home page, your default search engine, and various other database options. This document is complex enough that it warrants a detailed explanation.

Setting Internet Options for the Web Navigator

You can set up Internet Options when you first set up your Web Navigator database, or you can return at a later time to set it up if the default values do not work for you. The Internet Options work with whatever Web browser you have set up in you Location document.

To display the Internet Options document, if you are not already there, highlight the Web Navigator database and select Actions | Internet Options from the menu bar. The top part of the Internet Options document is shown in Figure 14.5.

Figure 14.5.
Set up your Internet environment on the Internet Options page.

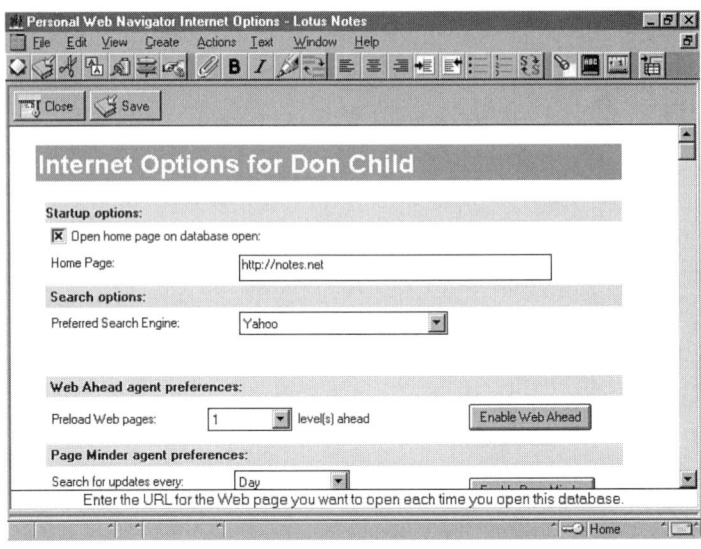

Setting Startup Options, Search Options, and Web Ahead

The options you can set up on the first part of the page include:

- *Startup Options.* If you check this, then the home page you identify in the Home Page field will be displayed when you first open your Web Navigator database. If you do not specify this, then the database will open up to a Notes view of the database. The default home page, http://notes.net, contains a lot of useful information, beta products, discussion databases, and news articles related to Notes. It's a good place to stay up-to-date with the latest happenings related to Notes.

- *Search Options.* You can specify the search engine that is used by default when you click on the Search button of the Web Navigator. You can select from one of the more popular search engines, or you can type in the URL of your own favorite search engine if it is not listed.

- *Web Ahead Agent Preferences.* Web Ahead is an agent that runs in the background on your Notes workstation. When you drop a Web page into an enabled Web Ahead folder, Notes downloads linked pages in the background for all URLs on the page down to the depth that you specify. You can then disconnect from the Web and work with the Web pages after you disconnect from the Web. Web Ahead will only run while your Notes workstation is running.

To enable Web Ahead, specify the number of levels to which Web pages should be preloaded (up to four levels deep), and then click on the Enable Web Ahead button. A dialog box will be displayed in which you specify the server on which the agent should run. After you specify the server, the Web Ahead agent will run every 30 minutes for any Web page that you put into the Web Ahead folder.

WARNING

Web Ahead can even run on an authenticated server or an authenticated proxy server. The first time you use the server during the session, you have to provide your user name and password, and the information is then stored in a field on the Web page. To ensure that the information is not stolen from a Web page, you should encrypt your Web Navigator database if you plan on using the Web Ahead agent on one of these servers.

Setting Up Page Minder, Purge, and Collaboration Options

Scroll down the Internet Options page to display the additional options shown in Figure 14.6.

Figure 14.6.
Define additional Internet Options, including Page Minder.

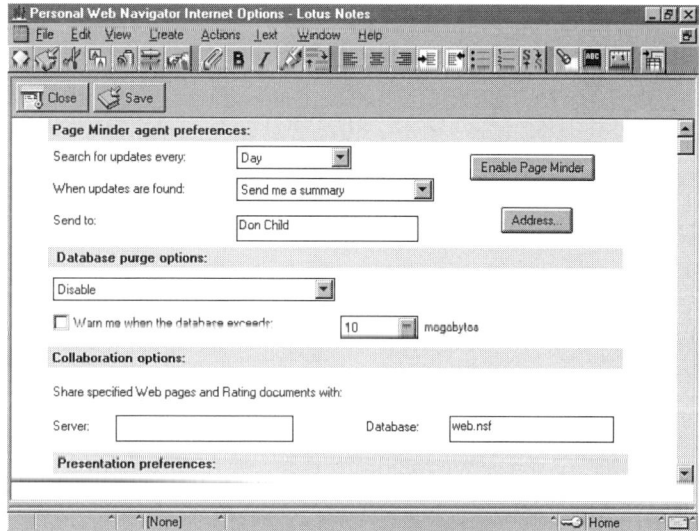

On this portion of the Internet Options document, you can define the following:

- *Page Minder Agent Preferences.* The Page Minder agent keeps track of changes to selected Web pages. You can set the agent to run once an hour, every four hours, once a day, or once a week, as long as your Notes workstation is running at the scheduled time. The Page Minder agent will inform you of changes by sending you a summary, or by sending you the entire page that has changed. You can also specify the address to which the summary or page is mailed.

  After you define the agent properties, enable the agent exactly the way you enabled the Web Ahead agent. The same caveat regarding authenticated servers and authenticated proxy servers applies. Encrypt your database if you use the agent on one of these servers.

- *Database Purge Options.* This option is disabled by default, but you can enable it so that Web pages are reduced to links or deleted from the database if they are not viewed in 15, 30, 60, or 90 days. You can also define when you want to receive size warnings regarding the Web Navigator database. If you elect to receive warnings, you can define a size limit of 5, 10, 25, or 50 megabytes before you receive a warning.

- *Collaboration Options.* You can share Web pages that you encounter in your Personal Web Navigator by copying the pages into the Server Web Navigator database, or by creating a Rating document in the Server Web Navigator database. On the Internet Options page, define the name of the Domino server and the database file name of the Server Web Navigator database where Web pages are to be shared.

Setting Up Presentation and Network Preferences

The final sections of the Internet Options document determine how various types of information get displayed, and there is a link to the Location document. This section of the document is shown in Figure 14.7.

The presentation options include:

- *Anchors.* Anchors are links to other documents.
- *Body Text.* Body text is the default font for text in the main body of a document. Whatever size you define for body text applies to all other text types defined in the Presentation Preferences section of this document.
- *Fixed.* Fixed text is text that is monospaced, that is, each character is the same width. This includes the following HTML tags: <CODE>, <SAMPLE>, <KBD>, and <TT>.
- *Plain.* Plain text specifies how the HTML tags <PLAINTEXT>, <PRE>, and <EXAMPLE> are displayed.

- *Address.* This is the text with the HTML tag <ADDRESS>.
- *Listing.* This is the text with the HTML tag <LISTING>.
- *Save HTML in Note.* If you want to be able to view the HTML source code for Web documents, you have to check the box in the Presentation Properties section of the document.

Figure 14.7.
Set up how Web pages are displayed in the Internet Options document.

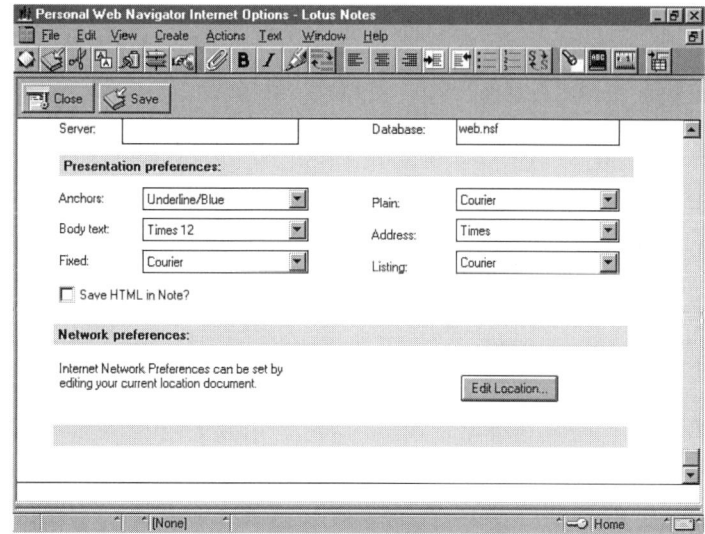

You already set up your preferred browser. The Internet Options apply to the Personal Web Navigator you just set up. If you want to use the Notes Navigator, you can click on the Edit Location... button to get to your current Location document from the Internet Options database.

Using the Personal Web Navigator

The Personal Web Navigator is a Web browser built into Notes, but it is also a Notes database with documents, replication, and ACL security. If you select Notes as your Web browser for the current location and then open a URL, Notes will use the PERWEB.NTF template to create a Personal Web Navigator database if one does not already exist.

Open the database, and press the Escape key, if necessary, to close the About Database document. Notes will display the default view of the database, shown in Figure 14.8.

Figure 14.8.
The default view of the Personal Web Navigator database.

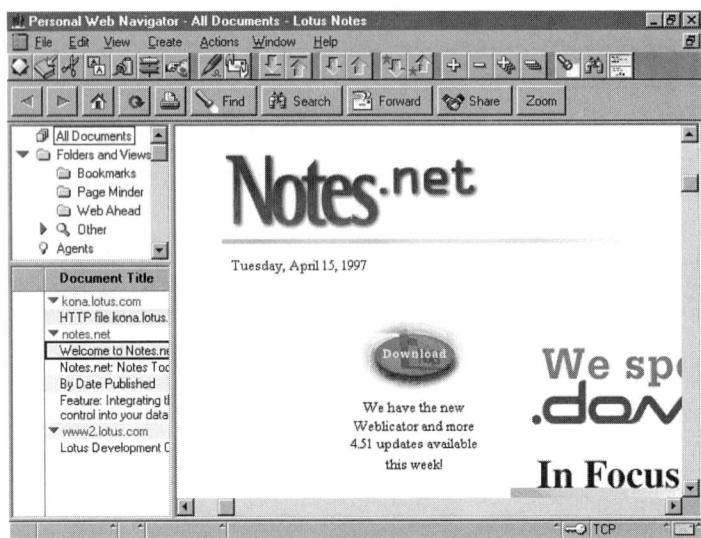

In this example, several documents have previously been opened, so you can see a list of open documents. The elements of the screen include:

- A standard Notes title bar, menu bar, and SmartIcon bar.
- A button bar that contains navigation buttons specific to the Web Navigator.
- A navigator pane in the upper-left corner of the screen, from which you can select different views, as with any Notes database.
- A view pane in the lower-left corner of the screen. This lists Web pages that have been previously downloaded and automatically saved as Notes documents.
- A preview pane on the right that shows the currently selected Web page.
- A standard Notes status bar.

NOTE The panes are in a different location than you may be used to, but are the standard panes available in a Notes view.

Navigating with the Button Bar

The icons on the button bar let you navigate through Web documents, just like the navigators on any of the popular Web browsers. Figure 14.9 shows the buttons.

Figure 14.9.
Buttons allow you to navigate on the document Web and work with Web pages as Notes documents.

The buttons, from left to right, include:

- Navigate to Next and Navigate to Previous document in the current session.
- Open the home page defined on the Internet Options page.
- Reload the current Web page from the Internet.
- Print the current document.
- Find a word or phrase within the currently selected document.
- Search the Web using the preferred search engine you defined in your Internet Options document.
- Forward the Web page as a Notes document. The Web page will be inserted into the Rich Text field of a regular Notes mail memo so you can address and send it to others.
- Share a page with others via the Shared Web Navigator database on the Domino server. The process of sharing pages is described below.
- Zoom lets you expand the Web page so it occupies the entire workspace, hiding the Navigator and View panes. When the Zoom view is showing, you can return to the Navigator view by closing the window (or by pressing Esc).

When you are on the zoomed page, an additional button gives you access to folders so you can move the current Web page into the Web Ahead or Page Minder folders, or into a Bookmarks folder, where you can locate frequently visited pages quickly and easily.

Sharing Web Pages with Others

If you want to share Web pages with others in your workgroup, you can do so by forwarding the page to Server Web Navigator database.

When you click on the Share button on the Navigator's button bar, the Share Options dialog box is displayed, as shown in Figure 14.10.

Figure 14.10.
Select how you want to rate and share a Web page with your coworkers.

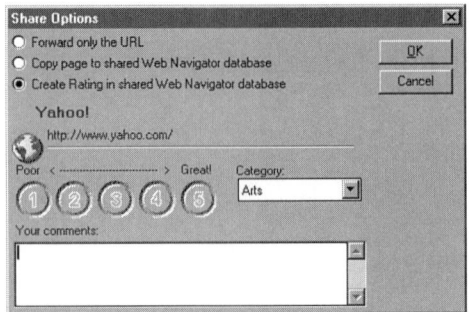

You can forward just the URL for a Web page to an individual or group; you can forward the entire document to the shared Web Navigator database; or you can create a Rating document in the Server Web Navigator.

Ratings are available in a special Ratings view that is only available in the Server Web Navigator database.

Taking a Web Tour

Okay, maybe the heading is a bit deceptive. You are going to create a Web tour for others to use, or for yourself to use when you are no longer attached to the Internet. You can create a Web Tour, and then recall the Web Tour later and replay all the pages you visited.

To create a Web Tour:

1. Use the Personal Web Navigator to visit all the Web pages you want to include in your tour.
2. When you are done with your tour, click on the History button on the Search Bar, or select Actions | History from the menu bar.
3. A dialog box will display a history that lists all the pages you have visited during your current session.
4. Click on the Save button to save the history as a Web Tour. Notes will display the Web Tour document, as shown in Figure 14.11.
5. Modify the list of sites, if you want to. You can delete Web pages, or rearrange them in the list using Copy and Paste commands.
6. Save the Web Tour when you are done.

Figure 14.11.
Save the history of your current session as a Web Tour document.

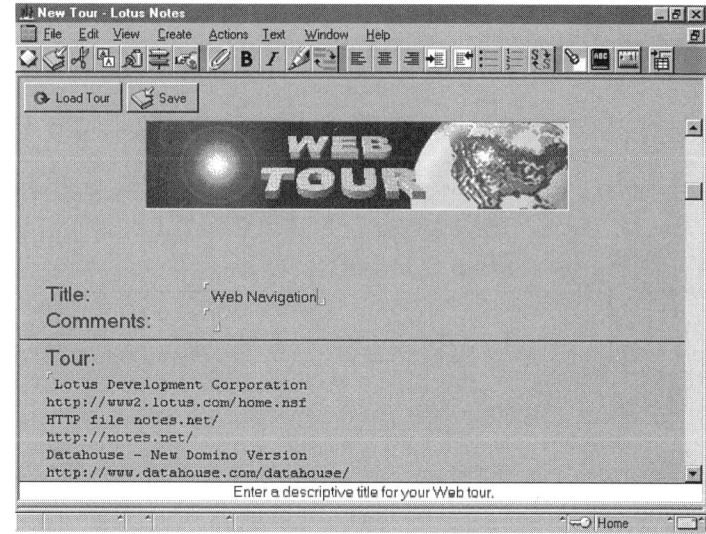

After you have saved a Web Tour, you can load it and rerun it. If you have specified No Retrievals on your Location document as an option for opening/retrieving Web pages, then the Web Tour pages will be loaded from the Web pages saved as Notes documents in your Web Navigator database.

To load and replay a Web Tour:

1. Select the Other | Web Tours view in the navigator pane of your Personal Web Navigator database.
2. In the view pane, locate and double-click on the tour you want to replay. The Web Tour document will be opened in the Preview pane.
3. Click on the Load Tour button.
4. The first page of the tour will be displayed in the Zoom view of the database.
5. Use the Next and Previous navigator buttons to move backward and forward through your Web Tour.

You can share your Web Tour with your coworkers by sharing the Web Tour document in the Server Web Navigator database. If the Web pages have not yet been loaded, have expired, or have been deleted from the database, Notes will load them in the background as you are looking at the tour.

Importing Favorites and Bookmarks from Other Browsers

If you are moving to the Notes Web Navigator from either the Microsoft Internet Explorer or from the Netscape Navigator, you can import your Favorites or Bookmark file into the Personal Web Navigator database.

To import the Microsoft Internet Explorer Favorite file:

1. Select Actions | Import Microsoft Favorites.
2. Specify the path to the Favorites file, such as `C:/Windows/Internet/Favorites`.

The top level of your Favorites file will be imported into the Bookmarks folder in your Personal Web Navigator.

To import the Netscape Navigator Bookmarks file:

1. Select Actions | Import Navigator Bookmarks.
2. Specify the path to the Bookmarks file, for example, `C:/Netscape/Bookmark.HTM`.

The entire Bookmarks file will be imported into the Bookmarks folder of your Personal Web Navigator database.

If your Favorites or Bookmarks have been cleared from the cache on your computer, you can still click on the title in the Bookmarks folder, and then click on the Refresh button to load the page into the Web Navigator database.

Viewing the HTML Source for a Document

If you have any amount of Web experience, you are probably well aware of the fact that you can borrow HTML design ideas from any Web site you visit. You do not have to know how to mark up a document using HTML, you do not have to know how to develop Java applets, all you have to know is how to download the HTML source for a document. You can then substitute your own graphics and text.

At the bottom of the Internet Options document, one of the options was to load the HTML source along with your Web pages. If you want to capture the HTML source for documents when using the Web Navigator, you have to check this option in the Internet Options document. The HTML source is then saved automatically along with the Web pages when you visit them.

The HTML source for a document is stored in a hidden field on the Notes form that holds a Web page. To view the HTML source:

1. Highlight the document in the View pane or open the Web page in the Web Navigator.
2. Display the Document Properties InfoBox and click on the Fields page.
3. Scroll through the list of fields, and highlight the HTMLSource field. The HTML source text will be displayed in the right panel of the InfoBox.

TIP The InfoBox panel is a bit cramped. You can copy the HTML source text to the clipboard and paste it into a word processing document or a Notes document to get a better look at the HTML source code.

Personal Web Navigator Folders and Views

Most of the folders and views have already been mentioned.

- The Bookmarks folder holds documents that you want to refer to again without having to search the entire database.
- The Page Minder folder holds pages for which you want to receive notification when there are changes on the page. The Page Minder has to be enabled in the Internet Options document, and your Notes workstation has to be running at the designated time before Page Minder will work.
- The Web Ahead folder holds pages for which you want the Web Navigator to automatically download links. The Web Ahead function has to be enabled in the Internet Options document, and your Notes workstation has to be running for Web Ahead to work.
- The Other/File Archive view holds graphic files associated with Web Pages, if you have Display Images After Loading checked in your User Preferences page, so that the text for Web pages gets displayed more quickly; after the text appears, the graphics are downloaded and displayed. The graphics are stored separately in the File Archive view.
- The Other/Housekeeping view holds elements that are scheduled to be purged from the database as a means of limiting the size of the database. You must enable the Purge agent in the Internet Options database for the documents to be automatically purged. The documents in this view include the graphic elements that are stored separately from documents when you select Display Images After Loading.
- The Other/Web Tours view holds the Web Tour documents you have created.

The one feature that distinguishes the Notes Web Navigator from Web browsers is the capability to manipulate the Web pages as Notes documents. Web pages are automatically converted to Notes documents, so they can be full text indexed, searched, forwarded to others, categorized, and manipulated with Notes agents—anything that can be done with a Notes document.

Weblicator: Notes Functionality without Notes

You will now do a 360-degree turn. Instead of using the Web from within Notes, as you were doing with the Personal Web Navigator, you will now be using the Weblicator, along with a Web browser, to achieve much of the functionality of Notes, even if you do not have a Notes client and do not have access to a Domino server aside from working with Web pages that are served up by Domino.

Weblicator, as of the time this is being written, is still a beta product. Some of the functionality that is obviously intended does not yet work smoothly, and there is little reliable documentation to go along with the product, but there is enough to give you a good solid understanding of the product. Hopefully, by the time you read this, the product will be on the market as a companion to Lotus Notes.

The Weblicator version I have used in the screen shots in this lesson is Weblicator BETA 4.B.1, downloaded from the Notes.Net site on the Web. There are two versions available: a Standard version for those who do not have a Lotus Notes client on their workstation, and a Lite version for those who already have a Notes client. The Weblicator uses a browser along with the Weblicator interface, all built on a subset of the Notes client. The subset provides access to Notes NSF files for storing Web information, as well as allowing access so you can perform two-way replication using a Web browser.

NOTE Because this is a beta product, the interface and even some of the functionality may change in the final product. However, this has been in beta through several generations, so the basic functionality is pretty well established.

If you have downloaded the Weblicator (downloaded as an installable EXE file) and installed it, you will see the splash screen shown in Figure 14.12.

Figure 14.12.
The Weblicator starts up a Web browser and then displays a splash screen.

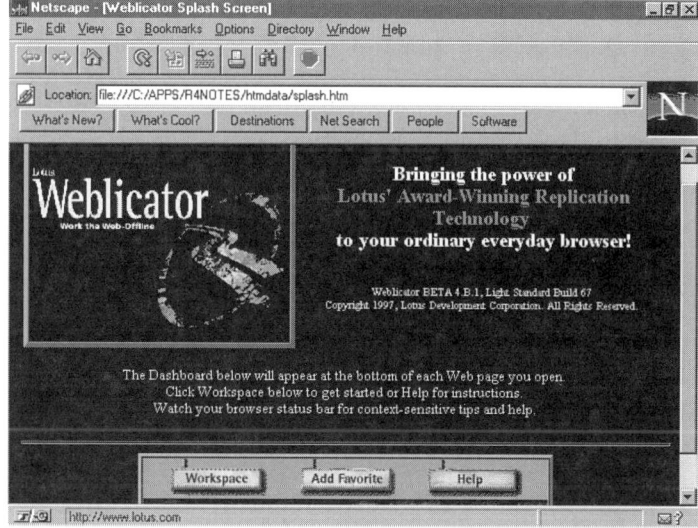

Notice the "dashboard" at the bottom of the splash screen. This same dashboard provides navigation shortcuts whenever you are looking at a "weblicated" page in the Weblicator.

Click on the Workspace button to get started with the Weblicator. The Weblicator workspace is shown in Figure 14.13.

Figure 14.13.
The Weblicator workspace provides access to all functions within the Weblicator.

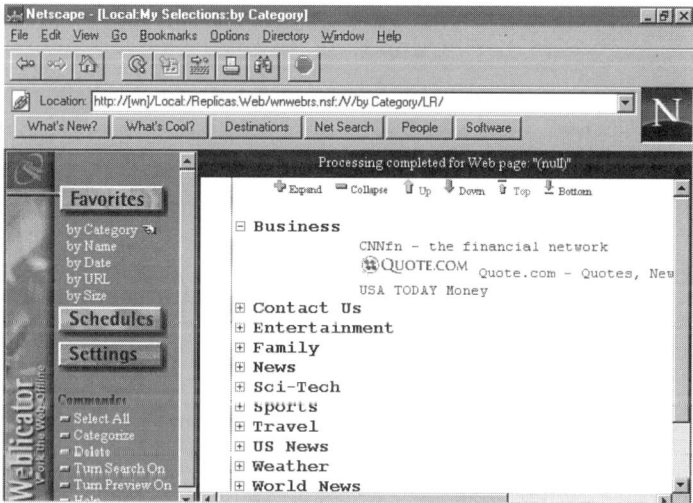

Verifying the Weblicator Settings

When you start up the Weblicator, you will want to make sure that everything is set up correctly. You can do this from the workspace page by clicking on the Settings button. The default page in the Settings view is the Weblicator Preferences document, part of which is shown in Figure 14.14.

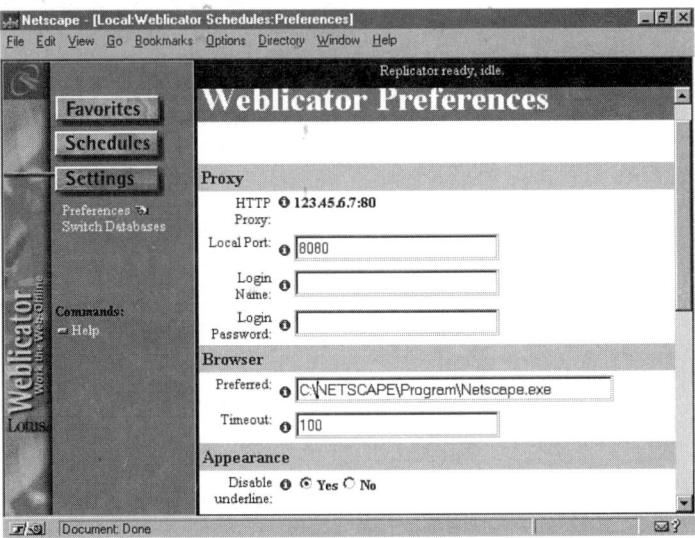

Figure 14.14.
The Weblicator Preferences page is used to set up your general Weblicator environment.

In this document, pay close attention to the field-level help, which you can access by holding the mouse pointer over the small Information icons beside each field. The information in this document includes:

- *Proxy Information.* If you access the Internet through an HTTP proxy server, the proxy server is already defined in your Web browser, and the number will be entered in the document. The proxy server will also require a local port so Weblicator (in the online help, it is referred to as WebNotes) can communicate with your browser. The proxy server may also require a login and password, which you can store here.

- *Browser Information.* In this section, you store the full path to the EXE file for the browser you use, and define how long to wait on the browser before assuming that an Internet connection has been lost.

- *Appearance Information.* In this section, you define how weblicated information is displayed and stored. You can turn off underlining for URL links; you can store parts of a document as separate parts so the document can be sorted and categorized using background Notes agents; and you can define a start-up URL, which is the first Web page that is displayed when Weblicator is launched.

☐ *Replicator Information.* In this section, you define how replication results are categorized, and whether they are automatically added to the full text index for the database.

If you change any information on the Weblicator Preferences page, you have to save your changes by clicking on the Save button at the bottom of the form, and then quitting and restarting the Weblicator.

NOTE When you save the form, the information is validated to ensure that it meets the format requirements for the document. You will have a chance to re-enter data if it is not in the correct format.

Selecting a Local Database

You have one more setup option—deciding which database to put your replication results into. By default, results are stored in an NSF file named REPLICAS.WEB\WNWEBRS.NSF, or My Selections. Any database created with the WNWEBRS.NTF template can be used, so you can have multiple databases and select which database you want to store replications to. To select one, click on Switch Databases and then locate the database you want.

Creating a Link to a Notes Database

You can also use the Switch Databases function to create a link to a Notes database and then access the database from Weblicator.

To create a link to a Notes database:

1. Click on the Rebuild Server List command (only available when you are in the Switch Databases view).
2. Locate the Notes server on which the database resides, and click on it.
3. Enter the password for your Notes user ID to gain access to the Domino server. The password dialog box will be displayed on the screen, as shown in Figure 14.15.

Figure 14.15.
Enter your Notes password to access a Notes database through Weblicator.

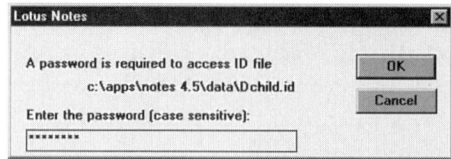

4. Locate the database you want to build a link to.
5. Click the database to open it. Weblicator will display a database summary and a list of available views, plus the About Database and Using Database documents. The database summary is shown in Figure 14.16.

Figure 14.16.
Weblicator will display a database summary when you select a new database.

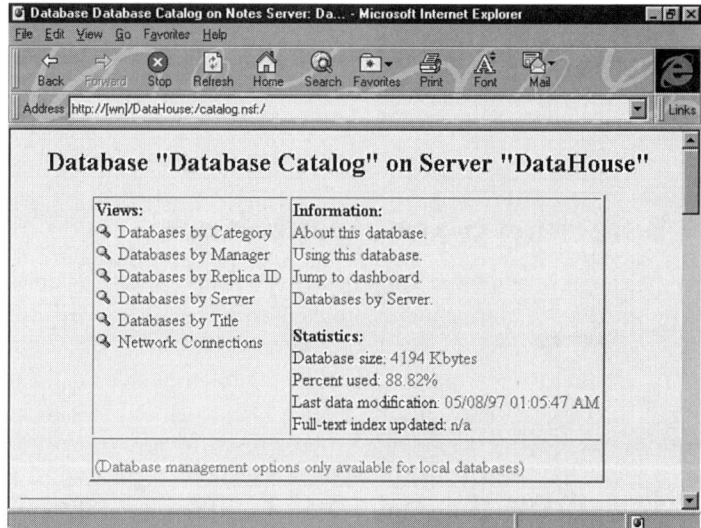

6. Click Add Favorite on the dashboard at the bottom of the document.
7. Enter the database title in the Replication Schedule document and save it.

You will find that you can open the database using the Weblicator, you can navigate through different views, you can compose documents—anything that you can do within Notes based on the ACL for the database.

> **NOTE**
> In other words, you can, if you really want to, use the Weblicator as a limited Notes client. However, aside from the novelty of being able to do so, you should stick with the Notes client if you want flexibility and ease of use.

Setting Up Replication Schedules

After you set up the Weblicator so it functions correctly with your Web browser, you can define replication schedules for your favorite Web sites.

To set up options for a site:

1. Click the Schedules button to view a list of Favorites for which you can set schedules.
2. If you want to create a new schedule, click on the New Schedule command.
3. If you want to modify an existing schedule, locate and click on the name of the Web page in the view.
4. The Edit Schedule and Copy Options dialog box will be displayed as shown in Figure 14.17.

Figure 14.17.
Select basic schedule and copy options in this dialog box, or go to more advanced settings.

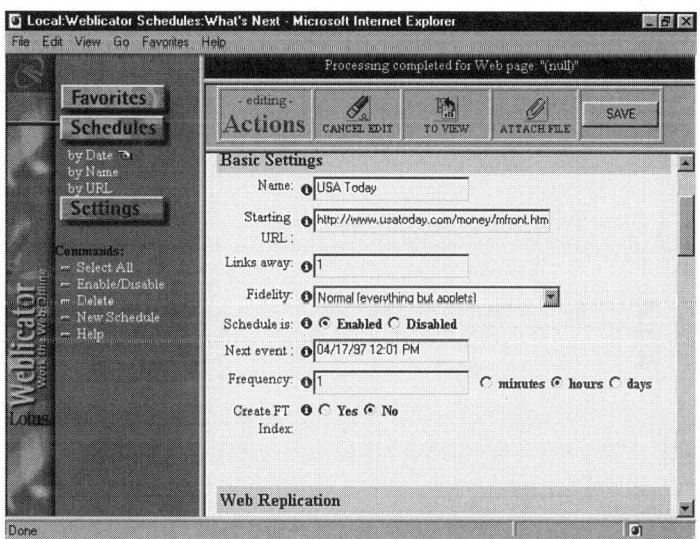

In this dialog box, you can check options to replicate (copy into your local favorites database) whole Web pages, replicate all pages that are *n* number of links away (that is, Web Ahead), and set a basic schedule for this particular favorite.

5. Click on OK to save your changes, or click on Advanced to see additional settings. The Advanced settings are entered on the Web Replication Settings page, part of which is shown in Figure 14.18.

Figure 14.18.
Set up advanced schedule and replication options on the Web Replication Settings page, which begins with Basic options.

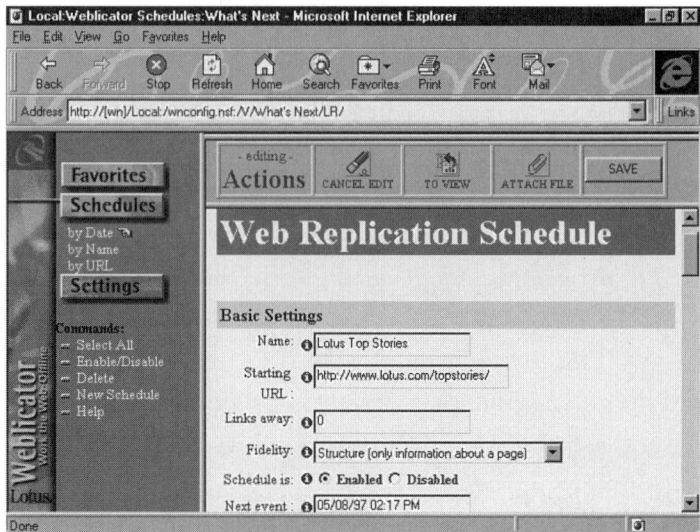

6. Enter the following information on the Web Replication Settings form:

    ☐ *Basic Settings.* This section includes the URL for the opening page, which information to replicate (Fidelity), scheduling details, and whether to full text index replicated pages.

    ☐ *Web Replication.* This section includes details such as which database to store replicated pages in, your login and password for the server if the replica is stored on a secure Notes server, and a number of parameters that let you control the amount of data that gets replicated.

    ☐ *Web Monitoring.* This section defines how the Weblicator informs you when it finds changes on the monitored pages. Even if you do not replicate copies of Web pages, you can still have the Weblicator monitor a Web site and inform you when there have been changes. You can then navigate to the site to view the newly revised Web pages online.

    ☐ *Notes Replication.* You can replicate Notes databases that are accessible through the Internet. In this section of the Scheduling document, you define the local replica database and the cutoff date for Notes replication. You can then replicate to and from a Notes database even when you do not have a Notes client available.

NOTE

Earlier beta versions of the Weblicator enabled you to replicate a Notes database even if the server was behind a firewall. This functionality is not available in BETA 4.B.1, and is not likely to be available in the gold release version of Weblicator.

☐ *Advanced.* This section defines specific programs that should be run at various times before, during, and after the replication process to condition the data that is being replicated. You can also specify whether to use Web compression, which is slower but saves space, and encryption.

All the fields on the form have a single-line help description that displays on the status bar in Netscape Navigator or in pop-up help on Microsoft Internet Explorer. Until more complete documentation is available, this online help will guide you as to the contents of specific fields.

When you are done setting up the parameters of your replication schedule, click on the Save button to submit your changes back to the Weblicator.

Enabling and Disabling Schedules

After you have created a schedule for a Favorite page, you have to enable the schedule before Weblicator starts monitoring and retrieving Web pages.

You can click in the left column beside Favorite pages to process them as a batch (see Figure 14.19).

Figure 14.19.
Select multiple Web pages to enable or disable their replication schedules.

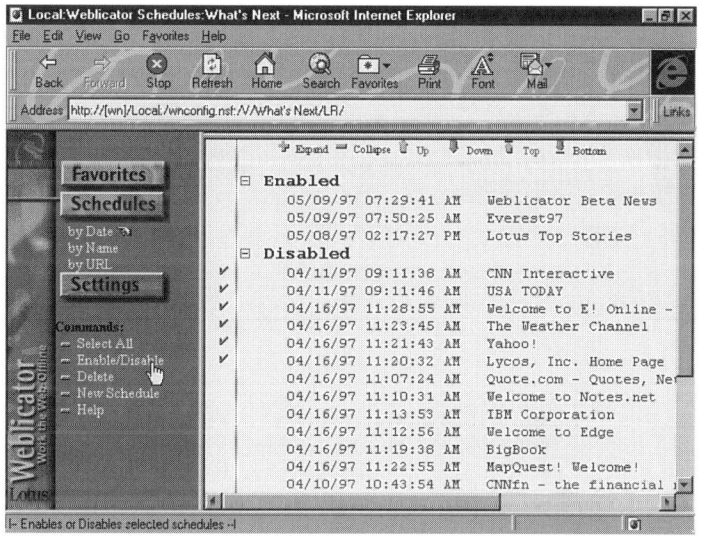

After selecting Web pages, click on Enable/Disable to enable or disable the schedule for those pages.

☐ If all of your selections are currently disabled, they will be enabled when you click on Enable/Disable.

- ☐ If all of your selections are currently enabled, they will be disabled when you click on Enable/Disable.
- ☐ If some selections are currently enabled and some are currently disabled, you will be given an option to disable all of them or enable all of them.
- ☐ You can also click on Select All to select all of your Favorites. If all Favorites are selected and some are enabled while others are disabled, you will be given the choice to enable everything or disable everything. Otherwise, your selections will toggle between enabled and disabled when you click on Enable/Disable.

Once enabled, pages will be replicated based on whatever schedule and parameters you defined.

Adding New Favorites to Your Weblicator

The Weblicator has two modes: online and offline. When you are offline, you can browse through Web pages or Web monitor documents using your Web browser, but you are looking at local documents, not at live Web pages.

When you are in the online mode, you can browse the Web as you normally do with your chosen Web browser, but the Weblicator dashboard gets embedded at the bottom of all documents you visit. The dashboard is shown in Figure 14.20. Note that the dashboard also contains a Java applet that displays a scrolling message within the dashboard.

Figure 14.20.
Use the Weblicator dashboard to add a new Favorite Web site.

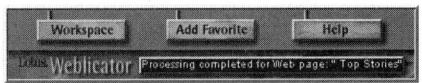

When you find a document that you want to save as a favorite so it can be replicated, click on the Add Favorite button on the dashboard. When you are done browsing, you can return to the Weblicator workspace and create a replication schedule for your new page.

If you want to replicate a single Web page, do not include any Web links when you set up your replication schedule. If you want to replicate an entire site, include a large number of Web links (99, for example—wildcards may work here, but I have been unable to test them; you may want to try this for yourself) and set the top level organization as the bounding URL. For example, if you wanted to replicate the entire Lotus Web site, you would set the bounding URL as *.lotus.com and you would then get anything below the top level, but you would also get links to www.kona.lotus.com.

TIP If you are working online and replicating a large number of Web pages, you may want to consider setting up Web monitors rather than replicating the entire page, unless you have plenty of disk storage. With the Web monitor, you can see when the page has changed and can visit the page by clicking on a link. Of course, this strategy will not work if you are reviewing Web pages offline.

Looking at Replicated Pages Offline

To look at your replicated Web pages or Web monitors, switch to the Favorites view. You will see a list of the Favorites you have stored in the currently selected My Favorites database.

You can sort the Favorites by clicking on the various views, listing them by category, by name, by last replication date, by URL, or by size. A categorized view is shown in Figure 14.21.

Figure 14.21.
The categorized view of Favorites is used to access Web pages offline.

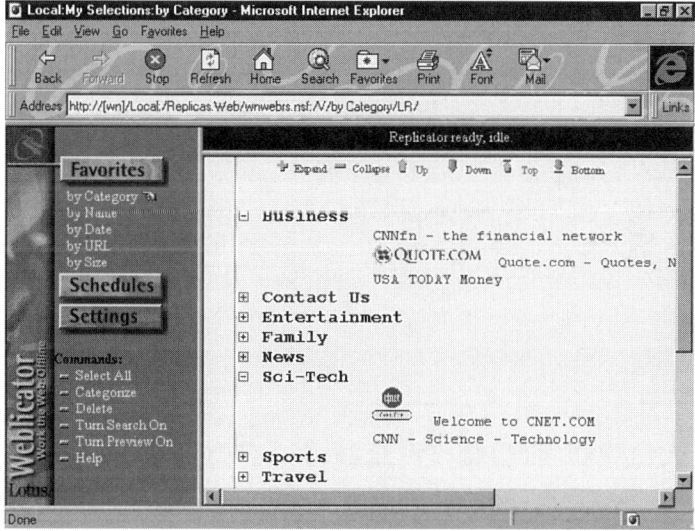

Click on titles to visit those pages. Depending on the options you have set for a page, you will see one of three things when you open a document:

- ☐ A link to the online document if the Web page has not been replicated.
- ☐ A Web monitor document that summarizes changes to the Web page and contains a link to the page.
- ☐ A local replica copy of the Web page (or pages, if you replicated links).

You can view any Web pages you have replicated. If you did not replicate graphics, then only the text and links will be shown.

If the Web page is a form, you can fill out the form offline and then replicate the form back to the Web server.

If the Web page happens to be a Notes page that was published to the Web from a Domino server, you can do a lot more. You can work with the document just as you would work with any Notes document through the Web browser environment. If you see an Edit button, you can put the document into Edit mode, modify fields in the Notes document, and then submit them back to the Domino server, even when you are working offline.

When you replicate with the Domino-based Web page, the replication is two-way, so your changes are submitted back to the original Notes database. If you have sufficient access in the database ACL, your changes will be made to the original Notes document. Likewise, you can fill out forms offline and submit them back to the Domino server.

This full two-way replication only works with Notes database served to the Web by a Domino server.

Warning

Caveat: The description of how to use the Weblicator is based on a beta version of the Weblicator application. The version of the Weblicator interface described in today's lesson was released in beta less than a week before this lesson was written, so the final functionality may not be as it is described above. The Weblicator may well be available by the time you read this, and should be available by downloading it from somewhere on the Lotus Web site (www.lotus.com) or through retail shops for a minimal cost.

Kona and Maui: The Future of Notes

While we are talking about beta releases, there is one more topic that has to do with the direction that Notes is going in relation to the Internet.

You have probably read about network computers (NCs), the computer with no local storage and only minimal built-in applications (a bit like the first IBM PC to hit the market back in the early 1980s, except that the NC has a built-in network connection, and a much faster processor than those early PCs). Everything you need will be downloaded over the network.

Whether NCs come to fruition remains to be seen, but the age of downloadable applications and downloadable interfaces is already here. Notes introduced embedded ActiveX applications called Lotus Components with Notes release 4.0. Then, just after the first release of Notes 4.5, Lotus announced a new breed of Web-enabled applications code-named "Kona."

If you are a coffee aficionado, you know that the Kona region on the Island of Hawaii is famous for its coffee beans. And Java is quickly becoming the *lingua franca* of the Internet. You should be able to fill in the blanks from there.

Kona is built out of downloadable Java applets (the same applications are also available in ActiveX for Microsoft Internet Explorer users). The Kona applets can be played in a Notes document or downloaded with a Web page and played in your Web browser.

The Kona applets can be downloaded to a PC or a Network Computer, so you do not need a disk drive that has separate applications for spreadsheets, word processors, charting, scheduling, or presentation graphics. These are all downloadable and can be embedded in documents so they are available through any Web browser. The applets can be "snapped" together to build more robust applications. It gives you basically a disposable light-weight version of software suites such as Lotus SmartSuite and Microsoft Office. The Suites still deliver a lot more functionality, but the Kona applets are tailored for download over the Web, and will run on any browser that runs as a Java virtual machine.

Figures 14.22 and 14.23 show examples of Kona applications from the Lotus Web site. You can download and play with Kona applications from www.kona.lotus.com.

Figure 14.22.

Lotus 1-2-3 and a chart applet can be downloaded as Kona applets.

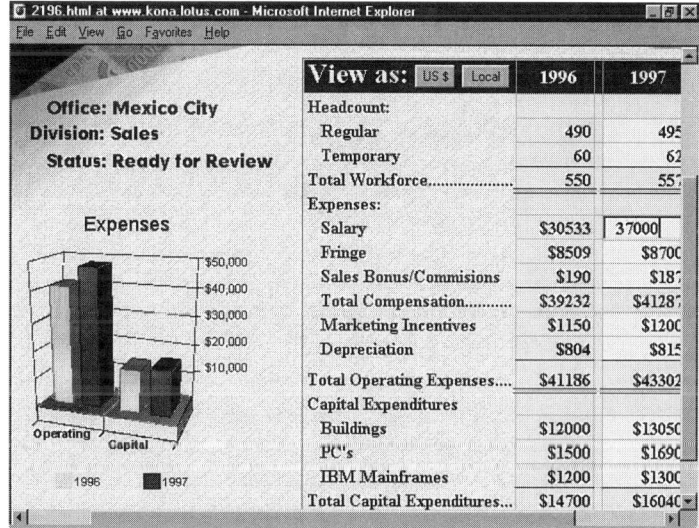

Figure 14.23.
Scheduling and Project Management can be downloaded as Kona applets.

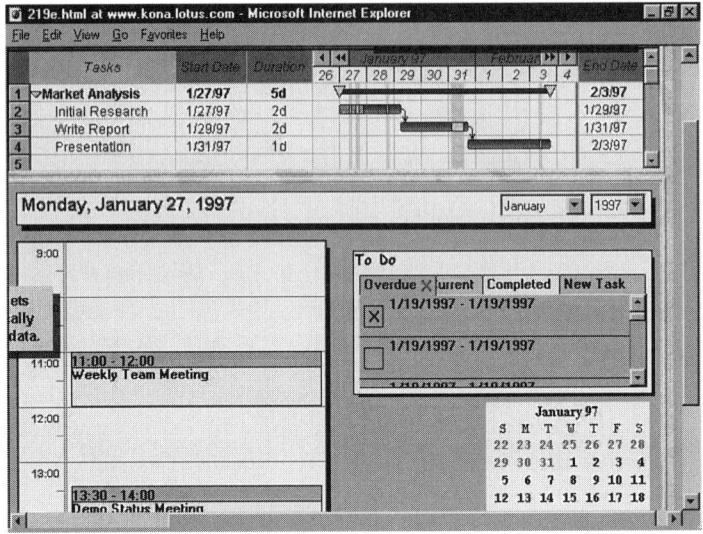

JavaBeans technology is being incorporated into Notes and Domino technology, and can be expected to be prevalent when Lotus releases the next version of Notes.

It is beyond the scope of this book to teach you how to use the Kona applets. Why are they beyond the scope of a book on Notes, if they are being delivered via Notes and Web browsers that give you access to Notes documents? Because you will not be using the Notes interface, you will be using a spreadsheet interface such as a light version of Lotus 1-2-3. You will be using a word processor interface such as a light version of WordPro, and a presentation graphics interface similar to Freelance.

With the Weblicator, you were using an interface that wrapped around basic parts of the Notes client back end. With the Kona applets, you will have the same thing: applets written in code that will make them available across all platforms, with the ability to work with data in Notes databases.

Let me give you another example. The Notes Personal Web Navigator was built into the Notes interface, and was able to save information from another environment, the Web, by translating the information into a Notes format. Another similar product that Lotus has mentioned, and has made available in an early beta version, is a Microsoft Internet Explorer client built into the Notes interface. The interface is being wrapped around the Notes back end instead of the Microsoft back end, giving you the leverage of the Notes environment, even if though you may prefer the IE interface. Likewise, when you embedded objects and launched them in a Notes Rich Text field, you saw the original application being opened up within the Notes interface.

This opens Notes up to a whole new world of possibilities. Are you using Notes if it looks like the Microsoft Internet Explorer? Are you using Notes if it looks like a word processor? Are you using Notes if it looks like a project manager? Notes is a powerful back end engine. It allows document-centric storage of information, with full text searching, automated agents, and easy access to the underlying design of the database. It can be published dynamically to the Web without having to be "published" to a separate directory. So you may be able to pick and choose your interface, but still take advantage of the full power of Notes.

That back end, code-named Maui, should be fully realized when Notes 5.0 becomes available. It will be a fully integrated Internet standards-based product, making it even easier to manage an enterprise using an intranet or extranet (an enterprise intranet with a customer connection) with the Notes client and the Domino server.

Summary

The future of Notes is the Internet. As the IBM/Lotus ads on television say, "Work the Web…" and "If you want to surf, move to Maui."

Notes is a powerful groupware communications package on its own, but today, communications and networking mean one thing: the World Wide Web.

Today, you learned how Notes uses the Web from two different perspectives: from within Notes looking out at the Web using the Notes Personal Web Navigator; and from the Web, building on the power of Notes to replicate Web data.

The Domino server makes it possible for Notes users to have the best of both worlds. Documents created and managed using the workflow capabilities of Notes can be opened from the Web via the Domino server. Notes uses the same server for database access, security, and administration of the Notes network as it uses to convert Notes documents to HTML on-the-fly. The converse is the Domino server takes HTML documents from the Web and saves them as Notes documents that can be managed with all the tools of a Notes user.

You learned how to define which browser you use. You learned how to use the Notes Web Navigator from within the Notes workspace. You then moved outside the Notes workspace and learned how to use the Lotus Weblicator to achieve much of the functionality of Notes from the Web using a browser. Finally, you had a glimpse of the Notes to come—a workspace interface that can change like a chameleon depending on which applet you are using, but always built upon a solid structure of ACL security, distributed authorship, and cross-platform functionality, along with a built-in application development environment that was barely touched upon in this book.

Workshop

The Workshop section presents questions and answers, quiz questions to help you cement your new knowledge, and exercises to give you experience using what you have learned. Try to understand the questions and exercises before moving on to the next lesson. Answers are in Appendix A.

Q&A

Q I worry that someone is going to send me a Java applet that contains a virus. How can I stop this?

A You do not need to accept Java applets. Most Web sites that have Java applets also provide a means of accessing data without the applets. To turn off Java applets, go to your User Preferences page and make sure that you have deselected running Java applets on your workstation. You can also define what types of access are allowed on your workstation by executable code from specific sources. This is done using an Execution Control List (ECL), accessed from the Security button on the User Preferences page.

Q I want to use non-Notes browser, but I like the idea of saving Web pages in a Notes database. Can this be done using another browser?

A As of the moment I'm writing this, no you cannot. By tomorrow morning, the answer may well be different, especially when the Notes back end has wrap-around Java interfaces such as the Microsoft Internet Explorer interface. I would imagine that will allow you to access Web pages as Notes documents.

You can use the Weblicator to retrieve Web pages, and then run Notes agents on them and full text search them. And remember, the Weblicator Favorites database is a Notes database. You can always open the database from within Notes, and work with documents using your Notes client.

Q When will all of the Kona and Maui stuff be available?

A Even if I knew, I couldn't tell you. By the time you read this, Kona should be available, at least in some form on some platforms. The latest from Lotus is that it will be available "this summer." And at LotusSphere, they announced that Maui may be available sometime later this year. Changes in the user interface are likely to reflect the opening of the Notes environment to JavaBeans, and you are likely to see more native Notes functionality available on the Web.

Q If I can do most Notes functions through a Web browser, why do I need a Notes client?

A The Notes client is essential for many system administration tasks and application development. The Notes client also gives you a lot of flexibility in working with documents that you do not have on the Web. In addition, you can use a Notes client to access the Web through a Server Web Navigator even if you do not have TCP/IP protocol on your workstation. This opens up the Web to organizations who already have a large network infrastructure, and do not want to retrofit all their workstations with TCP/IP.

Q Why don't Notes documents tell me when I've made a mistake entering data, if I'm accessing a Notes document on the Web using a browser?

A The only validations that can be done on the spot are those that can be written in HTML or can be performed by something like a JavaBeans. The only native Notes validation takes place when the document is "submitted" back to the Domino server.

Quiz

1. What type of communications port do you have to use to access the Internet from within Notes?
2. Can you use a browser other than the Notes Navigator, Netscape Communicator, or Microsoft Internet Explorer from within Notes?
3. Can you replicate a Notes database over the Internet?
4. What are the equivalents of a Page Minder and Web Ahead in the Weblicator?
5. Can you replicate a Notes database using the Weblicator?
6. How do you set up your Notes Web Navigator so it automatically purges documents?
7. How do you create a new Favorite Web page in the Weblicator?
8. Can you run a Kona applet through an HTTP proxy server?

Exercises

1. Set up different Location documents so you have different default Web browsers—Notes Web Navigator and another browser of your choice. Switch between locations retrieving your favorite Web pages. Compare them in both browsers. How easy is it to search for specific information when you saw it somewhere during the current session?

2. Use the Weblicator to open a local Notes database. Open the same database in Notes and compare functionality. When you rebuild your server list, can you see all of the servers in your organization? Why or why not?

3. Open the site at `http://kona.lotus.com` and navigate to the online demonstrations of Kona applets. Are you able to run them on your machine? If not, try to work through the setup for Java applet security, and see if you can get them to work.

In Review

Congratulations! You have now worked your way through an entire two weeks of learning Lotus Notes. When you began, what did the word "Lotus Notes" conjure up in your mind? Post-it notes? Glorified e-mail? A bulletin board application? A spreadsheet? Those are some of the responses I've heard before. If someone were to ask you the same question now, you could answer "Yes" to any of those answers. "Yes, but that doesn't even begin to scratch the surface."

With a little bit of practice, you can quickly move beyond being a novice user to being an advanced user. All of the material you need is contained in this book.

Let's take a look back over this second week and see what you've learned.

First, you learned that Notes is more than a container for documents. It is a way to store information in such a way that it becomes a corporate asset, not just a bunch of information. Notes is valuable for its workflow applications and for facilitating communication. And as you work your way through workflow applications or communicate with your colleagues, you begin to accumulate knowledge. Now, you need a way to mine that knowledge.

That is why an entire day's lesson was dedicated to indexing data and full text searching. You learned to create an index for a database, then used the Search Bar to perform a simple full text search. After that, you learned how to build complex searches using the Search Builder dialog box. You then learned how to leverage your newly acquired search skills by building a Site Search database so you could search through multiple databases with a single search.

On Day 9, you really got into the heart of workflow applications, but you did so by learning about the e-mail application that you probably use every day. You learned how to create and send a memo, and how to respond to mail that was sent to you.

You went through the different document types that are built into Notes Mail, and learned how to handle the flood of information that comes into your InBox. The information that comes in will stay in your InBox until you handle it one way or another. For that reason, you have folders that you can drop the memos into for future reference.

You then extended your knowledge of Notes Mail through an understanding of Notes address books. These address books control the flow of information throughout your organization, even in complex workflow applications, where hidden fields are used to mail information to other databases automatically. The Notes address books are also an essential part of the Notes security paradigm.

Mail is more than memos. You learned how to customize your mail, to give it a personal touch with your own letterhead. You learned how to create document templates, called Stationery in Notes.

And then, you put Notes Mail to work for you. You created a delegation profile that lets others access your mail in special circumstances. And you delegated to Notes itself the task of informing people that you were out of the office, and would respond to them when you got back.

Of course, not everyone who uses Notes uses it for e-mail. You can enable Notes for use with cc:Mail or Microsoft Exchange, for example. But even if you do use another mail system, you are still using Notes Mail as the backbone of your workflow applications.

And then you got to the calendar. It is a special view within the Notes Mail database. You could have used the calendar to track your progress through this book as you learned Notes, if you'd known about it earlier. The calendar is a great way to organize your time.

Within the calendar, you can convert memos into tasks, and you can even assign the tasks to others in your workgroup. You can schedule meetings, verifying that everyone you invited has a free timeslot on their calendar at the time of the meeting you set up. You can even attach documents to make sure they have read up on everything before the meeting. You can ask them to RSVP, and when they receive the invitation, and all they have to do is click on a button to say yes, they will be there. That is the sort of thing computers are made for. Quick, simple automation, and information put in front of you at the moment you need it.

One of the really strong points about Notes is that you can use it from anywhere, on just about any type of computer platform. It is great when you are attached to the office LAN and can have instant communication with everyone in your workgroup. But in today's business environment, chances are that you sometimes have to do work at least some of the time when you are not in the home office. You can still use Notes to send e-mail, do research in a Notes database, even browse the Web while you are cruising at 35,000 feet on your way to Europe, on your way to Japan, or on your way across the U.S. You can work from home while your child is sick, without missing a beat.

To set up your computer for mobile computing, you learned to set up the communications ports, set up Server Connection documents, and define which phone numbers Notes should call to connect to your Domino server. You created replica copies of the databases you wanted to work with on the road, then used the Replicator page to set up one-step replication from your current location. If you change locations, all you have to do is change to a new Location document and you have all of the phone numbers and database you need at that location ready to go.

You should begin to see a pattern by now. You sometimes need to take a little time out, concentrate, and set up Notes correctly. Once you have done the setup, you never have to worry about it again. Most of the automated functions are no more than a step or two away, once you get them set up to function the way you want.

That is also true of the agents and actions that you learned about. These are powerful tools for automating Notes. You can do things like sort through incoming e-mail and have Notes put it into folders for you automatically. You can have Notes search discussion databases and inform you whenever there is a new document posted that might interest you. You can have Notes summarize a database and send a library of DocLinks sent to people based on their profiles. You can archive documents to a new database, and then delete them from a more heavily used database based on inactivity or the age of the document.

Just remember, when you create agents, do it carefully. Test the agent on a single document, or do it using a test database. Once an agent makes a change in a database, there is no "undo" button.

Finally, you learned about Notes and the Internet. Notes has had the option of using TCP/IP, the communications protocol of the Internet, since well before the first mention of the World Wide Web in the press. In a flash, the Web has gone from being an experimental environment on the Internet, to ubiquity. Most information on the Web is created as a static document, then published to the Web. But Lotus did something different.

Notes is a dynamic workflow environment. Lotus, with the Domino server, made it possible to selectively expose documents from that workflow environment directly to the Web, without even having to *publish* them first. That means that as soon as information is saved in the form of a Notes document, it becomes available to users on the Web.

Notes, as you have seen, is fully Web-enabled. You can browse the Web from within Notes using either the Notes Web Navigator or your choice of browsers. When you use the Notes Web Navigator, you have a couple of advantages, though. You can save Web pages as Notes documents, and then run Notes agents against those pages, full text search the information in the pages, mail the pages to coworkers...in short, anything you can do with a Notes document. You can also use the Web Navigator on your Domino server. This opens up Web browsing to anyone in the organization, whether they have TCP/IP on their computer or not, as long as they have access to a Notes 4.5 client and to the Domino server. They can use NetBEUI, they can use AppleTalk, and still they can work the Web.

You saw just how fully Web-enabled Notes really is with the Weblicator. Here, the Notes backend has been made available to anyone with a Web browser and a copy of the Weblicator. You can do two-way replication of documents over the Web, and you can work with Web pages using a full text index and functions like Web Ahead and Page Minder to keep up with changes, whether the Web pages are Notes documents or not.

The Notes environment is rich. It is being Java-enabled, so by the time you finish this book, if you know the right programming languages, you can start to customize your Notes and Web desktops with JavaBeans and ActiveX controls, pushing the envelope by leveraging the strengths of the Notes environment to manage information from virtually anywhere, using the interface of practically any client you want. If that day is not here yet, it is coming.

Appendix A

Workshop Answers

Day 1

Quiz

1. Notes licenses include the full Lotus Notes client, which is needed for application development in Notes; Lotus Notes Desktop client, used to run Notes applications; and Notes Mail. The full Lotus Notes client is also used to perform administrative tasks on the Domino server.
2. No. There is no way you can talk to another Notes workstation on a peer-to-peer basis. You must go through a Domino server.
3. Yes. When security is enforced locally, you cannot open the database without the correct Notes user ID and password.
4. Yes. There is no file locking in Notes, and multiple users can open and edit the same document at the same time. If the same data is edited by two different users, both copies of the document are saved, one as the original and one as a Replication or Save Conflict. There is an exception to this, where the designer elects to Merge Replication Conflicts using a particular form, thus allowing two documents to be merged as long as edits were made to different fields on the document.
5. You can modify documents that you created, or that have your name in the Author Names field.
6. You cannot read any documents when you have Depositor access. All you can do is create documents.
7. You can modify or delete any document in a database if you have Manager, Designer, or Editor access.

Exercises

1. In this exercise, pay attention to the protocols that are being used. You can only communicate with a Domino server if your workstation and the server share a protocol that Notes recognizes. Are there multiple networks in a WAN? Are there laptop users?
2. Probably most users would have Author or Reader access. With Author access, they could be allowed to modify certain data in their own file, such as a "hobby" list. The Personnel department would need to have Editor access, but may not be able to delete documents. The person who maintains policies and procedures would need at least Author access. And obviously somebody would have to have Manager access to the database so that the ACL and database design can be changed, if necessary.

Day 2

Quiz

1. The font, size, and style are only available when you are editing a Rich Text field.
2. You can put a database on your desktop if you type in the full path to the database. In some instances, the Notes Administrator may also use a directory link to make it look like databases are in the default data directory on the Domino server, even though the databases may be stored elsewhere.
3. You have to type in the full path and file name.
4. There are six by default, but you can add or delete pages (but you cannot delete the Replicator page). You can have up to 32 folders on your desktop.
5. Deleting the icon does not effect the database itself. You can add the database back onto your desktop using File | Database | Open from the menu bar.

Exercises

1. Create the database from the Document Library template. After the database is created, select File | Database | New Copy. Delete the original by highlighting the icon and selecting File | Database | Delete.
2. Copy an existing SmartIcon, and then edit the formula. For example, if you copied the Lotus Freelance SmartIcon, the formula associated with the SmartIcon is @PostedCommand([Execute]; "c:\\flw\\flw.exe"). All you have to do is change the pathname (c:\\flw\\) and the name of the EXE file used to launch your word processor.

Day 3

Quiz

1. Open the Printed Documents view in the Help database. Expand the End User book and select the individual document you want to print, and then send it to the printer.
2. Go to the Search view and look for Default Font, or look for Font and then narrow the search by looking for Default.
3. Click anywhere in the view, and type **hor** to bring up the Quick Find dialog box. Press Enter to go to the correct place in the index to start looking.

Exercises

1. The purpose of this exercise is to help you learn how to search efficiently. You will use this ability in most Notes applications.
2. Notes Help Lite is designed for the mobile user. It should have everything you need.

Day 4

Quiz

1. The Author Name field is used to define which users with author access can edit the document. The Reader Name field is used to define a specific list of individuals who can read a document. A Names field is used to hold names for other purposes, such as a lookup in the Public Address Book.
2. Dialog list keywords, check boxes, radio buttons. The fourth type is a variation on the dialog list—a lookup in the a Notes address book.
3. The document uses hide-when features to display one version when you are editing, and another version when you are viewing a document. Another possibility is that Notes is using a different form to display the document than it used to create the document.
4. Main documents, responses to main documents, and response to response documents that can be under either a main document, a response document, or another response to response document.
5. Text fields cannot be formatted, and can only contain ASCII characters. Rich text can be formatted, and can contain various attachments and embedded or pasted objects.

Exercises

1. You will be using the documents created in this exercise during later lessons.
2. Hint: Use the Create menu to see what types of documents you can create. Use the Field Properties InfoBox to see what type of data a field contains.

Day 5

Quiz

1. Click on the Permanent Pen to enable it. Wherever you start typing, the Permanent Pen will be your font.
2. Tables can only be created in a Rich Text field.
3. Named styles are valid only in the database in which they were created.
4. Use the hide-when page in the Document Properties InfoBox to hide the page under specific circumstances.
5. When editing the table, you will be able to make selections from the Table menu on the menu bar.
6. You can, but you have to do it manually by creating a table and pasting in the data.

Exercises

1. This is just to give you practice, but you will be using these documents in later lessons, for example when you learn full text searching.
2. Again, this is just practice.
3. You are using three functions here: creating a table, creating a section, and using the hide-when features.

Day 6

Quiz

1. You can only import into a Rich Text field. You can, however, import into a view, and data can be put into non-Rich Text fields that the designer has defined.
2. You can import the documents, you can cut and paste text into a Notes document, you can attach the files in Notes documents, or you can embed them so they can be launched from within Notes.
3. You can create a View link to move to a particular view in a database. Although the InBox is technically a folder and not a view, the view link still works.

4. Yes, you can create a DocLink to any document in a database, but the document has to be visible at the time the DocLink is created.
5. No. You can only update the source of an object if it is linked.
6. No. You can create formula hotspots without formulas by using simple actions.

Exercises

1. If the object is from an OLE2 compliant application, Notes will display OLE2 controls that let you edit the object from within Notes. Otherwise, Notes will open and use the environment in which the embedded object was created when you edit the object.
2. The button will have two simple actions. The first will move the document to the new database. The second action will delete the document after the first action has been performed. This is like a manual archive function that can be performed on a single document.
3. If you successfully linked the document, the changes will be saved to the source file on the file server.
4. This exercise not only reinforces what you have learned in today's lesson, but it seeds the database with documents that you will use in later lessons.

Day 7

Quiz

1. Documents appear in a view automatically if certain selection criteria are met. A folder holds only the documents that you place there.
2. Nothing. The documents are still available in views.
3. Yes, you can have nested categories.
4. Yes, sometimes a document will be categorized in a view, so you can expand it to see any other documents contained in that category.
5. Hold the mouse button down and drag it down the selection column, past all the documents you want to select.
6. Click in the selection column to toggle the document between selected and unselected.

7. You can create database headers and footers, or document headers and footers if you are a reader. If you are a designer or manager, you can also create form headers and footers.

8. Change the name of a database in the Database Properties InfoBox. Changing the name has no effect on the content of the database, and it does not effect the ability of other Notes clients or servers to recognize the database.

Exercises

1. You can mark documents as read or unread by using the Edit | Unread Marks menu. You can also mark documents as read by selecting the setting Mark Documents Read When Opened In Preview Pane in the User Preference dialog box, and then working with the documents in the Preview pane.

2. Select Create | View, define the name of your view, and then enter Select Conditions so that you are selecting by date, by date modified, or within the last five days. Those selections are all available within the Select Conditions Search Builder dialog box.

3. Headers and footers print in both draft and regular modes. You create the database header and footer in the Database Properties InfoBox on the Printer page. You can suppress the printing of a header or footer by creating a document header/footer, adding a single blank space as a place holder. The document header and footer will supersede the database header/footer.

Day 8

Quiz

1. You can search on an unindexed database, but matches are not highlighted in documents, and the search is slower and not as versatile.

2. A graduated bar is displayed beside documents found by the search. The darker the bar, the higher the number of hits on the search string.

3. The full text index is stored in a separate directory beneath the data directory where the database is stored.

4. If you are a designer or manager, you can save a search on a server-based database. On local databases, you can save a search for yourself.

5. Only if you have manager or designer access to the database.
6. True. Databases do not have to be indexed before they can be included in a Site Search, but a property has to be set to include the database in site search indexes.

Exercises

1. This exercise is just to help reinforce what you learned about creating full text indexes.
2. You will have to set the database properties for any databases you want included in the search. When the search is done, you will see links to documents in individual databases, so when you open the document, you are opening it in its original format.
3. This exercise reinforces what you have learned.
4. This exercise reinforces what you have learned. You will have to use a local database in this exercise unless you have manager or designer access on a server-based database.

Day 9

Quiz

1. Yes. Save it without sending, and it will be saved in your draft folder. You can then reopen it, make further edits if necessary, then send it.
2. When you open a memo to read it, you can click on the Reply to All button to create a new blank memo addressed to anyone whose name was in the From or cc: field.
3. Yes and no. You cannot use a North American Notes license overseas unless you have a temporary export certificate. The certificate can be created and printed from within Notes.
4. You can copy archived documents from the archive database back into your Mail database, or you can copy them over from a replica of your mail database as long as you have not yet replicated the deletions to it. But otherwise, there is no way to recover deleted documents in Notes.

5. You can create an archive for any Notes database.
6. A serially routed document only gets sent to the next person when the reader clicks on the Send to Next Person button. If you track the progress of the document, you can remind people to forward the document if it sits in their mailbox for too long a period.

Exercises

1. You should see no difference in responses. When a user receives e-mail and responds, it does matter if they were addressed in the To, cc:, or the bcc: field.
2. Open the Archiving view in the Mail database, and click on the Setup Archive button. Fill out the Archive Profile document and the archive database will be created automatically based on the information you provide.

Day 10

Quiz

1. Documents are created from stationery by opening the stationery document in the Drafts view. When you send and save the document, a new document is sent, and the Stationery template remains in the Draft folder.
2. The Notes Public Address Book resolves names as long as there is enough information to uniquely identify the individual. If the name cannot be resolved, Notes will display a list of possibilities so you can choose.
3. You can use as many address books as you want. Notes uses as many Personal Address Books as you register, when doing name lookups for addressing mail, plus it does lookups in one Public Address Book. However, only the first local address book is used for Location documents.
4. To register a new address book so you can look up names in it, enter the name on the Mail page of the User Preferences dialog box. Notes uses the database with the name NAMES.NSF as the default, but you can enter other address book names, separated by commas. Notes uses them in the order in which they are entered in the User Preferences dialog box.
5. A delegated mail user cannot read your encrypted mail, because they do not have access to your Notes user ID, which is needed in order to read encrypted mail.
6. The out-of-office profile sends only one message to an individual, no matter how many memos they send to you.

Exercises

1. You create the Personal Address Book using a template. Give it a name, and then enter the name in the User Preferences dialog box. To make sure Notes uses the Personal Address Book for lookups, verify the setting in the Mail section of your current Locations document.
2. Select Create Stationery under Mail Tools on the Actions menu, and then design your status report the way you want it to look. When you save it, it will be saved to the Drafts folder. Open the stationery there, make any changes you want, and send it.
3. The rich text formatting will be lost in cc:Mail.
4. Your workmate should receive a message saying you are out of the office. You will receive the memo from your workmate, as usual.

Day 11

Quiz

1. A user who is allowed access to your calendar cannot see any of your other mail documents.
2. People can tell that the time is blocked, but they cannot see what you have scheduled.
3. Yes, you can change just the current, the current and all future occurrences, or all past, present, and future occurrences.
4. Tasks do not show up in the Meetings view, nor do they show up on the calendar unless you clicked on the action button to place the item on your calendar. Otherwise, Tasks can only be seen in the To Do view or in the All Documents view.
5. They automatically receive a notification of the change. They can RSVP, acknowledging the change and indicating if they can attend at the new time.
6. Create an invitation and invite every one. Be sure to click on the box to create a checkmark indicting that you do not want responses from the invitees.
7. An appointment blocks out a set time on a specific day. An event does not have a set time, it only identifies the date of the event.
8. Notes saves the new meeting, but it is saved as a conflict. You can then look at both activities you have planned, and decide which one should have the highest priority.

Exercises

1. You can see, from within the original invitation, who has accepted and who has declined. You also receive individual notification from users. They receive the original invite, but they do not receive any further information unless the meeting is changed.
2. You will discover that you cannot convert Calendar entries into Tasks, but you can make Tasks from any other Notes document. If you want To Do items on your calendar, click on the Display in Calendar button when the task is created.
3. This exercise helps to reinforce what you learned about the Calendar. Once you set up reminder parameters, you do not have to change them unless you want to.

Day 12

Quiz

1. Yes. On a LAN, you have one called Office. On a mobile or stand-alone workstation, you have Home, Island, Office, and Travel. And if you have TCP/IP and a dial-up connection, you will probably also have an Internet location.
2. You have to replicate with a database on the Domino server, and the other user also has to access data through the Domino server. There is no peer-to-peer replication.
3. False. Databases can only replicate if they have the same Replica ID.
4. You can open your User Preferences document to the Ports page, and do a Trace Connection to see if the call is going through.
5. Yes, as long as your workstation and the Domino server you are connecting to both have TCP/IP, and you have rights to access the server.
6. Yes. The replication schedules are very flexible.

Exercises

1. You set these up in the Phone Dialing section of a Location document that is set up for dialing.
2. Create a replica, but do not replicate immediately. After the replica stub is created, select File | Replication | Settings and set you replication settings before you replicate for the first time.
3. You may want to work with your mail database if you do not have a discussion database you can replicate. Create and save documents, and then replicate and verify that your changes were replicated to the version on the server.

Day 13

Quiz

1. False. You can create personal agents even if you only have reader access.
2. Shared agents only work on a Domino server. Personal agents can be run on any Notes database to which you have access.
3. The database has to be indexed before you can run an agent against all documents in the database, or all documents in a view.
4. The type of agent that mails out a list of DocLinks and a summary of all new documents in a database is called a Newsletter agent.
5. The agent at the top of the list gets run first, and the one at the bottom gets run last. Therefore, you should always place actions that delete documents last in the list.
6. Yes, running other agents is one of the allowable actions for an agent.

Exercises

1. This exercise involves creating two agents. Create the first one, a Newsletter agent, in the Discussion database. Create another one in your mail database. When a Newsletter summary is mailed into your e-mail database, place it into a folder (which you will also have to create).
2. You could create a mail archive database from the Archiving view, but the purpose of this exercise is to learn the process that goes into building an archive database. Create the database, then create an agent that copies documents to the database, and deletes them from your original mail database. Remember to use caution so you don't inadvertently delete the wrong documents.

Day 14

Quiz

1. If you want to access the Internet directly, you have to use TCP/IP. If you access the Internet through the Server Web Navigator, you can use any protocol that lets you talk to the server.
2. Yes. In the Location document, you can define the path to the EXE file that launches the browser of your choice.

3. You can replicate over the Internet as long as you can gain authorized access to the Domino server where the database is stored. You can also replicate using the Weblicator.

4. You can do the same thing with the Weblicator. Set the number of levels you want to Weblicate, or set up a Monitor in the Weblicator to tell you when the content of a Web page changes.

5. Yes, as long as the database is being served by a Domino server.

6. Enable the purge options in the Internet Options document.

7. With the Weblicator running, navigate online to a Web page, then click on "Add Favorite" on the Weblicator dashboard.

8. The applet must be able to run on the server, and you have to access it from the server. You cannot run the applet directly from your workstation via an http proxy server.

Exercises

1. You will find that each browser has its own strengths and weaknesses. The obvious advantage of the Notes Web Navigator is the ability to work with Web pages as Notes documents.

2. The Weblicator lets you create, modify and delete documents, but not all functions work within the documents over the Web. When you rebuild your server list, you can only see the servers within your Domain. If you use different protocols on your Notes network, you will not be able to see those servers that use a different protocol.

3. If you have the correct sort of setup, this exercise will give you a chance to experience the future of Notes. Depending on when new versions of Notes are released, the Kona applets may well be the present generation of Notes.

INDEX

A

About documents, 34
About This Database document, 169
Accept option (meetings), 293
Accept SSL Site Certificates (Web Retriever configuration), 371
access
 Manager, 353
 shared agents, 341
accessing calendars (assigning permissions), 281-282
ACL (Access Control List), 17, 21-22
 Author level access, 21
 Depositor level access, 21
 Designer level access, 21
 document creation, 85-86
 Editor level access, 21
 levels, 21
 local databases, 187
 Manager access, 85
 Manager Level Access, 21
 No Access level access, 21
 Reader level access, 21
 restricions, 21
 status bar icon, 43
acoustical modems, 322
Action bar options, 332
 Calendar view, 278
 replication, 332
action hotspots, 159
Action Bar

actions, 352-359
 action buttons in forms, 353-357
 Add Action dialog box, 349-351
 copying, 359
 deleting, 352, 359
 editing, 358
 hotspots, 353
 inserting, 352
 Manager access, 353
 moving, 352
 single (multiple), 352
 views, creating, 357-359
Actions menu commands
 Edit Document, 102
 Retrieve Entire Document, 324

Add Action dialog box, 349-351
Add Icon (database placement), 36
Additional Setup dialog box (modems), 310
address books
  browsing, 51
  selecting, 260-261
addresses
  Person document, 258-259
  Personal Address Book, 257-260
  Public Address Book, 18, 22, 256-257
  shortcuts (Group documents), 259-260
  see also URLs
addressing e-mail, 231-232
advanced options
  Basics page, 47
  Replication Settings dialog box, 326
Advanced Settings section (Location documents), 318
Agent Builder window, 343
Agent command (Create menu), 343
agents, 339-341
  copying, 342
  creating, 342-349, 352
  defining, 345-348, 351-352
  local (scheduled), 45
  naming, 343-345
  numbering, 344
  overview, 340-341
  personal, 341
  running against documents, 347-348
  shared, 341
  shortcut keys, 344
alarms
  appointments, 287-288
  scheduling options, 283
  types, 284
alignment, 109-110
All Documents view, 84-87, 229, 246

anchors (links), 376
animation (Web pages), 364
anniversaries (Calendar entries), 296
Appearance Information (Weblicator), 386
Append Column command (Table menu), 136
appending tables, 136
applets, 144
applications
  launching with icons, 32
  Web-enabled, 364-367
appointments
  alarms, 287-288
  creating, 284-286
  Pencil-in option, 286
  repeating, 286-287
archiving e-mail, 248
  creating databases, 249-250
  procedures, 250-251
  reading, 251
Archiving view (Mail), 230
arrows (menu options), 28
ASCII text, exporting, 141
attached files, 151-152
attachments
  files, 151-152
  replication, 333
authentication (ID file), 365
  see also security
Author field (Search Builder), 216-217
Author level access (ACL), 21
Author Name field (security), 17
authorization, *see* security
authors fields (documents), 94-95

B

background indexing, 45
background replication, scheduling, 329
backward compatibility, 23
Basics page, 44-50

Basics section (Location documents), 313-314
body text (Web Navigator), 376
bookmarks
  e-mail, 241
  Netscape, 382
Boolean searches, 214-215
borders (tables), 120-121, 136
breaking links, 150
broadcast meetings, 292
Browser Information (Weblicator), 386
browsers, 367-371
  default, 368-370
  downloading, 369
  installation, 369
  Internet Explorer, 11
  launching, 367-368
  Location document, 369
  Netscape, 11
  pages, retrieving, 369
  preferred, 369
  selecting Location documents, 314
  Web, 9-11
  windows, multiple, 370
  see also Notes Web Navigator
browsing address books, 51
bubble help, 29 , 77
bulleted lists, 109
button bar (Personal Web Navigator), 378-379
buttons, 76
  creating, 155-157
  deleting, 157
  editing, 157
  links, 155-157

C

caches (Web Navigator), 370
Calendar entries
  anniversaries, 296
  appointments, 284-286
  alarms, 287-288
  repeating, 286-287
  brodcast meetings, 292

creating, 284
default, 284
events, 296, 298
invitations
    creating, 288-289
    responding, 293
meetings
    free time, 289-291
    modifying, 295
    viewing, 297-298
reminders, 296
To-Do lists, 298-299
viewing, 301-302
Calendar Profile document
configuring, 280-282
displaying, 280
meetings, 290-291
scheduling options, 283-284
Calendar view, 278-280
Calendar view (Mail), 229
Calendaring and Scheduling overview, 277
calendars
access, 281-282
alarms, 284
data, entering, 284-297
days, viewing hourly increments, 279-280
navigation
    moving to a specific day, 279
    moving to another page, 278
opening, 282
Call Server dialog box, 321
cancelling editing, 106
cascading agent names, 344
Case Sensitive Index option, 207
case sensitivity in passwords, 166
cc:Mail, 270-272
cells (tables), 136
borders, 120-121
shading, 136
splitting, 136
centered tabs, 110

CERT.ID file, 20
check box keywords, 92
clients, 8-9
desktop menu options, 29
Domino server, 8
full menu options, 29
full Notes client, 9
Notes Desktop client, 9
Notes Mail client, 9
troubleshooting, 9
Clipboard, 139
closing
documents, 100-101
Help documents, 66
Notes, 53
Collaboration Options (Web Navigator), 376
color
graphics, 139
pages (workspace), 40
text, 108-109
workspace pages, 41
columns
databases
    resizing, 177
    views, 176-177
tables
    appending, 136
    deleting, 136
    inserting, 136
    resizing with ruler bar, 123, 136
    width, 121-124
commands
Actions menu
    Edit Document, 102
    Retrieve Entire Document, 324
Button menu (Edit Button), 157
Create menu
    Agent, 343
    Hot Spot, 155
    Hotspot, 159-160
    Main Topic, 87
    Object..., 143
    Page Break, 136
    Section, 136

Table, 119
Workspace Page, 41
Edit menu
    Copy as Link, 158
    Undo, 106
File menu
    Database, 33, 82
    Export, 141
    Import, 140
    Tools, 29, 44
Table menu
    Append Column, 136
    Insert Column, 136
    Insert Row, 136
    Merge Cells, 136
View menu (Ruler), 110
communications, 22
Internet connections, configuring, 312
Location documents, creating, 312-313
modem setup, 310-311
ports (TCP/IP), 369
protocols (TCP/IP), 310
Server Connection
    configuring, 318-320
    testing, 321-322
setup (data sharing), 309-312
workgroups, 4-5
Communications ports, 52
compatibility, 23
cross-platform, 8
e-mail formatting, 234
UserID, 23
complex documents, 99-100
compressing workspace, 41
Computed fields, 96
Computed for Display fields, 97
Computed When Composed fields, 97
Concurrent Retrievers (Web Retriever configuration, 370
conditionally hiding paragraphs, 114
Conditions field (Search Builder), 215

configuration
   Calendar Profile document, 280-282
   Internet connections, 312
   printers (default), 182
   Server Connections, 318-320
   Web Retriever Configuration, 370-371
   workstations, locations, 334-335
connections (Internet), 369
connectivity icon (status bar), 43
Contents view (Help), 67-68
context icons (SmartIcons), displaying, 30
context-sensitive Help, 73-74
context-sensitivity in menus, 28
controls, creating, 144
Copy as Link command (Edit menu), 158
copying
   actions, 359
   agents, 342
   databases, 202
Create Folder dialog box, 178
Create menu commands
   Agent, 343
   Hotspot
      Action Hotspot option, 159
      Button option, 155
      Text Pop-up option, 160
      URL Link option, 159
   Main Topic, 87
   Object..., 143
   Page Break, 136
   Section, 136
   Table, 119
   Workspace Page, 41
Create Object dialog box, 143
cross-platform compatibility, 8
customizing
   Notes, 28
   SmartIcons, 30-33

D

DATA directory, 15
data sharing
   communications setup, 309-312
   Location documents, 312-313
   overview, 308-309
   replication, 308
Database command (File menu), 33, 82
Database Icons, 27
database links, 153
Database Properties InfoBox, 322
   first page options, 188-189
   full text indexes, 206
   overview, 187-188
   second page options, 189-191
Database Purge Options (Web Navigator), 376
databases, 11
   access, multiple, 16
   adding/deleting (Replicator Page), 333-334
   browsing for, 36
   columns, resizing, 177
   copying, 202
   creating with templates, 33-35
   Database Properties InfoBox
      first page options, 188-189
      overview, 187-188
      second page options, 189-191
   default opening pages, 169
   deleted documents (placeholders), 189
   deleting, 22
   desktop, 82-83
   documents
      determining quantity, 171
      navigating unread, 173
   Domino server, 15-16
   e-mail archives, 249-250
   features, 187
   fields, 12
   folders
      adding documents, 177-178
      changing/removing, 179
      creating, 178-179
      overview, 177
      private, 180-181
   forms, 12
   full text indexes
      creating, 206-207
      customizing, 207-209
      procedures, 210-211
      removing, 209-210
   full text search, 204
   headers/footers, 184
   Help, 58-60, 75
      Contents views, 67-68
   icons, 33-39
      changing information, 38-39
      deleting, 39
      moving, 37-38
      moving on workspace, 37
   links, 387
   listing, 36
   local, 13-14, 34
      ACLs, 187
      folders, 46
      limitations, 13
      security, 14
   locating, 84
   Mail, 228-230
   mail (sharing), 265-267
   naming, 34
   Notes, 13-16
   Notes Help Lite, 58
   NSF files, 12
   opening, 84, 171, 202
   overview, 169
   passwords overview, 166-167
   Personal Notes Navigator, 373
   Replica ID numbers, 322
   replica stubs, 326-329
   replicas, 13, 308-309

replication, 323-324
    Action bar options, 332
    attachments, 333
    background, 329
    efficiency considerations, 332-333
    icon stacking, 328
    merging changes, 332
    modes, 327
    overview, 322-323
    results, 387
    size/content control, 324-326
Search Bar
    displaying, 204-205
    overview, 205
Search Builder, 214
search strings, 213
searches, 202
    Boolean logic, 214-215
    displaying results, 211-213
    multiple, 219-220
    printing documents, 214
security, 17, 208
simple searches, 202-203
site searches, 220-223
size
    determining, 189
    limits, 34
startup, 48-49
statistics, obtaining, 190
storing, 13
unread marks, 171-172
views
    columns, 176-177
    default, 170-171
    workspace, 35-37
databases Notes, 14
Date field (Search Builder), 217
days (Calendar), 279-280
decimal numbers, 93
decimal tabs, 110
Decline option (meetings), 293
Default Appointment/Meeting Duration field, 283
default printers, configuring, 182

defaults
    browsers, 368-370
    Calendar entries, 284
    database opening pages, 169
    databases, views, 170-171
    passwords, 167
defining
    agents, 345-348, 351-352
    styles, 115-117
Delegate option (meetings), 293
Delegation Profile, 280
deleting
    actions, 352, 359
    buttons, 157
    columns (tables), 136
    databases, 22
    databases (Replicator Page), 333-334
    documents/folders, 177-179
    e-mail, 239
    hotspots, 162
    icons
        databases, 39
        SmartIcon set, 31
    page breaks, 136
    rows (tables), 136
    Search Builder, 219
    sections, 136
    SmartIcon sets, 31-32
delivery options (e-mail), 234-236
Depositor level access (ACL), 21
Designer level access (ACL), 21
desktop
    client, 29
    databases, 82-83
    Personal Address Book, 257
    Personal Notes Navigator database, 373
dial-up connections (Internet), 369
dialog boxes
    Add Action, 349-351
    Additional Setup (modems), 310
    Call Server, 321
    Create Folder, 178

    Create Object, 143
    External Links, 149
    File Print, 182
    Formula, 32
    Free Time, 289
    Full Text Create Index, 207-209
    New Database, 33
    Page Setup, 183
    Properties, 40
    Quick Search, 64
    Replication Settings, 324-326
    Set Password, 168
    SmartIcon, 29
    User Activity, 190
    User Preferences, 44, 236
    Workspace Properties, 39-41
dialog list keywords, 92-93
dictionary, 49-50
direct connections (Internet), 369
Discussion threads view (Mail), 230, 247-248
displaying
    agent names, 344-345
    objects as icons, 144
    profiles (Calendar), 280
    scroll bars, 171
    Search Bar, 204-205
    server names (icons), 39
    SmartIcons, 30
    unread documents, 38
DocLinks, 153
documents, 81-82
    About This Database, 169
    alarms, 284
    Calendar Profile
        configuring, 280-282
        free time replication, 291
        free time setup, 290-291
        scheduling options, 283-284
    closing, 100-101
    collapsible sections, 136
    complex, 99-100
    creating, 83-90
    databases, 171, 189
    deleted (placeholders), 189

deleting from folders, 177
e-mail
   archive databases,
     249-250
   archiving, 248
   archiving procedures,
     250-251
   reading archived, 251
   types, 241
editing, 101-102, 203-204
embedded objects, pasting,
  145-146
fields
   authors, 94-95
   editing, 96-98
   Keyword, 99
   keywords, 91-93
   Names, 95-96, 99
   Number, 100
   numbers, 93-94
   Readers, 95
   Rich Text, 91
   text, 90-91, 99
   time, 94
folders, 177-178
forms (Main Topic), 87-89
headers/footers
   creating, 184-186
   positioning, 186
Help, 75-77
   closing, 66
   links, 64-65
   reading, 64-66
   saving to folder, 66
importing to, 140-141
Location
   Advanced Settings section,
     318
   Basics section, 313-314
   creating, 312-313
   defining servers, 314-315
   Mail section, 316-317
   Phone Dialing section,
     315-316
   Replication section,
     317-318
   selecting browsers, 314

mail, customizing, 261-263
marking multiple, 173-174
previewing (hiding paragraphs), 113
printing
   configuring default
     printer, 182
   headers/footers, 184
   overview, 181
   page setup, 183-184
   single, 181-182
read-only (editing objects),
  147
removing from folders, 178
responding to, 89-90
running agents against,
  347-348
saving, 100
   Web pages as, 372
search strings, 213
searching, 203, 214
security, 13, 17
types, 86-87
unread
   displaying number, 38
   navigating, 173
   scanning for, 45
views, changing, 174-176
Domino server, 8
   clients, 8
   file server comparison, 36
   listing, 36
   security, 13, 17
   Usenet groups, 5
**downloading from browsers,
  369**
Drafts view (Mail), 229
dragging icons, 31

E

e-mail
   addressing to groups, 232
   All Documents view, 246
   archiving
     procedures, 250-251
     reading, 251

   bookmarks, 241
   content, creating, 233
   deleting, 239
   Discussion Threads view,
     247-248
   documents
     archive databases,
       249-250
     archiving, 248
     types, 241
   expiration dates, setting, 252
   forwarding, 239
   icons, 238
   memos
     addressing, 231-232
     creating, 230-231
     databasse managers, 246
     delivery options, 234-236
     sending, 233
     universal delivery options,
       236-237
   opening, 238-239
   overview, 227-228
   phone messages, 242
   replying, 240
   serial route messages,
     242-243
   temporary export certificates,
     244-245
   To-Do list tasks, creating,
     299
**Edit Button command (Button
  menu), 157**
**Edit Document command
  (Actions menu), 102**
Edit menu commands
   Copy and Link, 158
   Undo, 106
editable fields, 97
editing
   actions, 358
   buttons, 157
   documents, 101-102
   fields in documents, 96-98
   hotspots, 161
   icons (formulas), 32
   linked objects, 151

links, 150
objects (embedded), 146-147
SmartIcons, 32-33
undoing, 106
Editor level access (ACL), 21
ellipses in menus, 207
embedded objects
creating, 143-147
editing, 146-147
pasting into documents, 145-146
Enable Alarm Notifications field, 283
Enable Local Background Indexing startup option, 45
Enable Scheduled Local Agents startup option, 45
enabling
ports, 52
replication schedules, 391-392
encryption, 18
full text searches, 208
mail messages, 52
network data, 53
temporary export certificates, 244
environment (Notes), 7-11
events (Calendar), 296-298
Exclude Words in Stop Words File option, 208
Execution Control List (security), 47-48
exiting Notes, 53
expiration dates (e-mail), 252
Export command (File menu), 141
exporting
graphics, 141
to files, 141-142
External Links dialog box, 149
extranets, 6

F

Favorites (Internet Explorer)
adding to Weblicator, 392-393
importing, 382
field level help, 77
field names (Search Builder), 217
fields
Computed, 96
Computed for Display, 97
Computed When Composed, 97
databases, 12
documents
authors, 94-95
editing, 96-98
keywords, 91-93
Names, 95-96
Number, 100
numbers, 93-94
Readers, 95
Rich Text, 91
text fields, 90-91
time, 94
editable, 87, 97
inherited data, 97-98
Keyword, 99
Names, 99
required data, 98
Rich Text, 106-118
graphics, 138-139
pagination, 111-112
printing, 111-112
tables, 118-123, 136
security, 18
Text, 99
File menu commands
Database, 33, 82
Export, 141
Import, 140
Tools
SmartIcons... option, 29
User Preferences option, 44
File Print dialog box, 182

file servers/Domino server comparison, 36
files
attached files, 151-152
creating objects from, 145-147
exporting to, 141-142
importing, 140
objects, creating, 143
finding/replacing documents, 203-204
flat file names, 292
flow control (modems), 311
folders
changing/removing, 179
compared to views, 180-181
creating, 178-179
documents, 177-178
Help documents, 66
local databases, 46
Mail, 229-230
overview, 177
private, 180-181
Web Navigator, 383-384
fonts, 43, 108
footers
creating, 184-186
positioning, 186
printing, 184
formatting
alignment, 109
bulleted lists, 109
e-mail compatibility, 234
indents, 109
importing formats, 140
margins, 110
paragraph formatting, 109-110
spacing, 110
styles, 115-118
tables
menus, 136
SmartIcons, 136
Table Properties InfoBox, 119-123, 136
text, 106

forms
    action buttons, 353-357
    actions, copying, 359
    databases, 12
    documents, 81, 87-89
    Main Topic, filling in, 88
    Search Builder, 218
    security, 17
    Web pages, 364-365
Formula dialog box, 32
formulas (icons)
    custom icons, 33
    editing, 32
forwarding e-mail, 239
Free Time dialog box, 289
full Notes client, 9, 29
Full Text Create Index dialog box, 207-209
full text indexes
    creating, 206-207
    customizing, 207-209
    procedures, 210-211
    removing, 209-210
full text search
    Help, 70
    overview, 204
    Search Bar
        displaying, 204-205
        overview, 205

G

glyphs in passwords, 167
graphics
    color, 139
    exporting, 141
    icons, 32
    importing, 140
    pasting, 139
    Picture Properties InfoBox, 138
    Rich Text fields, 138-139
    sizing, 138
grayed out menu options, 28
Group documents (mail), 259-260
groupware, 3

H

headers
    creating, 184-186
    printing, 184
Help, 57-77
    accessing through buttons, 74
    bubble, 29, 77
    context-sensitive, 73-74
    database level, 75
    document level, 75-77
    documents
        closing, 66
        links, 64-65
        saving to folder, 66
    field level, 77
    Index view, 60-73
    opening, 60
    preview pane, 61-62
    Quick Search, 64
    read documents, 64-66
    screen titles, 75
    searches, 70
    views, categories, 62
    Visual Index view, 69-70
Help database, 58-60
    Contents view, 67-68
hiding
    paragraphs, 112-115
    sections, 136
Hotspot command (Create menu)
    Action Hotspot option, 159
    Button option, 155
    Text Pop-up option, 160
    URL Link option, 159
hotspots, 158-161
    action hotspots, 159
    actions, 353
    deleting, 162
    editing, 161
    link hotspots, 158-159
    pop-up, 160-161
    see also links
hourly increments, viewing days, 279-280
How Do I...? view (Help), 67

HTML (HyperText Markup Language), 364
    source code, viewing, 382-383
HTTPS protocol, 371
hypertext link, 10

I

Icon bar (SmartIcons), displaying, 30
icons
    ACL (status bar), 43
    connectivity (status bar), 43
    custom (formulas), 33
    Database Icons, 27
    databases, 33-39
        changing information, 38-39
        deleting, 39
        moving, 37-38
        moving on workspace, 37
    dragging in SmartIcon set, 31
    e-mail, 238
    formulas, editing, 32
    graphics, 32
    Help, 58
    launching applications, 32
    launching macros, 32
    mail (status bar), 43
    objects, displaying as, 144
    positioning in SmartIcon set, 31
    server names, displaying, 39
    SmartIcons, 29-33
    stacking replicas from databases, 328
    unread documents, 38
    see also SmartIcons
ID file (authentication), 365
Import command (File menu), 140
Importance icons (e-mail), 235
importing, 140-142
    bookmarks (Netscape), 382
    Favorites (Internet Explorer), 382

files, 140
formats, 140
graphics, 140
to documents, 140-141
to views, 140
Inbox folder
e-mail, 238-239
Mail, 229
Include Word Variants option, 212
indents, 109
Index Attachments option, 208
Index Breaks option, 209
Index Encryptes Fields option, 208
Index view (Help), 60-73
indexes
full text
creating, 206-207
customizing, 207-209
procedures, 210-211
removing, 209-210
refreshing, 211
Information page (Database Properties InfoBox), 189-191
inherited data, 97-98
Insert Column command (Table menu), 136
Insert Row command (Table menu), 136
Insert Row SmartIcon, 136
inserting
actions, 352
columns (tables), 136
icons in SmartIcon set, 31
installing browsers, 369
international users, 50-51
Internet, 6, 363-397
connecting to (Personal Web Navigators), 10
connections
configuring, 312
dial-up, 369
direct, 369
TCP/IP, 369
example, 366-367

Internet Explorer, 11
browser options, 11
Favorites, importing, 382
InterNotes, 372
intranets, 6, 365-366
invitations (Calendar), 284
broadcast meetings, 292
creating, 288-289
meetings
automating responses, 294-295
free time, 289-291
modifying, 295
reserving rooms/resources, 292
responding, 293
responses, 295

J-K

Java/Notes compatability, 11
Java Applet Security fields (Locations document), 371
Java Bean, 11
keyword fields (documents), 91-93, 99
keywords
check box, 92
dialog list, 92-93
options, 93
radio button, 91-92
Kona, 394-397

L

labeling pages (workspace), 39-40
LANs (local area networks), 3
launching
applications with icons, 32
browsers, 367-368
macros with icons, 32
Notes, 26
Search Builder, 218
letterhead stationery, 264-265
link hotspots, 158-159

linked objects, 147-151
breaking links, 150
creating, 148
editing, 151
managing links, 148-150
updating manually, 149
links
anchors, 376
breaking, 150
buttons, 155-157
creating, 153
database links, 153
databases, 387
DocLinks, 153
editing, 150
external elements, 153-154
Help, 76
Help documents, 64-65
hypertext, 10
underlining, 368
views, 153
see also hotspots
links management, 148-150
listing databases, 36
local agents (scheduled), 45
local area networks, *see* LANs
local databases, 13, 34
ACLs, 187
folder, 46
see also databases
locating databases, 84
location (status bar), 43
Location document, 369
Location documents
Advanced Settings section, 318
Basics section, 313-314
browsers, selecting, 314
creating, 312-313
Mail section, 316-317
Phone Dialing section, 315-316
Replication section, 317-318
servers, defining, 314-315
locations (workstations), 334-335

locking (security)
  documents, 13
  UserID, 46
log files (modems), 310
Login, 18
Lotus Notes, *see* **Notes**
Lotusphere, 9
LotusScript compatibility, 23

M

macros, launching with icons, 32
  see also agents
Mail
  bookmarks, 241
  compatibiltiy, 234
  database, 228-230
  e-mail, opening, 238-239
  forwarding, 239
  memos, 230-232
  messages
    delivery options, 234-236
    sending, 233
    universal delivery options, 236-237
  overview, 227-228
  replying, 240
mail, 255-273
  address books
    browsing, 51
    selecting, 260-261
  addresses (Person document), 257
  cc:Mail, 270-272
  checking for messages, 51
  database sharing, 265-267
  documents, customizing, 261-263
  Group documents, 259-260
  hidden uses, 273
  Microsoft Exchange, 272-273
  Microsoft Mail, 272-273
  notification, 52
  Out of Office Profile document, 267-269
  Person document, 258-259
  Personal Address Book, 257-260
  preferences, 51-52
  Public Address Book, 256-257
  saving messages, 51-52
  sending messages automatically, 267-269
  signatures, 52
  stationery, 261-263
  trash folder, 47
  VIM programs, 270-272
Mail database, creating, 82
mail icon (status bar), 43
mail programs, 51
Mail section (Location documents), 316-317
mail systems, 269-273
main document type, 86
Main Topic, 87-89
Main Topic command (Create menu), 87
Main Topic form, 87-88
Manager access (actions), 353
Manager level access (ACL), 21, 85
managing links, 148-150
margins, 110
  Ruler, 110
  tables, 121-124
marking documents, multiple, 173-174
mathematical operators, 93
Maui, 394-397
maximum Search Results, 212
Meeting view, 297-298
meetings (Calendar)
  broadcast, 292
  free time, 289-291
  invitations, 293-295
  modifying, 295
  responses, handling, 295
  rooms/resources, reserving, 292
Meetings view (Mail), 230
memos
  content, creating, 233
  delivery options, 234-236
  e-mail, 230-232
  forms, 261-262
  sending, 233
  stationery, 264-265
  universal delivery options, 236-237
menu bar, 27-29
menus
  arrows, 28
  context-sensitivity, 28
  ellipses, 207
  grayed out options, 28
  options, 29
  pull-down, 27
  table formatting, 136
Merge Cells command (Table menu), 136
messages
  mail, 51-52
  system messages (status bar), 43
Microsoft Exchange, 272-273
Microsoft Internet Explorer, *see* **Internet Explorer**
Microsoft Mail, 272-273
modems
  acoustical, 322
  hardware flow control, 311
  log files, 310
  setup, 310-311
  speaker volume, 310
  testing, 311
modes (database replication), 327
moving
  actions, 352
  database icons, 37-38
  sections, 136

N

named styles
  formatting, 115-118
  Text Properties InfoBox, 115-118
Names fields (documents), 95-96, 99

naming
  agents, 343-345
  databases, 34
  servers, displaying in icons, 39
  SmartIcon sets, 31
  Web Navigator Database, 370
navigating
  calendar, 278-279
  documents, unread, 173
navigators
  Notes Web Navigator, 371-384
  Personal Web Navigator, 10
  Web, 10
Netscape, 11
  bookmarks, importing, 382
networks
  data sharing, 308-312
  encrypting data, 53
  Internet connections, configuring, 312
  modem setup, 310-311
  security, 17
New Database dialog box, 33
No Access level access (ACL), 21
Notes
  closing, 53
  customizing, 28
  environment, 7-11
  exiting, 53
  overview, 3-7
  launching, 26
Notes Desktop client, 9
Notes Help Lite database, 58
Notes Mail client, 9
Notes Web Navigator, 371-384
NSF (Notes Storage Facility), 12
  see also databases
number fields, 100
  documents, 93-94
numbering agents, 344

O

Object... command (Create menu), 143
objects, 137
  creating from files, 143
  displaying as icon, 144
  embedded, 142-147
    creating, 143-145
    creating from files, 145-147
    editing, 146-147
    Paste Special, 145-146
  linked, 147-151
    breaking links, 150
    creating, 148
    editing, 151
    managing links, 148-150
    updating manually, 149
One Week view (hourly increments), 279-280
opening databases, 84, 171, 202
  e-mail, 238-239
  Help, 60
Out of Office Profile document (mail), 267-269

P

Page Break command (Create menu), 136
page breaks, 136
Page Minder Agent Preferences (Web Navigator), 376
page setup (printing), 183-184
Page Setup dialog box, 183
pages (tabs), 27
pages (workspace)
  Basics, 44-50
  color, 40-41
  creating, 41
  deleting, 41-42
  inserting, 41-42
  labeling, 39-40
  tabbed, 39-42
pagination (Rich Text fields), 111-112

panes (Windows), 61
paragraphs
  formatting
    alignment, 109
    bulleted lists, 109
    indents, 109
    margins, 110
    spacing, 110
    styles, 115-118
  hiding, 112-115
    conditionally, 114
    previewing documents, 113
    printing, 113
    Read mode, 113
passthrough servers, defining, 314-315
passwords, 19-20
  authentication, 19
  case sensitivity, 20, 166
  changing, 167-168
  character restrictions, 20
  characteristics, 20
  encrypted, 20
  glyphs, 167
  length, 19
  multiple, 20
  overview, 166-167
  recovering, 169
  retrieval, 23
  selecting, 20
Paste Special (embedded object creation), 145-146
pasting, 139
  embedded objects, 145-146
  graphics, 139
paths (formulas), icons, 32
Pencil in option
  appointments, 286
  meetings, 293
Permanent Pen (text color), 108
Person document (mail), 257-259
Personal Address Book, 257-260, 312
  adding people, 258-259

desktop, 257
e-mail memos, addressing, 231
see also Location documents
personal agents, 341
Personal Notes Navigator, 373
personal stationery, 262-263
Personal Web Navigator, 371-384
   button bar, 378-379
   connecting to Internet, 10
Phone Dialing section (Location documents), 315-316
phone messages, 242
Picture Properties InfoBox, 138
placeholders (deleted documents), 189
pop-up hotspots, 160-161
pop-ups, 77
ports
   communication, 52, 369
   enabling, 52
   modem setup, 310
   preferences, setting, 52-53
   reordering lists, 52
   User Preferences dialog box, 309-310
positioning
   icons (SmartIcon set), 31
   SmartIcon bar, 30
preferences
   Basics page, 44-50
   mail, 51-52
   ports, setting, 52-53
   user preferences, setup, 44-53
presentation options (Web Navigator), 376-377
preview pane (Help), 61-62
previewing documents (hiding paragraphs), 113
Printed Books view (Help), 72-73

printing
   default printer, configuring, 182
   documents
      overview, 181
      single, 181-182
   headers/footers, 184
   hiding paragraphs, 113
   page setup, 183-184
   Rich Text fields, 111-112
private folders, 180-181
profiles
   Calendar
      configuring, 280-282
      displaying, 280
      free time replication, 291
      free time setup, 290-291
      scheduling options, 283-284
   Delegation, 280
Prompt for Location startup option, 45
properties, 40
   Database Properties InfoBox, 322
   sections, 136
   Text Properties InfoBox, 107-118
Properties dialog box, 40
Propose Alternative option (meetings), 293
protocols
   HTTPS, 371
   TCP, 310
Proxy Information (Weblicator), 386
Public Address Book, 22, 256-257
   creating, 82
   e-mail memos, addressing, 231
   URLs, 18
   UserID, 18
public Web Navigator, 10
pull-down menus, 27

Q-R

Quick Search requirements, 202
Quick Search (Help), 64, 70-72
Quick Search dialog box, 64
radio button keywords, 91-92
Read mode (hiding paragraphs), 113
read-only documents (editing objects), 147
Reader level access (ACL), 21
Reader Name field, security, 17
Readers fields (documents), 95
reading Help documents, 64-66
recovering passwords, 169
refreshing pages (Web Navigator Database), 370
reminders in Calendar entries, 296
reordering port lists, 52
repeating appointments (Calendar), 286-287
replica icons, stacking, 328
Replica ID numbers, 322
replica stubs, 324-329
replicas, 13, 16
replication, 13, 308
   Action bar options, 332
   attachments, 333
   background, scheduling, 329
   databases, 16, 323-324
   efficiency considerations, 332-333
   free time (meetings), 291
   merging changes, 332
   modes, 327
   replica stubs, creating, 326-329
   selective, 322
   size/content control, 324-326
   viewing pages offline, 393-394
Replication Page (adding/ deleting databases), 333-334

replication schedules
(Weblicator), 389-392
Replication section (Location
documents), 317-318
Replication Settings dialog
box, 324-326
Replicator Information
(Weblicator, 387
Replicator Page, 329
  database line items, 330-331
  overview, 330
replying to e-mail, 240
required data (fields), 98
resources
  flat file names, 292
  meetings (reserving), 292
responding to documents,
  89-90
response document type, 86
response to response document
  type, 87
restricted sections (security), 18
restrictions (ACLs), 21
Retrieve Entire Document
  command (Actions menu),
  324
Retriever Log Level (Web
  Retriever configuration), 370
reversing editing, 106
Rich Text fields (documents),
  91
  graphics, 138-139
  pagination, 111-112
  printing, 111-112
  tables, 118-123, 136
  text, 106-118
rooms (meetings), 292
rows (tables), 136
RSA security, 371
Ruler, 110
ruler bar, 123, 136
Ruler command (View menu),
  110
running agents, defining,
  345-347

S

saving
  documents, 100
  Help documents to folder, 66
  Location document, 369
  mail messages, 51-52
  Search Builder, 219
  SmartIcon sets, 31
  Web pages as Notes
    documents, 372
scanning for unread documents, 45
scheduled local agents, 45
scheduling options, 283-284
screen titles, 75
Scripts and Formulas view
  (Help), 69
scrollbars, displaying, 171
Search Bar, 204-205
Search Builder
  Author field, 216-217
  Boolean searches, 214
  Conditions field, 215
  Date field, 217
  deleting, 219
  field names, 217
  forms, 218
  launching, 218
  saving, 219
Search Options (Web Navigator), 374
Search view (Help), 70-72
search strings, locating, 213
searches
  full text indexes, procedures,
    210-211
  Help (full-text search), 70
  Stop Word files, creating, 209
searching
  Boolean logic, 214-215
  databases, 202
    multiple, 219-220
    site searches, 220-223
  documents, 203, 214
  finding/replacing, 203-204
  full text search overview, 204

results, displaying, 211-213
Search Builder, 214
Section command (Create
  menu), 136
sections, 136
secure sites, 371
security, 16-20
  Access Control List, 17
  ACL, 21-22
  clients, 9
  databases, 14, 17
  documents,13 , 17
  Domino server, 13, 17
  e-mail, temporary export
    certificates, 244-245
  encryption, 18
  Execution Control List,
    47-48
  fields, 17-18
  forms, 17
  full text searches, 208
  networks, 17
  passwords, 19-20
    authentication, 19
    changing, 167-168
    default, 167
    multiple, 20
    overview, 166-167
    recovering, 169
  restricted sections, 18
  RSA, 371
  shared networks, 13
  UserID, 18-19
  users, multiple, 20
  views, 17
selecting
  address books, 260-261
  menu options, 28
selective replication, 322
sending mail messages
  automatically, 267-269
  saving messages, 51
Sent view (Mail), 229
serial route messages, creating,
  242-243
server connections
  configuring, 318-320
  testing, 321-322

**Server Web Navigator,
371-384**
SERVER.ID file, 20
servers
    defining (Location documents), 314-315
    Domino, 8, 36
    file servers (Domino server comparison), 36
    names, displaying in icons, 39
    passwords (overview), 166-167
Set Password dialog box, 168
setup, 26
    user preferences, 44-53
    Web Navigator, 370-373
shading cells (tables), 136
shared agents, 341
sharing
    databases (mail), 265-267
    graphics (Rich Text fields), 138
    Web pages (workgroups), 379-380
shortcut keys (agents), 344
signatures (mail messages), 52
simple searches in databases, 202-203
sites (security), 371
size limits (databases), 34
sizing
    columns (tables), 123, 136
    graphics, 138
    panes, 61
    SmartIcons, 30
    tables (fitting to window), 121-122
SmartIcon bar, 27-30
SmartIcon dialog box, 29
SmartIcons, 29-33
    bubble help, 29
    context icons, displaying, 30
    custom, creating, 32-33
    descriptions, 30
    displaying, customizing, 30
    editing, 32-33
    Icon bar, displaying, 30

Insert Row, 136
menu options, 29
sets, 31-32
sizing, 30
spacers, 31
table formatting, 136
unread documents, navigating, 173
see also icons
Sort by Newest First, 212
Sort by Oldest First option, 212
Sort by Relevance, 212
source code (HTML), viewing, 382-383
spacing in tables, 121-123, 136
spacing (formatting), 110
speaker volume in modems, 310
spelling dictionary, 49-50
SSL site certificates, 371
startup databases, 48-49
Startup Options, 44-45
Startup Options (Web Navigator), 374
stationery
    creating
        from memo forms, 261-262
        personal stationery, 262-263
    mail, 261-263
    memos (letterhead), 264-265
status bar, 27, 42-43
storing
    databases, 13
    personal agents, 341
    Web pages, 370
styles
    formatting, 115-118
    Text Properties InfoBox, 115-117
styles (formatting), 115-118
system messages (status bar), 43

T

tabbed workspace pages, 39-42
Table command (Create menu), 119
Table menu commands, 136
Table Properties InfoBox, 119-123, 136
tables
    borders, 120-121
    cells, 136
    columns
        appending, 136
        deleting, 136
        inserting, 136
        resizing, 123, 136
        width, 121-124
    formatting
        Table Properties InfoBox, 119-123, 136
        with menus, 136
        with SmartIcons, 136
    margins, 121-124
    page breaks, 136
    Rich Text fields, 118-123, 136
    rows, 136
    sizing, 121-122
    spacing, 121-123
tabs, 110-112
    centered, 110
    headers/footers, positioning, 186
    pages, 27
    Ruler, 110
tasks (To-Do lists), 299-300
TCP/IP (Transmission Control Protocol), 10, 310, 369
team surfing (InterNotes), 372
Tell Me About... view (Help), 68
templates (databases), 33-35
temporary export certificates (e-mail), 244-245
testing
    modems, 311
    Server Connections, 321-322

text
  alignment, 109
  characteristics, 108-109
  color, 108-109
  fonts, 108
  formatting, 106
  paragraph formatting, 109-110
  Rich Text fields, 106-118
  sections, 136
  size, 108
  style (status bar), 43
  type style, 108
Text fields, 90-91, 99
Text Properties InfoBox, 107-118
  named styles, 115-118
  Permanent Pen, 109
time fields (documents), 94
title bar, 27-28, 75
titles (sections), 136
To Do view (Mail), 229
To-Do lists
  creating, 298-299
  tasks
    creating in e-mail, 299
    delegating, 299-300
    viewing, 300
toolbars
  menu bar, 27-29
  SmartIcon bar, 27
  status bar, 27
  title bar, 27-28
Tools command (File menu)
  SmartIcons... option, 29
  User Preferences option, 44
topics (Help), 63-73
trash folder (mail), 47, 230
troubleshooting clients, 9
Troubleshooting view (Help), 69
Two Day view (hourly increments), 279-280
Two Week view (hourly increments), 279-280
type style (text), 108

U

underlining links, 368
Undo command (Edit menu), 106
Uniform Resource Locators, *see* **URLs**
universal delivery options (e-mail), 236-237
unread documents
  displaying in icons, 38
  navigating, 173
  scanning for, 45
unread marks (databases), 171-172
Update Cache (Web Retriever Configuration), 370
updating linked objects maually, 149
URLs (Uniform Resource Locators), 10, 18, 364
  link hotspots, 158-159
  see also addresses
Use Thesaurus option, 212
Usenet groups, 5
User Activity dialog box, 190
user ID, 166-167
user preferences
  Basics page, 44-50
  mail, 51-52
  setup, 44-53
User Preferences dialog box, 44, 236
  communications setup, 309-310
  International settings, 50-51
User Preferences page, 368
UserID, 18-19
  compatibility, 23
  locking, 46
  name change, 18
  Public Address Book, 18

V

View menu commands, 110
viewing
  About This Database document, 170
  Calendar entries, 301-302
    meetings, 297-298
  mail database, 229
  replicated pages offline, 393-394
  source code (HTML), 382-383
  To-Do list tasks, 300
views
  actions
    copying, 359
    creating, 357-359
  All Documents, 84-87
  Calendar, 278-280
  compared to folders, 180-181
  databases
    columns, 176-177
    default, 170-171
    documents, changing, 174-176
  Help categories, 62
  importing to, 140
  Index (Help), 60-62
  links, 153
  Mail, 229-230
  Quick Search requirements, 202
  scrollbars, displaying, 171
  security, 17
  Web Navigator, 383-384
VIM programs (mail), 270-272
Visual Index view (Help), 69-70

W

WANs (wide area networks), 4
Web
  browsers, 9-11
  navigators, 10
Web Ahead Agent Preferences (Web Navigator), 374

Web Navigator
   body text, 376
   Collaboration Options, 376
   Database Purge Options, 376
   folders, 383-384
   HTML source code, viewing, 382-383
   options, 373-377
   Page Minder Agent Preferences, 376
   Personal Web Navigator, 377-384
   presentation options, 376-377
   Search Options, 374
   setup, 370-373
   Startup Options, 374
   views, 383-384
   Web Ahead Agent Preferences, 374

Web Navigator Database, 370

Web Navigator Database field (Web Retriver configuration), 370

Web Navigator view (Help), 68

Web pages
   animation, 364
   forms, 364-365
   retrieving, 369
   saving as Notes documents, 372
   sharing (workgroups), 379-380
   storing, 370

Web Retriever Configuration, 370-371

Web Tours, creating, 380-381

Web-enabled applications, 364-367

Weblicator, 11, 384-394
   Appearance Information, 386
   Favorites, 392-393
   Proxy Information, 386
   replication schedules, 389-392
   Replicator Information, 387

What's New view (Help), 69

wide area networks (WANs), 4

windows
   Agent Builder, 343
   browsers, multiple, 370

workgroups
   communications, 4-5
   Web page sharing, 379-380

workspace, 26-43
   compressing, 41
   databases, 35-38
   Help database, 58-60
   pages, 27
      color, 41
      creating, 41
      deleting, 41-42
      inserting, 41-42
      labeling, 39-40
      tabbed, 39-42
      tabs, 27

Workspace Page command (Create menu), 41

Workspace Properties dialog box, 39-41

workstations (locations), 334-335

A V I A C O M  S E R V I C E

The Information SuperLibrary™

Bookstore **Search** **What's New** **Reference Desk** **Software Library** **Newsletter** **Company Overviews**

Yellow Pages **Internet Starter Kit** **HTML Workshop** **Win a Free T-Shirt!** **Macmillan Computer Publishing** **Site Map** **Talk to Us**

CHECK OUT THE BOOKS IN THIS LIBRARY.

You'll find thousands of shareware files and over 1600 computer books designed for both technowizards and technophobes. You can browse through 700 sample chapters, get the latest news on the Net, and find just about anything using our massive search directories.

All Macmillan Computer Publishing books are available at your local bookstore.

We're open 24-hours a day, 365 days a year.

You don't need a card.

We don't charge fines.

And you can be as **LOUD** as you want.

The Information SuperLibrary
http://www.mcp.com/mcp/ ftp.mcp.com

 **Support:**

If you need assistance with the information in this book or with a CD/Disk accompanying the book, please access the Knowledge Base on our Web site at **http://www.superlibrary.com/general/support**. Our most Frequently Asked Questions are answered there. If you do not find the answer to your questions on our Web site, you may contact Macmillan Technical Support **(317) 581-3833** or e-mail us at **support@mcp.com**.

Lotus Notes and Domino Server 4.5 Unleashed, Second Edition

Randall A. Tamura, et al.

Lotus Notes is a versatile groupware package that offers document management, e-mail, and other features across multiple operating environments, including OS/2, Windows NT, Macintosh, UNIX, and NetWare. Because of its complex development platform, it is difficult for uninformed users to manipulate and customize the various products. This book shows the 4.5 million registered Notes users how to work with and customize Lotus Notes 4.5. The CD-ROM contains various utilities, toolkits, and two best-selling books in HTML format.

Price: $55.00 USA/$77.95 CDN   1,000 pp.
ISBN: 0-672-31004-X

Peter Norton's Complete Guide to Windows 95, 1997 Edition

Peter Norton & John Mueller

Following the success of the best-selling *Peter Norton Premier* series, this complete reference provides users with in-depth, detailed insights into this powerful operating system. Users will master all the tricks of the trade as well as learn how to create a Web page.

Price: $35.00 USA/$49.95 CDN   1,224 pp.
ISBN: 0-672-31040-6

Teach Yourself Windows NT Server 4 in 14 Days

Peter Davis & Barry Lewis

There is a major move in the marketplace from Windows and OS/2 to Windows NT. As more and more people make the transition, they need a book that can get them up and running quickly and easily. Using the proven elements of the best-selling *Teach Yourself* series, users will master everything they need to know to successfully develop and maintain a Windows NT Server. The CD-ROM includes authors' source code and third-party software designed to work with Windows NT Server.

Price: $35.00 USA/$49.95 CAN   700 pp.
ISBN: 0-672-31019-8

Teach Yourself Windows NT Workstation 4 in 24 Hours

Martin Kenley, et al.

This beginner-level book shows readers how to use the Windows 95-like environment of Windows NT Workstation. Many corporations soon may be migrating to this powerful new crash-proof Windows operating system. This book shows end-users, not system administrators, the differences between Windows 3.1 and Windows NT Workstation 4.

Price: $19.99 USA/$28.95 CAN   400 pp.
ISBN: 0-672-31011-2

Robert Cowart's Windows NT 4 Server Workstation Unleashed, Professional Reference Edition

Robert Cowart

The only reference Windows NT administrators need to learn to configure their NT systems for maximum performance, security, and reliability. This comprehensive reference explains how to install, maintain, and configure an individual workstation as well as how to connect computers to peer-to-peer networking. Includes comprehensive advice for setting up and administering an NT server network, and focuses on the new and improved administration and connectivity features of version 4.0. The CD-ROM includes source code, utilities, and sample applications from the book.

Price: $59.99 USA/$84.95 CDN 1,400 pp.
ISBN: 0-672-31001-5

Programming Windows NT 4 Unleashed

David Hamilton, Mickey Williams, & Griffith Kadnier

Readers get a clear understanding of the modes of operation and architecture for Windows NT. Everything—including execution models, processes, threads, DLLs, memory, controls, security, and more—is covered with precise detail. The CD-ROM contains source code and completed sample programs from the book.

Price: $59.99 USA/$84.95 CDN 1,200 pp.
ISBN: 0-672-30905-X

Red Hat Linux Unleashed

Kamran Husain, Tim Parker, et al.

Programmers, users, and system administrators will find this a must-have book for operating the Linux environment. Everything from installation and configuration to advanced programming and administration techniques is covered in this valuable reference. The CD-ROM includes source code from the book and powerful utilities.

Price: $49.99 USA/$67.99 CDN 1,176 pp.
ISBN: 0-672-30962-9

Windows NT 4 Web Development

Sanjaya Hettihewa

Windows NT and Microsoft's newly developed Internet Information Server is making it easier and more cost-effective to set up, manage, and administer a good Web site. Because the Windows NT environment is relatively new, there are few books on the market that adequately discusses its full potential. *Windows NT 4 Web Development* addresses that potential by providing information on all key aspects of server setup, maintenance, design, and implementation. The CD-ROM contains valuable source code and powerful utilities.

Price: $59.99 USA/$84.95 CDN 744 pp.
ISBN: 1-57521-089-4

Add to Your Sams Library Today with the Best Books for Programming, Operating Systems, and New Technologies

The easiest way to order is to pick up the phone and call
1-800-428-5331
between 9:00 a.m. and 5:00 p.m. EST.
For faster service please have your credit card available.

ISBN	Quantity	Description of Item	Unit Cost	Total Cost
0-672-31004-X		Lotus Notes and Domino Server 4.5 Unleashed, Second Edition (Book/CD-ROM)	$55.00	
0-672-31040-6		Peter Norton's Complete Guide to Windows 95, Second Edition	$35.00	
0-672-31019-8		Teach Yourself Windows NT Server 4 in 14 Days (Book/CD-ROM)	$35.00	
0-672-31011-2		Teach Yourself Windows NT Workstation 4 in 24 Hours	$19.99	
0-672-31001-5		Robert Cowart's Windows NT 4 Server Workstation Unleashed, Professional Reference Edition (Book/CD-ROM)	$59.99	
0-672-30905-X		Programming Windows NT 4 Unleashed (Book/CD-ROM)	$59.99	
0-672-30962-9		Red Hat Linux Unleashed (Book/CD-ROM)	$49.99	
1-57521-089-4		Windows NT 4 Web Development (Book/CD-ROM)	$59.99	

❏ 3 ½" Disk
❏ 5 ¼" Disk

Shipping and Handling: See information below.	
TOTAL	

Shipping and Handling: $4.00 for the first book, and $1.75 for each additional book. Floppy disk: add $1.75 for shipping and handling. If you need to have it NOW, we can ship product to you in 24 hours for an additional charge of approximately $18.00, and you will receive your item overnight or in two days. Overseas shipping and handling adds $2.00 per book and $8.00 for up to three disks. Prices subject to change. Call for availability and pricing information on latest editions.

201 W. 103rd Street, Indianapolis, Indiana 46290

1-800-428-5331 — Orders   1-800-835-3202 — Fax   1-800-858-7674 — Customer Service

Book ISBN 0-672-31080-5